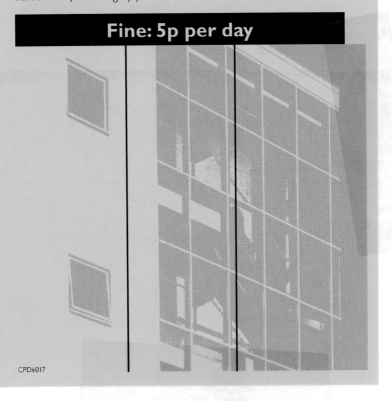

THE

GENE
Brian

ASSOC
A. R.

From
Camb
Brian
Gibbo

THE

The T
magic
and p
and pa
The T
Blackf
and u

THE NEW CAMBRIDGE SHAKESPEARE

All's Well That Ends Well, edited by Russell Fraser
Antony and Cleopatra, edited by David Bevington
As You Like It, edited by Michael Hattaway
The Comedy of Errors, edited by T. S. Dorsch
Coriolanus, edited by Lee Bliss
Hamlet, edited by Philip Edwards
Julius Caesar, edited by Marvin Spevack
King Edward III, edited by Giorgio Melchiori
The First Part of King Henry IV, edited by Herbert Weil and Judith Weil
The Second Part of King Henry IV, edited by Giorgio Melchiori
King Henry V, edited by Andrew Gurr
The First Part of King Henry VI, edited by Michael Hattaway
The Second Part of King Henry VI, edited by Michael Hattaway
The Third Part of King Henry VI, edited by Michael Hattaway
King Henry VIII, edited by John Margeson
King John, edited by L. A. Beaurline
The Tragedy of King Lear, edited by Jay L. Halio
King Richard II, edited by Andrew Gurr
King Richard III, edited by Janis Lull
Macbeth, edited by A. R. Braunmuller
Measure for Measure, edited by Brian Gibbons
The Merchant of Venice, edited by M. M. Mahood
The Merry Wives of Windsor, edited by David Crane
A Midsummer Night's Dream, edited by R. A. Foakes
Much Ado About Nothing, edited by F. H. Mares
Othello, edited by Norman Sanders
Pericles, edited by Doreen DelVecchio and Antony Hammond
The Poems, edited by John Roe
Romeo and Juliet, edited by G. Blakemore Evans
The Sonnets, edited by G. Blakemore Evans
The Taming of the Shrew, edited by Ann Thompson
The Tempest, edited by David Lindley
Timon of Athens, edited by Karl Klein
Titus Andronicus, edited by Alan Hughes
Troilus and Cressida, edited by Anthony B. Dawson
Twelfth Night, edited by Elizabeth Story Donno
The Two Gentlemen of Verona, edited by Kurt Schlueter

THE EARLY QUARTOS
The First Quarto of Hamlet, edited by Kathleen O. Irace
The First Quarto of King Henry V, edited by Andrew Gurr
The First Quarto of King Lear, edited by Jay L. Halio
The First Quarto of Othello, edited by Scott McMillin
The First Quarto of King Richard III, edited by Peter Davison
The Taming of a Shrew, edited by Stephen Roy Miller

THE TEMPEST

Edited by
DAVID LINDLEY
University of Leeds

CAMBRIDGE
UNIVERSITY PRESS

CAMBRIDGE UNIVERSITY PRESS
Cambridge, New York, Melbourne, Madrid, Cape Town, Singapore, São Paulo, Delhi

Cambridge University Press
The Edinburgh Building, Cambridge CB2 8RU, UK

Published in the United States of America by Cambridge University Press, New York

www.cambridge.org
Information on this title: www.cambridge.org/9780521293747

First published 2002
Tenth printing 2007

Printed in the United Kingdom at the University Press, Cambridge

A catalogue record for this publication is available from the British Library.

Library of Congress Cataloguing in Publication Data

Shakespeare, William, 1564–1616.
The Tempest / edited by David Lindley.
    p.   cm. – (The New Cambridge Shakespeare)
Includes bibliographical references and index.
ISBN 0 521 22159 5 – ISBN 0 521 29374 X (pbk)
  1. Survival after airplane accidents, shipwrecks, etc – Drama.   2. Fathers and daughters – Drama.
3. Magicians – Drama.   4. Islands – Drama.   I. Lindley, David, 1948–   II. Title.
PR2833.A2 L56 2002   2001035632
822.3′3 – dc21

ISBN 978-0-521-22159-7   hardback
ISBN 978-0-521-29374-7   paperback

CONTENTS

ILLUSTRATIONS

Illustrations 1 and 22 are reproduced by permission of the photographer, Keith Pattison; 3 by permission of Leeds Library and Information Services; 4 and 14 by permission of the Shakespeare Centre Library, Stratford-upon-Avon; 5, 8, 10, 11, 12, 15, 23, 24 by permission of the Brotherton Library, University of Leeds; 7 by permission of the photographer, Michael Le Poer Trench; 9, 13, 17, 20 from the collections of the Theatre Museum, London, by permission of the Board of Trustees of the Victoria and Albert Museum; 10 by permission of the British Library (shelfmark c.38); 16 by permission of the photographer, Zoe Dominic; 18 by permission of Shakespeare's Globe; 19 by permission of the photographer, John Haynes; 21 by permission of the photographer, Mike Kwasniak.

ACKNOWLEDGEMENTS

The Tempest has been part of my life for some forty years, since I took the part of
Miranda in a production at Wolverhampton Grammar School in 1959. Studied for
A-level, and again during my undergraduate career, the play has continued to figure
in my academic life ever since. During this continual, if intermittent, preoccupation,
my view of the play has inevitably been influenced directly and indirectly by more
people than it is possible to recall. Nonetheless my deepest debts are to two teachers
– Ken Parker, who produced that initial performance and taught me at A-level, infus-
ing the fundamental love of literature which propelled me to university, and then
Emrys Jones, whose rigorous teaching at Oxford profoundly challenged and stimulated my reading of Shakespeare. It is to them that I dedicate this edition.

Former colleagues at Stirling University have undoubtedly long forgotten the research paper on the use of music in the play which initiated my efforts to understand
this aspect of the work's dramatic power – but its ghostly presence is still there in the
Introduction to this edition, and owes something to the encouragement they offered
to a young scholar. Audiences at conferences and seminars in Oxford, Reading and
Durham have in their comments and criticisms sharpened my approach to the play,
as have colleagues in the School of English at Leeds, whose responses to various
papers over the years have affected substantially the development of ideas and
approaches to the text. More immediately I am deeply grateful to them for their tolerance of my obsessive editorial preoccupation in the last few years. They might have
dreaded incessant enquiries beginning with the words 'In *The Tempest* . . .', but have
always offered continuous good-humoured support. I thank them collectively and
whole-heartedly, but must record special thanks to David Fairer for his scrupulous
reading of the Introduction which purged it of many stylistic infelicities.

The staffs of the British Library, the Bodleian Library and the Brotherton Library
at Leeds have been unfailingly helpful. I am especially grateful to the last, my 'home'
library, for their generosity in supplying photographs. My work on the play's performance history would have been impossible without the assistance of the librarians and
staff of the Shakespeare Centre at Stratford, the Bristol University Theatre Collection and the Theatre Museum in London; the archivists of the National Theatre in
London and the Shared Experience Theatre Company. A grant from the British
Academy enabled me to conduct much of the research on music in the performance
history of the play. I am especially grateful to Christine Dymkowski for allowing me
to see her Shakespeare in Production edition of the play at proof stage; her work
effortlessly swallowed up most of my own, and has immeasurably strengthened the
elements of performance history in both Introduction and Commentary.

Individuals have generously offered assistance with enquiries of various kinds,
and simply to list them in alphabetical order is not to diminish my gratitude to them.
I thank Jerry Brotton, Andrew Gurr, Jonathan Hope, Richard Proudfoot, Barbara

Ravelhofer, Jonathan Sawday, Debora Shuger, Jerry Sokol and Brian Vickers. Richard Strier kindly let me see an advance copy of his challenging essay on the play, and Reaktion Books provided a pre-publication copy of the collection of essays edited by Hulme and Sherman, both of which helped me in the last stages of the preparation of this edition. To Tom Craik I am especially beholden, not only for his suggestion of a brilliant emendation, but for his kindly thoroughness in reading through the whole of the text and Commentary, and saving me from error, prevarication and evasion.

I was privileged to be allowed by Jude Kelly to attend a number of rehearsals for her production at the West Yorkshire Playhouse, Leeds, in 1999. The members of the 'Courtyard Company' were not only unfailingly tolerant of a loitering academic presence during their extremely tight period of rehearsal, and generous in allowing me to interview each of them, but the experience of watching the play come together made me sensitive to its theatrical problems and potencies in a way which would otherwise have been impossible, and has affected my thinking about it much more than I ever anticipated. I thank Susie Baxter, Claire Benedict, Paul Bhattacharjee, Claudie Blakley, Will Keen, Peter Laird, Sir Ian McKellen, Willie Ross, Rashan Stone, Clare Swinburne, Timothy Walker.

My final debts are to Brian Gibbons, for his patience in this edition's long gestation, his advice and his sharp general editorial eye, to Sarah Stanton for her tolerant encouragement, and to the copy-editors for Cambridge University Press, Paul Chipchase and Margaret Berrill, for their heroic efforts in saving me from inconsistency and error.

Leeds   David Lindley

ABBREVIATIONS AND CONVENTIONS

Shakespeare's plays, when cited in this edition, are abbreviated in a style modified slightly from that used in the *Harvard Concordance to Shakespeare*. Other editions of Shakespeare are abbreviated under the editor's surname (Orgel, Bevington) unless they are the work of more than one editor. In such cases, an abbreviated series name is used (Cam., Ard3). When more than one edition by the same editor is cited, later editions are discriminated with a raised figure (Rowe²). All quotations from Shakespeare, other than those from *The Tempest*, use the lineation of *The Riverside Shakespeare*, under the textual editorship of G. Blakemore Evans.

1. Shakespeare's works

Ado	*Much Ado About Nothing*
Ant.	*Antony and Cleopatra*
AWW	*All's Well That Ends Well*
AYLI	*As You Like It*
Cor.	*Coriolanus*
Cym.	*Cymbeline*
Err.	*The Comedy of Errors*
Ham.	*Hamlet*
1H4	*The First Part of King Henry the Fourth*
2H4	*The Second Part of King Henry the Fourth*
H5	*King Henry the Fifth*
1H6	*The First Part of King Henry the Sixth*
2H6	*The Second Part of King Henry the Sixth*
3H6	*The Third Part of King Henry the Sixth*
H8	*King Henry the Eighth*
JC	*Julius Caesar*
John	*King John*
LLL	*Love's Labour's Lost*
Lear	*King Lear*
Luc.	*The Rape of Lucrece*
Mac.	*Macbeth*
MM	*Measure for Measure*
MND	*A Midsummer Night's Dream*
MV	*The Merchant of Venice*
Oth.	*Othello*
Per.	*Pericles*
PP	*The Passionate Pilgrim*
R2	*King Richard the Second*
R3	*King Richard the Third*
Rom.	*Romeo and Juliet*
Shr.	*The Taming of the Shrew*
Son.	*The Sonnets*
STM	*Sir Thomas More*
Temp.	*The Tempest*

TGV	*The Two Gentlemen of Verona*
Tim.	*Timon of Athens*
Tit.	*Titus Andronicus*
TN	*Twelfth Night*
TNK	*The Two Noble Kinsmen*
Tro.	*Troilus and Cressida*
Wiv.	*The Merry Wives of Windsor*
WT	*The Winter's Tale*

2. Other works cited and general references

Works mentioned once in the Commentary appear there with full bibliographical information; all others are cited by the shortened titles listed below.

Abbott	E. A. Abbott, *A Shakespearian Grammar*, 3rd edn, 1870; references are to numbered sections
adj	*adjective*
adv	*adverb*
AEB	*Analytical and Enumerative Bibliography*
Arcadia	Sir Philip Sidney, *The Countess of Pembroke's Arcadia*, ed. Maurice Evans, 1977
Ard3	*The Tempest*, ed. Virginia Mason Vaughan and Alden T. Vaughan, 1999 (Arden Shakespeare)
Barton	*The Tempest*, ed. Anne Barton, 1968 (New Penguin Shakespeare)
Bevington	*The Tempest* in *The Complete Works of Shakespeare*, ed. David Bevington, 4th edn, 1997
Blount	Thomas Blount, *Glossographia* (1656). Early Modern English Dictionaries Database at http://www.chass.utoronto.ca./english/emed/emedd.html
Boteler	*Boteler's Dialogues*, ed. W. G. Perrin, Navy Records Society, 1929
Brissenden	Alan Brissenden, *Shakespeare and the Dance*, 1981
Brotton	Jerry Brotton, ' "This Tunis, sir, was Carthage": contesting colonialism in *The Tempest*', in Ania Loomba and Martin Orkin, eds., *Postcolonial Shakespeares*, pp. 23–41, 1998
Bullough	Geoffrey Bullough (ed.), *Narrative and Dramatic Sources of Shakespeare*, 8 vols., 1957–75
Burton	Robert Burton, *The Anatomy of Melancholy*, ed. Holbrook Jackson, 1932; references are to section numbers
Cam.	*The Tempest* in *The Works of William Shakespeare*, ed. W. G. Clark and W. A. Wright, 9 vols., 1891–3 (Cambridge Shakespeare)
Capell	*The Tempest* in *Mr William Shakespeare, his Comedies, Histories and Tragedies*, ed. Edward Capell, 10 vols., 1767–8
Collier	*The Tempest* in *The Works of William Shakespeare*, ed. J. Payne Collier, 8 vols., 1842–4
Collier MS.	John Payne Collier, *Notes and Emendations to the Text of Shakespere's Plays from Early Manuscript Corrections in a Copy of the Folio*, 2nd edn, 1853
conj.	conjecture, conjectured by
Dent	Robert W. Dent, *Shakespeare's Proverbial Language: An Index*, 1981; references are to proverbs by letter and number

Dryden   John Dryden and William Davenant, *The Tempest, or The Enchanted Island*, 1670

Dryden²   John Dryden, William Davenant and Thomas Shadwell, *The Tempest, or The Enchanted Island*, 1674

Dyce   *The Tempest* in *The Works of William Shakespeare*, ed. Alexander Dyce, 6 vols., 1857

Dymkowski   *The Tempest*, ed. Christine Dymkowski, 2000 (Cambridge Shakespeare in Production series)

ed., eds.   editor(s), edited by

ELH   *ELH: A Journal of English Literary History*

ELR   *English Literary Renaissance*

Erasmus, *Adagia*   Desiderius Erasmus, *Adagia*, trans. Margaret Mann Phillips, *Collected Works*, vol. XXXI, 1982

Erasmus, 'Shipwreck'   Erasmus, *Colloquies*, trans. Craig R. Thompson, 1965, 'Naufragium' ('The Shipwreck')

F   *Mr William Shakespeares Comedies, Histories, and Tragedies*, 1623 (First Folio)

F2   *Mr William Shakespeares Comedies, Histories, and Tragedies*, 1632 (Second Folio)

F3   *Mr William Shakespeares Comedies, Histories, and Tragedies*, 1663–4 (Third Folio)

F4   *Mr William Shakespeares Comedies, Histories, and Tragedies*, 1685 (Fourth Folio)

Falconer   Alexander Frederick Falconer, *Shakespeare and the Sea*, 1964

Folger   *The Tempest*, ed. Barbara A. Mowat and Paul Werstine, 1994 (New Folger Library Shakespeare)

Fraunce   Abraham Fraunce, *The Third Part of the Countess of Pembroke's Yvychurch*, 1592

Furness   *The Tempest*, ed. Horace Howard Furness, 1892 (New Variorum)

Gillies, *Geography*   John Gillies, *Shakespeare and the Geography of Difference*, 1994

Gillies, 'Masque'   John Gillies, 'Shakespeare's Virginian masque', *ELH*, 53 (1986), 673–707

Grant White   *The Tempest* in *The Works of William Shakespeare*, ed. Richard Grant White, 12 vols., 1857–66

Grey   Zachary Grey, *Critical, Historical, and Explanatory Notes on Shakespeare*, 2 vols., 1754

Gurr, 'Industrious Ariel'   Andrew Gurr, 'Industrious Ariel and idle Caliban', in Jean-Pierre Maquerlot and Michèle Willems, eds., *Travel and Drama in Shakespeare's Time*, 1996, pp. 193–208

Gurr, 'Tempest'   Andrew Gurr, '*The Tempest*'s tempest at Blackfriars', *S.Sur.*, 41 (1989), 91–102

Hakluyt   Richard Hakluyt, *The Principal Navigations, Voyages, Traffiques and Discoveries of the English Nation*, 12 vols., Glasgow, 1903–5

Halliwell   *The Tempest* in *The Works of William Shakespeare*, ed. James O. Halliwell, 16 vols., 1865

Halliwell, *Notes*   J. O. Halliwell, *Selected Notes upon Shakespeare's Comedy of The Tempest*, 1868

Halpern   Richard Halpern, ' "The picture of nobody": white cannibalism in *The Tempest*', in David Lee Miller, Sharon O'Dair and Harold Weber, eds., *The Production of English Renaissance Culture*, 1994, pp. 262–92

Hanmer	*The Tempest* in *The Works of William Shakespeare*, ed. Thomas Hanmer, 6 vols., 1743–4
Harrison	William Harrison, *The Description of England*, ed. Georges Edelen, 1968
Harsnett, *Declaration*	Samuel Harsnet(t), *A Declaration of egregious Popish Impostures*, 1603
Hoeniger	F. David Hoeniger, *Medicine and Shakespeare in Renaissance England*, 1992
Hudson	*The Tempest* in *The Works of Shakespeare*, ed. N. H. Hudson, 11 vols., 1851–9
Hulme and Sherman	Peter Hulme and William Sherman, eds., *'The Tempest' and its Travels*, 2000
Johnson	*The Plays of William Shakespeare*, ed. Samuel Johnson, 8 vols., 1765
Jones	*The Tempest*, ed. Frank Jones, 1913
Jowett, 'Directions'	John Jowett, 'New created creatures: Ralph Crane and the stage directions in *The Tempest*', *S.Sur.*, 36 (1983), 10–20
Kermode	*The Tempest*, ed. Frank Kermode, 1954 (Arden Shakespeare)
Kittredge	*The Tempest*, ed. George Lyman Kittredge, 1939
Langbaum	*The Tempest*, ed. Robert Langbaum (Signet Classic Shakespeare), 1964
Mainwaring	*The Seaman's Dictionary*, in *The Life and Works of Sir Henry Mainwaring*, ed. G. E. Mainwaring and W. G. Perrin, Navy Records Society, 2 vols., 1920–1
Malone	*The Tempest* in *The Plays and Poems of William Shakespeare*, ed. Edmond Malone, 10 vols., 1790
Monson	*The Naval Tracts of Sir William Monson*, ed. M. Oppenheim, Navy Records Society, 5 vols., 1902–14
Montaigne	Michel de Montaigne, *The Essayes, or Morall, Politick and Militarie Discourses*, 3 vols., trans. John Florio, 1603
N&Q	*Notes and Queries*
n	*noun*
NLH	*New Literary History*
Noble	Richmond Noble, *Shakespeare's Use of Song*, 1923
Norton	*The Tempest* in *The Norton Shakespeare*, ed. Stephen Greenblatt et al., 1997 (based on the Oxford edition)
OED	*Oxford English Dictionary*, 2nd edn, 1989
om.	omitted by
Orgel	*The Tempest*, ed. Stephen Orgel, 1987 (Oxford Shakespeare)
Oxford	*William Shakespeare: The Complete Works*, gen. eds. Stanley Wells and Gary Taylor, 1986
P&P	*Past and Present*
Peacham	Henry Peacham, *The Garden of Eloquence*, 1593 edn
Pope	*The Tempest* in *The Works of Mr William Shakespeare*, ed. Alexander Pope, 6 vols., 1723–5
Pulton	Ferdinando Pulton, *De Pace Regis at Regni*, 1609
Puttenham	George Puttenham, *The Arte of English Poesie*, 1593
Q	quarto
Rann	*The Tempest* in *The Dramatic Works of Shakspeare*, ed. Joseph Rann, 6 vols., 1786
RenQ	*Renaissance Quarterly*
Ripa	Cesare Ripa, *Nova Iconologia*, 1618 edn
Riv.	*The Riverside Shakespeare*, ed. G. Blakemore Evans, 1974

Rowe	*The Tempest* in *The Works of Mr William Shakespear*, ed. Nicholas Rowe, 6 vols., 1609
Rowe[2]	*The Tempest* in *The Works of Mr William Shakespear*, ed. Nicholas Rowe, 9 vols., 1614
RSC	Royal Shakespeare Company
Sandys	George Sandys, *Ovid's Metamorphoses: Englished, mythologiz'd, and represented in figures*, 1632
SB	*Studies in Bibliography*
Scot	Reginald Scot, *The Discoverie of Witchcraft*, 1584
sig.	signature (printers' indications of the ordering of pages in early modern books, often more accurate than page numbers)
Smith	Bruce R. Smith, *The Acoustic World of Early Modern England*, 1999
SQ	*Shakespeare Quarterly*
S.St.	*Shakespeare Studies*
S.Sur.	*Shakespeare Survey*
Stanyhurst	Richard Stanyhurst, *The First Foure Bookes of Virgils Aeneis*, 1583
Staunton	*The Tempest* in *Routledge's Shakespeare*, ed. Howard Staunton, 3 vols., 1857–60
Steevens	*The Tempest* in *The Plays of William Shakespeare*, ed. Samuel Johnson and George Steevens, 10 vols., 1773
Strier, 'Politics'	Richard Strier ' "I am power": "normal" and magical politics in *The Tempest*', in *Writing and Political Engagement in Seventeenth-Century England*, ed. Derek Hirst and Richard Strier, 2000, pp. 10–30
Sturgess	Keith Sturgess, *Jacobean Private Theatre*, 1987
sv	sub verbum – Latin for 'under the word', used in dictionary citations
Theobald	*The Tempest* in *The Works of Shakespeare*, ed. Lewis Theobald, 7 vols., 1733
Thomas	William Thomas, *The History of Italy*, ed. George B. Parks, 1963
Tilley	M. P. Tilley, *A Dictionary of Proverbs in England in the Sixteenth and Seventeenth Centuries*, 1950; references are to numbered proverbs
v	*verb*
Vaughans	Alden T. Vaughan and Virginia Mason Vaughan, *Shakespeare's Caliban: A Cultural History*, 1991
Warburton	*The Tempest* in *The Works of Shakespear*, ed. William Warburton, 8 vols., 1747
Williams	Gordon Williams, *A Dictionary of Sexual Language and Imagery in Shakespearean and Stuart Literature*, 3 vols., 1994
Wilson	*The Tempest*, ed. John Dover Wilson, 1921 (The New Shakespeare)

Unless otherwise specified, biblical quotations are given in the Geneva version, 1560.

INTRODUCTION

The Tempest is an extraordinarily obliging work of art. It will lend itself to almost any interpretation, any set of meanings imposed upon it: it will even make them shine.

(Anne Barton)[1]

I've never felt so strongly in a play that the meaning does not belong to the actor's perception
of what the play is . . . The audience's imagination is much, much less controlled by the actors,
I think, in this play than in almost any other.   (Sir Ian McKellen)[2]

Anne Barton's observation on the critical fortunes of *The Tempest* is amply borne out
in the history of its reception. It has at various times been read as a romance of reconciliation, a Christian allegory of forgiveness, a meditation on the powers of the
imagination and the limits of art, a psychological drama of fatherhood, a play about
Jacobean politics, and a dramatisation of colonialist or patriarchal ideology (to name
but the commonest approaches). Sir Ian McKellen's comment, that of an experienced
Shakespearean actor reflecting on the problems of acting the part of Prospero (illustration 1),[3] interestingly suggests that this openness is not simply a consequence of
readerly ingenuity, but is fundamental to the theatrical experience of the performed
play itself. One aim of this introduction is precisely to represent and attempt to
explain the range of readings and stagings that *The Tempest* has provoked in the course
of its transmission from the seventeenth century to the present. But, as an early
seventeenth-century play, *The Tempest* is rooted in the culture of its period. It draws
upon, moulds and responds to other texts both classical and contemporary; it participates in and reflects on issues and debates current at the time; and it was designed
for performance in particular theatres. The exploration of the play's originating contexts is the other principal thread of this introduction, and it is where we begin.

The experimental *Tempest*

The Tempest's first recorded performance was at court on 'Hallomas nyght', 1 Novem-
ber 1611.[4] Whilst it is conceivable that this was its 'opening night', it would have been
unusual if the play had not already been performed publicly by the King's Men.[5] The
earliest date for its composition has usually been set as 1610, on the grounds that the

---

[1] Barton, p. 22.
[2] Interview with the editor, February 1999.
[3] In the production by Jude Kelly at the West Yorkshire Playhouse, Leeds, 1999.
[4] E. K. Chambers, *William Shakespeare: A Study of Facts and Problems*, 2 vols., 1930, II, 342. The performance may have been in the Banqueting House.
[5] Leeds Barroll, *Politics, Plague and Shakespeare's Theater*, 1991, p. 203, suggests spring or autumn 1611
for its first performance. The fact that the only recorded performances were at court, in 1611 and again
in 1613, has led some to see it as having been designed specifically for court performance.

1 Sir Ian McKellen as Prospero in the production by Jude Kelly at the West Yorkshire Playhouse, Leeds, 1999

reports reaching London in that year of the wreck of Sir Thomas Gates's ship in the Bermudas, and the providential survival of his company, were a specific inspiration for the action of the play (but see below, pp. 30–1), and it is generally accepted that the play was the last Shakespeare wrote as sole author, a fact which has encouraged generations of critics to see it as a summation and a distillation of his dramatic career.[1] But to treat *The Tempest* as the grand finale to a writing life obscures the fact that in many respects this is as experimental a play as Shakespeare ever wrote. Though it revisits ideas, themes and topics explored in earlier plays, and though it has obvious generic affinities with the 'romances' which immediately preceded it, in its dramatic shaping, and in its deployment of music and spectacle in particular, *The Tempest* breaks new Shakespearean ground.

DRAMATIC DESIGN

Whereas *Pericles*, *Cymbeline* and *The Winter's Tale* accept in their narrative and dramatic form the traditional expansiveness of romance, ranging over the Mediterranean world and spanning many years, *The Tempest*, unlike any other Shakespeare play since the early *The Comedy of Errors*, observes the classical unities of time and place. The resulting concentration of action is intensified by symmetries at every level of the play's narrative. There are two sets of father and child and two pairs of brothers; the two conspiracies within the play replicate the original deposition of Prospero from the dukedom of Milan; Prospero's arrival on the island with his daughter parallels the earlier arrival of Sycorax and her son Caliban; Alonso, Antonio and Sebastian, the three men of sin (3.3.53), are echoed by the trinity of Stephano, Trinculo and Caliban – to offer but a few obvious instances. The play seems like a hall of mirrors[2] in which reflection is added to reflection in a curiously claustrophobic dramatic world. This sense of confinement is furthered by Prospero's domination of the action. Shakespeare had used 'manager figures' in earlier plays, and in some ways Prospero is a reworking of Oberon in *A Midsummer Night's Dream* or of the Duke in *Measure for Measure*. In *The Tempest*, however, Prospero's control of the narrative is not only more complete than that of his dramatic predecessors, but, unlike theirs, is directed to a personal and particular end – the triumph over the 'enemies' whom fortune has placed at his mercy.

The play's concentrated dramatic form may reflect a self-conscious effort on Shakespeare's part to imitate the 'New Comedy' of Plautus and Terence.[3] Robert Miola points out the way its structure echoes 'the principle of binary construction' that characterises classical comedy,[4] and suggests that a specific influence is Plautus' *Rudens* ('The Rope'), which, he argues, 'may function as a seminal subtext, frequently

[1] See, for example, G. Wilson Knight, *The Crown of Life*, 1947, ch. 5. The persistence of the tradition is also to be seen in Neil Gaiman and Charles Vess's *Sandman* graphic novel, *The Tempest* (DC Comics, 1996).
[2] Harold Brooks's phrase in '*The Tempest*: what sort of play?', *Proceedings of the British Academy*, 64 (1978), 27–54; p. 37. He gives a comprehensive account of the play's repetitions (pp. 34–41).
[3] See, especially, Leo Salingar, *Shakespeare and the Traditions of Comedy*, 1974, and Robert S. Miola, *Shakespeare and Classical Comedy: The Influence of Plautus and Terence*, 1994.
[4] Miola, *Shakespeare and Classical Comedy*, p. 155.

mediated and reconstituted, which offered dramatists a generic set of romance pos-sibilities'.[1] Italian drama may have been one route for such mediation between Shake-speare and the classics. K. M. Lea's suggestion of the influence of the improvised scenarios of the *Commedia dell'arte* has been extended by Louise Clubb, who points out that 'the magician with rod and book, the spirits, the urban refugees, wandering lost and hallucinated, the transformations . . . the boisterousness of self-infatuated clowns with their minds on drink and license' are all found in the Italian literary pas-toral.[2] G. K. Hunter argues that the blending of tragedy and comedy which is so marked a feature of all the late plays owes something to fashionable Italian practice.[3] The point here is not that *The Tempest* derives from a particular Italian original,[4] but, as Clubb suggests, that an awareness of its classical and Italian models is 'especially important for doing justice to Shakespeare, whose work . . . demands recognition as avant-garde drama in which the latest theatrical fashions were appropriated in dazzlingly new combinations'.[5]

One motivation for Shakespeare to attempt a 'dazzlingly new' play was the acqui-sition by the King's Men of the indoor theatre at Blackfriars in 1608 (see illustration 2). Andrew Gurr suggests that *The Tempest* was the first Shakespeare play indubitably designed for performance at Blackfriars,[6] and there were two important practical con-sequences, each of which may have stimulated Shakespeare to dramatic experiment. First, the King's Men were able to call on the services of the consort of musicians who had previously played there for the boy companies. The importance of this newly extended theatrical resource will be discussed shortly. Secondly, the custom in hall theatres like Blackfriars was for each act-break to be marked by a pause of a few minutes which provided time to trim the candles. That such act-breaks were expected in *The Tempest* is made obvious by the fact that Prospero exits at the end of Act 4, but returns at the beginning of Act 5, an immediate re-entry unique in Shakespeare's work.[7] Shakespeare turns this practical necessity to dramatic account. At the most obvious level, the play is deliberately designed to emphasise the shape imposed by the four breaks between acts. Each act builds to a powerful dramatic moment: the first ends with the subjection of Ferdinand (virtually the only dramatic *action* in the long second scene); the second culminates in Caliban's song and celebration of

---

[1] Ibid., p. 156. An extended case for Plautus' play as a specific source is offered by Bruce Louden, '*The Tempest*, Plautus and the *Rudens*', *Comparative Drama*, 33 (1999), 199–223, but the more the detailed case is pressed the less compelling it becomes.

[2] K. M. Lea, *Italian Popular Comedy*, 2 vols., 1934, II, 443–53; Louise George Clubb, *Italian Drama in Shakespeare's Time*, 1989, p. 20.

[3] G. K. Hunter, 'Italian tragicomedy on the English stage', *Renaissance Drama*, NS 6 (1975), 123–48. See also Robert Henke, *Pastoral Transformations: Italian Tragicomedy and Shakespeare's Late Plays*, 1997.

[4] Just as no compelling argument has been produced for a single romance as a source. Bullough put forward *The Mirror of Knighthood* (1578), while Gary Schmidgall has argued for *Primaeleon*, originally appearing in Spanish in 1512, in '*The Tempest* and *Primaeleon*: a new source', *SQ*, 37 (1986), 421–40 – but neither is very close.

[5] Clubb, *Italian Drama*, p. 157.

[6] Gurr, 'Tempest', p. 92. I am indebted to this article in what follows.

[7] In the modern theatre, where the play is customarily played with one interval, some cutting and rearrangement is frequently made at this point to enable the action to flow smoothly.

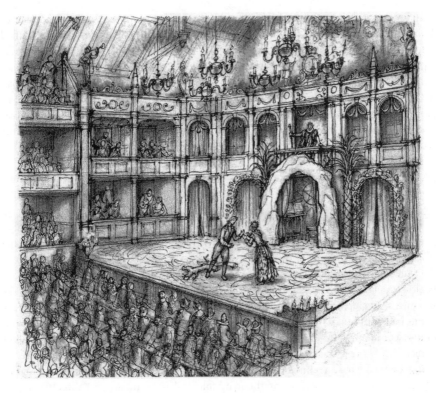

2 3.1 on the Blackfriars stage: drawing by C. Walter Hodges

freedom; the third with the frenzied reaction of the lords to Ariel's appearance as a
harpy; and the fourth with Caliban and his co-conspirators driven out, pursued by
dogs. Thus, at the close of each act, service and freedom are emphasised as central
themes.

The action of the three main plot-strands is neatly interlaced. The developing relationship of Ferdinand and Miranda, the conspiracy of Antonio and Sebastian and the
torment of the 'three men of sin', and its parodic counterpart in the plot of Stephano,
Trinculo and Caliban, are tidily interleaved. For a theatrical company *The Tempest*
easily lends itself to an economical rehearsal schedule, so little do the groups of characters intersect before Act 5. But while alternation of plots is characteristic of Shakespeare's dramatic structures – as in the movement between the court and Eastcheap
in the *Henry IV* plays, or between the Lear and Gloucester plots in *King Lear* – in
this play the narrative disconnection of its stories seems particularly extreme and
mannered. In the absence of a narrative continuity, it is the presence of Prospero
or Ariel, or both, which links the scenes (they both are absent only from 1.1 and
2.2), thus focusing attention firmly on the fact of their control rather than on the

individual development of each plot-strand. It is as if the conjunction of the romance genre's traditional interlacement of plots, the neo-classical prescription for a unified action, and the new theatre's demand for clearly marked, structural act-breaks, precipitated Shakespeare into this experimental design.[1]

Nothing in the play, however, more clearly manifests its dramaturgical bravura than its first act. Storm or shipwreck had traditionally initiated the action in romance or epic, from Virgil's *Aeneid* to Sidney's *Arcadia*, and a prologue of retrospective narration is a common feature of classical drama;[2] but on both these conventional elements Shakespeare plays extraordinary variations.

Storms were not unusual in the drama of the period, and in *Macbeth*, *Lear* and *Pericles* Shakespeare had already used them to powerful theatrical effect. In mounting a tempest complete with a shipwreck before the spectators' eyes, however, Shakespeare was not merely going further than he himself had done before, but attempting an unprecedented theatrical coup.[3] Confronted with such a scene an audience would have readily been disposed to understand it symbolically. Leslie Thomson suggests that '*Thunder and Lightning* was the conventional stage language – or code – for the production of effects in or from the tiring house that would establish or confirm a specifically supernatural context in the minds of the audience'.[4] More generally, the storm-tossed ship as a metaphor for the vicissitudes of human life, and the shipwreck as an 'image of surrender of self-control, or helplessness before fortune', were commonplaces in emblem books and elsewhere.[5] But *The Tempest*'s opening scene appears determined to resist such symbolic readings in its turbulent physical action, precise and technical naval commands, and the almost prosaically 'realistic' entrance of Mariners, wet.[6] This mixture of the symbolic and naturalistic, and the challenge it offers to an audience to find a secure interpretative vantage-point, is to be characteristic of the play which follows.

The scene's dialogue, however, initiates important thematic threads by establishing a parallel between the disordered elements and the inversion of social hierarchy on board the ship. Refusing to countenance the authority of the king, and ridiculing the impotence of Gonzalo's courtly counsel in commanding the tempest, the Boatswain raises questions of power and control that will reverberate throughout the play.[7] The arrogant resistance of both Antonio and Sebastian to the Boatswain's suggestion that

[1] See Barbara Mowat, *The Dramaturgy of Shakespeare's Romances*, 1976.

[2] The action of Plautus' *Rudens* is precipitated by an off-stage storm.

[3] Gurr, 'Tempest'. He suggests also that it would have challenged the audience at Blackfriars 'accustomed to the quieter indoor conditions of the hall playhouses' (p. 95).

[4] Leslie Thomson, 'The meaning of *Thunder and Lightning*: stage directions and audience expectations', *Early Theatre*, 2 (1999), 11–24.

[5] Lawrence Otto Goedde, *Tempest and Shipwreck in Dutch and Flemish Art: Convention, Rhetoric and Interpretation*, 1989, p. 170. Though its focus is on pictorial art, this book is comprehensive in its survey of literary storm depictions.

[6] Goedde notes that even in emblems with a clear moral purpose 'the depictions possess an internally consistent realism that may permit but does not appear to require a particular metaphorical interpretation' (p. 12).

[7] See David Norbrook, '"What cares these roarers for the name of King?": language and Utopia in *The Tempest*', in Gordon McMullan and Jonathan Hope, eds., *The Politics of Tragicomedy*, 1992, pp. 21–54.

they should set to work is a proleptic contrast with Ferdinand's readiness to endure his 'mean task' in 3.1.[1] Gonzalo's desire for 'an acre of barren ground' is fulfilled (in a way he does not anticipate) by the 'desert' he first sees the island to be (2.1.34). The thematic significance of the opening scene was recognised by an anonymous lecturer who, before F. R. Benson's first performance of the play at Stratford in 1891, instructed his audience in its political resonance.[2] Unfortunately for him, the actual performance cut the entire scene, and substituted the music of Haydn's *Der Sturm*, played while Prospero stood before a painted backdrop 'waving his wand', with 'spirits seen in mid-air'.[3]

In cutting the words of the opening scene Benson was following the usual practice of eighteenth- and nineteenth-century performances,[4] and the substitution of music is a device employed both earlier and in more recent productions.[5] The storm could nonetheless be advertised as one of the highlights of a production, even if, as was frequently the case, it became the play's second scene. The poster for a performance at the Royal Amphitheatre, Leeds, in October 1865, for example, declared that the 'Great Storm at Sea' was 'Pronounced to be one of the best scenes and the nearest approach to reality ever witnessed in a Theatre' (illustration 3).[6] This boast finds an echo in reviewers' response to the Stratford staging by Bridges-Adams some seventy years later, when the *Birmingham Mail* commented that 'Stratford has never seen anything more realistic than this disaster, with the ship lurching sickeningly to her final doom, the wind howling'[7] (illustration 4). Giorgio Strehler's famous Italian production of the play began with a 'powerfully physical tempest' which lasted 'five full minutes', though it was 'contextualised by a conspicuous theatricality' as the billowing sea of silken cloth, first seeming an effort of quasi-realistic illusion, was, as the storm ended, broken up by Prospero, and revealed as having been produced by sixteen stage-hands.[8] That a striking effect does not depend upon such elaborate staging, however, was demonstrated in the success of the 1951 Mermaid Theatre production, played on a stage designed by Michael Stringer and C. Walter Hodges as a generalised imitation

[1] But Strier, 'Politics', p. 22, observes that their contempt for labour is replicated in Prospero's unwillingness to 'fetch his own wood or make his own fire', and to be contrasted with the willingness of all on board the *Sea Venture* to assist in the storm (and see 1.1.37 n.).

[2] *Stratford-upon-Avon Herald*, 17 April 1891.

[3] Ibid., 24 April 1891. Haydn's music has no connection with Shakespeare's play.

[4] Dymkowski, p. 11, notes that 'apart from partial retention of the dialogue in David Garrick's 1757 text and in William Burton's 1854 production, none of Shakespeare's opening scene was heard on stage until the beginning of the twentieth century'.

[5] Thomas Linley's fine setting of a chorus, 'Arise, ye spirits of the storm', replaced the first scene in Sheridan's 1777 production, as did Sibelius's dramatic storm-music in a 1926 performance in Finland.

[6] Kean in 1857 had a notably spectacular storm as a virtually detached prologue. See Mary M. Nilan, 'Shakespeare, illustrated: Charles Kean's 1857 production of *The Tempest*', *SQ*, 26 (1975), 196–204.

[7] 17 April 1934.

[8] Dennis Kennedy, *Looking at Shakespeare*, 1993, p. 305. The device was imitated in Noble's 1998 Stratford production, and anticipated, interestingly, in Jonson's 1605 *Masque of Blackness*, which featured 'an artificial sea' which 'was seen to shoot forth, as if it flowed to the land, raised with waves which seemed to move, and in some places the billow to break' (David Lindley, ed., *Court Masques*, 1995, p. 1). See also Pia Kleber, 'Theatrical continuities in Giorgio Strehler's *The Tempest*', in Dennis Kennedy, ed., *Foreign Shakespeare*, 1993.

3 Part of an advertising poster for a performance at Leeds Royal Amphitheatre in 1865.
Note the emphasis on the realism of the storm scene, and that it is the actress playing Ariel who gets 'star' billing

4 The realistic set designed for Bridges-Adams's production at the Shakespeare Memorial Theatre in 1934
(photographer Ernest Daniels)

of the Jacobean hall theatre. One reviewer commented on 'the surprising number of
effects which can be got on the platform stage', and another described the scene
enthusiastically: 'The play opened with a clap of thunder, rigging fell from the
heavens, mariners tumbled up through a trap-door, courtiers reeled through side-
entrances, everybody acted high seas and hurricanes, and not a word was lost.'[1] In
many subsequent productions, although mimetic realism has given way to a more min-
imalist staging, directors have been so tempted by the possibility of amplified sound-
effects that the words have been obliterated almost as completely as by Benson's
cutting of them. Peter Hall in 1988 tried to avoid the scene's 'becoming what it always
is, just a lot of desperate noise', by deploying sound as punctuation of, rather than
ground-bass for, the action, so that it was 'a quiet scene about an external storm, followed by a noisy scene about an internal storm'.[2] It is certainly important to the play
that we should both be persuaded of the tempest's ferocity, and yet aware, through
the dialogue, of the collapse of social distinction under its overwhelming threat.

[1] Theatre Museum, London; the source of the reviews is not specified. William Poel in his late nineteenth-
century attempt to imitate the 'original' Shakespearean staging had also eschewed stage illusion, but
according to William Archer made 'a side gallery or balcony, cut in the very cornice of the lofty hall, to
represent the ship at sea, and . . . Miranda watch the wreck from the stage . . .'. *Theatrical World of 1897*,
1898, p. 315.
[2] Roger Warren, *Staging Shakespeare's Late Plays*, 1990, pp. 160–1. Hall also argued that the scene was
much less naturalistic than is generally supposed.

Benson also anticipated what has become almost a cliché of modern performance in having Prospero or Ariel, or both, present on stage throughout.[1] At one level this device seems to integrate the storm narratively into the play which follows and simultaneously to emphasise its meta-theatricality as an event, yet it profoundly changes the relationship, and therefore the effect, of the first two scenes. Peter Holland objected that it was 'a mistake to have Ariel visibly controlling the storm . . . for there are few effects in Shakespeare quite as thrilling as the realisation that the hyper-realism of the opening scene is really only a trick of the play's magician'.[2] The relationship between the play's first two scenes, however, is even more complex than Holland suggests. It is not simply that 'realism' turns out to be merely 'theatrical illusion' – watching the bare Blackfriars stage an audience knows full well that it must, in Gower's words: 'In your imagination hold / This stage the ship' (*Per.* 3, Prologue, 58–9). When Miranda opens the second scene with the words 'If by your art . . .' it is not stagecraft she means, but the arts of magic; and in both benign and malign forms it was believed that the magician (or witch) had the power to command 'real' tempests. Her 'If' registers that she reacts, not only to the horror of the storm, but also to the fearful possibility that it has been generated by her father, thus raising a question, which haunts the play, as to how magic power can and should be used.

In shifting to retrospective report, her rhetorical set-piece also prepares us for what is to be the dominant narrative mode of the second scene. It does not, however, anticipate the extraordinary virtuoso display by which Shakespeare so extends the exposition that it is only at line 375 that the present action of the play, suspended after the storm, recommences.[3] It is worth considering carefully the way Shakespeare constructs this second scene, for in many different ways his elaborate descant on a classically conventional exposition sets up both the central thematic concerns and the characteristic dramatic patterns of the play.

The scene is built out of a historical recapitulation in three instalments which move successively closer to the present moment. Each of these sections is, as it were, framed and suspended within a narrative loop. The first runs for 175 lines before Prospero answers his daughter's implied question about the reason for raising the storm by telling her that his enemies are 'Brought to this shore' (180). The second begins as Prospero summons Ariel with the words 'I'm ready now. Approach, my Ariel. Come!' (187–8). But these instructions are postponed, and finally delivered (in a whisper we do not hear) only after Ariel's history has been recapitulated. In the third 'loop' Prospero summons Caliban to work, only to plunge again into some thirty lines of retrospection before demanding that he fetch fuel (rather than undertake the 'other business' he had said he required him for). Though action is repeatedly deferred, the scene is nonetheless organised to sustain dramatic momentum. Each bout of remi-

---

[1] As, for example, in Stratford productions in 1951, 1957 and 1993; Leeds, 1999; Shakespeare's Globe, 2000; and many more.

[2] Peter Holland, *English Shakespeares*, 1997, p. 172. The same view is expressed by Barton, p. 8, though E. M. W. Tillyard, *Shakespeare's Last Plays*, 1938, p. 82, thought 'Nugent Monck had the right instinct when he put Prospero and Miranda on the stage from the beginning.'

[3] Its precedent in *The Comedy of Errors* (clearly modelled on Plautus) is a mere 150 lines.

niscence is shorter than the one before, thus accelerating up to the moment when past and present finally come together with Ferdinand's entrance, and the whole is articulated by the successive crescendos of Prospero's fury.[1] This ensures that although the scene functions formally as a *protasis*, introducing us to the principal characters of the play, it is focused upon Prospero's carefully differentiated feelings towards those characters.[2] In the first movement his anger is directed both at the brother who usurped him, and at himself for having made that usurpation possible; in the second it is aimed at Ariel's lack of gratitude and refusal of agreed terms of service; in the third at Caliban's violation of his daughter. The final exercise of Prospero's angry control comes with his treatment of Ferdinand. The crucial difference here is that Prospero allows us to be aware that this is a simulated anger. He pretends that it is derived from fear of Ferdinand's usurping him as lord of the island, but lets the audience know that its motivation is to test his suitability as a potential husband for his daughter.[3] That this is a self-consciously staged fury neatly links the end of the act to its beginning in an angry tempest that is also a simulated elemental rage.

Carefully designed though it is, 1.2 poses an enormous technical challenge to the actor playing Prospero. In part this is simply a matter of his total domination of the scene, but it is rendered more difficult by the fact that throughout its length he is never engaged in conversation, speaking either to himself, or else aggressively to dominate Ariel and Caliban.[4] The danger, therefore, is that he can appear a tedious or tiresomely tetchy bore. In older productions the narrative was almost always severely cut, and the tradition of playing Prospero as a dignified, other-worldly figure inhibited much variety in his representation.[5] Dymkowski suggests that it was Gielgud's 1957 performance which decisively 'broke the nineteenth-century mould', and in her survey of subsequent productions she notes the emergence of a Prospero tormented by inner conflict – as in Derek Jacobi's 1982 performance, which emphasised 'his internal struggle between omnipotence and humanity'.[6] But the astonishing demands Shakespeare makes on his principal actor issue a challenge to every production.

[1] For discussion of Prospero's anger in the light of Seneca's treatise *De Ira*, where it is condemned as 'temporary madness', see Ben Ross Schneider, Jr, '"Are we being historical yet?": colonialist interpretations of Shakespeare's *Tempest*', *S.St.*, 23 (1995), 121–45; pp. 132–4.

[2] Dymkowski notes that a number of recent productions bring on stage in dumb-show the characters of whom we only hear by report, both to vary the visual nature of the scene and to make recognition easier for the audience.

[3] Though, of course, one might see Ferdinand's marriage to Miranda as a different kind of 'usurpation' – of fatherly, rather than political, authority.

[4] McKellen commented that 'what is difficult about Prospero . . . is that he's a loner, he doesn't communicate well . . . there are no proper scenes in which there's an interchange of the kind that you expect'. Though Prospero insists on Miranda's attention, this seems to be to ensure that she fully recognises what the story means to him. Philip Voss discusses the actor's problems with this scene in his essay on playing Prospero in Robert Smallwood, ed., *Players of Shakespeare, 5*, (forthcoming).

[5] A tradition summed up by a reviewer in the *Observer*, 30 May 1940, as a 'mixture of Father Christmas, a Colonial Bishop, and the President of the Magician's Union'; more pithily by Ivor Brown as 'a bore with a beard' (Dymkowski, p. 18). Theodore Fontane, though recommending the introduction of the play onto the continental stage, yet considered Prospero 'not a role in which one can make much of an impression on the audience' (*Shakespeare in the London Theatre, 1855–58*, trans. Russell Jackson, 1999, p. 68).

[6] Dymkowski, pp. 19–34.

The sequence of Prospero's angry outbursts unambiguously places at the centre of the play questions of authority and obedience. Its structure, in persistently thwarting the anticipated movement to the present time, also sets in place what is to become a continuing feature of the play's narrative. Throughout *The Tempest* both the characters on stage and the audience who watch them repeatedly experience frustration and disappointment as action is halted or deferred. The assassination threatened in 2.1 is postponed by the 'stagiest' of devices, Sebastian's 'O, but one word' (293). In 3.3, the offered banquet suddenly vanishes *with a quaint device*, and the celebratory betrothal masque of 4.1 ends prematurely in *a strange, hollow and confused noise*.[1] The frustration of expectation adumbrated in 1.2 pervades the play and provides its narrative 'deep structure'.

Perhaps the most obvious feature of this second scene is its insistence upon memory. This too initiates one of the play's thematic strands. Ariel's later injunction to the 'three men of sin' to '. . . remember – / For that's my business to you' (3.3.68–9) enforces its centrality. Conversely, the moment when Prospero's memory fails him, in his absent-mindedness about Caliban's conspiracy, causes the dissolution of the masque and precipitates his meditation on oblivion. Once the anger fuelled by recollection of his usurpation is converted to forgiveness, Prospero turns to Alonso at the play's end and instructs him: 'Let us not burden our remembrances with / A heaviness that's gone' (5.1.199–200). As Michael Neill points out, this turn from vengeance to forgiveness is also a revision of revenge tragedy into romance, and 'marks the conclusion not just of [Prospero's] moral pilgrimage, but of his creator's long meditation on man's relation with his past, on the significance of remembrance and revenge'.[2]

Memory for Miranda, peering backwards across the 'abysm of time', is a guarantor of fixity, its certainty set against the delusion of dreams (1.2.44–50); but for the audience its status is more ambivalent. They are offered no means of testing Prospero's stories (though, equally, no evidence to mistrust them), and the play seems at times to remember more than the characters themselves can know, teasing us to construct a prior narrative which would authenticate the knowledge they appear to have. So, for example, Prospero gives us a detailed description of Sycorax and her history, yet he himself can never have seen her. L. C. Knights famously rebuked those who went about to remedy a text's silences with supplementary narratives,[3] but it is not only the desire of readers brought up on novelistic completeness, or the need of actors to create a possible past as motivation for the characters they play, which invite us to fill in the blanks. Our understanding of the play's action depends crucially upon the interpretation we have of the stories that precede and motivate it, yet those narratives are marked by lacunae and by information denied. That the text's silences should have invited later writers to repair and to build upon them is not surprising, and the substantial volume of rewritings and supplementations of the play is a testament to its provocative withholdings. But, as we shall see, the distinctly varied interpretations of

---

[1] See Brian Gibbons, '*The Tempest* and interruptions', *Cahiers Elisabéthains*, 45 (1994), 47–58.
[2] Michael Neill, 'Remembrance and revenge: *Hamlet*, *Macbeth* and *The Tempest*', in Ian Donaldson, ed., *Jonson and Shakespeare*, 1983, p. 35.
[3] L. C. Knights, 'How many children had Lady Macbeth?', 1933.

The Tempest have often derived from the different ways in which critics have fleshed out in their imaginations the play's pre-history.[1]

SPECTACLE AND MASQUE

The theatrical experiment of the opening act is continued in the deployment of spectacle throughout the play. Ariel's appearance as a harpy in 3.3, the extended masque in 4.1, and the 'trumpery' and dogs at the end of that scene, are all staged by Prospero as emblematic scenes intended to instruct or manipulate characters, and thereby to bring his project to its conclusion. Entertainments featuring allegorical figures were commonplace in both courtly and popular pageantry, and most members of the audience would readily have comprehended their symbolic significance. Not all would have been familiar with the substantial handbooks that collected together the frequently contradictory allegorisations of classical figures, but whereas Ben Jonson published some of his court masques encrusted with scholarly footnotes, and castigated those spectators who lacked the learning fully to understand his allegories, Prospero's entertainment for Ferdinand and Miranda would have required comparatively little exegesis.

It is not, however, mythologically imprecise. Its deities are chosen to celebrate elemental concord. Iris, the 'watery' goddess of the rainbow, brings down Ceres, goddess of the earth, and introduces Juno, goddess of the air and patroness of marriage (see illustration 5), and the subsequent dance of fiery reapers and watery naiads enacts the fusion of male heat and female coldness in the ideal temperate marriage.[2] The exclusion of lustful Venus from the masque makes an equally straightforward symbolic point.

This celebratory set-piece is carefully framed. Before it begins Prospero warns Ferdinand that consummation of his love for Miranda must wait upon the 'holy rite' that will legitimate their union. The masque's vision is therefore provisional, its blessings conditional on their proper behaviour. This betrothal masque functions as the court masque was conventionally supposed to do – the 'spell' that Prospero creates is intended by its harmonious charm to educate his audience in the virtue it represents. It is as morally purposeful as Ariel's apparition as a harpy to bring the lords to repentance. But its discordant ending in *a strange, hollow and confused noise*, and the meditation its dissolution precipitates, signals its implication in wider contemporary debates about the nature of the court masque.

The masque had come to occupy a central place in the Christmas festivities of the Jacobean court, and in Ben Jonson it had found its most determined apologist.[3] In the Preface to *Hymenaei* (1605), he confronted those critics who bemoaned the fact that

---

[1] On the ways in which all critical activity can be seen as an act of supplementation, see Frank Kermode, *The Genesis of Secrecy: On the Interpretation of Narrative*, 1979, ch. 4.

[2] As Jonson explains in his masque, *Hymenaei*, 'Like are the fire, and water, set; / That, ev'n as moisture, mixt with heat, / Helps everie naturall birth, to life; / So, for their Race, joyne man and wife' (C. H. Herford, Percy and Evelyn Simpson, eds., *Ben Jonson*, 11 vols., 1925–52, VII (1941), p. 215).

[3] For useful introductions to the genre see Stephen Orgel, *The Jonsonian Masque*, 1967; David Lindley, ed., *The Court Masque*, 1984; David Bevington and Peter Holbrook, eds., *The Politics of the Stuart Court Masque*, 1998.

Imagine di Giunone inuentrice ò protetrice del matrimonio, detta Giunone giugale, & del giogo & vcelli à lei sacrati, significanti l'vssitio de maritati, & la successione ò prole che ne viene dal matrimonio concorde.

5 An image of Juno as goddess of marriage from Cartari's compendium of the allegories attached to the pagan gods, *Le imagini de gli dei degli antichi*. This picture is from the 1608 edition

vast effort and expenditure was lavished on one single night's performance, by arguing that the transitoriness of the masque could be overcome by 'high and hearty inventions . . . which, though their voice be taught to sound to present occasions, their sense or doth or should always lay hold on more removed mysteries'.[1] By its learning and scholarship, he suggests, the masque genre has the capacity to transcend the particu-

[1] Lindley, *Court Masques*, p. 10. This masque was written for the marriage of Frances Howard and Robert Devereux, Earl of Essex, and some details of Shakespeare's masque may derive from it.

lar and aspire to a permanent wisdom. In this Preface, however, Jonson was also aiming critically at Samuel Daniel, who in his Introduction to the previous year's entertainment, *The Vision of Twelve Goddesses*, had explicitly eschewed learned allegory, claiming that he chose his deities 'according to some one property that fitted our occasion, without observing other their mystical interpretations'.[1] Daniel returned to the fray in the preface to *Tethys Festival* (1610), characterising masque-writers, including himself, as 'poor engineers for shadows' who 'frame images of no result'.[2] The most exquisite lyric in his entertainment concludes:

> Feed apace then, greedy eyes,
> On the wonder you behold.
> Take it sudden as it flies,
> Though you take it not to hold.[3]

Where Jonson seeks to transcend the evanescence of the masque's occasion, Daniel instructs his audience to embrace it. Prospero's masque is imagined in Daniel's rather than Jonson's terms, in the transparency of its allegory, the self-deprecatory tone in which he asks Ariel to prepare 'Some vanity of mine art' (4.1.41) and in the way he instructs Ferdinand, 'Be cheerful' (147), in contemplating the fact of its dissolution.[4] More profoundly, the vision Prospero's masque offers of an idealised world predicated on the proper control of the passions touches on the play's central preoccupations, but does so only to expose the limits of Prospero's 'art' in the face of the reality of Caliban's remembered rebellion. The dismay shared by Ferdinand and the audience at its evaporation is the most extreme version of the disappointment which, I have suggested, is pervasive in the play.

It is possible to argue that the influence of the masque extends further into the fabric and design of the play than this. After 1609 the usual form of the court masque included an 'antimasque' depicting some kind of threat to courtly order, which was overturned by the entry of the main masquers, and the *shapes* who bring in the banquet in 3.3 might recall such figures (see illustration 6), so that the scene functions as an analogue to the antimasque, and, by extension, characterises the 'three men of sin' as figures of moral disorder. Some critics, however, argue that it is Caliban, Stephano and Trinculo who should be seen as antimasquers, so that their irruption reverses the normal masque sequence and becomes a 'generic cue' through which '*The Tempest* enacts its meaning, in large part silently, by depending on a sophisticated audience to recognize, and respond to, a significant rearrangement of masquing structure.'[5] This may be to press the argument too far. In 1610–11 the form of the masque

---

1 Samuel Daniel, *The Vision of Twelve Goddesses*, ed. Joan Rees, in T. J. B. Spencer and Stanley Wells, eds., *A Book of Masques*, 1967, p. 26.
2 Lindley, *Court Masques*, p. 55.
3 Ibid., p. 63, lines 355–8.
4 *The Tempest* certainly seems to have irritated Ben Jonson, as is indicated by the derogatory comments in both the Prologue to the revised *Every Man In His Humour* and the Induction to *Bartholomew Fair*. It is not perhaps fanciful to conjecture that some of the animus derived from Shakespeare's very qualified view of the masque.
5 Ernest B. Gilman, '"All eyes": Prospero's inverted masque', *RenQ*, 33 (1980), 214–30; p. 218. Mendes's 1993 RSC production dramatised this possibility by having the straw-hatted reapers reveal themselves as the conspirators in disguise.

"... Enter several strange shapes
bringing in a banquet ..."

"... and with a quaint
device the banquet
vanishes."

6 C. Walter Hodges's representation of the *shapes*, and of Ariel as a harpy, draws on Inigo Jones's designs for antimasque figures. He imagines the *quaint device* by which the banquet vanishes as a reversible table-top

had barely stabilised into the dialectic of masque and antimasque, so that one cannot be certain that Shakespeare or his Blackfriars audience would have responded to it in these terms. It is also important to recognise that Prospero's masque is not an *example* of the court masque, but a partial *representation* of it. Nonetheless the function of this 'harmonious vision' within the play cannot be fully comprehended without an awareness of how it draws on, and therefore contributes to, contemporary debates about the ambitions and limitations of the genre.[1]

It is precisely because the masque as a literary genre is so deeply embedded in the culture of the early seventeenth century that subsequent productions have had difficulty in finding a theatrical vocabulary capable of suggesting to an audience its full significance. Dryden and Davenant simply cut it from their redaction, substituting a different pageant at the play's end, whereas in the nineteenth century it was frequently amplified as a self-contained spectacle, with multiple changes of scenery and hosts of additional dancers.[2] In more recent productions material has been substituted for, or added to, the text;[3] it has been radically pruned, or entirely cut.[4] When staged, it has not infrequently been a theatrical flop.[5] In that the masque is a deliberate introduction into the play of a distinct and different theatrical vocabulary, directors have attempted to find some analogous modern generic equivalent. So, for example, Mendes flew in a kind of pop-up theatre, and his goddesses imitated puppets (illustration 7), whereas a New York production by George C. Wolfe transformed the masque into 'a blissful celebration of the rites of marriage . . . presented as a jubilant Brazilian carnival'.[6] Some of the most successful recent stagings have established its theatrical distinctiveness by giving it a through-composed quasi-operatic setting. Hall's 1988 National Theatre production had 'a masque of beauty and charm, much of which is provided by Harrison Birtwistle's music',[7] while Stephen Oliver's brilliant pastiche score for the RSC in 1982 made the masque 'the showpiece of this magical production', and gave real celebratory weight to its idealised vision of fertile marriage.[8]

The theatrical problem of what to do with the masque echoes the unease which has provoked literary critics to argue that it must be a late addition, or simply non-

---

[1] Stephen Orgel argues that the play offers 'the most important Renaissance commentary' on the masque (*The Illusion of Power: Political Theater in the English Renaissance*, 1975, pp. 45–9). John Gillies, 'Shakespeare's Virginian masque', *ELH*, 53 (1986), 673–707, reads Shakespeare's masque against Chapman's *Memorable Masque* of 1613, which is explicitly about Virginia, to explore the play's treatment of the idea of the Americas.

[2] Sixty dancers were used in the Leeds 1865 production, and Beerbohm Tree added a supplementary danced narrative.

[3] The Old Vic performance of 1962 imported additional lyrics from Jonson and others, for example, whereas an American production substituted readings of some of the Sonnets (Dymkowski, p. 26. She describes other alternatives adopted by modern directors).

[4] As it was in Strehler's production, which otherwise sought to emphasise the meta-theatrical qualities of the play as a whole.

[5] See Dymkowski, pp. 288–91. Flops include Hytner's 1988 RSC production, where 'Prospero conjures up busy little figures bearing black plastic hampers, and allows a soft-focus harvest to be projected onto the back of the stage. The rich and strange is briefly overtaken by the rich and kitsch' (Kate Kellaway, *Observer*, 30 July 1988), and Hall's 1974 National Theatre production, which drew on the theatrical vocabulary of the Jacobean masque, but was dominated by a 'Juno whose [false] breasts are so enormous that whilst they are on the stage they absorb the attention to the exclusion of all else in fascinated horror' (Harold Hobson, *Sunday Times*, 10 March 1974).

[6] Dymkowski, p. 289.

[7] Charles Osborne, *Daily Telegraph*, 21 May 1988. It is curious, but revealing of the general temper of much stage history, that Warren's valuable, detailed discussion of this production in *Staging Shakespeare's Late Plays* yet makes no mention of the music.

[8] *New Statesman*, 20 August 1982.

7 Siân Radinger (Iris), Virginia Grainger (Juno) and Johanna Benyon (Ceres) imitating puppets as they perform the masque for Mark Lewis Jones (Ferdinand) and Sarah Woodward (Miranda) in Sam Mendes's production at the RSC, 1993 (photographer Michael Le Poer Trench)

Shakespearean (see Textual Analysis, pp. 220–2). Yet the theatrical and critical anxiety about this scene paradoxically directs our attention to its central thematic significance, and underlines the experimental nature of the play as a whole. Though Shakespeare had deployed classical figures in plays such as *As You Like It* and *Cymbeline*, had poked fun at Elizabethan courtly masking in *Love's Labour's Lost*, and had used plays-within-the-play in a variety of ways throughout his career, the masque in *The Tempest* is more elaborate and more complex in its effect than any of them.

MUSIC AND SONG

The Tempest is also exceptional because music is more fundamental to its action and its symbolism than it is in any other Shakespeare play, and its treatment engages profoundly with his culture's understanding of its significance and power. At one end of the spectrum of that understanding was the traditional, neo-platonic view that human music imitated divine harmony and the music of the spheres. Insofar as it shadowed that celestial pattern it was imbued with the power to harmonise the disorderly passions of humankind, and, in the hands of its mythic practitioners, Orpheus, Amphion and the rest, could charm wild beasts, even rocks, stones and trees.[1] This is the view

[1] See Gretchen Ludke Finney, *Musical Backgrounds for English Literature: 1580–1650*, 1962; John Hollander, *The Untuning of the Sky: Ideas of Music in English Poetry, 1500–1700*, 1961; James Anderson Winn, *Unsuspected Eloquence: A History of the Relations between Poetry and Music*, 1981.

that Lorenzo articulates in his dialogue with Jessica in Act 5 of the *Merchant of Venice*, and that Antonio and Sebastian mockingly allude to in this play (2.1.82–3). But it is one which *The Tempest* determinedly sets out to question.

When Ferdinand enters he comments that:

> This music crept by me upon the waters,
> Allaying both their fury and my passion
> With its sweet air.   (1.2.391–3)

This seems a straightforward enunciation of standard neo-platonic theory, but we know, as he does not, that the song has been designed by Prospero to 'draw' him towards Miranda, and detach him from his father, and therefore functions as a means of human rather than divine control. It is followed by 'Full fathom five', which, whatever its symbolic resonance in this play of transformations, tells a lie – Alonso is not dead, but it is important to Prospero's purposes that Ferdinand should think him so. In analogous fashion, when Prospero calls for 'heavenly music' to cure the frenzy of the lords in Act 5 he invokes the same power that Cerimon summons to awaken the apparently dead Thaisa in *Pericles*, 3.2.88–91, or the quarto text of *Lear* requires to cure Lear's madness (4.7.24). But he explicitly commands this music 'To work *mine end* upon their senses' (5.1.53; emphasis added), and we are uncomfortably reminded that he had himself characterised Antonio's subornation of his subjects as setting 'all hearts i'th'state / To what tune pleased his ear' (1.2.84–5).[1] By stressing the essentially rhetorical nature of music and dramatising the way in which it is used to manipulate and control, Shakespeare questions the traditional view of its God-derived power.

Caliban's most frequently quoted speech in praise of the island's music (3.2.127–35) introduces a further set of complications. It has often been argued that his sensitivity to 'sweet airs' is a mark of Shakespeare's intention to elevate him above the merely brutish. But Puttenham's observation that 'the American, the Perusine and the very Canniball, do sing and also say, their highest and holiest matters in certaine riming versicles and not in prose'[2] should give pause to too sentimental a reading – it is precisely the point of the Orpheus myth that even animals respond to musical sound. Stephano and Trinculo's fear, like Antonio and Sebastian's apparent deafness to the music which charms the other lords to sleep in 2.1, is a mark of their declination from human virtue in that they do not even have the brute's instinctive response. It is sometimes asserted that this is the music 'of the island', and therefore that Caliban forlornly responds to something Prospero has taken from him. But Caliban's young ears can have heard only the cries of the imprisoned Ariel, with their grotesque inversion of Orphic myth in making 'wolves howl' (1.2.288). It is Sycorax who confined the musical spirit, Prospero who released him. Nonetheless the poetry Caliban speaks is resonant, and his response is similar to the wonder Ferdinand exhibits towards the

---

[1] For discussion of the identification of royal and musical power in the court masque, see David Lindley, 'The politics of music in the masque', in David Bevington and Peter Holbrook, eds., *The Politics of the Stuart Court Masque*, 1998, pp. 288–91.

[2] George Puttenham, *The Arte of English Poesie* (1589), p. 7.

masque. But just as the masque dissolves, so the riches of Caliban's dream are illusory, and confounded in the mantled pool to which this music actually leads him and his fellows.

At the other end of the spectrum from neo-platonic idealisation, music was considered as the source of riot and disorder. As Prynne later fulminated:

Such songs . . . deprave the manners of those that heare or sing them, exciting, enticing them to lust, to whoredome, adultery, prophanes, wantonnesse, scurrility, luxury, drunkennesse, excesse, alienating their mindes from God, from grace and heavenly things.[1]

Characteristically, however, Shakespeare offers a much more ambivalent picture of the rebels' 'depraved' music. If Stephano's first songs render his maudlin drunkenness comic, Caliban's 'No more dams I'll make for fish' (2.2.156–63) is powerful and assertive, for by singing his celebration of freedom he commands empathy from the audience. As Mark Booth points out, 'most songs of protest do not appeal to an audience as jury but invite the already sympathetic into collective accusation'.[2] And that is also the effect of the 'catch' sung by Stephano, Trinculo and Caliban to the words 'Flout 'em, and scout 'em' (3.2.114–16). The musical nature of the 'catch' – a round in which the same tune is picked up in turn by each singer – is symbolically appropriate for a conspiratorial combination.[3] The unaccompanied, proletarian song stands for that which opposes Prospero's harmonious purposes; but Ariel, playing the popular instruments of pipe and tabor (see illustration 8) co-opts its music, thereby controlling its rebellious energy and transforming it into a means of leading characters in a direction dictated by Prospero.

The distinction between the rebelliously popular and the harmoniously courtly is further blurred by the way in which Caliban's freedom song in 2.2 is echoed by Ariel's song of release in 5.1. They employ different musical vocabularies, but articulate the same feeling. 'Where the bee sucks' (5.1.88–94) accompanies the narrative climax of the play, the moment when Prospero's triumph is signalled by his resumption of his ducal robes, but the song seems pointedly inappropriate to the action. It is not simply the hedonistic triviality of Ariel's ambition which undercuts Prospero's robing, but the contrast the song sets up between the insouciant future Ariel imagines for himself and the heaviness of Prospero's resumption of his political duties.[4] That there is indeed a tension between the song and the action it accompanies is suggested by the fact that in production they are not infrequently separated one from the other, as, for example, in Tree's 1904 production, the RSC 1982, where it was recomposed for the Newcastle and London performances and moved to the beginning of Act 5, and

[1] William Prynne, *Histriomastix* (1633), p. 267.
[2] Mark W. Booth, *The Experience of Songs*, 1981, p. 16.
[3] Shakespeare uses the same musical form in *Twelfth Night* for the subversive below-stairs revelry of Toby Belch, Andrew Aguecheek and Feste.
[4] For a fuller exposition of this argument see my 'Music, masque and meaning in *The Tempest*', in Lindley, *The Court Masque*, pp. 47–59. This view has been challenged by, among others, Robin Headlam Wells, 'Prospero, King James and the myth of the musician-king', in *Elizabethan Mythologies*, 1994, pp. 63–80, Howell Chickering, 'Hearing Ariel's songs', *Journal of Medieval and Renaissance Studies* (1994), 131–72; Jacquelyn Fox-Good, 'Other voices: the sweet, dangerous air(s) of Shakespeare's *Tempest*', *S.St.* (1996), 241–74.

8 Bacchus, the god of drink, playing the three-hole pipe and tabor in an illustration from the 1614 edition of Alciati, *Emblemata*. The pipe and tabor were associated with popular revelry

Leeds, 1999, where Ariel directed the song to the lords, rather than to Prospero, as he charmed them into the magic circle. But the disjunction of song and action is precisely the point. Music may throughout the play have been commandeered for manipulative purposes, but it finally resists such domination. Mark Booth writes that: 'A song, set in a play, but set out of the play too by its music, facilitates our indulgence in feelings that may be undercut before and after the music plays.'[1] The undercutting may equally go the other way; and as we identify with the singer, rather than the robing duke, this song disrupts the closure at which the play is aiming. Furthermore, insofar as music is associated with Prospero's magic, then Ariel as the musical intermediary and agent of Prospero's plans must be released once that magic is disowned.[2] In the

[1] Booth, *Experience of Songs*, p. 118.
[2] See D. P. Walker, *Spiritual and Demonic Magic from Ficino to Campanella*, 2nd edn 1975; Gary Tomlinson, *Music in Renaissance Magic*, 1993.

end, the music of the island is not Prospero's (or Caliban's, for that matter), but Ariel's. In this respect the play seems to suggest that music is of itself morally neutral, and both the precariousness of Prospero's control of music, and the seductive but impossible fantasy of total freedom it suggests, are imaged in this final musical event of the play.

How the music functions within the performed play, however, depends upon the nature of the music actually provided in the theatre, and its character will, in turn, derive from cultural assumptions and historically determined theatrical and musical conventions.[1] There is an enormous difference, for example, between the effect of Ariel's final song in the brevity and directness of the early, probably original, music by Robert Johnson (printed in Appendix 1), in the fugitive minimalism of Tippett's modernist setting first employed in the Old Vic production of 1962, or in the ample and familiar baroque setting by Thomas Arne.[2] Differences of musical language lead to very different dramatic effects. If Ariel's songs are given full-scale quasi-operatic treatment (as they were throughout the eighteenth century and beyond),[3] then the balance between song and surrounding action is profoundly changed. This may be seen in Mrs Charles Calvert's account of her husband's Manchester production of 1864, where his decision to use Arthur Sullivan's recently composed music was opposed by Julia St George as Ariel:

When she found that Sullivan's music was to be used, she pleaded with great earnestness that she might retain Dr Arnold's [sic] and Purcell's settings of Ariel's songs – knowing what she could do with the old music and fearing the new. She gained her point, and her singing of 'Where the Bee sucks' was the success of the evening . . . not until she had sung it for the third time was the play allowed to proceed.[4]

Not only does this illustrate the way in which the musical settings were deployed as part of a segmented series of set-pieces in nineteenth-century production, it also testifies to the astonishingly tenacious hold familiar settings had on the theatre. The songs attributed to Purcell (now generally ascribed to Weldon) from the late seventeenth century,[5] Arne's eighteenth-century settings, and Sullivan's mid nineteenth-century music were all still to be heard on the stage well into the twentieth century, often in random combination one with another.[6] Though in most modern performances the music is entrusted to a single composer, the question raised by the his-

---

[1] My 'Tempestuous transformations', in Shirley Chew and Alistair Stead, eds., *Translating Life: Studies in Transpositional Aesthetics*, 1999, pp. 99–121, is a preliminary attempt to investigate these questions.

[2] Tippett's setting was published in a concert version in *Songs for Ariel*, 1964.

[3] For the chronology and the music of eighteenth-century adaptations, see Julia Muller, 'Music as meaning in *The Tempest*', in A. J. Hoenselaars, ed., *Reclamations of Shakespeare*, 1994, pp. 187–200; Irena Cholij, ' "A thousand twangling instruments": music·and *The Tempest* on the eighteenth-century London stage', *S.Sur.*, 51 (1998), 79–94.

[4] Mrs Charles Calvert, *Sixty-Eight Years on the Stage*, 1911, p. 70. (By 'Arnold' she meant 'Arne', who was always afforded the title 'Dr'.)

[5] Margaret Laurie, 'Did Purcell set *The Tempest*?', *Proceedings of the Royal Musical Association*, 90 (1963–4), 43–57.

[6] Interestingly, it was 'Purcell' and Arne's settings which were claimed as 'the original music' for the play throughout much of the nineteenth century – see the poster for the Leeds 1865 performance (illustration 3).

9 Act 3, Scene 2 from William Poel's production of the play, c. 1897. He was an early advocate of attempts to perform Shakespeare 'authentically' without elaborate scenic effects. The pipe and tabor Ariel plays were in fact a mock-up, and the music was played on a tin whistle

torical unspecificity of the music in earlier productions is still a pertinent one. For in creating a soundscape for Prospero's island the composer or musical arranger is mediating between the seventeenth-century text and the twentieth-century audience in a fashion exactly parallel to the designer, the director and the literary critic.[1]

William Poel, the early proponent of 'authenticity' in Shakespeare performance, employed Arnold Dolmetsch, founder of the early music movement in Britain, to arrange music from early sources for his 1897 production, and played it on 'authentic' instruments (illustration 9).[2] Most earlier twentieth-century productions, however, continued to use the resources of the standard theatre orchestra, a sound neither Jacobean, nor in any way likely to suggest that it is generated by Ariel and his 'quality'. In the last fifty years, as ensembles have become smaller, yet the instrumental palette wider, the effort has frequently been to create, in an unambiguously modern musical vocabulary, an unusual soundscape that underpins the strangeness of the

[1] It is, however, one of the curiosities of modern theatre audiences that they are much more aware of the precise historical semiosis of costume and setting than they are of music.

[2] On Poel, see Marion O'Connor, *William Poel and the Elizabethan Stage Society*, 1987, pp. 54–7. The programme, in the Poel collection at the Theatre Museum, London, specifies 'the original songs and instrumental pieces performed upon the original instruments of Shakespeare's time' which were the virginals, three viols, pipe and drum. (Orgel wrongly states that only the pipe and tabor were used.) Walter Bergmann, very much a successor of Dolmetsch, provided music similarly arranged from early sources for the 1951 Mermaid performance mentioned above, pp. 8–9.

island. The advent of electronic resources has extended such musical possibilities. One of the earliest electronic 'scores' was assembled by Peter Brook for his 1957 production (described by Kenneth Tynan as 'like a combination of glockenspiel, thundersheet, Malayan nose-flute and discreetly tortured Sistine choirboy').[1] This refusal of a conventional score was entirely deliberate on Brook's part. The alienness of the sounds suited his emphasis upon the darker potential of the play, and created an appropriately strange soundscape, but it was also a product of his beliefs about the function of incidental music itself. In a newspaper article he wrote:

It is no longer the ideal to go to an eminent composer . . . and ask him to write a score to accompany a play . . . A good incidental score nowadays is more a matter of timbre and tone colour than of harmony or even of rhythm; it has to appeal to a mind which has at least one and three-quarter ears fully occupied with following the dramatic narrative; it is, in fact, quarter-ear music.[2]

There are, however, two problems raised here. First, the emphasis on subordinating the music to dramatic continuity, though it certainly avoids the dangers of quasi-operatic amplification, yet risks undermining the potential for the songs to 'speak' fully in their own right. Secondly, as is demonstrated by the mixed reviews of Brook's score, the music that is chosen, however carefully matched to a directorial vision, will still be interpreted and responded to independently by audiences *as* a musical language in a way that is not within directorial control.[3]

These problems surface repeatedly in critical reaction to other scores. One example will serve for many. Michael Tippett's music for the 1962 Old Vic performance was designed not to impede the action – the songs of Ariel are short, and the suggestion of strangeness is there in the modernist musical language they employ. Yet reviewers commented unfavourably that the music 'is too thin to create any atmosphere', and that Tippett 'has rarefied his art to the point of non-existence', and though one considered the musical language 'a happy compromise between the idiom of Shakespeare's and our own day', another thought that 'the cast of "Beyond the Fringe" could and should gleefully parody [it]'.[4] Reviewers are rarely unanimous about anything, but their divergence here is witness to the special indeterminacy of musical effect.

There is, however, a third problem to consider. All these scores are now performed in an environment where audiences are accustomed to the convention of 'incidental' music, whereby they know and accept that what they hear is not necessarily heard by characters on stage. It exists, therefore, simultaneously as something 'in' the play, as

---

[1] *Observer*, 18 August 1957.

[2] *Sunday Times*, 22 September 1957.

[3] The very different, positive response to the electronic score for the Shared Experience 1996–7 production, where all sound was generated by Ariel, and fed through a sophisticated computer sound-system, perhaps indicates how much more pervasive, and therefore comprehensible, electronically generated sound is in our culture.

[4] Respectively *Time and Tide*, 7 June 1962; John Warrack, *Sunday Telegraph*, 10 June 1962; Martin Cooper, *Daily Telegraph*, 31 May 1962; *Scotsman*, 4 June 1962. The reaction, of course, might well have been influenced by the fact that this seems to have been a generally unsuccessful production, and by the apparent vocal imperfections of the actor playing Ariel.

a commentary upon it, and as a series of emotional and interpretative cues supporting a directorial perspective. In Shakespeare's theatre, however, there is no clear evidence that music was employed in this fashion.[1] In the modern theatre, therefore, the
sense of the music in the play as the means of Prospero's (rather than the director's)
control is defused. For us the manipulation of an audience's emotions by music is so
commonplace, and film and television have so habituated us to pervasive sound, that
we undervalue the uniqueness of this island 'full of sounds and sweet airs', and,
perhaps more importantly, miss the important questions Shakespeare's play asks about
the nature and limits of music's power.

Thus far, then, I have suggested that attention to the features of *The Tempest* which
mark out its experimental nature directs us to some of its major thematic preoccupations. But implicit in this discussion are two further questions: the first is the extent
to which the play delivers its significance by deliberate reference to the knowledge
and expectations that its contemporary audience brought to it; the second is how far
a modern critic can accurately and fully recreate that environment. Both of these
questions can be clarified and further explored in considering the play's relationships
to its sources and contexts.

Sources and contexts

One of the most substantial changes in critical approach in recent decades has been
a revision of the notion of what constitutes a 'source'. Where once it was assumed
that the term could apply only to those texts with demonstrable verbal connection,
critics are no longer content merely to use sources as instances of the ' "raw material" that the artist fashioned',[2] and have insisted instead upon the dialogue that an
individual text conducts both with its recognisable sources and analogues, and with
the wider culture within which it functioned. Nonetheless, it remains important to
establish a clear sense of the different relationships that may subsist between text,
source and context, and of their consequently varied implication for our response to
the play.

Renaissance writers were familiar with the idea that to recollect a particular literary text was in some way to conduct a conversation with it. Imitation was the foundation of a writer's training,[3] and Thomas Greene has usefully categorised the various
kinds of relationship that such imitation may initiate with an originating text, ranging
from insignificant echo, through passing allusion, to a sustained dialogue.[4] For a critic,
to note the most fleeting of citations may be of interest in mapping the mind of an

---

[1] Martin White disagrees. He writes: 'After experimenting extensively with music, language and action in
a range of plays . . . I am certain that music would have been used . . . in a manner not dissimilar to the
way it was used to accompany action in early cinema and in film scores today' (*Renaissance Drama in
Action*, 1998, p. 154).

[2] Stephen Greenblatt, *Shakespearean Negotiations*, 1988, p. 95.

[3] As Jonson noted in *Discoveries*: 'The third requisite in our poet or maker is imitation, to be able to convert
the substance or riches of another poet to his own use' (*Ben Jonson* (The Oxford Authors), 1985, ed. Ian
Donaldson, p. 585).

[4] Thomas M. Greene, *The Light in Troy: Imitation and Discovery in Renaissance Poetry*, 1982, ch. 3.

author and suggesting his or her creative preoccupations, but in the theatre it is only when a text assumes an audience's recognition of its source that the relationship between the two becomes an essential constituent of meaning. The question is then to decide how far the presence of individual local echoes encourages the reader or audience to perceive a more sustained relationship with the source-text. Not the least unusual feature of *The Tempest*, however, is that – like only two other of Shakespeare's plays, *Love's Labour's Lost* and *A Midsummer Night's Dream*[1] – it has no dominant narrative source, though it is generally agreed that it makes substantial allusion to Virgil, Ovid and Montaigne, and to reports of the wreck of the *Sea Venture* in the Bermudas.

VIRGIL, OVID AND MONTAIGNE

Virgil's presence in *The Tempest* is announced by a number of clear recollections. Ferdinand's first comment on seeing Miranda: 'Most sure the goddess / On whom these airs attend' (1.2.420–1) echoes *Aeneid*, 1.128; Francisco's speech at 2.1.108–17 draws details from the description of serpents swimming towards the shore in *Aeneid*, 2.203–8;[2] and Ariel's vengeful appearance as a harpy in 3.3.52 SD parallels the Celaeno episode in Book 3. (See Appendix 2, pp. 254–5 for texts.) How far these references actually bring Virgil's text as a whole into substantial play, however, is debatable. The single famous phrase 'O dea certe' had become sufficiently disconnected from its original context to be intellectual common property, while Francisco's speech is so unlike the Virgilian original in its context as to suggest that Shakespeare was simply consulting his commonplace-book for a treatment of the topic 'swimming'. Even in the harpy episode Prospero emphasises, in praising Ariel's 'grace', his spirit's difference from the disgusting Virgilian prototype, and it is to the subsequent allegorising of the mythic figure of the harpy, derived as much from Ovid as Virgil, that we seem to be directed.[3] (See Commentary and illustration 10.)

The most incontrovertible link, however, is that made by Gonzalo's likening of Claribel's arrival in Tunis to that of Dido in Carthage, which seems, as Jonathan Bate puts it, to be 'vigorously waving a flag marked *Aeneid*'.[4] The subsequent wrangling with Antonio, Sebastian and Adrian (2.1.70–81) then sets up a contest between Virgil's story and the older historical account of Dido (see Commentary), and it is the tension this establishes between a view of the Carthaginian queen as an icon of idealised chastity on the one hand and illicit sexuality on the other which is of most consequence for the story of Ferdinand and Miranda. They are defined through the way their relationship is linked to, but distinguished from, Virgil's epic. The cave in which Dido and Aeneas consummated their love is invoked, only to be dismissed, as Ferdinand asserts that 'the murkiest den' (4.1.25) will not tempt him to lust. It is teasingly

---

[1] Jonathan Bate suggests that *Titus Andronicus* should be added to this list (Arden edn, 1995, p. 85).

[2] A parallel pointed out by Donna B. Hamilton, *Virgil and 'The Tempest': The Politics of Imitation*, 1990, pp. 21–3.

[3] For the Ovidian connection see Anthony DiMattio, '"The figure of this harpy": Shakespeare and the moralized Ovid', *N&Q*, NS 38 (1991), 70–2.

[4] Jonathan Bate, *Shakespeare and Ovid*, 1993, p. 243.

115   *In repetundos, et adulatores.*

O F Virgins face, with winges, and tallants ſtrong,
    Vpon thy table, *P H I N E V S* here behold,
Ovid: Metam: lib: 6. A monſtrous *Harpie*, that hath præied long,
    Vpon thy meates, while thou art blind, and old,
      And at all times, his appetite doth ſerue,
      While vnregarded, thou thy ſelfe doſt ſterue.

    The Courtes of Kinges, are ſaid to keepe a crew
    Of theſe * ſtill hungry for their private gaine:
* Hirudines æra- The firſt is he, that carries tales vntrue,
rii, Cic: ad Atti- The ſecond, whome baſe * bribing doth maintaine,
cum 1.   The third and laſt, the Paraſite I find,
* Nihil in penati-   Who bites the worſt, if Princes will be blind.
bus eius ſit væna-
le, aut ambitioni
pervium. Tacitus Inſidit dapibus voluecris fœdiſſima Phineu   Crimina qui deſert, repetundus, Gnato notantur
Annal: 13. (Harpyiam vocitant) vngue rapace tuis :   Vile genus fucos, quos alit Aula ſuos.

Baſilie: Doron.   Eſt et apud Reges rudis, invida, ruſtica turba,
                  Hiſtrio, ſcurra, quibus virtus odioſa, Poetas
B: Mantuan: in   Mille modis abigunt, vt quando cadavera corvi
Æglog: Invenere, fugant alias volucreſque feraſque.

                                            Salomone

10 This rather domesticated and disconsolate harpy is from Peacham's *Minerva Britanna*, 1612. The allegory suggests it stands for the rapacious favourites of kings

recalled by the cell in which Ferdinand and Miranda are finally revealed, and the potential parallel is intensified in Miranda's challenge to her future husband, since the adjective 'false' was frequently and formulaically applied to Aeneas. The affinity, however, is quickly repudiated, and the reversal of the Virgilian story is reinforced in the mythology of their betrothal masque, where Venus, who had presided over Dido and Aeneas' union, is banished, and they are blessed by Juno, Aeneas' enemy. An audience capable of recognising these cues would readily respond to Ferdinand and Miranda as a revised, antithetical version of Virgil's lovers.

Since J. M. Nosworthy first suggested that these particular recollections implied that the play conducts a more systematic engagement with Virgil, an increasing number of critics have elaborated and debated the implication of the connection.[1] So, for example, the storm at the play's opening has been related to the storm which initiates the epic's action (see illustration 11), and the interrupted journey of Alonso from Tunis to Italy is seen as a miniature parallel of Aeneas' journey. Virgil's epic theme of the founding of a nation has been linked to the colonial enterprise (as it was in contemporary discussions of imperial expansion). Barbara Mowat suggests that this last link places 'sixteenth-century New World exploration, expansion and plantation within the old, old story of finding, conquering and dominating New Worlds'.[2] But not everyone has found these claims persuasive. Jonathan Bate, for example, argues that 'it is extremely difficult to make the pattern fit'. For him 'Shakespeare's play could be described as a romance-style reworking of epic material. His precedent for such a reworking was Ovid's *Metamorphoses*, the later books of which cover some of the same ground as the *Aeneid*, but in a revisionary way.'[3]

The single direct borrowing from Ovid is Prospero's renunciation of magic in 5.1.33–57. His words are taken from *Metamorphoses*, 7.197–209, and Shakespeare drew on Golding's translation in composing his own version of the speech. (See Appendix 2, pp. 255–6, for the text.) Given the prominence Medea's speech had both in the literature of magic and on the stage,[4] it is certain that a significant number of the original audience would immediately have recognised its provenance, and been able to register its departures from its original. So, for example, where Medea summons the 'spirits of the groves and of the night' to 'be present' in order to aid her magic, Prospero, in one of his characteristic *anacolutha*, loses the syntax of the sentence, and forgets to give the 'elves' he apparently invokes any action to perform. (Not for the first time, recollection induces in him a syntactical indigestion.) This prepares for the departure from Ovid that no moderately learned audience could miss,

[1] J. M. Nosworthy, 'The narrative sources for *The Tempest*', *Review of English Studies*, 24 (1948), 281–94. Jan Kott, 'The *Aeneid* and *The Tempest*', *Arion*, NS 3/4 (1976), 424–51, and '*The Tempest*, or repetition', *Mosaic*, 10:3 (1977), 10–36; Hamilton, *Virgil and The Tempest*; Heather James, *Shakespeare's Troy: Drama, Politics and the Translation of Empire*, 1997; Margaret Tudeau-Clayton, *Jonson, Shakespeare and Early Modern Virgil*, 1998.
[2] Barbara A. Mowat, '"Knowing I loved my books": reading *The Tempest* intertextually', in Hulme and Sherman, pp. 34–5.
[3] Bate, *Shakespeare and Ovid*, p. 244.
[4] It is used, for example, in Jonson's *Masque of Queenes*, lines 218–47, and Middleton's *The Witch*, 5.2.25–9, as well as being cited in witchcraft treatises.

11 The storm in Book 1 of Virgil's *Aeneid* from an early edition of 1502. Juno, Aeneas' enemy, instructs
Aeolus, the god of the winds, to raise the storm, and the four winds in the top left-hand corner may be
said to 'Blow till thou burst thy wind' (1.1.6–7)

Prospero's renunciation of his magic. At the most obvious level, then, just as Ferdinand and Miranda are 'not-Dido-and-Aeneas', Prospero is 'not-Medea'. But the effect
of this invocation is more complicated than that. As Prospero begins the speech, and
as the fact of its recollection of the archetypal witch becomes apparent, we respond
directly to its power and intensity, perceiving the similarity without yet knowing that
it is to be disowned. As Prospero amplifies Medea's claim to have 'made the ghosts
walk', so the potential blasphemy of his magic power becomes frighteningly apparent. Through variation of an extremely well-known original, the issue of the legiti-
macy of Prospero's powers is brought sharply into view, not simply as a matter of
debate, but as something experienced by the audience. To the issue of magic we will
return later, but, as with the *Aeneid*, the next question is how far the dialogue with
the classical poet extends beyond this specific reference. Jonathan Bate sees in *The
Tempest* both a characteristic emphasis on metamorphosis (imaged, for example, in
the song 'Full fathom five'), and a substantial recollection of Ovid's Silver Age of
agriculture and marriage in the masque of Act 4.[1] The Ovidian Golden Age is invoked
by Gonzalo's speech in 2.1, with its vision of a world of communal ownership and an
absence of the need for law and regulation.

The wording of Gonzalo's speech, however, is not taken directly from the first book
of *Metamorphoses*, but from the version of its vision contained in Montaigne's Essay
'Of the Cannibals'. Montaigne is clearly Shakespeare's 'source' here, and yet it is
extremely unlikely that he expected the audience to recognise the fact. Any exploration of Montaigne's significance, therefore, is either a traditional consideration of
'influences' upon Shakespeare as author, or else to be conducted as part of a wider
consideration of contexts for the play. Both of these approaches are sustainable, for
Montaigne's account of the inhabitants of the Americas is explicitly interested in the
nature of tale-telling and the veracity of report – both central concerns of the play –
and at the same time it uses the figure of the cannibal to conduct a critique of the
political and social structures of European society, which brings it within the wider
orbit of discussion of colonialism.[2]

COLONIAL CONTEXTS

This returns us to the material which has for the last two hundred years been consistently claimed as a direct 'source' for the play. Malone first argued that Shakespeare's play was influenced by the reports of the wreck of the *Sea Venture* on the
coast of the Bermudas in 1609, the company's escape from death and final arrival in
Virginia in May 1610.[3] Subsequent scholars have suggested that three texts in particular were absorbed by Shakespeare: Sylvester Jourdain's *Discovery of the Barmudas*
(1610), the Council of Virginia's *True Declaration of the state of the Colonie in Virginia*

---

[1] Bate, *Shakespeare and Ovid*, pp. 239–63.
[2] 'Of the Cannibals', vol. I, no. 30; on Montaigne's influence on the play, see Arthur Kirsch, 'Montaigne
and *The Tempest*', in Gunnar Sorelius and Michael Srigley, eds., *Cultural Exchange between European
Nations during the Renaissance*, 1994, pp. 111–22.
[3] Edward Malone, *An Account of the Incidents, from which the Title and Part of the Story of Shakespeare's
Tempest Were Derived*, 1808.

(1610), and a letter by William Strachey, known by the title of *True Reportory of the Wrack*, which is dated 15 July 1610, was not published until 1625 in *Purchas His Pilgrimes*, but is assumed to have been available to the playwright in manuscript. In fact there is virtually nothing in these texts which manifests the kind of unambiguous close verbal affinity we have seen in the other sources so far considered. Strachey's account of the storm is itself a variation on a standard set-piece topic,[1] and, as the Commentary indicates, many other literary parallels are equally close to Shakespeare's text. Kenneth Muir was not convinced that these accounts were necessarily sources,[2] and Arthur Kinney has suggested that James Rosier's earlier pamphlet, *A True Relation* (1605), is more important to the play than any of them.[3] Whilst it is certainly possible that the apparently miraculous preservation of Sir Thomas Gates, Sir George Summers and their company did influence Shakespeare, and whilst it is indisputable that for an audience in 1611 the apparent parallel would have given the play an irresistible topicality, it is difficult to demonstrate that any of these individual texts were direct sources for the play. They need, rather, to be seen as examples of the many works concerned with colonial adventure – both Spanish and English – which were available to Shakespeare and may have affected the play in less specific, though no less important, ways.

The argument that the action of the play and the issues it raises are connected to the 'New World' of the Americas has been present in discussions of the play at least from the early nineteenth century, and it has become in the last twenty or thirty years the dominant critical perspective upon it.[4] Colonial and postcolonial readings focus on the representation of the relationship between Caliban and the other characters of the play, and the intersection of those relationships with contemporary accounts of New World exploration. Thus the history Prospero and Caliban relate in 1.2, of a friendly relationship deteriorating into one of domination and rebellion, can be paralleled in many accounts of Spanish and (later) English dealings with the native populations of South and North America, and the way in which Trinculo and then Stephano see Caliban as a potential exhibit from which they can derive profit (a perception repeated by Antonio in Act 5) alludes to the way in which Native Americans were indeed shipped back to England as 'booty of a successful voyage'.[5] Most powerfully, whereas Prospero in his brief narrative to Alonso in Act 5 casually asserts that he arrived upon the island 'To be the lord on't' (5.1.162), Caliban's cry: 'This island's mine by Sycorax my mother, / Which thou tak'st from me' (1.2.332–3), brings into the play the debates in the Early Modern period about the rights of conquest and colonisation.

There are other less direct ways in which colonialist concerns might be seen as informing the play. The confrontation with the New World of the Americas, as

---

[1] As Mowat points out ('Reading *The Tempest*', pp. 31–2).
[2] Kenneth Muir, *The Sources of Shakespeare's Plays*, 1977, pp. 278–83.
[3] Arthur F. Kinney, 'Revisiting *The Tempest*', *Modern Philology*, 93 (1995/6), 161–77.
[4] See Charles Frey, '*The Tempest* and the New World', *SQ*, 30 (1979), 29–41.
[5] Kinney, 'Revisiting *The Tempest*', p. 167. See Alden T. Vaughan, 'Trinculo's Indian: American Natives in Shakespeare's England', in Hulme and Sherman, pp. 49–59.

Anthony Pagden demonstrates, raised fundamental problems for European civilisation in incorporating its discoveries 'into their cosmographical, geographical and, ultimately, anthropological understanding'.[1] Not the least of those problems was that of
finding a language in which this world might be represented. As Pagden puts it: 'the
difficulty was to distance [the] account of a new and seemingly bizarre world from
those described in the romances of chivalry'.[2] The difficulty for the travel-writer
was, however, an opportunity for the dramatist, enabling him to address the new in
an old literary vocabulary, familiar to his audience. This fusion is evident in *The
Tempest*, for example, in the confrontation between the lords and the *shapes* who
bring in the banquet at 3.3.19 SD. Alonso's exclamation 'What were these?' leads the
others to talk of travellers' tales being proved true, and Gonzalo to remark of these
'islanders':

> though they are of monstrous shape, yet note
> Their manners are more gentle, kind, than of
> Our human generation you shall find
> Many, nay almost any. (31–4)

The distinction Gonzalo attempts to make between the 'monstrous' islanders and
'Our human generation' points directly towards one of the central debates concerning the nature of the peoples of the Americas. (And his sense of their greater civility
gestures towards the argument of Montaigne's essay from which he had earlier
quoted.) Confronted by the radical difference of Amerindian societies, the first
explorers debated whether they were to be regarded as human or as animal, whether
they were examples of civilisation in its early stages and therefore capable of being
led towards the 'higher' state of European evolution, or simply incommensurable with
all existing norms. These questions were central to the debate about the colonial
project.[3]

Recently a number of critics have pointed to the way the discussion of empire in
the New World echoes English preoccupation with a colony much nearer home, in
Ireland.[4] The same issues, the same questions of categorisation, the same strategies
of 'othering' and the same justifications of violent suppression were being deployed
in a context which had perhaps a more immediate relevance, and a rather clearer vis-
ibility for most of the population, than the faltering, small-scale adventures of the
English in Virginia. But whether Virginia, or Ireland, or both, are taken as the points
of reference, it is clearly important to the reading of *The Tempest* to recognise that

---

[1] Anthony Pagden, *European Encounters with the New World: From Renaissance to Romanticism*, 1993, p. 5.
[2] Ibid., pp. 61–2.
[3] See Anthony Pagden, 'Dispossessing the barbarian: the language of Spanish Thomism and the debate
over the property rights of the American Indians', in Anthony Pagden, ed., *The Languages of Political
Theory in Early-Modern Europe*, 1987, pp. 99–123.
[4] Paul Brown, '"This thing of darkness I acknowledge mine": *The Tempest* and the discourse of colonialism', in Jonathan Dollimore and Alan Sinfield, eds., *Political Shakespeare: Essays in Cultural Materialism*, 2nd edn 1994, pp. 48–71; Barbara Fuchs, 'Conquering islands: contextualizing *The Tempest*', *SQ*, 48
(1997), 45–62; David J. Baker, 'Where is Ireland in *The Tempest*?', in Mark Thornton Burnett and Ramona
Wray, eds., *Shakespeare and Ireland: History, Politics, Culture*, 1997, pp. 68–88; Dympna Callaghan,
Shakespeare Without Women, 2000, ch. 4.

these were matters of dispute and controversy in the period, and to argue that it is the *debate* which the play enacts. For whereas the Virginia Company in 1609 decided not to publish a justification of the plantation out of nervousness that 'ther is much of a Confession, in every unnecessary Apology',[1] Shakespeare, especially in the ambiguous representation of Caliban, stages the debate before his audience's eyes.

COLONIAL CALIBAN

Prospero's first intention to educate Caliban is echoed by Robert Johnson's advice in *The New Life of Virginia* (1612), to 'Take their children, and train them up with gentleness; teach them our English tongue and the principles of religion' in order to 'win them by way of peace and gentleness'.[2] But this hope is converted into abuse and punishment by the attempted rape of Miranda which disrupts the relationship between them. Caliban's crime, it can be argued, is deployed exactly in the way that the narratives of native 'treachery' were customarily used, to evade the charge of unjust expropriation by making the conduct of the natives responsible for their own repression. But if this seems firmly to locate the play within the patterns of colonialist discourse, and, by demonising Caliban, to uphold it, the very excess of Prospero's threatened punishments and the expressiveness of Caliban's language permit an audience to question the justice of his treatment.

Indeed, since Shakespeare's text was restored in the nineteenth century, replacing the unambiguously comic Caliban of Dryden and Davenant's adaptation which dominated the eighteenth-century stage, audiences have found it difficult to resist some degree of sympathy for Caliban, and reviewers have complained at representations which failed to bring out the suffering and pathos the part can sustain.[3] So, for example, Benson's performance, which, under Darwinian influence,[4] treated Caliban comically as an ape-like 'missing link', provoked one reviewer to observe that it 'prevented the audience from rightly sympathizing with the "ill-used, down-trodden wretch" who is "wantonly tortured and tormented for not obeying the despot" Prospero'.[5] In 1934 Ivor Brown responded positively to Roger Livesey's Caliban (the first in which black make-up seems to have been used) arguing that 'Caliban should be the oppressed aboriginal as well as the lecherous monster, a case for the radical politician's sympathy as well as for Prospero's punishment'.[6]

During the twentieth century the move was generally to encourage such sympathy by making Caliban less and less monstrous. It was not a uniform process, however – whereas in 1938 Wilson Knight adopted a costume that emphasised strangeness,

[1] B. J. Sokol and Mary Sokol, '*The Tempest* and legal justification of plantation in Virginia', *Shakespeare Yearbook*, 7 (1996), 353–80; p. 368.
[2] Quoted in H. C. Porter, *The Inconstant Savage: England and the North American Indian 1500–1600*, 1979, p. 342.
[3] The stage history of Caliban's representation has been comprehensively treated by Trevor R. Griffiths, '"This island's mine": Caliban and colonialism', *The Yearbook of English Studies*, 13 (1983), 159–80, and by the Vaughans. See also Orgel and Dymkowski.
[4] Mediated through Daniel Wilson, *Caliban: The Missing Link*, 1873.
[5] Dymkowski, p. 53. Benson considered the role of Caliban his 'pet part' and played it from the 1890s to the end of his career in the 1930s in what seems to have been a largely unchanged fashion.
[6] Ibid., p. 55.

rather than monstrosity (illustration 12), two years later the Old Vic performance still represented Caliban as clearly monkey-like (illustration 13). In 1974, however, Denis Quilley's Caliban had a 'bisected' make-up, 'on one half the ugly scrofulous monster whom Prospero sees, on the other an image of the noble savage',[1] and the increasing use of black actors to play the part has further debarred perception of him as a grotesque.[2] But sympathy for Caliban need not extend to an understanding of the play as a political drama, nor, conversely, need a recognition of the colonial politics of the play lead to a sympathetic view of Caliban.

In the Collins School and College Classics edition of the play in 1875 the Rev. D. Morris casually observes that:

At a time when colonization was taking hold of the public mind in England, the contrast of savage and civilized man would do much to justify the formation of colonies in lands inhabited by rude races, and this probably may have been one of Shakespeare's objects in the delineation of Caliban.

(p. 10)

Wilson Knight's performance of the part presumably reflected his belief that *The Tempest* was 'a myth of the national soul', and reflected Britain's 'colonizing, especially her will to raise savage peoples from superstition and blood-sacrifice, taboos and witchcraft and the attendant fears and slaveries, to a more enlightened existence'.[3]

Obviously enough, how one responds to a colonised Caliban will depend crucially on how one responds to colonialism itself. Beerbohm Tree's much-reshaped version of *The Tempest* in 1904 placed the actor-manager's performance as Caliban at its centre.[4] To underline his view of the part he rearranged the ending so that the play concluded with a tableau in which Prospero's ship is seen leaving (illustration 14), and:

Caliban creeps from his cave, and watches the departing ship bearing away the freight of humanity which for a brief spell has gladdened and saddened his island home, and taught him to 'seek for grace' . . . As the curtain rises again, the ship is seen on the horizon, *Caliban* stretching out his arms towards it in mute despair. The night falls, and *Caliban* is left on the lonely rock. He is a King once more.

(p. 63)

Tree explains that 'in his love of music and his affinity with the unseen world, we discern in the soul which inhabits the brutish body of this elemental man the germs of a sense of beauty, the dawn of art'. This is a 'sympathetic' but yet 'pro-imperial' reading of Caliban's situation, and one to which contemporary reviewers were alert. The *Daily Telegraph* commented:

---

[1] Ibid., p. 59, quoting Irving Wardle.

[2] This has been true at least since 1970, when an audience properly sensitive to endemic racism would see a black actor playing a grotesque Caliban as unacceptable stereotyping. (But see below, p. 43 n.2.)

[3] Knight, *Crown of Life*, p. 255. Knight was later to modify his views – see 'Caliban as a red man', in Philip Edwards et al., eds., *Shakespeare's Styles*, 1980, pp. 205–20.

[4] Tree's text was first published in a souvenir programme on the occasion of the fiftieth performance in 1904, and later that year as an 'Acting Edition'. It can be accessed at http://www.leeds.ac.uk/english/staff/projects/treestempest/. For discussions of this performance see Mary M. Nilan, '*The Tempest* at the turn of the century: cross-currents in production', *S.Sur.*, 25 (1972), 113–23 (which also discusses Benson's and other performances); Brian Pearce, 'Beerbohm Tree's production of *The Tempest*, 1904', *New Theatre Quarterly*, 11 (1995), 299–308.

12 G. Wilson Knight as Caliban in a performance in Toronto, 1938. He made up with green body-paint and purple highlights. Throughout his academic career Wilson Knight performed in Shakespeare's plays with colleagues and students

13 John Gielgud as Prospero and Jack Hawkins as a monkey-like Caliban complete with tail, in George Devine's production at the Old Vic, 1940 (photographer Edwin Smith)

If there is one thing more certain than another about 'The Tempest', it is that it marks the beginning of England's colonising impulses, and raises in literary form social and ethical questions, concerned with the right of the conquering race to subdue an inferior one.[1]

More strikingly, W. T. Stead remarked:

I felt a sting of conscience . . . when Caliban proceeded to unfold a similar case to that of the Matabele. It might have been the double of old King Lobeguila rehearsing the blandishments which led to his doom . . . Who could help sympathising with his outburst after recollecting how he had helped the newcomer? The spectacle of Caliban as he crawled crouching on all fours, ravenously eating a fish, brought back reminiscences of mealtime in a Johannesburg compound . . . It was as if I saw represented on the stage, in dramatic form, the history of the last few years.[2]

Yet a review in the *New York Tribune* argued that Tree

has not thrown any light upon the erudite theory that the poet was attempting to satirize the moral right of a conquering race to impose its will upon an inferior one, nor has he lent his

[1] 15 September 1904.

[2] *Review of Reviews*, October 1904, where it appears anonymously as the account of a 55-year-old's first visit to the theatre to see a play he has read often. It continues with bizarre allegorisation of the play in terms of contemporary politics, concluding that Caliban coming to his senses 'prefigures a Liberal victory next year'.

14 Charles A. Buchel's illustration of the concluding tableau in Beerbohm Tree's 1904 production from the souvenir programme of the fiftieth performance

authority to the fantastic idea that the master of the drama, with prophetic insight, was teaching Englishmen to think imperially at a time when they were entering upon their colonial enterprise.[1]

Apart from showing that colonial readings of the play were already in place at the beginning of the twentieth century, these reviews indicate that the perception of such a resonance relies crucially on the mind-set of the reviewer rather than the intent of the actor (bearing out McKellen's comment at the beginning of this introduction), and that the response to a 'colonial' reading is conditioned by the cultural assumptions of the period. But Stead's review is also remarkable for the way it reads the play in terms of a specific memory that he brings to it. To very different effect George Lamming makes a similar point:

I cannot read *The Tempest* without recalling the adventure of those voyages reported by Hakluyt; and when I remember the voyages and the particular period in African history, I see *The Tempest* against the background of England's experiment in colonisation . . . *The Tempest* was also prophetic of a political future which is our present. Moreover, the circumstances of my life, both as a colonial and exiled descendant of Caliban in the twentieth century, is an example of that prophecy.[2]

[1] *New York Tribune*, Weekly Review, 8 October 1904.
[2] George Lamming, *The Pleasures of Exile*, 1960, p. 13.

For this Caribbean writer the play offers an image in, through and against which he can represent his own situation.[1] Oscar Mannoni's *Psychologie de la colonisation*, 1950, translated under the title *Prospero and Caliban*, attempted 'to explain and account for the mentality of colonization and racism in general', and deployed reference to Shakespeare's play as a myth through which that mentality might be understood.[2] Though his analysis of the 'dependency complex' of the colonised has been strongly challenged, the importance of his work to the postcolonial reading of *The Tempest* has been enormous. Jonathan Miller's 1970 production was avowedly influenced by it, especially in its representation of Ariel and Caliban as different versions of the colonised subject.[3] Yet it was possible for the anti-colonial perspective of this production to be resisted, even as it was acknowledged. One reviewer commented: 'Norman Beaton's Ariel is the lordly African colonized by European Prospero, impatient for independence. Rudolph Walker's Caliban is the ex-African degraded into the New World slave, used solely for Prospero's profit. Mr Beaton and Mr Walker speak the lines with a sensitive precision exceptional among West Indian actors.'[4] In this reviewer's account the challenge of the production is defused by astonishing condescension towards the black actors – who have at least learned to speak properly, and so may be returned to the mainstream of 'Shakespearean' acting style.

POSTCOLONIAL APPROACHES

American, Caribbean and African 'writing back' to *The Tempest*, like Miller's production, anticipated the subsequent explosion of postcolonial literary criticism of it.[5] Whereas older critics simply, and approvingly, saw the play as one which unproblematically represented colonial relationships, more recent writers use postcolonial theory to read 'against the grain' of the text in order to reveal its underlying, unconscious assumptions, and, as a consequence, to enable a hostile critique, especially of Prospero. This critical perspective offers 'an explanation of features of the play either ignored or occluded by critical practices that have often been complicit, whether consciously or not, with a colonialist ideology'.[6] What for the reviewer of Tree's pro-

---

[1] See also Roberto Fernández Retamar, 'Caliban: notes towards a discussion of culture in America', *Massachusetts Review*, 15 (1973–4), 11–16; Edward Kamau Brathwaite's poems 'Caliban', in *The Arrivants*, 1973, and 'Letter Sycorax' in *Middle Passages*, 1992. For other examples see Thomas Cartelli, *Repositioning Shakespeare: National Formations, Postcolonial Appropriations*, 1999; Rob Nixon, 'Caribbean and African appropriations of *The Tempest*', *Critical Inquiry*, 13 (1987), 557–78; Chantal Zabus, 'Prospero's progeny curses back: postcolonial, postmodern, and postpatriarchal rewritings of *The Tempest*', in Theo D'haen and Hans Bertens, eds., *Liminal Postmodernisms*, 1994, pp. 115–38.

[2] Oscar Mannoni, *Prospero and Caliban: The Psychology of Colonization*, trans. Pamela Powesland, 1956, reissued with a new foreword by Maurice Bloch, 1990, p. v.

[3] See Jonathan Miller, *Subsequent Performances*, 1986, pp. 159–61. His was a reading influenced by 'the recent history of Nigeria', rather than the story of New World colonisation. For discussion of this production see David L. Hirst, *The Tempest: Text and Performance*, 1984, pp. 41–68, where it is one of four productions treated in some detail.

[4] *Punch*, 24 June 1970. The *Illustrated London News* commented that 'Miller has theories about colonialism . . . We need not worry over this.'

[5] See Jonathan Bate, 'Caliban and Ariel write back', *S.Sur.*, 48 (1995), 155–62.

[6] Francis Barker and Peter Hulme, 'Nymphs and reapers heavily vanish: the discursive con-texts of *The Tempest*', in John Drakakis, ed., *Alternative Shakespeares*, 1985, pp. 236–48; p. 204. See also Peter Hulme, *Colonial Encounters*, 1986, for a more extended and nuanced account of the play.

duction was a 'fantasy' is, for the postcolonialist critic, a self-evident truth – *The Tempest* is not only a colonialist text, but has functioned historically to support and validate a colonialist ideology.

But if it is a play about colonialism, Prospero is a very odd colonist indeed. He did not choose to voyage to his island, has no interest in founding an outpost of Milan, and no desire to turn the riches of the island which Caliban has made known to him into tradeable commodities – aims which were absolutely central to the Virginia propaganda. In many respects he seems closer to Duke Senior, reluctant inhabitant of the Forest of Arden in *As You Like It*, than to Sir Thomas Gates, and generically his island functions rather more like the 'green worlds' of earlier Shakespearean comedy, from *Two Gentlemen of Verona* onwards, than it does as a colonised territory.[1] As Robert Miola remarks: 'The island setting of *The Tempest* constitutes the *locus amoenus*, or "pleasant place" of the pastoral genre' and 'provides the conventional retreat from civilization and the courtly world'.[2] One might also argue that Caliban is not an indigenous native, but rather a first-generation colonist himself. His enslavement by Prospero repeats his mother's earlier imprisonment of Ariel, who might be considered the island's 'real' indigenous inhabitant. In sum, as Jeffrey Knapp puts it: 'the action of Prospero's Mediterranean isle, controlled as it is by Prospero's magic, steadfastly resists the colonial analogy it nevertheless suggests'.[3] For some writers this is evidence enough to dismiss postcolonial interpretation altogether. Brian Vickers concludes: 'If modern critics want to denounce colonialism they should do so by all means, but this is the wrong play.'[4]

A distinction, however, needs to be made between critical readings of the play itself, and its rewritings by authors who use it as a source-text – one which allows them both to articulate their own postcolonial position and to undertake the larger cultural enterprise of subverting Shakespeare's function as 'the quintessence of Englishness and a measure of humanity itself'.[5] For Lamming, Césaire and many other writers, *The Tempest* was emphatically the 'right' play and their work generates its power through a contestatory dialogue with Shakespeare's text.[6] But many recent critics have not been prepared to allow such a separation between *The Tempest* and its later appropriations and rewritings. Peter Hulme argues that 'postcolonial reading claims to locate its local analyses in the words of the text, not in its own decision to

[1] See, for example, C. L. Barber, *Shakespeare's Festive Comedy*, 1959, Northrop Frye, *A Natural Perspective*, 1965. The view of the play as a 'pastoral comedy' was once the dominant perception of it.
[2] Robert S. Miola, *Shakespeare's Reading*, 2000, p. 144. Unlike the earlier comedies, however, the 'archetypal movement from court to country, in fact, has already happened before the beginning of the play'.
[3] Jeffrey Knapp, *An Empire Nowhere*, 1992, p. 221. Gillies, *Geography*, however, suggests that the narrative of the play in moving from a 'dispersal myth', through a 'plantation myth' to a 'myth of renewal' has 'an obvious resonance with the discourse of the New World in general and that of Virginia in particular' (pp. 141–7).
[4] Brian Vickers, *Appropriating Shakespeare: Contemporary Critical Quarrels*, 1993, p. 246.
[5] Ania Loomba and Martin Orkin, eds., *Postcolonial Shakespeares*, 1998, p. 1.
[6] On Césaire, see, for example, James Arnold, 'Césaire and Shakespeare: two *Tempests*', *Comparative Literature*, 40 (1978), 236–48; Laurence M. Porter, 'Aimé Césaire's reworking of Shakespeare: colonialist discourse in *Une Tempête*', *Comparative Literature Studies*, 32 (1995), 360–81.

find postcolonial themes present, to land a seventeenth-century play with a late-twentieth-century agenda'.[1] Richard Strier goes further by insisting that in deploying the writings of Mannoni or Césaire as interpretative tools he is not 'exploring the "political unconscious" of the play, or finding meanings in it that the play does not want us to notice. I understand the meanings that I ascribe to the play as conscious and intended.'[2]

For these and many other contemporary critics, then, the perspective afforded by postcolonial criticism reveals something that is intrinsic to the seventeenth-century play, and its rewritings provide a clarification of its implication in the politics of colonial expansion. I would argue, however, that consideration of Césaire's play – one of the most important and powerful of such rewritings – actually questions these claims, and demonstrates the ways in which a postcolonial reading depends upon a particular selection and weighting of aspects of Shakespeare's play. The absence of any overt colonial motivation in Shakespeare's Prospero, for example, is remedied by an early scene in which Césaire's Prospero declares that he had been banished because: 'I had discovered the precise location of these lands that had been sought for centuries, and I was preparing to take possession of them.'[3] This purposeful supplementation is evident also in modifications Césaire introduces in two closely linked moments in the play, of particular significance for postcolonial critics.

In a speech attributed to Miranda in the Folio (see Commentary) she claims:

> I pitied thee,
> Took pains to make thee speak, taught thee each hour
> One thing or other. When thou didst not, savage,
> Know thine own meaning, but wouldst gabble like
> A thing most brutish, I endowed thy purposes
> With words that made them known. (1.2.353–8)

To which Caliban responds:

> You taught me language, and my profit on't
> Is, I know how to curse. (363–4)

This exchange has been taken as symptomatic of the way in which the coloniser deprives the indigenous population of its language, and comparisons have frequently been made with the practices of Spanish colonisers in the Americas, and the English attempt to extirpate the language of the Irish. The sense that control of language is a means of ensuring that the subjected can articulate their subjection only in a language which already defines their subordinate relationship to the powerful is one which speaks directly to the condition of the colonised.[4] But in order for Caliban's

---

[1] Hulme and Sherman, p. 234.
[2] Strier, 'Politics', p. 11.
[3] Aimé Césaire, *A Tempest*, translated by Philip Crispin, 2000, p. 16. Césaire further consolidates the colonial reading by having Alonso and the rest set out on their journey to discover Prospero's new territories, rather than as a consequence of the marriage of Claribel.
[4] See Edward Kamau Brathwaite, *The Colonial Encounter: Language*, 1984; Stephen Greenblatt, *Learning to Curse*, 1990, pp. 16–39.

situation to be understood in these terms the assumption must be that he himself had a prior language which was displaced by Prospero's. In Césaire's rewriting of the play, this is unambiguously asserted, since his Caliban enters uttering the word 'Uhuru' (meaning 'freedom' in Swahili). The subsequent dialogue underlines the significance of that theft of his native tongue. Yet, as so often in *The Tempest*, there is an alternative frame of reference, which derives from a different understanding of the situation before the play opens.

If Caliban has a language of his own, then he can have learnt it only from Sycorax, and the fact that Caliban seems to know of her magic powers, and the name of her god, Setebos, might suggest that he had indeed acquired a speech from her, which Miranda arrogantly misinterpreted as 'gabble'. Yet Miranda's words will sustain a very different reading. E. J. Ashworth writes that: 'Medieval and Renaissance philosophy of language is characterised by two central doctrines, which can only be fully understood in conjunction: the doctrine that spoken language is purely conventional and the doctrine that spoken language corresponds to a mental language, which has natural signification.'[1] The second of these 'doctrines' corresponds exactly to Miranda's comment that though Caliban possessed ideas and thoughts, he had no language in which to 'make them known'. If language is 'conventional', then meaning exists only by social agreement – a belief commonly held from classical times onwards.[2] Caliban's orphan situation, then, can be interpreted as that of one denied the social environment essential to the acquisition and development of language. Only when Prospero and Miranda arrive on the island does the 'society' exist within which Caliban can find the ability to communicate. A further complication in the Renaissance view of language, however, was introduced by the biblical suggestion of a divine origin for language, when Adam names every creature that God puts before him (Genesis 2.19–20). Caliban recollects that Prospero would 'teach me how / To name the bigger light, and how the less' (1.2.335–6) – phrases that recall the Bible, and cast Caliban as a kind of paradisal innocent. His speech – especially in his description of the delights of the island to Stephano and Trinculo at 2.2.137–49 – is characterised by an Adamic pleasure in naming physical objects with a verbal caress. In either event, however, it is perfectly possible to argue that Prospero and Miranda were not depriving Caliban of his own pre-existing language, but providing for him the society within which he could learn language at all. The need Césaire feels to supplement and thereby clarify Shakespeare's presentation by affording Caliban an ability to speak Swahili paradoxically emphasises that this is not the only possible reading of the story of his acquisition of language.

But the plural possibilities that the text may sustain for the reader must, in performance, be focused by an actor's choice of an appropriate voice for Caliban on stage. In earlier productions a savage Caliban was characterised by an utterance 'half snarl, half hiss' in William Burton's 1854 New York performance,[3] or by Benson's 'grinning

---

[1] Charles B. Schmitt and Quentin Skinner, eds., *The Cambridge History of Renaissance Philosophy*, 1988, p. 155.
[2] See Jane Donawerth, *Shakespeare and the Sixteenth-Century Study of Language*, 1984, p. 52.
[3] Dymkowski, p. 52.

and chattering and making a series of discordant, inarticulate noises'.[1] Trevor R. Griffiths cites a number of performances in the 1920s and 30s in which actors 'tried to get the monstrous character by breaking up all the lines into pieces',[2] but, as Caliban has been treated with greater sympathy in more recent productions, other possibilities have been explored. David Suchet, who played the part at Stratford in 1978–9, wrote that 'the voice I used was slightly stilted as I tried to make it clear that I had been taught to speak'.[3] Timothy Walker, in the Leeds 1999 production, answered Stephano's question, 'Where the devil should he learn our language?' (2.2.60–1), in the most straightforward fashion – he learnt his language from Prospero and Miranda, and therefore spoke as they did. This Caliban had no memory of any other language, but the contrast between his upper-class accent and the curses he delivered, and the juxtaposition of his courtly language with the regional accents of Stephano and Trinculo, served admirably to register the problematic position of a Caliban who *only* has the language of his master in which to articulate his rage.[4]

If the question of Caliban's language is important to postcolonial readings of the play, then equally central is the accusation Prospero levels at him of the attempted rape of Miranda. It is this reported act which, in the play, is held to justify the treatment he receives. In Shakespeare's text the charge is not denied; the unrepentant Caliban simply wishes ''t had been done' (1.2.349). In Césaire's play, however, Caliban responds to the accusation with the words:

Rape! Rape! Listen, old goat, you've foisted your own lustful cravings on me. Know this: your daughter means nothing to me, your cave neither. (p. 21)

The problematic nature of the charge for a positive reading of Caliban is amply demonstrated by Césaire's flat denial of it. Literary critics, however, cannot so peremptorily write it out of the play; instead they adopt a range of strategies to defuse or redirect its significance. Dympna Callaghan, for example, suggests that 'What is suppressed by Prospero and Miranda's version of history is the reality of colonial desire, here transformed into and demonized as rape',[5] whilst Joan Pong Linton argues that 'For Caliban, [Miranda's] education of him thus operates as a form of cultural rape, to which his attempted rape of her serves as a symbolic playback.'[6] The metaphorical ingenuity of such readings, however, downplays the physical reality of characters on stage. If we accept – as we must – the fact of attempted rape, then it is not surprising that Miranda 'does not love to look on' Caliban, nor is the revulsion expressed in her speech to him inappropriate, especially if we imagine that it is a

---

[1] Quoted in Griffiths, '"This island's mine"', p. 167.

[2] Ibid., p. 174. This comment is on Henry Baynton's 1926 Caliban.

[3] Philip Brockbank, ed., *Players of Shakespeare*, 1985, p. 179. David Troughton in the 1993 RSC production similarly savoured his words, generating both a sense of the alienness of the language he spoke, and yet his fascination with it.

[4] This was further intensified as Caliban reacted with horror to Stephano's promise that his liquor would 'give language to you'.

[5] Callaghan, *Shakespeare Without Women*, p. 126.

[6] Joan Pong Linton, *The Romance of the New World*, 1998, p. 155. See also David Dabydeen's controversial poems in *Coolie Odyssey*, 1988, where he dramatises the 'encounter with whites' as a sexual encounter with 'the "White Woman" (Miranda/Britannia)'.

relatively recent event. From Miranda's perspective at least, Susan Bennett's assertion that 'the rape *only* has significance insofar as it proves the savagery of the colonial subject' is scarcely adequate.[1]

I am not challenging the force of Césaire's creative and theatrically powerful rewriting of Shakespeare's play – it would be as silly to contend that he got the play 'wrong'
as it would be to complain at Shakespeare's 'falsification' of Ovid's Medea speech. I
do not seek to deny the usefulness and importance of *The Tempest* to postcolonial
writers more generally, nor to suggest that questions of colonial relationships would
have been invisible to the original audience or ought to be excluded from modern
interpretations.[2] I suggest only that analysis of the ways in which Césaire creatively
rewrites *The Tempest* indicates the kinds of supplementation and adaptation that are
necessary to sustain a univocal reading of the play as a 'colonialist' text.

The colonial reading of the play has not gone uncontested. In the first place, the
figure of Caliban can be placed in other contexts. He can, for example, be situated
within the period's fascination with monstrous births and prodigies, as David Cressy
and Mark Thornton Burnett have suggested.[3] He also draws upon a much older tradition of the 'wild man', who had figured in romance literature throughout the Middle
Ages, upon the fantastic creatures of the bestiaries (illustration 15) and upon the classical satyr, half man, half beast in his predatory sexuality.[4] That these symbols of
society's liminal figures were, as Wittkower puts it, to 'migrate' westward and be
visited upon the indigenous populations of the Americas,[5] and that the African
stereotype at the time included sexual potency, does not mean that this was the only
understanding of them available to the first audience of *The Tempest*.[6] It is precisely

---

[1] Susan Bennett, *Performing Nostalgia: Shifting Shakespeare and the Contemporary Past*, 1996, p. 126 (my italics).

[2] Though it seems to be the case that the theatre has begun to move away from colonial readings. Ralph Berry commented in 1993, 'this reading is less popular today. I suspect that directors have become bored with Caliban as a victim of colonial oppression . . . the colonial framework is a constriction of the play, which may have outlived its usefulness' (*Shakespeare in Performance*, p. 129). The recent trend towards gender- and colour-blind casting is also beginning to subvert postcolonial critiques of the play. When, as in the Leeds 1999 production, a black Ferdinand is reunited with a father who is played by a white female actor, or when Vanessa Redgrave at Shakespeare's Globe in 2000 plays Prospero 'as a man', the effect is quite different from Miller's use of black actors in 1970, or Retallack's 1981 production with a female Prospero which introduced textual changes to 'lady', 'mother', 'mistress' (Dymkowski, p. 119). Peter Brook's multinational 1990 Paris performance chose a German Caliban 'to bring a new vision to the part, so often presented either as a monster made up of rubber and plastic or as a Negro, exploiting the colour of his skin to illustrate in a very banal way the notion of a slave' (*There Are No Secrets*, 1993, p. 107).

[3] David Cressy, *Travesties and Transgressions in Tudor and Stuart England*, 2000, ch. 3; Mark Thornton Burnett, ' "Strange and woonderfull syghts": *The Tempest* and the discourse of monstrosity', *S.Sur.*, 50 (1997), 187–99; Katharine Park, 'Unnatural conceptions: the study of monsters in sixteenth- and seventeenth-century France and England', *P&P*, 92 (1981), 20–54.

[4] See, for example, Spenser, *The Faerie Queene*, 3.10, where prodigious sexual performance is attributed to the satyrs. Robert Henke notes that the pastoral satyr of Italian drama also embodies the ambivalent and contradictory possibilities of Shakespeare's Caliban (*Pastoral Transformations*, p. 108).

[5] Rudolf Wittkower, *Allegory and the Migration of Symbols*, 1977, ch. 5, 'Marvels of the East: a study in the history of monsters'.

[6] Ania Loomba, *Gender, Race, Renaissance Drama*, 1992, p. 150, sees Caliban stereotyped as the 'black rapist', and as Peter Fryer, *Staying Power: The History of Black People in Britain*, 1984, p. 7, points out, the notion that 'every male African had an enormous penis' is attested by the 'tiny naked figures of

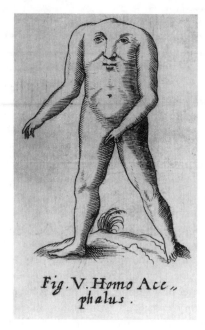

15 Two monsters – a headless man, and a manlike fish – from Gaspar Schott, *Physica Curiosa* (1662), drawing on standard images with antecedents stretching back to the Middle Ages and beyond. (Compare 3.3.46–7: 'such men / Whose heads stood in their breasts', and Trinculo's question, 'What have we here – a man, or a fish?' (2.2.23))

what Marina Warner calls the 'contradictory zoology' of the character, made up of 'shuffling and overlapping pictures', which has 'made Caliban notoriously difficult to cast and dress', and which permits readers and audiences to respond very differently to him.[1]

A number of critics have gone further in insisting that the invocation of an American context is inappropriate or anachronistic,[2] and recently several writers have argued

Africans on more than one fifteenth-century map'. See *H8* 5.3.32–4: 'Or have we some strange Indian with the great tool come to court, the women so besiege us'.

[1] Marina Warner, '"The foul witch" and her "freckled whelp": Circean mutations in the New World', in Hulme and Sherman, pp. 97–113; pp. 98–9.

[2] See, for example, Elmer Edgar Stoll, *Poets and Playwrights: Shakespeare, Jonson, Spenser, Milton*, 1930; Meredith Anne Skura, 'Discourse and the individual: the case of colonialism in *The Tempest*', *SQ*, 40 (1989), 42–69; Tristan Marshall, '*The Tempest* and the British Imperium in 1611', *The Historical Journal*, 41.2 (1998), 375–400.

that the colonial reading of the play masks the Mediterranean contexts which are much more obvious on the play's surface.[1] Certainly the play emphasises that its island is located between Italy and the North African coast. Not only are the lords ship-wrecked on their journey back from Tunis, but, in an exchange whose very redundancy suggests its significance, Prospero solicits from Ariel the information that Sycorax originated from Algiers. Both places were under the control of the Ottoman Empire, and had been the scene of attempted conquest by the Spanish. Algiers in particular was noted as a haven for pirates and as a place where Europeans were themselves enslaved. The function and effect of these pointers to an African dimension for the play seems, however, elusive. There is little agreement between critics on how they are to be read. Where Fuchs emphasises the 'outrageousness' of the forced marriage of Claribel to the King of Tunis in order to argue that the gender politics of the play 'participates in the text's containment of Islamic expansionism', Wilson contends that the wrecking of Alonso's ship makes Prospero 'a king of pirates', and identifies him with the renegade son of the Earl of Leicester, Robert Dudley. Kastan focuses more generally on the world of European dynastic politics, and notes, as others have done, the similarity of Prospero to the Holy Roman Emperor, Rudolf II, who was deposed by his brother because of his preoccupation with study and magic.[2] While it might seem self-evident that the audience in 1611 would have had an awareness of the significance of Algiers and of Tunis that was more precise – and quite possibly more immediately threatening – than a modern readership readily recognises, efforts to make the North African dimension of the play yield more than passing resonances struggle as yet to be fully convincing.

MAGIC AND RELIGION

There can, however, be little argument that magic and religion are topics central to the play, even if they have tended to slip into the background of recent criticism. Thomas Blount defined magic thus:

Magick Art (magia) in general, is wisdom or contemplation of heavenly Sciences, and is two fold; Natural, which is lawful, and is the ground of all true Physick, and the occult wisdom of nature, without which all mans Reason and Knowledge is Ignorance; The other is Diabolical, superstitious and unlawful, and is called Necromancy: whereby men attain to the knowledge of things by the assistance of evil spirits.[3]

This seems to offer a convenient formula for a reading of magic in *The Tempest* in which Prospero's good version is simply set against Sycorax's bad. Kermode influentially argued for such a binary opposition, though he characterised it as one of Sycorax's 'natural magic' as opposed to Prospero's 'holy magic'.[4] That he uses

---

[1] Fuchs, 'Conquering islands'; Richard Wilson, 'Voyage to Tunis: new history and the old world of *The Tempest*', *ELH*, 64 (1997), 333–57; Brotton, pp. 23–42; David Scott Kastan, *Shakespeare After Theory*, 2000, ch. 10.

[2] Fuchs, 'Conquering islands', p. 61, Kastan, *Shakespeare After Theory*, pp. 192–3.

[3] Thomas Blount, *Glossographia* (1656). Early Modern English Dictionaries Database at http://www.chass.utoronto.ca./english/emed/emedd.html

[4] Kermode, p. xl.

Blount's positive term negatively is an indication of the problem of nomenclature in the period. As Nicholas Clulee puts it: 'the magical heritage of the Renaissance was exceedingly complex and . . . the distinctions between various types of magic had become blurred through frequent intermingling'.[1] Nonetheless, some definitions must be risked. 'Natural magic' was essentially 'a practice consisting in the knowledge of hidden things and the art of working wonders',[2] and occupied a legitimate place within the aspirations of the intellectual elite. As Allen Debus observes, the 'student of nature might learn to acquire natural powers not known to others and thus astonish the populace, even though these powers were known to be God-given and available to all'.[3] The natural magician's 'marvels' might extend from mechanical devices, such as John Dee's flying scarab for a Cambridge performance of Aristophanes' *Peace*, to the control over tempests, the seasons and harvests that Bacon promised in the *Magnalia Naturae*.[4] Both Prospero's theatrical magic (including the *quaint device* by which the banquet in 3.3 is made to disappear) and his ability to generate storms might, therefore, be included in this category.

In the writings of neo-platonists and Hermeticists, however, 'natural magic' was but the first stage of an aspiration to wisdom that ascended via celestial or astrological magic to ceremonial or religious magic.[5] This ascent involved the purification of the adept himself, and led finally to the possibility of converse with angelic spirits. Insofar as Prospero's 'secret studies' are devoted to the 'bettering of my mind' he casts himself as a 'white' theurgist,[6] and that he exercises his power through the agency of the spirit Ariel indicates that he practises the highest, 'ceremonial' magic.[7] Such magic, however, veered dangerously towards the black arts of diabolic inspiration, and Shakespeare devotes some effort to bleaching Prospero's art of such contamination. Prospero performs no conjuration on stage, and though he has the traditional cloak, book and staff of the magus, and at the end of the play traces a magic circle on the stage,[8] we see his magic simply in its effects without attention to its generation. Not all critics, however, have been prepared to accept that Prospero's magic is so clearly 'white', arguing that prevailing legal and religious attitudes of the period would have made it intrinsically suspect.[9]

But other traditions, as Barbara Mowat reminds us, also feed into the portrayal of Prospero.[10] As a 'magician-on-stage', his freezing of Ferdinand's sword recalls

---

[1] Nicholas H. Clulee, *John Dee's Natural Philosophy: Between Science and Religion*, 1988, p. 134.
[2] Quoted in Stuart Clark, *Thinking with Demons: The Idea of Witchcraft in Early Modern Europe*, 1997, p. 216.
[3] Allen G. Debus, *Man and Nature in the Renaissance*, 1978, pp. 12–13.
[4] Quoted in Orgel, p. 20.
[5] See Wayne Shumaker, *The Occult Sciences in the Renaissance*, 1972, for a clear, if relentlessly sceptical, account.
[6] See Karol Berger, 'Prospero's art', *S.St.*, 10 (1977), 211–39.
[7] Robert H. West, *Shakespeare and the Outer Mystery*, 1968, p. 84.
[8] According to the stage direction – though it is not explicit in the text. C. J. Sisson, wanting to advocate firmly Prospero's benevolence, overstates his case by claiming that 'he does not draw circles or utter spells'. 'The magic of Prospero', *S.Sur.*, 11 (1958), 70–8; p. 71.
[9] See, for example, D'Orsay W. Pearson, '*The Tempest* in perspective', *S.St.*, 7 (1974), 253–82.
[10] Barbara A. Mowat, 'Prospero, Agrippa, and hocus pocus', *ELR*, 11 (1981), 281–303.

Greene's *Friar Bacon and Friar Bungay*, Scene 5, for example,[1] and Ariel's teasing of the conspirators in 3.2 gestures towards the comic episodes in *Doctor Faustus* and recalls analogous scenes in the *commedia dell'arte* tradition. Such theatrical familiarity might have worked to defuse his potential menace, as would his similarity to 'the streetcorner "art-Magician" or "Jugler", or fairground illusionist with his boy assistant'. Prospero's renunciation of his magic, Mowat argues, places him in yet another tradition, that of the 'wizard' who 'delights in his magic powers; however, as a human in a Christian world, he must eventually admit the "roughness" of his magic'. But her contention that Prospero's magic is 'likely to be taken far too seriously and treated in far too ponderous a manner' plays down the theatrical force and thematic significance of his renunciation of his powers.[2]

Prospero's decision to drown his book is immediately preceded by his conversion from vengeance to forgiveness. It is one of the strangenesses of the play that this narrative and moral turning-point is curiously underplayed, passing by in a shared half-line (5.1.20) in which Prospero declares that he will follow Ariel's advice, followed by a summary of his reasons for doing so.[3] In performance, of course, more can be made of this moment; in Benthall's 1951 production, 'Prospero's sudden shamed repentance and strong prayer for the power to forgive, turn[ed] a speech which sometimes seems merely smug self-righteousness into a decisive, victorious struggle.'[4] But even so, the contrasting, powerful rhetoric of the 'Ye elves' speech makes us feel that he renounces an emotional as well as an intellectual investment in his dominion over nature, and that its surrender costs him far more than does the abandonment of his desire for vengeance which preceded it.[5]

Less than sixty years after the first performance of *The Tempest*, the Prologue to Dryden and Davenant's adaptation suggested that to found a play on magic would no longer be acceptable, and apologised that Shakespeare 'then writ, as people then believ'd'.[6] This embarrassment suggests that as early as 1669 it was problematic to convey in the theatre the reality of Prospero's magic. The traditional representation of the magician with cloak and staff has nonetheless had a long life. Peter Hall's 1974 production, for example, costumed John Gielgud in a fashion intended to suggest John Dee, the Elizabethan magus (see illustration 16), and other earlier productions gave Prospero a distinctly Eastern character (see illustrations 17 and 20). But many recent Prosperos – including John Wood in 1988, and Ian McKellen in 1999 – have eschewed

---

[1] Scott McMillin and Sally-Beth MacLean have suggested that Shakespeare may have been associated with the Queen's Men, and thus familiar with this, one of the company's plays (*The Queen's Men and their Plays*, 1998, pp. 155–69).
[2] Mowat, 'Prospero', pp. 297, 290, 282. See also her 'Prospero's Book', *SQ*, 52 (2001), pp. 1–33.
[3] To see the peculiarity of the moment, one only has to imagine how much more effortfully introspective – and perhaps how much more conventional – it would have been if the order of the speech were reversed, and the questions were explored *before* he announced 'And mine shall.'
[4] Dymkowski, p. 301. She lists a number of other, similarly powerful, theatrical representations.
[5] Whether or not Prospero intended forgiveness all along has been a topic of critical debate. He can be played either way.
[6] John Dryden and William Davenant, *The Enchanted Island*, in Sandra Clark, ed., *Shakespeare Made Fit*, 1997, p. 88.

16 1.2.24: 'pluck my magic garment from me'. John Gielgud in his fourth and final stage performance as Prospero at the National Theatre in 1974, with Jenny Agutter as Miranda. Gielgud's costume was intended to suggest the figure of John Dee, Elizabethan magus (photographer Zoe Dominic)

such trappings; the former clad in a contemporary, informal costume, with a long dressing-gown as magic cloak, the latter in battered hat, cardigan and breeches, with a magic stole of plastic (illustration 1).[1] In productions of this kind Prospero's magic is simply a 'given', but others have attempted to find a contemporary analogy for it. In Liviu Ciulei's 1981 Minneapolis production, for example, Ken Ruta's Prospero was depicted as 'a modern scientist of genius . . . [who] could pass for Einstein'.[2] This,

[1] McKellen did, however, carry three dolls in the opening scenes, and throughout pored over a battered book which was both a book of spells, and a kind of record of his past, containing pictures of Antonio etc.

[2] Dymkowski, p. 27.

17 Felix Aylmer as an Eastern Prospero in John Drinkwater's production at the Birmingham Repertory Theatre in 1915

and other similar representations, may have been influenced by the 1956 science-fiction film adaptation of the play, *Forbidden Planet*, in which Prospero becomes Dr Morbius, a scientist settled in another world, Altair-IV. This translation is in many ways a felicitous one, for the aspiration of modern science to comprehend the mysteries of the universe is similar to the ambition of the Renaissance natural magician, and it encounters the same ambivalent response of fascination and fear (and never more so than in the H-bomb-menaced, Cold War atmosphere of the 1950s).[1] The modern analogy also valuably reminds us that magic in *The Tempest* was not only a metaphor for something else – for monarchical, colonial or theatrical power – but formed in itself a subject for the play's investigation.

This investigation is conducted in religious terms. As Clark observes, 'Demonology in all its manifestations was not merely saturated with religious values; it was inconceivable without them.'[2] Yet West claims that the play 'does not connect Prospero's magic and spirits overtly with religion . . . Shakespeare keeps his dramatic world secular and empirical'.[3] Superficially this may seem true, but in the play there are more unambiguous references to the Bible and the Prayer Book than to the Virginia tracts, those texts confidently regarded as its sources, and of all the play's recollections it is these which are the most likely to have been picked up by every member of its contemporary audience. As Debora Shuger suggests, it is scarcely likely 'that the popular drama of a religiously saturated culture could, by a secular miracle, have extricated itself from the theocentric orientation informing the discourses of politics, gender, social order and history'.[4] Perhaps the most obvious of such references are to be found in 3.3, where the end of Ariel's 'three men of sin' speech (53–82) reorientates its Virgilian antecedent by its echoes of St Paul.[5]

Ariel insists to the lords: '. . . remember – / For that's my business to you'. In standard thinking about sin and confession, to recall trespasses committed is the first stage in the process of contrition. John Donne, for example, wrote that 'the art of salvation is but the art of memory'.[6] This memory is directed to the goodness of God, as compelling gratitude, and also to the inward self-examination that is a prelude to repentance. As Hooker put it:

A generall perswasion that thou art a sinner, will neyther soe humble, or bridle thy soule: as if the catalogue of thy sinnes examined severally, bee continually kept in minde . . . The minde, I know, doth hardly admitt such unpleasant remembrances, butt wee must force it, wee must constraine it thereunto.[7]

The 'desperation' that follows Ariel's 'forcing' of their recollection belongs to this same process, since theologians argued that the memory of sin itself generated the

[1] See J. P. Telotte, 'Science fiction in double focus: *Forbidden Planet*', *Film Criticism*, 13.3 (1989), 25–36. Judith Buchanan, however, has argued that the affiliation of the film to Shakespeare's play is less secure than many have supposed ('*Forbidden Planet* and the retrospective attribution of intentions', in Deborah Cartmell et al., eds., *Retrovisions*, 2001).
[2] Clark, *Thinking with Demons*, p. 437.
[3] West, *Shakespeare and the Outer Mystery*, p. 84.
[4] Debora K. Shuger, 'Subversive fathers and suffering subjects: Shakespeare and Christianity', in Donna B. Hamilton and Richard Strier, eds., *Religion, Literature, and Politics in Post-Reformation England, 1540–1688*, 1996, p. 46.
[5] Robert Hunter, *Shakespeare and the Comedy of Forgiveness*, 1965, pp. 234–5, suggests that the banquet earlier in the scene is a version of the Eucharistic feast, from which the Prayer Book reminded congregations that sinners were barred.
[6] Evelyn Simpson and George Potter, eds., *The Sermons of John Donne*, 10 vols., 1953–62, II, 78. This quotation is noted by Michael Neill, whose article 'Remembrance and revenge: *Hamlet*, *Macbeth* and *The Tempest*' in Donaldson, *Jonson and Shakespeare*, pp. 35–56, has influenced my argument in this section.
[7] Richard Hooker, *The Folger Library Editions of the Works of Richard Hooker*, ed. Georges Edelen et al., 7 vols., 1977, III, 20.

inward bitings of guilt, whether or not it was acknowledged or repented. As Joseph Hall commented: 'Consciences that are without remorse are not without horror; wickedness makes men desperate.'[1] In the period, then, the compulsion of memory has a powerful religious resonance which Ariel's speech summons up.

But yet Prospero's solicitation of repentance at this stage of the play seems in its execution very like an exercise in magical control. Its effect is to 'knit up' the lords, in the same way Prospero had earlier threatened to 'peg' Ariel in an oak, had 'styed' Caliban in a rock, and manacled Ferdinand. It is this absolute, punitive control which Ariel challenges when he later tells Prospero that his own affections towards the lords would become most tender 'were I human' (5.1.20).[2] Prospero's response to Ariel turns on the recognition of the humanity he shares with his enemies, and it is that recognition which precipitates the rejection of his magic.[3]

His forgiveness, however, is offered to, and received by, his various enemies very differently. Alonso works fully through the paradigm of repentance: he remembers, he repents and then provides the 'satisfaction' that Hooker spoke of as essential to the process:

> Our offences sometymes are of such nature as requireth that particular men bee satisfyed, or else repentance to bee utterly voide and of none effect. For if . . . a man have wittingly wronged others to enrich himselfe: the first thing evermore in this case required . . . is restitution: for lett noe man deceyve himselfe; from such offences wee are not discharged . . . till recompense and restitution to man accompanie the poenitent confession wee have made to Almightie God.[4]

Alonso, immediately upon awaking from Prospero's spell in Act 5, makes this restitution, when he says, 'Thy dukedom I resign, and do entreat / Thou pardon me my wrongs' (118–19). One of the most striking consequences of this repentance is Prospero's subsequent observation: 'Let us not burden our remembrances with / A heaviness that's gone' (199–200). For the first, indeed the only time in the play, Prospero commands a forgetting, freeing both himself and Alonso from the destructive corrosiveness of recollection. Though Prospero imitates the divine amnesia of the Epistle to the Hebrews 8.12, where God declares: 'I will be merciful to their unrighteousness, and their sins and their iniquities will I remember no more', he disowns the divine parallel by including himself as needing a blessed forgetfulness.

In his confrontation with Antonio and Sebastian, however, there is little sign of such generosity. He hoards the memory of their murderous designs upon Alonso as a politically valuable tool to ensure their future compliance, and he forgives Antonio's

---

[1] Joseph Hall, *The Works*, ed. Philip Wynter, 10 vols., 1863, I, 20.

[2] In F this word is spelt 'humane'; Renaissance spelling and pronunciation did not distinguish between the two words. A modern-spelling edition is compelled to choose, and clearly Ariel's conditional remark turns on the fact that he is a spirit, not a human being. But the secondary meaning is also tellingly present. Philip Davis, *Sudden Shakespeare*, 1996, writes of this moment: 'Just one word, but it is here the greatest and most powerful word in Shakespeare: it opens up the world and its whole history again, it makes a godlike figure again a man' (p. 180).

[3] A similar reading, though not religiously loaded, is offered by Margreta de Grazia, '*The Tempest*: gratuitous movement or action without kibes and pinches', *S.St.*, 14 (1981), 249–65, who argues that Prospero's 'practice of magic has imprisoned him . . . because it removes him from other men' (p. 261).

[4] Hooker, *Works*, III, 61.

'rankest fault' with considerable effort. Many critics have seen the absence of any signal that Antonio repents as a mark of Prospero's final 'failure'. There is, however, another way of reading this moment. In his earlier exchange with Ariel, Prospero had suggested, 'They being penitent, / The sole drift of my purpose doth extend / Not a frown further' (28–30), recalling the priestly words of the absolution at Morning and Evening Prayer (see Commentary). But the forgiveness there offered to a congregation 'being penitent' is not in the priest's power to command or bestow, but only for God to afford. Prospero finally accepts that he, likewise, cannot set conditions on forgiveness, recognising instead that he is bound by another biblical imperative – to forgive a brother, not seven times, but seventy times seven.[1] With gritted teeth and in grudging words Prospero acknowledges that his human (or humane) 'virtue' is to be found in a forgiveness which is unconditional. As John Hoskin put it in 1609: 'To pardon and forgive, is the part of a man, to revenge is the part of a beast.'[2]

Prospero's final confrontation with an apparently unrepentant Antonio is analogous to the way in which Duke Vincentio in *Measure for Measure* is ultimately, in the intransigent Barnardine, compelled to recognise the limits of his secular power.[3] To read either play as simply demonstrating the 'failure' of their respective dukes' projects is falsely to identify the purposes of the plays with the plans of their central characters. In both dramas the audience is required to question the aspirations of the dukes, and to recognise, as ultimately they both do, the limits of their powers. This, one might argue, is their triumph, rather than their failure.

James I observed in his 1610 speech to Parliament that 'Kings are iustly called Gods, for that they exercise a manner or resemblance of Divine power upon earth.'[4] With this axiom the Elizabethan preacher Henry Smith would have agreed, but in his sermon, *The Magistrates Scripture*, he took as his text verses 6 and 7 of Psalm 82: 'I have sayd ye are Gods . . . But ye shall dye as a man, and ye Princes shall fall like others.' In the course of his meditation on the common humanity of rulers in the face of death he addresses his congregation:

Where are they which founded this goodlie Cittie, which possessed these faire houses, and walked these pleasant fieldes, which erected these stately Temples, which kneeled in these seates, which preached out of this place but thirtie yeares agoe? Is not earth turned to earth, and shall not our Sunne set like theirs when the night comes?[5]

The sentiments are not unusual, but the coincidental pre-echo of Prospero in the phrase 'these stately Temples' suggests that as Prospero's earlier retirement from his dukedom for the 'bettering of my mind' (1.2.90) turns towards a retirement to it in which 'Every third thought shall be my grave' (5.1.309) he recognises in his own mortality the absolute limits on an aspiration to absolute power. It suggests also that the language of religion, necessarily implicated in the representation of magic, cannot be

---

[1] Matthew 18.21–2.
[2] *A Sermon upon the Parable of the King that taketh accompt of his servants* (1609), sig. B2.
[3] See David Lindley, 'The stubbornness of Barnardine', in *The Shakespeare Yearbook*, 7 (1996), 333–52.
[4] Johann P. Sommerville, *King James VI and I: Political Writings*, 1994, p. 181.
[5] *The Sermons of Maister Henrie Smith* (1593 edn), p. 814. Smith's text is taken from the Geneva Bible.

neglected in any comprehensive account of the play. This is not, emphatically not, to claim that *The Tempest* is a religious allegory; but rather to observe that its engagement with religious paradigms of repentance and forgiveness, power and its limitations, animates yet another 'discursive field' that must be taken as seriously as all the other contexts we have so far discussed.

It is somewhat paradoxical, perhaps, to approach *The Tempest*, a play without a single source, through such an extended account of its contexts. The play's concentrated spareness, however, joined to its teasing allusiveness, positively requires its readers or audiences to supply contexts within which it might define itself. Insofar as it partakes of the abstractions of romance it seems to invite a symbolic or allegorical reading, but its range of affiliations to varied sources inhibits the selection of any one of them as a secure vantage-point from which the whole play may be viewed. As we turn to consider the relationships between the play's characters, we see the same multiplicity of possible frames of reference similarly complicating any straightforward reading.

Authority and power

Whether it is in the authority of the ruler, master, father or colonist, Prospero's relationships with the other characters all turn on questions of command. Where it was once customary to see this as a necessary and benign authority directed to good ends, recent criticism has reacted with varying degrees of hostility to the manifestations of power in Prospero's actions.[1] If the older version of Prospero now seems partial and politically complacent, then the contemporary distaste for his crabbed harshness, and attempts to expose the ideological foundations of his authority, are equally a consequence of our own cultural moment, and embedded in the critical and political orthodoxies of our own time. One of the things that most divides us from the Shakespearean world is, indeed, our attitude to power. For though the foundation of kingly authority was much debated, in the early seventeenth century there was general agreement that, as Robert Bolton put it:

> Government is the prop and pillar of all States and Kingdoms, the cement and soule of humane affaires, the life of society and order, the very vitall spirit whereby so many millions of men doe breathe the life of comfort and peace; and the whole nature of things subsist.[2]

This 'government' was conceived of as necessarily hierarchical, and founded upon the overwhelming authority of God. As Debora Shuger has pointed out: 'To the extent that we cannot but perceive "oppressive systems" as bad and liberation as good, we are confused by a spirituality based on the duplication of political relations of domination and submission, one valorising obedience, guilt, and fear.'[3] Yet it is within this

---

[1] See Harry Berger, Jr, 'Miraculous harp: a reading of Shakespeare's *Tempest*', *S.St.*, 5 (1969), 253–83, for a powerful reading of the play's provisionality about Prospero's power.

[2] *Two Sermons preached at Northampton* (1635); quoted in J[ohann] P. Sommerville, *Politics and Ideology in England 1603–1640*, 1986, p. 17.

[3] Shuger, *Habits of Thought*, p. 163.

system of 'duplications' that we must attempt to understand the relationships of *The Tempest* and try to assess how the play directs us to respond to them.

CONSPIRACIES: ANTONIO AND SEBASTIAN

Questions of authority and power are most obviously raised by the three conspiracies lying at the heart of the play's narrative, each carefully distinguished one from another. The first, reported by Prospero, is Antonio's original usurpation of the dukedom of Milan. Here Prospero himself was partly to blame, in that it was his failure to exercise authority which 'Awaked an evil nature' in his brother, and 'did beget of him / A falsehood' (1.2.93–5). Antonio crept into usurpation by a gradual process of assuming a role.[1] Although we are made aware of the political deftness with which Antonio operated in dislodging the affections of Prospero's 'creatures', this first conspiracy is presented as a crime against nature and family bonds as much as a political act. It is the offence of the 'brother' that Prospero emphasises, whilst simultaneously casting himself as the 'good parent' whose trust is abused. This emphasis is underlined by the fact that though Prospero is a 'prince of power', there is no trace in his narrative of the religious language Shakespeare had deployed to characterise monarchical authority in his history plays. No divinity hedges this duke, even if he is later to acquire the magic power which might be read as a metaphor for royalty's god-like command. Far from 'mystifying' the basis of royal power in religious terminology, the play seems deliberately to expose its secular foundation.

When we witness Antonio's next foray into political action, we are on more familiar theatrical ground. He is a variation on a standard Shakespearean figure – the Machiavellian villain – and looks back to Richard III, Edmund and Iago. Like them, he is an opportunist, and in 2.1 we see confirmed Prospero's suggestion that he is, like them, a gifted persuader, both in his manipulation of Sebastian and his confidence that he can make all except Gonzalo 'take suggestion as a cat laps milk' (285). His repudiation of conscience and his total egotism are memorably elaborated in Auden's *The Sea and the Mirror* where Antonio's lyric concludes:

> *Your all is partial, Prospero:*
> *My will is all my own:*
> *Your need to love shall never know*
> *Me: I am I, Antonio,*
> *By choice myself alone.*[2]

But unlike the earlier villains (and Auden recalls the 'I am I' of Richard III here), there is nothing in the dramatic presentation of Antonio that is made attractive to the audience. In particular, he never speaks directly to us as they do, thereby defusing villainy by inviting our complicity with it, so that even the most determinedly anti-Prospero reading of the play has not made a case for Antonio as other than irreducibly evil.

---

[1] See Nora Johnson, 'Body and spirit, stage and sexuality in *The Tempest*', *ELH*, 64 (1997), 683–701; p. 688: 'Prospero invents the role of "Prospero", Antonio plays that role, and Antonio then becomes the role's inventor.'

[2] W. H. Auden, *Collected Poems*, ed. Edward Mendelson, 1976, p. 318.

But the evil of Antonio is somewhat muted by the dramatic presentation of 2.1. The musical control of the action suggests that Prospero has deliberately created the opportunity for Antonio's treason and is in command of its outcome. Moreover this is not a planned act growing out of a determined purpose. But perhaps the principal problem is the relentless, sometimes obscure, and often feeble punning of the earlier part of the scene. Throughout its theatrical history, most productions have responded by cutting some, if not virtually all, of this material; but that solution itself brings further problems, in that it gives the actors playing Antonio and Sebastian no jumping-off point for the second half.[1] A comparatively rare success was Peter Hall's 1988 National Theatre production in which 'Ken Stott's and Basil Henson's handling of Antonio's and Sebastian's sneering was a brilliant demonstration of Coleridge's point that "Shakespeare never puts habitual scorn into the mouths of other than bad men."'[2]

It is not simply the difficulty for a modern audience in comprehending Antonio and Sebastian's jokes which is the problem;[3] for our response is also complicated by the unclear status of Gonzalo. If played, as he often is, as a doddery, Polonius-like chatterer, then Antonio's dismissive estimate of him seems confirmed. It is important, however, that this scene should present a collision of habits of mind that is of a piece with the play's larger questionings. Whilst, as Simon Palfrey argues, Antonio 'articulates a corrosive assault upon the foundations of . . . romance',[4] it is an attack that should not simply lead to a victory. Their confrontation centres on Gonzalo's vision of the ideal commonwealth. His speech is oddly unmotivated – why it should suddenly occur to him to embark upon it is by no means clear, since it scarcely assists Alonso's mourning, and indeed is potentially offensive to his kingly position. This signals the literary derivation of its fantasy, and its picture of a non-hierarchical society (a picture which was sometimes painted of Amerindian societies) is not only punctured by Antonio, but was firmly rejected in Renaissance political thinking. But, at the same time, it allows us to hear, faintly and briefly, an alternative possibility. Its invocation of an alternative world is functionally not unlike the songs of Amiens in *As You Like It* (similarly ridiculed there by Jaques) which make the best of enforced pastoral retreat. In this play it is linked both to the fleeting vision of the masque and to Caliban's wistful lost dreams of riches. The fact that the 'materialist critique'[5] of Gonzalo's vision is offered by these immoral lords emphasises the human self-interestedness that renders all such utopian visions unsustainable, and paradoxically makes the necessity of a controlling 'sovereignty' all the more compelling.

[1] This became clear to me in talking to the Courtyard Company at Leeds in 1999, where the actors found it necessary to restore in rehearsal some lines originally cut (though much was still omitted).
[2] Warren, *Staging Shakespeare's Late Plays*, p. 175. Brook's 1957 actors also 'had a menacing quality these petty villains usually lack' (Dymkowski, p. 187). By contrast, in the RSC productions of 1993 and 1998 both Mendes and Noble seemed to have given up hope, so flat was this scene.
[3] Lynne Magnusson calls them 'deconstructionists' in an interesting essay on language in the play: 'Interruption in *The Tempest*', *SQ*, 37 (1986), 52–65.
[4] Simon Palfrey, *Late Shakespeare: A New World of Words*, 1997, p. 141. But it should be noted that they also resist the evidence of their own eyes in refusing to accept that their garments are indeed refreshed, not stained with water.
[5] Norbrook, 'Language and Utopia', p. 32. This essay contains a subtle discussion of the scene.

CONSPIRACIES: STEPHANO, TRINCULO AND CALIBAN

The complot of Stephano, Trinculo and Caliban is the second replay of attempted usurpation, but it is far from a simple repetition of Antonio's designs. Whereas his treasons were not justified by the imperfections of either Prospero or of Alonso as rulers, Caliban founds his appeal to Stephano on the claim that he is 'subject to a tyrant' (3.2.37). His choice of words is particularly pointed. Raleigh's posthumously published *The Prince: or Maxims of State* states that tyranny 'is the worst of all the Bastard States, because it is the perverting of the best Regiment, to wit, of a Monarchy'.[1] In his *History of the World* Raleigh defined tyranny as 'a violent form of government, not respecting the good of the subject, but only the pleasure of the commander', and suggested that 'the taste of sweetness, drawn out of oppression, hath so good a relish, as continually inflames the Tyrant's appetite, and will not suffer it to be restrained with any limits of respect'.[2] For many modern readers, and quite possibly for some of the seventeenth-century audience, Prospero's appropriation of the island and his apparent delight in continually tormenting Caliban give good reason to categorise him as tyrannical. But even if Prospero merits the epithet, it is, or was, a different matter to argue that Caliban therefore has the right to rebel. The official doctrine, articulated in the Elizabethan *Homily Against Disobedience and Wilful Rebellion*, and endlessly repeated, was that a tyrant was sent by God to punish the sins of a people, and consequently that they must not 'shake off that curse at their owne hand'.[3] Nonetheless, especially in the context of the pursuit of religious freedom, writers both Protestant and Catholic had argued in the last years of the sixteenth century for the right to remove tyrants.[4] By calling Prospero a 'tyrant' Caliban gestures towards this debate, and leaves room, however narrow, for a seventeenth-century audience to consider whether his revolt might be justified.

Caliban's servile status further complicates the debate. Aristotle in the *Politics* had argued that 'the lower sort are by nature slaves, and it is better for them as for all inferiors that they should be under the rule of a master'.[5] This theory had a long and continuous life – though not an uncontroversial or uncontested one.[6] That Caliban does not desire rule for himself, but merely wishes to change his master from Prospero to Stephano, might indicate that the play accepts this definition of his nature. Yet because Caliban offers as justification for his revolt the seizure of 'his' island, he brings into play the much-debated question of whether or not the Native Americans were

---

[1] Walter Raleigh, *The Prince: or Maxims of State* (1642), p. 4.

[2] Raleigh, *Selected Writings*, ed. Gerald Hammond, 1984, p. 219. In Shakespeare's works the term is used as an appellation for Macbeth, Richard III and Leontes (in descending order of frequency).

[3] An extract from the Elizabethan *Homily* is printed in David Wootton, ed., *Divine Right and Democracy: An Anthology of Political Writing in Stuart England*, 1986; the complete text is at http://www.library.utoronto.ca/utel/ret/homilies/elizhom.html. See also King James, *The Trew Law of Free Monarchies* (1598), in Sommerville, *Political Writings*, pp. 68–72.

[4] See Quentin Skinner, *The Foundations of Modern Political Thought: Volume Two The Age of Reformation*, 1978, for a detailed consideration of the evolution of a theory of justified rebellion.

[5] Stephen Everson, ed., *Aristotle: The Politics*, 1988, p. 7.

[6] See Peter Garnsey, *Ideas of Slavery from Aristotle to Augustine*, 1996, for detailed discussion of this 'battered shipwreck of a theory' (p. 107).

to be categorised as 'natural' slaves.[1] But even if for most of the audience these recondite questions of political philosophy were invisible, they would still have recognised that Prospero's treatment of his slave was questionable. In law,

> if a villaine wil not be justified by his Lord, nor obedient unto him, it is lawfull for the Lord to chastise, and beat him, or to imprison him, or to inflict any reasonable punishment upon him, so that he do not maihem [maim] or kill him . . . the master may strike his servant with his hand, fist, small staffe, or sticke for correction, and though he do draw blood.[2]

Nonetheless, Richard Robinson advised that

> the freeman which hath under him the government of servants, ought speciallye to thinke that they are men, and not brute beastes, and that he should not rage with crueltye against them, in scourging, evyll entreating, or chayning of them, for by scourging their hartes are made obdurate and hardened, neyther do they any thing but with evill wyl.[3]

Prospero's treatment of Caliban is open to Robinson's censure, and might well have been criticised by a seventeenth-century audience, though this, again, would not necessarily have led to endorsement of Caliban's conspiracy. As Thomas Forsett observed,

> . . . albeit their masters doe not well to deale hardly and evilly with them . . . yet if the mallice and perversenes of their maisters be such, they notwithstanding being servants must not shake off the yoake, set themselves at liberty, and depart when they list . . . because they have not power of their owne selves.[4]

Caliban's position is all the more threatening since he combines with Stephano and Trinculo, who are, or at least think themselves to be, 'masterless men', a category much feared and castigated in the period as the enemies of civil rule.[5] Their ambition is ridiculed by the way they set themselves up as a parody court, with Caliban kneeling to make his 'suit' to the drunken 'monarch' Stephano, and this satire is intensified if in production the 'trumpery' which they don with such enthusiasm in 4.1 contains rich or regal garments.[6] If it does, then the effect of the play's end, when they stand forlorn in their muddied finery, is yet more complicated. Their stolen garb imitates and parodies Antonio's usurpation of the robes of ducal authority, but it also reflects more uncomfortably upon the recognisability Prospero has just gained by adopting the hat and rapier which present him as he 'was sometime Milan' (5.1.86). The 'proper' relationship of the 'badges' of costume to social hierarchy is re-established,

---

[1] See Pagden, 'Dispossessing the barbarian'; *Cambridge History of Renaissance Philosophy*, pp. 407–8. Similar questions were raised in relation to the Irish (see p. 32, n. 4 above).
[2] Pulton, p. 6.
[3] Francesco Patrizi, *A Moral Methode of Civile Policie . . . done out of Latine into English by Rycharde Robinson* (1576), fol. 11ᵛ.
[4] Thomas Forsett, *The Servants Dutie* (1613), p. 19.
[5] Brown, '"This thing of darkness"', p. 63. See A. L. Beier, *Masterless Men: The Vagrancy Problem in England, 1560–1640*, 1985.
[6] As it did, for example, in the crowns they obtained in Mendes's 1993 and Noble's 1998 productions.

but at the same time the shakiness of the correspondence, already suggested in Antonio's exchange with Sebastian in 2.1, is hinted at.[1]

The restoration of social order and hierarchy fulfils Prospero's designs, but Curt Breight contends that: 'the audience exists *outside* Prospero's manipulation of characters and situations and is thereby enabled to perceive Shakespeare's clever demystification of various official strategies within the discourse of treason. The audience is allowed to see that conspiracy is often a fiction, or a construct, or a real yet wholly containable piece of social theatre.'[2] In his reading Prospero himself generates the treasonable plots of the play, and through his intelligencer, Ariel, maintains surveillance over them. The 'pinches' with which he threatens lords and low-class conspirators alike are, to Breight, 'euphemistic' versions of the torture that was actually used upon those suspected of treason and he suggests that, at the end of the play, Prospero 'instructs Ariel to bring in the writhing lower-class conspirators in a moment that is far from comic, although some modern directors complicit with hierarchical discourse attempt to represent it comically'.[3] His implied imperative for directors to resist 'hierarchical discourse' bears out Shuger's earlier-quoted observation about present-day problems in confronting Renaissance views of power and authority, but most revealing is the fact that he also wants to resist playing these parts for comic effect.

At one level this seems a wilful refusal to recognise the fact that Stephano and Trinculo are the play's comic parts. But his comment usefully directs attention to the fact that the theatrical representation of the relationship between the three conspirators is by no means straightforward. In the first place, as comic characters Stephano and Trinculo have none of the expansiveness and richness that make Falstaff's resistance to authority a powerful articulation of comic subversion in *Henry IV*, nor does their drunkenness carry the defiance that Sir Toby Belch offers to the prissy world of the 'puritan' Malvolio in *Twelfth Night*. Secondly, to generate comic effect in their scenes requires a good deal of actorly effort and well-constructed stage business, since, as Roger Warren observes: 'Stefano's and Trinculo's humour depends much less on what they say than on what they do.'[4] In the performance at Shakespeare's Globe, comedy was generated in by-play with the audience (illustration 18), and the delighted response of the 'groundlings' in 2000 was, one might think, closer to the kind of reaction that Robert Armin and the other members of the King's Men could have anticipated in 1611 than to Breight's desired class-based sympathy.

But in emphasising comedy at the expense of all else the Globe production flattened out the complexity of the relationships between the three figures. Throughout

---

[1] Throughout Shakespeare's work the relationship of robes and rank is a troubling issue – notably in *King Lear*, where 'robes and furred gowns hide all' (4.6.165).

[2] Curt Breight, '"Treason doth never prosper": *The Tempest* and the discourse of treason', *SQ*, 41 (1990), 1–28; p. 1. See also Frances E. Dolan, 'The subordinate('s) plot: petty treason and the forms of domestic rebellion', *SQ*, 43 (1992), 317–40.

[3] Breight, '"Treason doth never prosper"', p. 23.

[4] Warren, *Staging Shakespeare's Late Plays*, p. 183. As Will Keen observed to me while rehearsing as Trinculo for the Leeds production: 'I'm supposed to be a jester and I've got no [expletive deleted] jests!'

18 Jasper Britton (Caliban), watched by Geraldine Alexander (Ariel), engages directly with the audience in the performance at Shakespeare's Globe, 2000 (photographer Donald Cooper)

their scenes Trinculo maintains the traditional function of the jester as a detached and ironic commentator. He is well aware, for example, that Stephano's fantasy of power is built on tottering foundations, and his incredulity at Caliban's adoration of the drunken butler reflects on the vanity of the latter, as well as the foolishness of the former. The greater part of his commentary, however, is upon Caliban. Trinculo's crucial opening monologue is the one speech that is virtually guaranteed to raise a laugh from the audience in almost any performance, and, since it is directly spoken to us, it invites us to share his perspective on Caliban's appearance, and his revulsion at the fishy smell he gives off (illustration 19). Throughout the scenes which follow Trinculo insists upon a view of Caliban as a 'puppy-headed monster', a thing 'half a fish, and half a monster'. It is Trinculo's consistent denigration, quite as much as Prospero's contempt, which fixes Caliban as the alien 'other', and it is he and Stephano, rather than Prospero, who see Caliban as the exploitable colonial subject. Furthermore, as Stephano himself fantasises about his role as king, his will to power – and readiness to exercise it tyrannically on a dissentient Trinculo – comes into sharper focus.[1] A number of productions have chosen to underline this

---

[1] In Césaire's reworking, though Stephano begins by declaring himself a 'republican', his rapid intoxication with colonialist ambition is emphasised.

19 'a very ancient and fish-like smell' (2.2.25). Tony Haygarth (Caliban) and Tim Piggott-Smith (Trinculo) in Peter Hall's 1988 National Theatre production (photographer John Haynes)

darker view. Paul Moriarty in Clifford Williams's 1978 production, for example, was 'enflamed less with drink than with the ambition of repeating Antonio's coup', and Miller's Stephano and Trinculo 'exhibit[ed] colonialism in a brutally primitive form'.[1]

The parallel of Stephano and Trinculo with Antonio and Sebastian is underlined by the fact that they exhibit the same reductive materialism as their social superiors. Just as the lords puncture Gonzalo's Golden Age musings, so Stephano deflates Caliban's rapt meditation on the island's 'sounds and sweet airs' with the comment that 'This will prove a brave kingdom to me, where I shall have my music for nothing' (3.2.136–7).[2] In other respects, however, the sets of conspirators are very different. The contrast between Caliban's serious ferocity in the pursuit of his aim and the half-hearted frivolousness of his co-conspirators is a much stronger version of the difference between Antonio and the hesitant Sebastian, and the triangular relationship between Stephano, Trinculo and Caliban, which sees the jester becoming increasingly marginalised, so that he can be represented on stage with a plaintive pathos, has no parallel in the lords' scenes.[3]

[1] Dymkowski, p. 219.
[2] In the Shared Experience production the parallel was emphasised by doubling the parts of Antonio/Stephano and Sebastian/Trinculo.
[3] David Bradley at Stratford in 1993 played Trinculo as a lugubrious music-hall comic with oversized shoes, accompanied by a ventriloquist's dummy, which 'betrayed' him by seeming to voice Ariel's accusation that he lied in 3.2.

In Dryden and Davenant's adaptation the politics of this sub-plot are considerably simplified by its total disconnection from Prospero. It is represented only as a contest for power between Stephano, recast as the Master of the ship and accompanied by newly invented mariners, and Trincalo, the Boatswain.[1] This simplification serves by contrast to confirm the complexity of Shakespeare's treatment of questions of authority and power as they are refracted through the three conspiracies of the play. Stephano and Trinculo have received comparatively little critical attention; their life in the theatre depends upon the way they are animated by stage business and is therefore not readily susceptible to analysis derived entirely from the words they speak. The alcohol in which they swim renders them comic, yet the laughter it provokes is by turns complicit and contemptuous; their scenes consequently present shifting and unstable perspectives on questions of rebellion and rule, of fantasy, perception and misperception, and of journeys that end in disappointment.

CALIBAN AND ARIEL

Caliban is not only a slave and political rebel, but is also defined within Prospero's domestic economy by his relationship to Ariel. At the simplest level, where Ariel is represented as the indentured servant, bound to his master for a specific period before being freed, Caliban is the perpetual bondslave.[2] Prospero tells Miranda that they 'cannot miss' Caliban for the domestic service he performs (1.2.312), but it is equally true that he himself cannot do without Ariel as the executant of his magic designs. Prospero's treatment of the two is, however, very different. Though briefly berated in 1.2, nowhere in the play does Ariel endure the physical discipline that Caliban suffers, and at the play's end Ariel is freed to the elements, whereas Caliban is sent back to the cell, perhaps to be taken home with Prospero to Milan.[3]

The treatment of the relationship between these two characters has been one of the most interesting and variable features of the play's performance history. During the nineteenth century, when Caliban was fixed as a comic monster, Ariel could be the star part, as the poster for the Leeds Royal Amphitheatre indicates (illustration 3). In the final tableau of Kean's 1857 performance, 'The ship gradually sails off, the Island recedes from sight, and Ariel remains alone in mid-air, watching the departure of his late master.'[4] The emphasis was always on Ariel-as-fairy; she (and the part was always played by a woman) was usually costumed with wings; balletic grace and agility seem to have been more important than an ability to sing the songs (which were occasionally entrusted to another actress). This emphasis continued well into the

[1] For a sustained analysis of the politics of this adaptation see Katharine Eisaman Maus, 'Arcadia lost: politics and revision in the Restoration *Tempest*', *Renaissance Drama*, 13 (1982), 189–209. Michael Dobson, *The Making of the National Poet: Shakespeare, Adaptation, and Authorship, 1660–1769*, 1992, pp. 38–61, extends her analysis, though says nothing further about this part of the play.
[2] See Andrew Gurr, 'Industrious Ariel and idle Caliban', in Jean-Pierre Maquerlot and Michèle Willems, eds., *Travel and Drama in Shakespeare's Time*, 1997, pp. 193–208.
[3] The prevailing assumption that Caliban remains on the island is by no means a necessary one – powerful though it is in conditioning our view of him. If he is, as he promises to be, 'wise hereafter, / And seek for grace' (5.1.292–3), there is, surely, a strong implication that he accepts service to Prospero as his future.
[4] Kean, 1857. It is an interesting opposite to Tree's conclusion already discussed.

twentieth century, even after the part was again taken by a male actor. Leslie French, a frequent Ariel during the 1930s, 'was a highly skilled singer and actor who was also trained in ballet',[1] and illustration 20 suggests that graceful and mannered movement characterised his performance. It was Marius Goring's 1940 interpretation of the part as 'some weird immortal spirit imprisoned in mortal toils and painfully eager to be free'[2] which initiated a new direction, one taken up by many later performers. Alan Badel in 1951 was a 'really imprisoned Ariel – no tricksy elf, with none of the "child-like simplicity" that Coleridge found in the part, but an elemental spirit robbed of freedom and even tortured by the loss'.[3] Perhaps the apogee of resentful Ariels was reached in Simon Russell Beale's 1993 performance. A servant who betrayed no emotion, substantial of body, slow of movement, and clad in 'a blue silk Mao suit', at the end of the play 'Ariel met the benign gaze of Prospero by spitting full in his erstwhile master's face, a superb invention, pinpointing the patronising nature of our assumption that the perfect servant enjoys serving and that Prospero's treatment of him is not in its own way as brutal and humiliating a servitude as Sycorax's.'[4] It is no coincidence that an emphasis on Ariel's servitude should accompany an increasing stress on Prospero's anxious and angry command, and sit alongside a representation of the enslaved Caliban as human, rather than monstrous.[5] In recent productions it has been the human similarity of the two figures which has been explored, effecting a comprehensive revaluation of their natures, and leading to a rejection of the once-standard view of their symbolic difference one from the other.

And yet, where Ariel is 'but air', and associated with St Elmo's fire in the storm, Caliban is called 'Thou earth', and is custodian of the 'quick freshes' of water (5.1.21, 1.2.315, 3.2.61). The pair therefore combine, between them, all the four elements of which, in Renaissance thinking, the world was made. As A. D. Nuttall remarks, a perception of this relationship at the beginning of the nineteenth century 'open[ed] the doors to an allegory of the soul in terms of early seventeenth-century psychology',[6] and he charts the evolution of such readings up to the earlier twentieth century. Allegorical readings of this kind have fallen out of favour as materialist and political readings (allegories of a different temper) have come to dominate the critical landscape.[7] But romance is a genre inherently disposed to symbolic interpretation, and Renaissance culture at every level and in every literary kind was saturated with allegorical

[1] Dymkowski, p. 40. She notes that the first male Ariel was in the Birmingham Repertory Company's 1915 performance.

[2] Audrey Williamson, *Old Vic Drama*, quoted in Orgel, p. 78.

[3] *Manchester Guardian*, 27 June 1951, and see Dymkowski, pp. 140–2.

[4] Holland, *English Shakespeares*, pp. 172–3. The spit was loathed by many reviewers, and was actually cut towards the end of the run. At virtually the same time Olwyn Fouéré in the English Shakespeare Company's production was a reluctant circus performer who moved with resentful slowness until breaking into a run when given freedom.

[5] Dymkowski argues that the transformation of Ariel's role is also entwined in complicated ways with the change from female to male actors.

[6] A. D. Nuttall, *Two Concepts of Allegory*, 1967, p. 2.

[7] They have not, however, disappeared completely – see, for example, Michael Srigley, *Images of Regeneration: A Study of Shakespeare's 'The Tempest' in its Cultural Background*, 1985, which offers a reading of the play as an allegory of 'human life as an alchemical process of dissolution and regeneration as taught by the Paracelsan school of medicine' (p. 19).

20 Leslie French, who played Ariel on many occasions throughout the 1930s, exhibits his balletic training
before Harcourt Williams's turbaned Prospero at the Old Vic in 1933

figuration. It is hard to believe that in the creation of Ariel and Caliban Shakespeare did not anticipate such a reading of them. The question, indeed, may rather be why today's criticism should resist it.

One reason may be because, as Angus Fletcher remarks, allegory 'is hierarchical in essence, owing not only to its use of traditional imageries which are arranged in systems of "correspondences", but furthermore because all hierarchies imply a chain of command'.[1] It is this to which Lorie Leininger objects in the allegorisation of Caliban: 'The absorption of the native's inferiority into an allegorical scheme provides an unassailable strategy for excluding considerations of justice based upon the common humanity of those high and low on the social scale.'[2] That her observation is in some sense accurate is borne out by Gary Schmidgall's extended reading of Caliban as 'a creature of courtly allegory', representing the evils of rebellion, and of uncontrolled *furor*.[3] Sympathy becomes irrelevant as the dramatic figure is dissolved into the texts that explain him. Detailed and extended though Schmidgall's reading is, however, it yet finds little room for Ariel,[4] and this is a weakness, since allegory always establishes the significance of its figures by their relationship to each other within the narrative, as well as by their individual iconography. Furthermore, allegorical figures may represent simultaneously an external and an internal world, and one of the most persistent uses of allegory in the Middle Ages and the Renaissance was precisely to render visible the *psychomachia* or struggle within the mind and soul of the hero.

Ariel and Caliban, from this perspective, can be regarded as complementary figures functioning less as individuals than as representations of aspects of Prospero himself. To characterise Caliban in such a scheme is relatively easy – he may be taken as unregulated passion and rebellious flesh, the very qualities from which the contemplative Prospero seeks to withdraw. Ariel is more difficult to place, though a case can be made for considering him as the imaginative faculty of the mind, that which executes and bodies forth the ideas of the reason – since it is Ariel who comes 'with a thought' (4.1.164), and gives present life to Prospero's conceptions in the forms he adopts, as St Elmo's fire, sea-nymph, harpy and as Ceres.

Attempts to read these two characters as aspects of Prospero have in the twentieth century received further impetus through the application of psychoanalytic categories to them. The richest of such extensions is Auden's poetic descant, *The Sea and the Mirror*, and perhaps the most successful dramatic representation is in the film adaptation, *Forbidden Planet*, where Caliban is the unacknowledged, destructive 'id' of Morbius/Prospero.[5] The film succeeded in making the allegory work because Caliban had no bodily form, assuming only an outline shape at its climax, but in the theatre, as Timothy Walker observed: 'You can't as an actor play an extension of

[1] Angus Fletcher, *Allegory: The Theory of a Symbolic Mode*, 1964, pp. 22–3.
[2] Lorie Jerrell Leininger, 'Cracking the code of *The Tempest*', *Bucknell Review*, 25 (1980), 121–31; p. 125.
[3] Gary Schmidgall, *Shakespeare and the Courtly Aesthetic*, 1981, ch. 6.
[4] As he acknowledges in a long footnote, pp. 235–6, where he links Ariel with Mercury.
[5] See Tim Youngs, 'Cruising against the id: the transformation of Caliban in *Forbidden Planet*', in Nadia Lie and Theo D'haen, eds., *Constellation Caliban*, 1997, pp. 211–30.

Prospero.'¹ Nuttall sensibly declares that: 'Ariel and Caliban of all the characters in the play come nearest to being allegories of the psychic processes, but it would certainly be a mistake not to realise that they are very much more besides.'²

As readers, and even more as members of a theatre audience, we are confronted, therefore, by figures which demand to be comprehended in conflicting ways, both as 'characters' and as abstractions. In the case of Caliban this conflict is most clearly expressed at the ending, when Prospero says, 'this thing of darkness, I / Acknowledge mine' (5.1.274–5). Leininger expresses the duality clearly:

> The word 'acknowledge' implies self-discovery and revelation; it implies confession of guilt or acceptance of responsibility at some personal cost – specifically, here, for the darkness in one's own nature . . . The action in the play that gives rise to this sentence, however, is equivalent to no more than the identification of retainers. It is as though, after a public disturbance, a slave-owner said, 'Those two men are yours: this darkie's mine.'³

Everything, of course, turns on the inflection and action of actors on stage. Dymkowski notes that the line was often cut in nineteenth-century performances, but instances a number of relatively recent productions which have made it 'a fulcrum of the play', and a moment of mutual acceptance.⁴ Conversation with the Leeds Prospero and Caliban revealed that it is perfectly possible for the two actors/characters to intend and receive the line very differently. Sir Ian McKellen felt that 'Prospero makes no apologies about being wrong about Caliban or having treated him badly . . . I acknowledge it's my problem, but I don't know that it's acknowledged that it's of me.' But for Timothy Walker the moment triggered a self-recognition, so that his intention to 'seek for grace' was fully meant, and his gratitude at being permitted to return to the cell from which he had earlier been excluded was overwhelming. As is everywhere the case in this play, critical effort to confine its implications can be resisted by the plural possibilities available to actors and audience.

In nineteenth-century productions Ariel's freedom emblematised the happy ending of the romance, and the refrain of his concluding song, 'Merrily, merrily, shall I live now' (5.1.93), was often reintroduced as an epilogue which expressed the final mood of the play for all its characters. In more recent productions Prospero's farewell has been variously interpreted. The spectator's attention can be focused on Ariel's response to freedom, whether astonished, regretful or bitterly resentful. In Strehler's production Ariel moved with breathtaking grace, her feet never touching the ground, though 'on an obvious theatrical wire . . . a vivid signifier of her peculiar slavery; she could fly but not fly away'. In 'the most powerful emotional moment of the production' she was released, descending to stand on the ground and 'slowly and gleefully danced up the aisle of the auditorium, exiting through a spectator's door'.⁵ The focus

---

¹ Interview with the editor, February 1999. Interestingly, Timothy Walker had earlier played Prospero in Declan Donellan's Cheek By Jowl production, when he had found it possible to think of Caliban as a 'manifestation and extension' of himself.
² Nuttall, *Two Concepts of Allegory*, p. 159.
³ Leininger, 'Cracking the Code', p. 127.
⁴ Dymkowski, pp. 321–2.
⁵ Kennedy, *Looking at Shakespeare*, pp. 307, 309.

might equally be on Prospero's loss, as it was in Stratford in 1982, poignantly emphasised by the fact that Ariel had already departed before Jacobi gave him his final instruction and his freedom. Paul Bhattacharji in Leeds, 1999, walked impassively across a gallery at the back of the stage, his blue body-paint merging with the blue light of the sky; Prospero's wave to him was ignored.[1] In such performances the regret expressed in the statement 'I shall miss thee, / But yet thou shalt have freedom' (95–6), and the warmth of Prospero's final characterisation of Ariel as 'chick' (314), with its suggestion that he sees him as a child, opens yet another frame of reference into which the triangular relationship can be drawn.[2]

FAMILY RELATIONSHIPS

To recognise that *The Tempest* is concerned with the dynamics of family relationships leads to consideration of the ways in which the play reflects a distinctively Renaissance understanding of the nature and function of the family, which William Perkins succinctly described: 'this first societie, is as it were the Schoole, wherein we are taught and learned the principles of authoritie and subjection'.[3] In the hands of critics influenced by psychoanalytic theory, it can be directed towards a much less historically inflected study of the personal relationships in the play.[4]

When Prospero reassures Miranda of his intentions in raising the sea-storm, he insists: 'I have done nothing but in care of thee' (1.2.16); in handing her to Ferdinand he characterises her as 'that for which I live' (4.1.4), and as the play draws to its close he looks forward to the solemnisation of the nuptials of 'our dear-belovèd' (5.1.307). The good of his daughter is a motivation for his actions that runs in parallel with his own ambition to recover his dukedom, and the closeness of their relationship can be powerfully suggested in performance. Its achievement, however, is figured in terms as much political as personal – by marrying her to the King of Naples's son he brings together both his purposes. (Though, paradoxically, just as recovering Milan necessitates the abandonment of the learning he had 'prized above' his dukedom, so the marriage contract cements the subordination of Milan to Naples which he had earlier resented.) In securing an advantageous match for his daughter, Prospero achieved what any good Renaissance parent aimed for. The conclusion of the marriage of King James's daughter Elizabeth to the Elector Palatine in 1613 was, according to the Ven-

---

[1] In rehearsal the actors had explored the possibility of Ariel responding to Prospero, but concluded that a final distancing was the right solution.

[2] This 'warmth', however, is not present in performances where Prospero (despite 1.2.301–4) is imagined as himself unable to see Ariel. This was the line taken in Noble's 1998 production, and Gielgud claimed that 'In all the times I acted Prospero, I never looked at Ariel. He was always behind me or above me, and I saw him only in my mind's eye' (*Acting Shakespeare*, 1997, p. 95).

[3] William Perkins, *Christian Œconomie*, trans. Thomas Pickering (1609 edn), fol. 3ᵛ. See Jonathan Goldberg, 'Fatherly authority: the politics of Stuart family images', in Margaret W. Ferguson, Maureen Quilligan and Nancy J. Vickers, eds., *Rewriting the Renaissance: The Discourses of Sexual Difference in Early Modern Europe*, 1986, pp. 3–32.

[4] See, for example, Coppélia Kahn, 'The providential *Tempest* and the Shakespearean family', in Murray M. Schwartz and Coppélia Kahn, eds., *Representing Shakespeare: New Psychoanalytic Essays*, 1980, pp. 217–43.

etian ambassador, 'subject to the Princess's pleasure, who wishes first to see the Palatine and be wooed a while';[1] its motivation, however, was entirely political. Prospero is glad that his daughter falls in love with Ferdinand, but one cannot imagine that Miranda, any more than Princess Elizabeth, would have been allowed to refuse her proposed mate. From today's feminist perspective this makes the Ferdinand–Miranda relationship no more than a mystification of patriarchal ideology, representing as romantic and spontaneous that which is controlled and determined by (male) political ends. But this response insufficiently registers the importance of the theme of education to the play.

Prospero congratulates himself on his excellence as a teacher (1.2.171–4), but the 'profit' he brings his dutiful daughter is contrasted with the 'profit' his other pupil claims as the only benefit of his education. Caliban has learnt, he says, only to curse (264). For Prospero the failure is Caliban's own, since he has a nature upon which nurture cannot stick. But, as Jonathan Bate asks, 'is the lack of profit the result of Caliban's nature or the teaching method?'[2] Certainly severe punishments for recalcitrant pupils, though permitted in law and recommended by some in the educational establishment, were contrary to the prescriptions of humanist educators like Erasmus and Ascham.[3] The isolated island replays the detached world of the mind Prospero had fashioned for himself in Milan, and becomes the schoolmaster's dream classroom, free from distraction. But just as Milan was disrupted by political ambition, the island retreat is threatened by the irruption into it of lustful passion. Antonio's usurpation destroyed the original, and Caliban's attempted rape of Miranda exposes the limits of its successor. In both, Prospero's own indifference or unworldliness created the circumstances that made transgression possible. In the play he must put himself to school to find an appropriate response, and at the end of the play he pardons Caliban as he forgives Antonio, renouncing his excessive punishment as he reverses his desire for vengeance.

For critics who approach the play from a psychoanalytic perspective, the close relationship between father and daughter provides an important key to the play's meaning and shape. As Ruth Nevo puts it, both father and daughter must be saved

from the loveliest of all fantasies. To live thus, father and daughter, alone and together, with no rival to challenge, no rebellion to threaten, no sexual turmoil to overthrow the beatific enjoyment of beauty, of obedience, of affection, of consideration . . . what is this but the wishful fantasy of a Lear, who would sing like a bird in a cage in prison with Cordelia, or the fantasy of any parent.[4]

---

[1] *Calendar of State Papers (Venetian)*, p. 365. The second recorded performance of the play was as part of the celebration of this marriage.

[2] Jonathan Bate, 'The humanist *Tempest*', in Claude Peltrault, ed., *Shakespeare, 'La Tempête': Etudes critiques*, 1993, p. 12. He argues in this essay that the humanist discourse on education is a central context for the play as a whole.

[3] See Rebecca W. Bushnell, *A Culture of Teaching: Early Modern Humanism in Theory and Practice*, 1996. Pulton notes that an action of assault could be avoided by demonstrating that the accused was a teacher (p. 162).

[4] Ruth Nevo, *Shakespeare's Other Language*, 1987, pp. 133–4.

The parallel with *Lear* is a suggestive one; for Lear's representation of a prison as freedom enunciates a paradox that is also true for Prospero's island, an idealised space which yet itself must in the end be escaped.[1]

Prospero must surrender his daughter to marriage, and thereby acknowledge her sexuality. From this perspective his treatment of Ferdinand, his immobilising of the phallic sword in 1.2, his insistence on pre-marital chastity in 4.1, and, perhaps most obviously, his inflicting on him of the punishment of bearing logs, thereby identifying him with Miranda's other would-be violator, Caliban, mark out the father's 'symbolic victory over the younger man's confident sexuality'.[2] Only when chastened by labour, and instructed by the masque from which Venus is banished, will Ferdinand take Miranda as his wife. We have seen that he is defined against classical story as 'not-Aeneas'; and within the action of the play he is made to become 'not-Caliban'. But the play emphasises the sexual instinct's power in Ferdinand as well as in Caliban. The latter wishes to use Miranda as a means of 'peopling the isle' (and promises to Stephano that she will bring him 'brave brood') while fertility is also promised in the betrothal masque. The difference is one of obedience to society's ceremonial rites – but also, and crucially, it is the difference between attempted rape and mutual love.[3] But still, at the play's end, Prospero represents the giving of his daughter in marriage as a 'loss' – she will go to Naples, he return to Milan. The giving up of Miranda brings Prospero something of the same regret as does the liberation of Ariel.

For Nancy Meckler, 'Miranda is the catalyst of the story. Had it been possible for her to have remained forever a child in a child's body the tempest would have been unnecessary', and the play turns on the 'power that parents necessarily have over their children which must eventually be relinquished'.[4] In her production for the Shared Experience Company it enabled a presentation of Prospero's relationship with Ariel as analogous to that with his daughter.[5] Rachel Sanderson's Ariel was, in the words of one reviewer, 'a recalcitrant and other-worldly teenager bowed by parental expectation'.[6] The other-worldliness was emphasised by her computer-assisted generation of all musical sound, but the similarity with Miranda was a direct consequence of the female casting, and was underlined by the way Ariel at the end of the play signalled her freedom by stripping off her costume of white tabard with long sleeves to reveal the female body beneath (illustration 21). This was a variation on the current emphasis on Ariel's imprisonment,[7] but it also gave Prospero's final address to 'My Ariel,

---

[1] The island-as-prison was the dominant metaphor of the staging in Leeds, 1999, where the black-box set was hung with chains, and the rear wall was covered with chalk-marks crossed off to indicate the passing of days – Prospero added a fresh mark at the beginning of each performance.

[2] David Sundelson, '"So rare a wonder'd father": Prospero's *Tempest*', in Schwartz and Kahn, *Representing Shakespeare*, p. 46.

[3] In some productions Caliban's desire for Miranda has been given a softer quality and exploited for pathos. Dymkowski, p. 163.

[4] Nancy Meckler, 'Director's notes', in programme for Shared Experience Theatre production, 1996–7.

[5] More controversially, the performance opened with a dumb-show in which the attempted 'rape' was staged as a shared desire for sexual experiment, halted just in time by Prospero. This necessitated Miranda later performing the 'Abhorrèd slave' speech as if unwillingly under her father's command.

[6] Lyn Gardner, *Guardian*, 1 February 1997.

[7] Gardner commented on 'the sudden shocking realisation that the white designer number Ariel had floated about in all evening is in fact a straightjacket [sic]'.

21 Rachel Sanderson, Ariel in the Shared Experience Company production directed by Nancy Meckler (1996–7), has just been granted freedom, and has removed the long-sleeved tabard in which she had been clothed throughout (photographer Mike Kwasniak)

chick' a powerful emotional charge, underscored by its very inappropriateness to the mature woman to whom it was spoken.[1]

Some critics have viewed Prospero's acceptance of the need to let go of his daughter positively. David Sundelson argues that 'Prospero identifies with Ferdinand and surrenders to him the pleasure of possessing Miranda. The success of this surrender accounts in part for the deep harmony that distinguishes *The Tempest*.'[2] Janet Adelman, by contrast, laments the way in which, after *The Winter's Tale*, this play reinstates 'absolute paternal authority with a vengeance'. She emphasises the way in which 'the maternal body has been defined as dangerous and banished in the form of Sycorax', and notes the way Prospero arrogates the maternal function to himself as he 'gives birth' to Ariel, by releasing him from the pine.[3] Stephen Orgel has discussed the most glaring omission of all – that of Prospero's wife – and others have considered Claribel, the last of the shadowy and marginalised women who haunt the edges of the play, both as a female victim of male power politics, and, in her marriage to the African King of Tunis, as invoking the threat of miscegenation that Prospero thwarts in Caliban and surmounts in the marriage of his daughter to a European prince.[4]

These marginalised women trouble literary critics, perhaps, more than they concern an audience in the theatre, but in Peter Greenaway's film adaptation, *Prospero's Books*, Prospero's wife is given a name, Susannah, and an eerie presence, and Claribel is fleetingly and shockingly viewed. Derek Jarman reintroduced Sycorax briefly, with Caliban suckling at her breast.[5] Neither film explicitly contested the play's 'patriarchalism'. Other rewritings, however, expressly place Miranda at their centre, or give voice to the marginal Claribel and demonised Sycorax.[6] Marina Warner's *Indigo*, for example, presents the story of a modern Miranda framing those of Sycorax, Ariel and

[1] It also reflected interestingly on the theatrical tradition which, at least since Leslie French, has paradoxically suggested Ariel's other-worldliness by a conspicuous lack of clothing throughout.

[2] Sundelson, 'Prospero's *Tempest*', p. 47.

[3] Janet Adelman, *Suffocating Mothers: Fantasies of Maternal Origin in Shakespeare's Plays, 'Hamlet' to 'The Tempest'*, 1992, p. 237.

[4] Jyotsna G. Singh, 'Caliban versus Miranda: race and gender conflicts in postcolonial rewritings of *The Tempest*', in Valerie Traub et al., eds., *Feminist Readings of Early Modern Culture*, 1996, pp. 201–2.

[5] On Greenaway's film, from a growing bibliography, see Claus Schatz-Jacobsen, '"Knowing I lov'd my books": Shakespeare, Greenaway, and the prosperous dialectics of word and image', in Michael Skovmand, ed., *Screen Shakespeare*, 1994, pp. 132–47; Peter Donaldson, 'Shakespeare in the age of postmechanical reproduction: sexual and electronic magic in *Prospero's Books*', in Linda Boose and Richard Burt, eds., *Shakespeare the Movie*, 1997, pp. 169–85; 'Digital archives and sibylline fragments: *The Tempest* and the end of books', *Postmodern Culture*, 8.2. (1998); Douglas Lanier, 'Drowning the book: *Prospero's Books* and the textual Shakespeare', in James C. Bulman, ed., *Shakespeare, Theory and Performance*, 1996, pp. 187–209. On Jarman's film see Kate Chedgzoy, *Shakespeare's Queer Children: Sexual Politics and Contemporary Culture*, 1995, ch. 5. They are compared in Chantal Zabus and Kevin A. Dwyer, '"I'll be wise hereafter": Caliban in postmodern British cinema', in Lie and D'haen, *Constellation Caliban*, pp. 271–89.

[6] For feminist rewritings, especially in Canada, see Diana Brydon, 'Re-writing *The Tempest*', *World Literature Written in English*, 23 (1984), 75–88; 'Sister letters: Miranda's *Tempest* in Canada', in Marianne Novy, ed., *Cross-Cultural Performances*, 1993, pp. 165–84; '*Tempest* plainsong: retuning Caliban's curse', in Marianne Novy, ed., *Transforming Shakespeare: Contemporary Women's Re-visions in Literature and Performance*, 1999, pp. 199–216; Thomas Cartelli, *Repositioning Shakespeare*, ch. 5. H. D. (Hilda Doolittle) in her *By Avon River* (1949) adopts the voice of Claribel, as does Linda Bamber in 'Claribel at Palace dot Tunis', in Novy, *Transforming Shakespeare*, pp. 237–58.

Caliban before and after the seizure of their island by her colonial ancestors. Her novel is told through female voices, and presents a complex meditation on colonial and gender relationships (and the troubled intersection of the two).[1]

In Shakespeare's play, however, the absent female figures function, in part at least, to question rather than, by their marginalisation, merely to endorse Prospero's male power. If Prospero begins by defining his magic against the witchcraft of Sycorax, his use of Medea's words makes us aware of the precariousness of such a distinction. Magic, in the end, must be renounced because it is magic, not because it is 'female'. Claribel's politically arranged marriage, enforced by the will of her father, functions as a contrast with the marriage of Ferdinand and Miranda where such coercion is absent. That it is Sebastian who utters criticism of arranged marriages would not prevent a seventeenth-century audience recognising in his words a familiar attack on the practice, one with which many would have sympathised, and which had been staged in George Wilkins's play, *The Miseries of Enforced Marriage* (1607).[2]

But it is the representation of Miranda herself which has focused feminist hostility to the play. In the eyes of a number of critics she is a passive, dutiful daughter who willingly submits to Prospero's control of her chastity, and consents to her position as a pawn in political negotiations between men, in a marriage which reinstates the secure line of male inheritance threatened by Caliban's claim to inherit the island from his mother. This perception of Miranda as oppressed victim of patriarchy has also involved seeing parallels with Caliban. Lorie Jerrell Leininger ends her polemical assault on the play by fashioning a new 'epilogue' for Miranda, which concludes: 'I need to join forces with Caliban – to join forces with all those who are exploited or oppressed – to stand beside Caliban.'[3] Others have wished to negotiate parallels between them in subtler ways, for, as Kate Chedgzoy observes of the attempted rape, 'each is seen to be placed in an anomalous and uneasy position: Miranda disadvantaged by her gender, yet protected by and benefiting from colonialism; Caliban oppressed as the colonial subject, but empowered by his masculinity'.[4] (This argument, of course, depends upon the problematical prior categorisation of Caliban's status as 'colonial subject'.)

But feminist discontent with Miranda raises starkly the question of how far it is just to read Shakespeare's play in late twentieth-century terms. This problem is raised

---

[1] On Warner's novel see Chedgzoy, *Shakespeare's Queer Children*, pp. 123–9, and Caroline Cakebread, 'Sycorax speaks: Marina Warner's *Indigo* and *The Tempest*', in Novy, *Transforming Shakespeare*, pp. 217–36. Marina Warner herself revisits Sycorax's place in Shakespeare's play in '"The foul witch" and her "freckled whelp"', in Hulme and Sherman, pp. 97–113.

[2] The ideology of marriage was much more conflicted than can be fully developed here – King James himself, for example, inveighed against arranged marriage, even as he sought to organise politically suitable matches for his children. See, for example, Alan Macfarlane, *Marriage and Love in England, 1300–1840*, 1986, ch. 7; David Lindley, *The Trials of Frances Howard*, 1993, ch. 1.

[3] Lorie Jerrell Leininger, 'The Miranda trap: sexism and racism in Shakespeare's *Tempest*', in Carolyn Lenz et al., eds., *The Woman's Part*, 1980, pp. 285–94.

[4] Chedgzoy, *Shakespeare's Queer Children*, p. 99. Laura E. Donaldson, *Decolonizing Feminisms: Race, Gender and Empire-Building*, 1992, uses the term 'Miranda Complex' as a starting-point for her exploration. Singh, 'Caliban versus Miranda', produces a carefully nuanced account, aimed in part at the absence of any 'reconceptualisation' of the relationship in Césaire's play.

directly by Ann Thompson's emphatically contemporary perspective on the play, as she asks: 'what kind of pleasure can a woman and a feminist take in this text beyond the rather grim one of mapping its various patterns of exploitation?'[1] She argues that Miranda is so utterly unassertive that even Victorian women could find little in her to enthuse over, and that twentieth-century female students 'find Miranda an extremely feeble heroine and scorn to identify with her'.[2] Compared with Innogen or Perdita, let alone with Rosalind or Viola, the passivity of Miranda seems self-evident. Yet Prospero himself contrasts the courage of the baby Miranda with his own near-despair during their sea journey, and, though it offended eighteenth-century editors and is problematic to postcolonial critics, her attack on the Caliban who has attempted to rape her is not notably wilting. Indeed, in another context, one would have expected that her spirited resistance to her would-be assailant might command some respect. But it is her love for Ferdinand which most obviously provokes her to thoughts of self-assertive opposition to her father.

We are here in familiar comic territory. When Miranda says 'Pity move my father / To be inclined my way' (1.2.445–6), she echoes Hermia's words: 'I would my father look'd but with my eyes' (*MND* 1.1.56).[3] This opposition is confirmed in 3.1, where she utterly subverts Prospero's attempted control by actually marrying the man she thinks he is opposed to, for a clandestine, but valid, marriage is what takes place in this scene (see Commentary).[4]

Miranda's opposition should not be overstated, however, for she has certainly internalised her culture's premium upon virginity when she swears 'by my modesty, / The jewel in my dower' (3.1.54–5). Given that she exists in a world where a woman 'hath naught to see to but her chastity; when she is enfirmed of that she hath everything',[5] she would be foolish indeed not to recognise reality, even if it is a view that many now find offensive. But feminist dissatisfaction derives less from Miranda's own statements than from the view that 'Prospero must control Miranda's sexuality before he hands her over to Ferdinand.'[6] This seems to me at best a partial reading of the play's action. Prospero defends his daughter from attempted rape, and ensures that the man she falls for proves himself to be more than a courtly male on the make – not necessarily ignoble parental ambitions. More importantly, it is not Miranda's sexuality that he attempts to control in his introduction to the masque, but Ferdinand's. In

---

[1] Ann Thompson, '"Miranda, where's your sister?": reading Shakespeare's *The Tempest*', in Susan Sellers, ed., *Feminist Criticism: Theory and Practice*, 1991, p. 54.

[2] Ibid., p. 47.

[3] I have marked her speech at 1.2.443 ff. as an aside, but in the Leeds 1999 performance Claudie Blakley chose to address the whole speech directly to Prospero, and physically to confront him. To perform this speech in this way is almost certainly anachronistic, so complete a violation is it of the expectation of a child's obedience to a parent, but it does develop a clear implication of the text, and suggests how a less passive Miranda may be imagined, at least for a modern audience not fully attuned to the extent of her seventeenth-century daring in simply opposing her father's wishes.

[4] The varied responses that the watching Prospero might make – from amused tolerance, to genuine pleasure, to worry as Miranda offers herself as Ferdinand's wife – can significantly affect an audience's sense of what is at stake.

[5] Juan Luis Vives, *Instruction of a Cristen Woman*, trans. Richard Hyrde (c. 1529), sig. B2.

[6] Thompson, 'Miranda', p. 50.

refusing to countenance a double standard that is fiercely demanding of female chastity, but tolerant of male laxity,[1] Prospero chimes with Donne's argument that

> mariage should have no beginning before mariage; no half-mariage, no . . . lending away of the body in unchaste wantonness before. The body is the temple of the Holy Ghost; and when two bodies, by mariage are to be made one temple, the wife is not as the Chancell, reserv'd and shut up, and the man as the walks below, indifferent and at liberty for every passenger. God in his Temple looks for first fruits from both.[2]

Nor is it true that Miranda is unaware of her own sexual desire. Ferdinand's response to Prospero: 'The white cold virgin snow upon my heart / Abates the ardour of my liver' (4.1.55–6), and the iconology of the dance of reapers and nymphs, seem to concur with the period's assumption that, as Anthony Stafford put it: 'the woman should expect till heate bee infused into her by her husband[:] it being as much against the nature of an honest spouse, as of the coldest water, to boile of her selfe'.[3] But, though considerably more reticent than Juliet in her anticipation of her lover (*Rom.* 3.2.1), Miranda in 3.1.79–84 is perfectly aware of what it is she 'desire[s] to give', and what she 'shall die to want', and, far from 'expecting' till Ferdinand awake her, it is she who takes control of the scene in declaring 'I am your wife, if you will marry me.' On these grounds, then, it is possible to argue that the play presents a rather more assertive Miranda than some feminist critics have allowed.

But even this is to underplay the theatrical force of 3.1. Coleridge considered it 'a masterpiece', in which 'the first dawn of disobedience in the mind of Miranda to the command of her father is very finely drawn', and executed with 'exquisite purity'.[4] The delight and power of this scene is not merely a matter of character, however, but derives from the subtle architecture which its formal, rhetorical patterning generates.

Language and rhetoric

In order fully to appreciate the design of 3.1 a short detour is needed. When commenting on the language of *The Tempest*, formalist critics concentrate upon patterns of imagery as directions to the thematic centres of the play.[5] Anne Barton commented perspicaciously on the play's linguistic compression,[6] and Stephen Palfrey has recently offered a complex study of the 'new world of words' which he sees as characterising

---

[1] See, for example, Pettie's *The Civil Conversation of M. Stephen Guazzo* (1581): 'Though the Husband offende God as much as the Wyfe in vyolating the sacred band of Matrimonye, yet the wife ought firmelye to print this in her harte . . . that where the husband by this fault doth, according to the opinion of men, but a little blemish his honour, the wife altogether looseth her good name.'

[2] Simpson and Potter, *Sermons of John Donne*, III, pp. 247–8.

[3] *Niobe* (1611), sig. C2ᵛ–3.

[4] Terence Hawkes, ed., *Coleridge on Shakespeare*, 1969, p. 227. A slightly later writer was rather more troubled by it, remarking that: 'the plain acknowledgement of her thoughts, which in any other woman would be disgusting forwardness, proclaims in her the extreme of unsuspecting innocence', W. Oxberry, *The Tempest . . . as it is performed at Theatres Royal* (1823), pp. vi–vii. The early nineteenth-century Miranda was in trouble for saying too much, just as the late twentieth-century one was for saying too little.

[5] See, for example, Reuben A. Brower, *Fields of Light*, 1951.

[6] Barton, pp. 13–14. Russ McDonald, in 'Reading *The Tempest*', *S.Sur.*, 43 (1990), 15–28, concentrates on patterns of repetition in the play's language.

the late romances.[1] In Shakespeare language serves also as an index of character, as, for example, in the way the tangled syntax of Prospero's account of his brother's treachery imitates the disorienting horror he feels as he is plunged into his retrospective narrative and suggests at the same time that this is a narrative which he had not prepared, but is improvising hastily in response to the sudden appearance of his enemies within his reach. But useful though all these approaches are, the linguistic artistry of *The Tempest* cannot be fully comprehended without some exploration of its use of the disciplines of rhetoric.

Educational practice throughout the Renaissance was based on a belief in the centrality of artful language to a civilised society. Shakespeare would have been drilled in the arts of rhetoric at school, where he would have memorised the figures of speech, sought for them in his reading of classical texts and entered them in his commonplace-book. He would also have been trained in the organisation of an argument, and its rhetorical elaboration for best effect. Most modern students are alienated by the taxonomies of rhetorical figures in the handbooks, yet these treatises inculcated practices and habits of mind that underpinned all literary composition, and conditioned the response of readers and of audiences in the playhouses.[2]

A self-contained, but usefully typical, example is Francisco's speech in 2.1.108–17. He puts together a vivid picture of Ferdinand's escape from the sinking ship:

> Sir, he may live.
> I saw him beat the surges under him,
> And ride upon their backs; he trod the water
> Whose enmity he flung aside, and breasted
> The surge most swol'n that met him. His bold head
> 'Bove the contentious waves he kept, and oared
> Himself with his good arms in lusty stroke
> To th'shore, that o'er his wave-worn basis bowed,
> As stooping to relieve him. I not doubt
> He came alive to land.

This speech elaborates the simple proposition 'I saw Ferdinand swimming' in a coherent fashion in order to emphasise the swimmer's control of the threatening elements, moving purposefully from Ferdinand's feet treading water up through his breasting of the waves to his 'bold head' kept above them, and concluding with a metaphoric personification of the overhanging cliffs 'stooping to relieve him'. The speech is framed by an address to Alonso, and indicates clearly the way in which Francisco vividly refashions elements from the *Aeneid* to create a speaking picture of Ferdinand's heroic struggle which will persuade the king to abandon his grief. The point here is that this speech has nothing to do with 'character' – Francisco has none – but every-

---

[1] Palfrey, *Late Shakespeare*, passim.

[2] Students not deterred might pursue the subject through useful introductions in Brian Vickers, *Classical Rhetoric in English Poetry*, 1970, Gert Ronberg, *A Way with Words*, 1992. Comprehensive listing of the rhetorical figures is to be found in Richard Lanham, *A Handlist of Rhetorical Terms*, 2nd edn 1991, and Gideon Burton's *Silva Rhetoricae* web-site at http://humanities.byu.edu/rhetoric/silva.htm. The fullest account of what might have been Shakespeare's educational experience is to be found in T. W. Baldwin's monumental *William Shakespere's Small Latine and Less Greeke*, 1944.

thing to do with a verbal art which a rhetorically trained listener could enjoy for its own sake. It is precisely this self-conscious aesthetic pleasure that is essential to the larger-scale effect of Ferdinand and Miranda's wooing scene.

Ferdinand opens 3.1 with a set-piece structured by the figure of paradox. His situation is to toil, yet to delight in his labour because it confirms both his love for Miranda and hers for him. He thereby translates a service commanded by Prospero into service offered to his beloved. From line 38 onwards we witness the artful formality with which first Ferdinand, then Miranda, deliver praises of each other. Ferdinand, in courtly fashion, plays learnedly upon the Latin derivation of her name, and converts his past experience of women into a compliment to her peerlessness. In no less formal terms Miranda replies by turning her innocence to rhetorical account. Ferdinand's response then neatly explores the difference between the bodily servitude of his 'wooden slavery' to Prospero's commands, and the willing service of his heart to Miranda. It is into this ceremonious rhetoric that Miranda's blunt question 'Do you love me?' irrupts; but, as yet, her plain speech is answered by further formality. At line 79 Miranda again begins with a neatly balanced, rhetorically ordered explanation of her weeping, and it is only after she calls upon 'plain and holy innocence' that she utters the show-stopping line 'I am your wife', and answers Ferdinand's protestations that he is her slave with a parallel assertion that 'I'll be your servant / Whether you will or no.'

At the simplest level the rhetorical artfulness of this scene functions deliciously to postpone the mutual declaration of love that the audience anticipates from the moment it begins. If one does not draw pleasure from the ceremonious interchanges of the earlier part of the scene then one will miss the force of Miranda's 'plain' statement of her desire to marry and the ritual significance of the handclasping that follows. At the same time, lack of attention to the mutual rhetorical amplification and witty analysis of loving servitude produces an inadequate response to Miranda which characterises her as one who has merely internalised patriarchal assumptions of obedience. Judith Dusinberre is surely right to insist that in this scene 'Shakespeare uses reciprocal idolatry to reveal the nature of love rather than to create, as male idolatry does, preconceptions about the nature of women.'[1]

It is, furthermore, a remarkable scene in this play of frustrated anticipations precisely because the expectations it sets up are not thwarted but fulfilled, even exceeded, and this is part of the reason that it can work powerfully on stage. In the 1982 RSC production 'the young lover pair [made] the centrepiece of the play with the wonderment of sudden self-revelation and maturity',[2] and the same effect was achieved in the rapt intensity of feeling generated in the Leeds 1999 performance (illustration 22). But the scene is perilously balanced, and vulnerable equally to excessive naturalism, and to a modern audience's unease with formal speech. In many ways it has the

---

[1] Judith Dusinberre, *Shakespeare and the Nature of Women*, 1975, p. 157. Her 'soft' view of Shakespeare as proto-feminist has been much challenged.

[2] Dymkowski, p. 241. It is noticeable how often reviewers are surprised by the life actors can bring to the characters of Ferdinand and Miranda. Actors, it seems, find it much easier than literary critics might believe to give dynamism and attractiveness to the young lovers.

22 3.1.91–2 – Claudie Blakley (Miranda) and Rashan Stone (Ferdinand) take hands in the Leeds 1999 production (photographer Keith Pattison)

same qualities as the final ceremoniously patterned pairings of *As You Like It*, or the mutual recognition of Sebastian and Viola in *Twelfth Night*, and like them it requires a slightly distanced, but delighted, recognition on the part of the audience that they are witnessing a 'set-piece' scene, and a readiness on the part of actors to let the pattern of the words do the work. It is precisely, if paradoxically, because this scene is so self-consciously artful, so aware of its own rhetoric, that its celebration of mutual love is dramatically powerful, and the terms in which that love is expressed would have resonated even more strongly in a world where it was possible to believe that 'service is perfect freedom'.[1] But at the same time its rhetorical self-consciousness hints at an awareness of the fragility of the idealised relationship it constructs.

For though rhetoric was central to Renaissance thinking, it was frequently regarded with suspicion. Montaigne, in his Essay 'On the Vanity of Words', articulated an attitude that reached back to Plato when he wrote: 'those that maske and paint women, commit not so foule a fault: for it is no great losse, though a man see them not, as they were naturally borne and unpainted: Wheras these [rhetoricians] professe to deceive and beguile, not our eies, but our judgement: and to bastardize and corrupt the essence of things'.[2] When Prospero tells Miranda that the usurpers dared not destroy them,

[1] The phrase is taken from the second collect at Morning Prayer.
[2] Montaigne, I, 352. For the attacks on rhetoric see Brian Vickers, *In Defence of Rhetoric*, 1988.

'but / With colours fairer painted their foul ends' (1.2.142–3) he, like Montaigne, fuses the 'colours' of rhetoric with the deceitfulness of cosmetics to characterise his enemies' treachery, and his description of Antonio's manipulative skills is borne out within the play itself by the rhetorical subtlety his brother deploys in winding Sebastian up to murder.

But it is on the figure of Gonzalo, explicitly characterised as a rhetorician and 'spirit of persuasion' (2.1.231), that the ambivalent response to rhetoric is focused. On his first entrance, in an attempt to console Alonso for the loss of his son, he offers a set-piece comparison of their fortunes with the everyday situation of the sailor's wife or the merchant, and his subsequent meditation on recreating the Golden Age is carefully constructed, as he himself says, by means of 'contraries'. Though the contempt of Antonio and Sebastian may chime with a modern antipathy to such obvious rhetoric to encourage the view that he is emptily garrulous, yet Antonio himself fears his powers of persuasion enough to wish to assassinate him.

In the play as a whole, then, an awareness of rhetorical arts contributes to the pleasure that an audience takes in its language – in Ariel's account of the tempest (1.2) or his witty representation of the drunken conspirators (4.1) for example. Perhaps more significantly, we, like the characters on stage, experience the persuasive force of rhetorically organised language, its power to command a particular interpretation of events, in Prospero's narrative in 1.2, Ariel's persuasion to repentance in 3.3, and Prospero's effort to interpret for Ferdinand the dissolved masque in 4.1. And, as we have seen, persuasive rhetoric extends beyond the verbal to encompass the play's emblematic spectacular devices and the affective rhetoric of music. Precisely because we recognise the intention of rhetoric to work its end upon our senses, however, we are able to register also the ambivalences and limitations that Montaigne articulates. If the undercutting of the masque bespeaks a radical uncertainty about the effectiveness of theatrical art, then the same questioning of rhetorical control is evidenced in the final scene. There Gonzalo winds up to a peroration in his 'Was Milan thrust from Milan' speech (5.1.205–13). As the Commentary points out, this is a polished rhetorical performance. Gonzalo has earlier characterised the plight of the lords as entrapment in a maze (3.3.2, see Commentary), and his conclusion suits with the conventional moralisation of life's labyrinth as ultimately under divine control (see illustration 23). Yet we are uncomfortably aware of how his speech ameliorates events by writing out Claribel's discontent at her forced marriage and by benignly (and inaccurately) assuming that Antonio and Sebastian have now 'found themselves'. Moreover, as Orgel points out, his speech is in the 'wrong' place; it sounds like a formal conclusion to the romance narrative, the kind of summary one would expect right at the end of a play, yet it comes a hundred lines too early, before the entries of the mariners and of Caliban, Stephano and Trinculo.

'My ending is despair, unless . . .'

The problems raised by Gonzalo's speech take us back to the beginning of this introduction. The ambivalence of our reaction to his words is typical of the plural

Oh that my wayes were directed
to keepe thy Statutes. *P.f.119.5.*
W. Simpson Sculp:

23 The maze as an emblem of life's struggle, guided by the 'thread' that emanates from an angel, from Francis Quarles, *Emblemes*, 1643

possibilities of reading which *The Tempest* holds, and their formal oddity confirms the sense that such openness to interpretation is in part the result of the experimental shape of the work. Towards the end of *A Midsummer Night's Dream* Hippolita observes that 'all the story of the night told over . . . grows to something of great constancy; / But howsoever, strange and admirable' (5.1.22, 26–7). The late romances add to this comic resolution of confusion and pain the larger hope that the past, too, may be redeemed. In the theatre, however, the moment of reconciliation and recognition is always a perilous one, since it can easily seem a matter of mere contrivance. As Terence Cave observes: 'We never know whether to take *anagnorisis* seriously. We can't answer the question "when is a parody not a parody?".'[1] The knife-edge upon which such scenes can teeter is evidenced, for example, in the theatrical fortunes of the moment at the end of *The Comedy of Errors*, when the Abbess is revealed as Egeus' long-lost wife. This usually produces roars of laughter in the theatre, but in Tim Supple's production for the RSC in 1996 it moved its audience near to tears. In the three plays which immediately precede *The Tempest* Shakespeare had tried various strategies for handling this problem, in each of them generating a powerful affirmation of restoration. But in its ending, as in so much else, *The Tempest* is distinctive and experimental.[2]

The exclusion of Antonio and Sebastian from a full integration into the harmonious resolution is not without precedent – Shakespeare had often complicated his comic conclusions with figures such as Malvolio in *Twelfth Night* or Jaques in *As You Like It* who obstinately refuse to participate in the inclusive ending.[3] What is distinctive in *The Tempest* is the way Shakespeare insistently undercuts all of the gestures the play makes towards a fullness of restoration. 'Welcome my friends all', says Prospero to the lords – then immediately qualifies the warmth of his remark in the bitter exchange with his brother and Sebastian. The 'wonder' of Ferdinand and Miranda's reappearance is threatened by her accusation of falseness, and its characterisation as 'A most high miracle' is entrusted to Sebastian – to be uttered, one might imagine, with less than full-hearted joy. Miranda's 'brave new world' is briskly undercut as 'new to thee', and Alonso's reconciliation with his son and new daughter-in-law is cut short by Prospero's 'There, sir, stop.' None of these moments, each of which, in the earlier romances, might have expanded heart-warmingly, is allowed to resonate fully. The dramatic sequence is also peculiar, in that the mariners and lower-class conspirators are reintroduced *after* Gonzalo's speech has attempted to sum up the final situation. In its structure the scene is quite unlike *The Winter's Tale* which concludes so movingly with the restoration of Hermione, and different also from the complex

---

[1] Terence Cave, *Recognitions: A Study in Poetics*, 1988, p. 260.

[2] See R. S. White, *Let Wonder Seem Familiar: Endings in Shakespeare's Romance Vision*, 1985. Frank Kermode, *The Sense of an Ending*, 1967, offers a wide-ranging consideration of the nature and implication of endings.

[3] In the theatre, however, there are ways of including Antonio and Sebastian. Bridges-Adams, for example, had Prospero address 'Please you draw near' to Antonio, who then 'knelt and kissed his brother's hand' (Dymkowski, p. 329). In Leeds 1999, Miranda addressed the 'brave new world' speech directly to Antonio, and thereby precipitated his repentance. (The analogous case of Isabella's ambivalent status in *Measure for Measure* has prompted similarly varied theatrical solutions.)

resolution of *Cymbeline*, where, in just about the longest recognition scene in theatrical history, successive revelations form a rising sequence that leads to harmony at the widest political level. Instead, the final movement of *The Tempest* returns us to the play's beginning, reverses its opening storm with a command for calm seas and auspicious gales, but also promises (or threatens) yet another recapitulation of 1.2, when Prospero offers to make the night 'Go quick away' by retelling 'the story of my life, / And the particular accidents gone by / Since I came to this isle' (5.1.302–4). The speed with which they will catch up with the 'royal fleet' suggests that the last three hours have been but a brief, dream-like interlude. As is characteristic of Shakespeare, there are questions unanswered – whether or not Antonio is likely to remain under control in the future; what will happen to Ferdinand and Miranda as her idealism confronts the reality of a world where not all are 'brave'; whether a Prospero retiring to Milan to meditate on his end will be any more successful a duke than when he retired to pursue his secret studies; and, perhaps most puzzlingly, what happens to Caliban.[1] It is symptomatic of the play's resistant, wilful opacity that productions have in various ways felt it necessary to amplify this laconic conclusion, to give the audience, as we have seen, a triumphant Ariel, a wistful Caliban, or even an Ariel about to take command over Caliban, as in Miller's production.

However it might be realised on stage, the play could perfectly properly end here. The Epilogue which follows is, in the Folio, separated off by a double ruled line, and the last stage direction of the text, *Exeunt omnes*, implies that Prospero leaves with all the others. Excised from the Dryden–Davenant adaptation and its successors, the Epilogue was also omitted from many nineteenth and early twentieth-century productions, and there can be no assumption that it was always spoken on the stage of Blackfriars or the Globe.[2] And yet it provides, as Barton says, 'the last of the surprises which *The Tempest* has to offer, the last of its reminders that it stands on the frontiers of what is possible in the theatre'.[3] As an appeal for applause it is entirely conventional. The peculiar resonance of this epilogue compared with other Shakespearean examples derives from the ambiguous status of the speaker who stands before us. Puck, in *A Midsummer Night's Dream*, stays in character; Rosalind, in *As You Like It*, and the King, in *All's Well That Ends Well*, both step out of their roles and present themselves as, in turn, the male actor beneath the female disguise, and the beggar that an actor/king becomes when 'the play is done'. At the end of this play, however, a play that has continually teased its on-stage characters with the question 'What have we here?', the audience is placed in exactly the same position. Is it Prospero who speaks, or the actor beneath? Barton maintained that Prospero stays in character throughout, so that the Epilogue 'perpetuates this illusion and firmly, if with great deference and courtesy, involves the audience with it', but productions have in various ways modulated from character to actor as the Epilogue unfolds.[4] That these lines can

---

[1] In some ways the openness of this ending is more like that of a history play than of a comedy.
[2] See Tiffany Stern, *Rehearsal from Shakespeare to Sheridan*, 2000, pp. 113–21, for the suggestion that epilogues were most likely to be delivered at a first performance, or else, at least in the 1620s and 30s, at a second or third performance where the author received a substantial proportion of the takings.
[3] Barton, p. 51.
[4] See Dymkowski, p. 331.

be played either way is typical of *The Tempest*, but without some sense that both are implied their rich suggestiveness is diminished. The 'I' who lacks spirits to command is both a Prospero who has abandoned his magic, and the actor wanting to go home, and there is a clear difference between Prospero's 'project' and that of the actor/dramatist to 'please' his audience. The challenge of the Epilogue, however, comes in its final lines, where, whether or not magus has dwindled into actor, the demand for our consent to the play returns us to its central concern with forgiveness, and by its recollection of the Lord's Prayer places a moral responsibility upon us to answer Prospero's plea. The plangent final line then resonates eerily – who are we being asked to free from what, and what kind of freedom is it that we bestow? Even as we confer freedom on the actor/Prospero (who must, after all, return on the occasion of the next performance) we free ourselves from our voluntary imprisonment in the theatre, and give ourselves licence to return to the workaday world.

Orgel points out in his commentary to this passage that in the Epilogue 'Prospero puts himself in the position of Ariel, Caliban, Ferdinand and the other shipwreck victims.' But perhaps he has never been in any other. His retirement to his library in Milan was an effort to find freedom from the active life of office, but it delivered him to the imprisonment of the island. There, and only there, could he release an Ariel who enabled him to put his magic arts into practice, but the desire through magic to escape from human limitation must itself in the end be disowned. *The Tempest* has, especially in recent years, been seen as a play about power. Perhaps it should rather be regarded as a play about the illusion of freedom. For if romance offers the chance that time may be redeemed, that utopia may be found, this play's relentless scepticism – about Gonzalo's Golden Age, Ferdinand's paradise and Miranda's brave new world, no less than Caliban's delirious 'freedom, high-day' – seems radically to question its possibility. As its final words ring in our ears we recognise that no more than Ferdinand can we 'live here ever', no less than Prospero must we return from the world of contemplation to the world of the active life – even though, like Caliban, we may yet cry to dream again.

Coda

The Tempest is a challenging play. Its spareness of incident and characterisation invites a reader or theatre audience to piece out its silences with their thoughts, and whilst its patterned structual repetitiveness intimates a strict control, its rich allusiveness opens up multiple perspectives that resist easy synthesis. It is this paradoxical combination of qualities which has made the play so elusive, and, at the same time, perhaps, has given it a particular prominence in the literary criticism of the last half-century. For the old critical certainties have been displaced. Neither the formalist claim for a literary text as standing outside its historical moment and reaching for timeless human truths, nor the appeal to objective history as the guarantor of an original and 'authentic' meaning now seems adequate. We have become increasingly aware of the degree to which we bring our own culturally conditioned assumptions to the act of interpretation. As Tom Healy observes, 'Our relation with literary texts is formed through a complex intersection of past and present; moments of reception as well as moments of production are of equal importance.'[1] For some critics, analysis of the 'moments of reception' has been extended to suggest that there is no such thing as 'the text itself', only a series of historically determined appropriations of it – a position expressed in Terence Hawkes's pithy aphorism: 'Shakespeare doesn't mean: *we* mean *by* Shakespeare.'[2]

It is, of course, inevitable that we bring our own current preoccupations to the reading of the play, as we have seen in feminist, psychoanalytic and postcolonial approaches to it. It is true, furthermore, as Healy observes, that 'our interest in the past will be dictated by our involvement in the present'.[3] But this does not mean that reconstructions of the seventeenth-century contexts for *The Tempest* cannot be tested against empirical evidence. Nor does it imply that the text itself is incapable of exerting some control over the relevance of the particular contexts or approaches a critic brings to bear upon it. If the dismantling of boundaries between texts of different kinds has in recent years been enormously productive in enriching our understanding of cultural formation, the concomitant danger is that any bush may ingeniously be supposed a bear. So too, though proclaiming the undecidability of meaning, many recent critiques of the play are remarkably decided, even one-sided, in the readings they offer. *The Tempest*, as we have seen, alludes to a wide range of cultural, political and social issues and languages, and it is necessary to recognise their interplay rather than dilute the play's resonance by turning it into a single-stranded allegory.

The critical focus upon the the play's reception and appropriation accompanies the increased interest in production history which is so marked a feature of all the recent major editions of Shakespeare. But theatre history itself has undergone a transformation analogous to that observable in literary study. Where once it was primarily a way of illustrating the meaning that might inhere in the text, W. B. Worthen has recently argued that 'both texts and performances are materially unstable registers of signification, producing meaning intertextually in ways that deconstruct notions of intention, fidelity, authority, presence'.[4] It is certainly valuable to recognise the ways in which the theatrical history of the play reveals a good deal about the historically contingent meanings that have been afforded to it, and about the theatrical practices and cultural assumptions of the periods in which they were produced.[5] In analogous fashion, attention to adaptations such as Dryden and Davenant's *The Enchanted Island*, Césaire's *Une Tempête* or Greenaway's *Prospero's Books* may provoke some particular insight into the potential of Shakespeare's text, but is much more revelatory of the period of their own composition. They, like Browning's 'Caliban upon Setebos', Auden's *Sea and the Mirror* or Warner's *Indigo*, are independent works which generate their meaning in part out of their varied relationships with Shakespeare's play but

[1] Tom Healy, *New Latitudes: Theory and English Renaissance Literature*, 1992, p. 11.
[2] Terence Hawkes, *Meaning by Shakespeare*, 1992, p. 3.
[3] Healy, *New Latitudes*, p. 10.
[4] W. B. Worthen, *Shakespeare and the Authority of Performance*, 1997, pp. 189–90.
[5] As, for example, in Dennis Kennedy's magisterial study of twentieth-century production, *Looking at Shakespeare*.

neither displace nor absorb it. The history of the play's appropriations, critical, theatrical and literary, is fascinating and challenging, but the point of repeated return remains the text itself in all its obstinate particularity.

To read *The Tempest* is to enter into dialogue with it, one which requires scrupulous attention to both sides of the exchange: self-consciousness about our culturally determined assumptions on the one hand, but on the other an equal openness to the ways in which exploring its historical situation might challenge those assumptions. As Peter Brook observes, in describing the early, exploratory stages of theatrical rehearsal: 'The quality of the play, the enigma that it contains, makes it a stern judge. The play is the rigour, the austerity that helps to separate the valuable from the useless within the mass of undeveloped ideas.'[1] *The Tempest*, in other words, retains a perpetual capacity to answer back and to exceed our critical grasp – and that is precisely why it continues to solicit our attention.

---

[1] Brook, *There Are No Secrets*, p. 109. Brook has returned to this play at least four times in his directorial career; these comments are made in the context of his 1990 Paris production.

NOTE ON THE TEXT

The Tempest was published in the First Folio of 1623, where it appears as the first play in the volume. This text, carefully printed and offering comparatively few problems of substance, forms the basis of the present edition. Like the four comedies which follow it in the Folio, it derives from a manuscript transcription prepared by Ralph Crane, a professional scrivener closely associated with Shakespeare's company, the King's Men, from 1619 onwards. (He may also have been involved with the preparation of copy for other plays, including *Othello* and *Cymbeline*.) A good deal is known about Ralph Crane's working practices from the evidence of surviving manuscripts he prepared of other plays. From them it is evident that he intervened in the texts he transcribed not only by introducing his own characteristic spellings, but, more significantly, by imposing his own habits of punctuation, by employing elisions to rectify metre, and by modifying stage directions. So active does Crane seem to have been in his preparation of copy that it is possible, as Trevor Howard-Hill has suggested, to regard him as an 'editor', rather than mere transcriber of his texts. The thoroughness of his intervention makes it difficult to deduce exactly what kind of manuscript he had before him as he prepared the text of *The Tempest*, but it seems likely that it was an authorial manuscript, or a transcript of it; perhaps, as John Jowett has suggested, a late draft of the play. These questions are discussed more fully in the Textual Analysis (pp. 220–4), but some of the major implications for this edition of Crane's presence in the history of its transmission may be noted here.

First, Crane's habit of not extending prose lines to the extreme right of the page, and the fact that he did not always use initial capitals at the beginning of verse lines, may have contributed to the sometimes erratic lineation of the text. Though Crane's manuscript might not have been entirely clear in distinguishing verse from prose, it is nonetheless evident that he worried about versification, as is indicated by his efforts to indicate elisions in order to 'correct' the metre of his texts – though on occasion the printed elisions actually seem to introduce, rather than cure, irregularity. In subsequent generations, and particularly in the eighteenth century, metrical imperfection was often taken as of itself a sufficient cue for editorial intervention. Though modern practice has been far more ready to accept irregularity, particularly in the late plays, where Shakespeare's versification is much more varied and flexible than in his early work, it must be the case that Shakespeare would have anticipated an actor's readiness to elide syllables without his having to indicate exactly what was required. But many modern readers and actors find the 'tune' of Shakespearean verse elusive, and, without in any way wishing to return to the prescriptiveness of the eighteenth century, some effort has been made in the text, notes and collation of this edition to indicate where elision (or expansion of Folio elisions) might aid the realisation of the rhythm of a particular line. More substantially, there are a number of occasions when the lineation of the Folio text produces irregular verse lines. Some relineation introduced by eighteenth-century editors has been generally accepted by subsequent scholars; in this edition a few further suggestions have been introduced. The logic of these interventions is argued in the Textual Analysis, but proceeds from a basic assumption that Shakespeare was likely to write verse that generally conforms to the basic pentameter, and where that can be achieved by simple reorganisation of line-endings and standard elisions it is likely to conform to the original intention. There remain, however, many places – particularly in 2.1, 2.2 and 3.2 – where the dividing line between metrical verse and sometimes rhythmical prose is difficult to ascertain, and where caution has seemed appropriate. A further problem is created by the way in which editors since the eighteenth century have indicated by 'white space' in the text the relationships between short-line speeches and exchanges. This practice is extremely useful, especially in suggesting on some occasions the relationship between characters' utterances. As the Textual Analysis makes clear, however, decisions about how speeches may be accommodated together in pentameter lines are not always obvious and straightforward, and there are a number of places where this edition differs from its predecessors in the choices it makes. The collation records significant instances of departures from F's lineation. In some places the compositors set what is clearly intended as prose in broken lines. Only where there is some possibility that verse might have been intended are variations noted.

The fact that Crane punctuated heavily, where it would seem that Shakespeare's own habit was to point lightly, together with the fact that compositors themselves introduced their own preferences into the texts they set, has frequently been taken as giving an editor licence to make free with the Folio text in this respect. At the same time there has been a tendency amongst editors to regard the modernisation of punctuation as a merely routine activity, more or less comparable to the modernisation of spelling. But despite this double pressure to thin out the Folio punctuation, one should both consider carefully what Crane's pointing might indicate of the way in which a sophisticated contemporary of Shakespeare responded to the text in front of him, and at the same time recognise the significance of editorial decisions on commas, full stops and the like in shaping a reader's understanding of the text. In collation and Commentary, therefore, more attention than is perhaps customary is afforded to editorial decisions in matters of punctuation. The purpose of this attention is to ensure that readers are alert to the ways in which such apparently trivial matters can have important consequence.

Crane's practice of modifying the stage directions he found in his copy has been much discussed by editors, and in the case of *The Tempest* it has been suggested that he was attempting at times to represent a memory of actual performance through his descriptive directions. These matters are more fully discussed in the Textual Analysis, but it is likely that Crane's underlying purpose was to render such directions more 'readerly'. Though his criteria for adapting stage directions were no doubt different from those of the modern editor, he was nonetheless engaging in a similar activity, with analogous dangers. For in altering existing stage directions, or in supplementing them, every editor is attempting to present a practicable, stageable version of the text.

Yet attendance at any performance of the play immediately reveals how a director or acting company can easily come to quite different, but equally appropriate, solutions to theatrical problems and possibilities inherent in the text. In this respect, then, one might consider that descriptive adjectives in F's stage directions probably added by Crane should not carry any more or less authority than directions added by later editors. Any modifications of, or additions to, Folio stage directions are marked with square brackets in the text so that a reader may feel free to reimagine the theatrical decisions that these directions imply.

In line with the practice of this series, the collation is a selective one. It marks all substantive variations from F in this text, and notes those emendations suggested over the centuries which a reader might find worth remarking. Whilst an effort is made to indicate the first suggestion of an added stage direction, it is undoubtedly the case that in the many single-volume editions of the play produced since the latter part of the nineteenth century, only a few of which have been collated for this edition, there will be unnoticed anticipations of such additions.

Earlier drafts of this text were used for the Cambridge Schools Shakespeare and Shakespeare in Performance editions. Some few changes of lineation and punctuation have been introduced subsequently, and two substantive changes (at 2.1.76 and 3.1.47).

The Tempest

LIST OF CHARACTERS

ALONSO, *King of Naples*
SEBASTIAN, *his brother*
PROSPERO, *the right Duke of Milan*
ANTONIO, *his brother, the usurping Duke of Milan*
FERDINAND, *son to the King of Naples*
GONZALO, *an honest old councillor*
ADRIAN *and* FRANCISCO, *lords*
CALIBAN, *a savage and deformed slave*
TRINCULO, *a jester*
STEPHANO, *a drunken butler*
MASTER *of a ship*
BOATSWAIN
MARINERS
MIRANDA, *daughter to Prospero*
ARIEL, *an airy spirit*
IRIS
CERES
JUNO
NYMPHS
REAPERS
SPIRITS

The scene: an uninhabited island

Notes

The list of characters is placed at the end of the play in F and probably compiled by the scribe, Ralph Crane, who may well have added the descriptions of their roles.

PROSPERO The Latin verb *prospero* means 'I render fortunate, make happy, prosper.' The name may have been suggested by William Thomas's *Historie of Italie*, which tells of Prospero Adorno, established as governor of Genoa by Ferdinando, Duke of Milan, deposed and replaced by Antony Adorno.

ANTONIO The F spelling of the name is consistently 'Anthonio'.

GONZALO Though *gonzo* is Italian for 'simpleton' this does not seem to be part of the implication of the character.

CALIBAN It is generally assumed that the name is an anagram of 'cannibal', though many other more or less implausible suggestions have been offered, including the Romany word *caulibon* ('black, dark things'). See Vaughans, pp. 26–36.

TRINCULO His name may have some connection with the Italian verb *trincare*, 'to drink'.

MIRANDA Derived from the gerundive of the Latin verb *miror*, and meaning 'she who is to be admired, or wondered at', the English meaning of her name is the basis for rhetorical elaboration on several occasions in the play.

ARIEL If there is an allusion to Isaiah 29, where 'Ariel' is the name of the city of Jerusalem, and glossed
    by the Geneva Bible as 'the lion of God', its significance is by no means obvious. It is, more likely,
    simply a name that emphasises his 'airiness'.

IRIS The rainbow, mythologically the messenger of Juno, as Mercury was of Jupiter.

CERES Goddess of the harvest.

JUNO Queen of the gods, wife of Jupiter. The goddess of riches, the air, and of marriage.

THE TEMPEST

1.1 *A tempestuous noise of thunder and lightning heard. Enter a*
SHIPMASTER, *and a* BOATSWAIN [*and* MARINERS]

MASTER Boatswain!

BOATSWAIN Here, master. What cheer?

MASTER Good; speak to th'mariners. Fall to't yarely, or we run our-
selves aground. Bestir, bestir!   *Exit*

BOATSWAIN Heigh, my hearts! Cheerly, cheerly, my hearts! Yare, yare!   5

Act 1, Scene 1 1.1] *Actus primus, Scena prima.* F 0 SD.2 *and* MARINERS] *This edn; Enter mariners / following*
bestir! F 5 Cheerly, cheerly, my] F; cheerly my *Rowe*

Act 1, Scene 1

0 SD.1 *A tempestuous . . . heard* The formulation
of this direction may be the scribe Ralph Crane's
elaboration of the conventional *Thunder and Lightning*. The noise of thunder was produced by rolling
a cannonball down a wooden trough and/or by
drum-beats; lightning by squibs or fireworks. But
the smoke and smell of such fireworks was unpleasant in the indoor theatres, and so the SD's *heard* may
accurately reflect a performance in which only off-
stage noise was employed (See Gurr, 'Tempest',
p. 95). Sturgess (p. 81) suggests that there might
also have been 'sound effects from a sea machine
(small pebbles revolved in a drum) and a wind
machine (a loose length of canvas turned on a
wheel)'. Jonson referred scathingly to such effects
in the Prologue to the revised version of *Every Man
In His Humour* (1616), where he offered a play in
which no 'nimble squib is seen, to make afear'd /
The gentlewomen, nor roll'd bullet heard / To say,
it thunders, nor tempestuous drum / Rumbles, to
tell you when the storm doth come' (lines 17–20).

0 SD.1–2 *Enter . . .* MARINERS The directions for
this scene are incomplete, with a number of missing
exits. The Master and Boatswain probably enter
separately, with the Master, perhaps, appearing
above in the gallery. Some separation might be
implied by the fact that the Master and Boatswain
had distinct areas of command: 'As the master is to
be abaft the mast, so the boatswain, and all the
common sailors under his command, are to be afore
the mast' (Monson, III, 33). The manner in which

the scene might have been staged is a matter for
debate. It is often assumed that ropes were let down
from the music-room, and so the Mariners might
accompany the Boatswain on stage, and be in position as he speaks to them at line 5, subsequently to
be seen hauling on these ropes. But if, as Gurr suggests, there were no such ropes, then they might
enter at 5 as in F's SD and run off stage almost
immediately to execute the Boatswain's commands.
There must have been at least two Mariners, and
it is possible that more could have been available
(see Appendix 3, p. 260). Throughout the scene it
is possible that they might come and go singly or
together.

1 **Boatswain** Pronounced 'Bos'n' (F's spelling at
11). He was a significant figure on board ship: 'This
officer must needs be of much use and necessity for
the due disciplining, and ordering of the whole
company belonging to the ship; and it behoves him
to be strong, stout, and faithful' (Boteler, p. 16).

2 **What cheer** How are you (*OED* cheer *n*[1] 3b).

3 **Good** Either (1) the Master's acknowledgement of the Boatswain's presence and response to
him ('A superior acknowledged a report or answer
in this way' (Falconer, p. 59)), or (2) 'Good fellow'
as in 14. F's punctuation ('Good:') suggests the first.

3 **yarely** quickly.

5 **hearts** good fellows (naval speech – as in 'my
hearties').

5 **Cheerly** With a will. F's 'cheerely' might be
modernised as 'cheerily', for which *OED* gives 1616
as the first instance.

Take in the topsail. Tend to th'master's whistle. [*To the storm*] Blow
till thou burst thy wind, if room enough!

Enter ALONSO, SEBASTIAN, ANTONIO, FERDINAND,
GONZALO *and others*

ALONSO Good boatswain, have care. Where's the master? Play the
men.

BOATSWAIN I pray now, keep below.   10

ANTONIO Where is the master, boatswain?

BOATSWAIN Do you not hear him? You mar our labour – keep your
cabins. You do assist the storm.

GONZALO Nay, good, be patient.

---

6 SD *Orgel; not in* F   8 Play] F; ply *John Upton, 'Critical Observations on Shakespeare' (1746)*   11 boatswain]
Boson F

6 Take ... topsail Furl the topmost sail on the
mainmast. This is the first stage in reducing the
ship's speed. During a storm a balance needs to be
struck between carrying enough sail to maintain
momentum, and carrying so much that the wind
capsizes the ship. Many of the details in this scene
might suggest a realistic knowledge of seafaring
practices, but there was an extensive literature of
storm descriptions on which Shakespeare could
have drawn. See, for example, Ovid's *Metamorphoses*, 11, where, in Golding's translation, 'Anon
the Mayster cryed strike the toppesayle, let the
mayne / Sheate flye' (lines 558–9).

6 Tend Pay heed.

6 whistle A whistle was customarily carried by
both Master and Boatswain as a badge of office and
as a means of giving commands. William Monson
describes how 'upon the winding of the master's
whistle, the boatswain takes it with his, and sets the
sailors with courage to do their work, every one of
them knowing by their whistle what they are to
do' (Monson, III, 33). Perhaps during this scene
the Boatswain might pipe in imitation of the
Master's whistle heard off stage in addition to his
shouted orders to the Mariners, the sound of
both whistles contrasting with the noise of the
storm (cf. *H5* 3, Chorus, 9–10, where the audience
is invited to 'Hear the shrill whistle, which doth
order give / To sounds confused', and *Per.*
4.1.63–4: 'The boatswain whistles and / The master
calls').

6–7 Blow ... enough You can blow as hard as
you like, provided we have enough sea-room
between ship and rocks. As in *Lear* 3.2.1, 'Blow,

winds, and crack your cheeks', the winds were often
imagined as faces puffing out their cheeks (cf. *Per.*
3.1.44, and see illustration 11).

7 SD. 2 and others This 'permissive' SD may be a
mark of Shakespeare's draft lying behind Crane's
transcript. Attendants are not absolutely necessary,
but at least two actors – those later named as Adrian
and Francisco – could have been available to swell
Alonso's retinue (see Appendix 3).

8 have care Ralph Berry suggests that this 'may
mean that the Boatswain has bumped into Alonso,
or is bidden, superfluously, to manage things
properly' (*Shakespeare and Social Class*, 1988,
p. 180).

8–9 Play the men Either (1) Alonso speaks to
the Mariners, contemptuously urging them to act
like men; or (2) he speaks to the Boatswain, asking
him to 'play' his whistle to give orders to the
Mariners (though I have found no other example of
this usage in the period); or (3) Upton's emendation, 'ply', would mean 'Keep the men to their
tasks.'

12 hear him i.e. hear his whistle sounding off-
stage. Barton suggests, however, that it is the noise
of the storm, heard in the 'slight pause between
the question and the next sentence' which is 'the
Master' that they acknowledge.

13 assist the storm i.e. by interfering with
the Mariners' work. The same idiom is used in
Per. 3.1.19: 'Patience, good sir, do not assist the
storm.'

14 good my good man.

14 be patient be composed in enduring misfortune (*OED* Patient *adj* 1).

BOATSWAIN When the sea is. Hence! What cares these roarers for the   15
name of king? To cabin. Silence! Trouble us not.

GONZALO Good, yet remember whom thou hast aboard.

BOATSWAIN None that I more love than myself. You are a councillor;
if you can command these elements to silence, and work a peace of
the present, we will not hand a rope more – use your authority. If   20
you cannot, give thanks you have lived so long, and make yourself
ready in your cabin for the mischance of the hour, if it so hap. [*To
the Mariners*] Cheerly, good hearts. [*To the courtiers*] Out of our way,
I say.

[*Exeunt Boatswain with Mariners, followed by Alonso,*
Sebastian, Antonio, Ferdinand]

GONZALO I have great comfort from this fellow. Methinks he hath no   25
drowning mark upon him, his complexion is perfect gallows. Stand
fast, good Fate, to his hanging; make the rope of his destiny our

---

15 cares] F; care *Theobald*   18 councillor] *Wilson*; Counsellor F   19–20 a peace . . . present] *This edn;* the peace . . .
present F; the peace . . . presence *Kermode (Maxwell conj.);* peace . . . present *Oxford*   22–3 SD *Orgel, not in* F   23 SD
Orgel, not in F   24 SD *Exeunt . . . Ferdinand*] *This edn; Exit* F

15 **cares** One of a number of examples of a
plural subject with singular verb in the play (Abbott
332, 333, 335). Though emendation is not necessary, since this was a permissible construction in
Early Modern English, it would be an easy compositorial or scribal misreading to make. (See
Textual Analysis, p. 228.)

15 **roarers** The waves, but carrying a subsidiary
association with disorderly people (known as
'roaring boys'). There is, then, a metaphoric link
between the chaos in nature and the upsetting of
social hierarchy in the Boatswain's speeches.

16 **Silence . . . not** The Boatswain's words
emphatically challenge social decorum. Sidney
offers a parallel image when remarking that Pyro-
cles 'no more attentively marked his friend's discourse than . . . the diligent pilot in a dangerous
tempest doth attend the unskilful words of a pas-
senger' (*Arcadia*, p. 111).

18 **None . . . myself** 'I am nearest to myself'
was proverbial (Tilley N57).

18 **councillor** F's spelling, 'Counsellor', contains
the senses both of an official position in the
monarch's Privy Council, and of 'one who gives
advice'. In this context the first is perhaps the dominant meaning, though the second is clearly present.

19–20 **work . . . present** manufacture peace out
of the present turmoil. There are no contemporary
parallels for the F reading 'work the peace', whereas
'work a peace' occurs in many places, including, for
example, Milton's 'Ode on the Morning of Christ's

Nativity', line 7. (See Textual Analysis, pp. 228–9.)
Maxwell's emendation, adopted by Kermode, suggesting 'the peace of the [royal] presence' founders
on lack of any evidence for such a usage.

20 **hand** handle (there would be no further need
of their efforts).

22 **hap** happen, befall.

24 SD F's *Exit* here and at line 29 are singular,
but the lords need to leave the stage in order to re-
enter at 31, and the Mariners must leave the stage
at some point in order to re-enter *wet* at 44. The
Boatswain's plural 'out of *our* way' suggests that
he is accompanied by Mariners as he pushes past
the lords. Some of the lords themselves might
exit earlier, or leave the stage here, or else after
Gonzalo's speech. But whether or not some or
all of the lords are on stage, Gonzalo's ensuing
speech is perhaps best treated as an aside delivered
directly to the audience, whereas the recapitulation
of the same idea below, 40–1, is in answer to
Antonio.

25 **Methinks** It seems to me.

25–6 **he hath . . . gallows** Alludes to the
proverb, 'He that is born to be hanged shall never
be drowned' (Tilley B139). Proteus uses the same
commonplace in *TGV* 1.1.148–50.

26 **complexion** (1) face, appearance, (2) tem-
perament, character.

27 **rope of his destiny** The hangman's rope for
which he is destined, but Gonzalo also perhaps
alludes to the thread of life spun by the Fates.

cable, for our own doth little advantage. If he be not born to be
hanged, our case is miserable.   *Exit*

Enter BOATSWAIN

BOATSWAIN Down with the topmast! Yare, lower, lower! Bring her to   30
try with main-course.

A cry within

Enter SEBASTIAN, ANTONIO *and* GONZALO

A plague upon this howling! They are louder than the weather, or
our office. [*To the lords*] Yet again? What do you here? Shall we give
o'er and drown? Have you a mind to sink?

SEBASTIAN A pox o'your throat, you bawling, blasphemous, in-   35
charitable dog.

BOATSWAIN Work you then.

ANTONIO Hang, cur, hang, you whoreson, insolent noisemaker, we are
less afraid to be drowned than thou art.

30–1 to try with] F; to: try wi' th' *Grant White*   31 SD.1 *Following* plague *in* F   31 SD.2 *Enter . . .* GONZALO] *As* F; *Re-enter . . . Gonzalo / following* office. *Kermode*   33 SD *To the lords*] *This edn; not in* F   35–6 incharitable] F; uncharitable *Theobald*

---

28 **cable** Three-twisted rope for an anchor.

28 **our own . . . advantage** our ship's anchor gives us little help.

30 **topmast** Topmost section of the main-mast.

30–1 **Bring . . . main-course** 'Trying is to have no more sail forth but the mainsail, the tack aboard, the bowline set up, the sheet close aft, and the helm tied down close aboard . . . A ship *a-try* with her mainsail . . . will make her way two points afore the beam' (Mainwaring, II, 250). The crew are attempting to maintain some momentum away from the rocks but with the minimum of sail, in order to avoid capsizing.

31 SD.1–2 *A cry . . .* GONZALO In F this direction follows the word 'plague'. Editors have frequently separated the two parts of the direction, and had the lords enter after the word 'office'. It makes obvious sense to place *A cry within* before the Boatswain's comment, since he must hear a noise before he can respond to it. But it is equally appropriate for the lords to enter in time to overhear the Boatswain's words, which then motivate their objection to his speech. (See Textual Analysis, p. 244.)

32 **A plague** Followed by a long dash in F (see illustration 24), which editors have suggested could

indicate omission of profanities that might give cause for the nobles' comments on the Boatswain's bad language here and at 5.1.218. Whilst it is possible that Crane might have censored the text, the likeliest explanation for the dash is a technical one. (See Textual Analysis, pp. 244–5.)

32–3 **or our office** or we are at our work.

34 **give o'er** stop working.

mind purposeful intention.

35 **A pox . . . throat** The conventional curse (literally wishing disease to affect the throat) is aimed at the Boatswain's organ of disrespectful speech.

35–6 **bawling . . . dog** Regulations forbade swearing at sea, and it was specifically the Boatswain's job to enforce this discipline. Whether Sebastian is responding to some (now lost) profanity, or whether his abuse of the Boatswain is unjustified, these are real insults to one in his position.

37 **Work . . . then** Richard Strier notes that the aristocrats' unwillingness in this scene to 'work' is in sharp contrast to Strachey's narrative of the shipwreck in the Bermudas (see Introduction, p. 31), where 'the better sort, even our governor and admiral themselves' did not refuse to toil ('Politics', p. 15).

GONZALO I'll warrant him from drowning, though the ship were no   40
stronger than a nutshell, and as leaky as an unstanched wench.
BOATSWAIN Lay her a-hold, a-hold; set her two courses. Off to sea
again; lay her off!

Enter MARINERS, *wet*

MARINERS All lost! To prayers, to prayers, all lost!
BOATSWAIN What, must our mouths be cold?   45
GONZALO The king and prince at prayers! Let's assist them,
For our case is as theirs.
SEBASTIAN   I'm out of patience.

40 from] *Theobald;* for F   42 courses. Off] *Grant White;* courses; off *Steevens;* courses off F   46–7 *As Pope;* Them, /
for . . . theirs. / *Sebas.* I . . . patience F; Them . . . theirs *as prose Ard3*   46 prince at] F4; prince, at F; prince are at *Rowe*
46 prayers! Let's] *Pope;* prayers, let's F   47 I'm] F (I'am)

40 warrant . . . drowning I guarantee he will
not drown. Gonzalo returns to the conceit in 25–29.
F's 'for' has generally been retained in modern editions, and explained as meaning 'against'. 'Warrant
for' in the period, however, almost always carries
its positive modern sense: 'I guarantee that he will
drown' – which is quite opposite to what is
required. 'Warrant from' was a customary phrase,
giving the necessary sense, and it would be an easy
misreading for scribe or compositor, especially if
the manuscript read 'fro' (cf. Dekker and Webster,
The famous history of Sir Thomas Wyat (1607), line
250: 'I thanke thee, and will warrant thee from
death').
41 leaky . . . wench The 'leakiness' of women
was a commonplace, deriving from medical theory
which believed their bodies to be 'moister' than
men's, and therefore 'notable for the production of
liquids – breast milk, menstrual blood, tears and
[urine]' (Gail Kern Paster, *The Body Embarrassed*,
1993, p. 39). The reference here may be specifically
to menstruation, with the flow of blood
'unstaunched', and 'unstanched' could also mean
'insatiable, unsatisfied', and was associated more
generally with moral looseness and sexual vora-
ciousness, as, for example, in the widely circulated
epigram on Frances Howard, described as a vessel
'Which sore did leake but did not sinke'. The for-
mulaic nature of the phrase may explain the inex-
actness of this unsavoury simile, referring to leaking
water out, where the boat leaks water in.
42 Lay . . . a-hold 'To bring a vessel close to the
wind so as to hold it or keep it' (Falconer, p. 39).
This is a unique literary use of the term, but Falconer claims it is still in use in New England.
42 set . . . courses raise the foresail as well as the
mainsail. This is a last desperate attempt to sail
away from land – to 'lay her off'. Many editors

choose to follow F's punctuation, implying that
the sails are set in a particular way to aid the
manoeuvre.
43 SD Enter . . . wet F gives no exit for the
Mariners. They might pass directly across the stage,
so that they could make the *confused noise within* at
52. The stage must be cleared for Gonzalo's solilo-
quy at the end, but exactly where and when is
a matter for a director's decision. The specificity
of the SD has a few parallels in other drama of
the period, most closely in Greene and Lodge's *A
Looking Glass for London and England* (1594): 'Enter
. . . some Sailers, wet from sea', though more often
the entry of a character 'wet' is a matter for comedy,
as it is later in 4.1. See, for example, Marlowe,
Doctor Faustus: 'Enter the Horse-courser, wet'
(B-text, 4.4.26), or Dekker et al., *The Witch of
Edmonton*, 3.1, where the Clown's entry 'wet'
provokes hilarity.
44 To prayers . . . lost A standard motif in
storm descriptions. In Seneca's *Agamemnon*, for
example, Newton's translation reads: 'To prayer
then apace we fall, when other hope is none' (*Seneca
His Tenne Tragedies*, ed. Charles Whibley, 1927, p.
121).
45 mouths . . . cold Either (1) 'must we die', or
(2) indicating that the Boatswain takes a (warming)
drink – explaining Antonio's comment at 49. The
first meaning is the more likely.
46 The king . . . them Oxford rightly suggests
that to follow F's punctuation, giving the sense 'The
king and prince being at prayers, let's assist them',
lacks urgency. The speech might, however, be punctuated as 'The king and prince! At prayers . . .' with
the implication that Gonzalo suddenly realises
that Alonso and Ferdinand are no longer with
them, exclaims in alarm and then suggests joining
them.

ANTONIO   We're merely cheated of our lives by drunkards.
          This wide-chopped rascal – would thou mightst lie
              drowning
          The washing of ten tides!
GONZALO   He'll be hanged yet,   50
          Though every drop of water swear against it,
          And gape at wid'st to glut him.
                          [*Exeunt Boatswain and Mariners*]
                 A confused noise within
                                 Mercy on us!
[VOICES OFF STAGE] 'We split, we split!' – 'Farewell, my wife and
              children!' –
          'Farewell, brother!' – 'We split, we split, we split!'
ANTONIO   Let's all sink wi'th'king.
SEBASTIAN   Let's take leave of him.   55
                          [*Exeunt Sebastian and Antonio*]
GONZALO   Now would I give a thousand furlongs of sea for an acre of
          barren ground – long heath, brown furze, anything. The wills above
          be done, but I would fain die a dry death.   *Exit*

48–50 *As Pope; We . . . drunkards, / This . . . drown- / ing . . . Tides* F; *as prose Ard3*   48 We're] *Pope;* We are F   52 SD
Exeunt . . . Mariners] *This edn; Exit Boatswain / Dyce; not in* F   52–4 *As Capell; all attributed to Gonzalo in* F; 'Mercy on
us' *Steevens (as prose)*   53 SH *This edn; not in* F   55 wi'th'] *Grant White;* with' F   55 SD *Exeunt . . . Antonio] Cam. subst.;
Exit* F   57 long heath, brown furze] *Rowe;* ling, heath, broom, furze *Hanmer;* long heath, broom, furze *Kermode (Tannenbaum conj.);* Long heath, Browne firrs F

48 We're The elision regularises the metre.

48 merely utterly.

49 wide-chopped big-mouthed.

49–50 lie drowning . . . tides Pirates were tried by the Court of Admiralty, and punished by being hanged on the shore at the low-water mark and their bodies left there until three tides had flowed over them. Antonio's 'ten' is an exaggeration.

52 glut swallow.

52 SD.1 Exeunt . . . Mariners There is no exit marked in F for the Boatswain. He might leave here, accompanied by the Mariners if they have not already gone, but could exit at any point after his final line at 45.

52–4 Mercy . . . split These lines are printed as verse in F, continuous with Gonzalo's speech. Johnson noted that they 'should be considered as spoken by no determinate characters', and Capell set it out as here. Later editors included 'Mercy on us' as one of the off-stage exclamations, but the phrase, which completes Gonzalo's verse line, can be taken as his response to the noise he hears, which is then represented in the lines which follow. (See

Textual Analysis, p. 234.) Many parallels for these cries of distress can be found. In Ovid's *Metamorphoses*, 11.623–6 in Golding's translation, 'Too God another makes his vow . . . The thought of this man is upon / His brother and his parents . . . Another calles his house and wyfe and children untoo mynd.' In Sidney's *Arcadia*, after a similar characterisation of differing responses to impending shipwreck, 'a monstrous cry begotten of many roaring voices was able to infect with fear a mind that had not prevented it with power of reason' (p. 263).

56 a thousand furlongs A furlong is literally $\frac{1}{8}$ of a mile (about 200 m) – but the phrase means 'any distance or amount'.

57 long heath A kind of heather.

57 brown furze gorse. The modernisation of F's 'firrs' has been questioned, but it is a characteristic Crane spelling variant. So too, 'brown' has been emended to 'broom' (another heathland shrub), on the grounds that gorse is an evergreen, but since its lower leaves do go brown in winter, the emendation is unnecessary.

58 fain gladly.

1.2 *Enter* PROSPERO *and* MIRANDA

MIRANDA If by your art, my dearest father, you have
        Put the wild waters in this roar, allay them.
        The sky it seems would pour down stinking pitch,
        But that the sea, mounting to th'welkin's cheek,
        Dashes the fire out. O, I have suffered   5
        With those that I saw suffer! A brave vessel,
        Who had no doubt some noble creature in her,
        Dashed all to pieces. O, the cry did knock
        Against my very heart! Poor souls, they perished.
        Had I been any god of power, I would   10
        Have sunk the sea within the earth, or ere
        It should the good ship so have swallowed, and
        The fraughting souls within her.
PROSPERO   Be collected;
        No more amazement. Tell your piteous heart

Act 1, Scene 2   1.2] *Scena Secunda.* F   7 creature] F; creatures *Theobald*

Act 1, Scene 2

1–13 Prospero must enter wearing his 'magic' cloak. His subsequent disrobing at 24 could imply that the noise of the storm is still being produced during the first part of the scene, only to be fully allayed as he lays his 'art' aside. But though Miranda's speech suggests that the waters are still in a 'roar' (and in many productions the thunder persists as she speaks), her words form a rhetorical set-piece, with many literary precedents, designed verbally to recreate a picture of the storm and to register the reaction of pity. (The technical rhetorical term for such a description is *ecphrasis* or *enargia*.) The ability to raise storms was commonly ascribed to both magicians and witches – it is one of the abilities that Marlowe's Faustus anticipates as a consequence of his study of the secret arts (A-text, 1.1.61), but it is also a characteristic manifestation of the power of God, and of Jupiter (see 290 below).

1 art learned arts, magic powers. It is clear that Miranda is aware of her father's magical abilities. 'Art' has an initial capital throughout in F, a possible indication of its specialised sense in the play.

2 roar noisy tumult (cf. 1.1.15).

2 allay quieten, appease.

3–5 The sky . . . out The blackness of the sky suggests that it will disgorge tarry pitch (which would become liquid when heated by the fire of the lightning), except that the violence of the storm pushes waves up to the sky to douse the flames.

4–5 But . . . out The conflict and disorderly mingling of the elements of air, fire and water is a standard topos of storm descriptions.

4 welkin's cheek face of the sky.

6 brave fine.

7 creature person, human being (not, in the period, used solely of animals). Modern editors have rejected Theobald's emendation to 'creatures' (though there are many instances in the play where there could be scribal or compositorial misreading of final 'es' and in this case it may be of some interpretative significance – see Textual Analysis, p. 228).

10 Had I . . . power Miranda's remark makes an implicit challenge to her father and his lack of pity.

11 or ere before.

13 fraughting souls the people who were the cargo.

13 Be collected Compose yourself.

14 amazement bewildered anguish, fear and alarm (*OED* sv *n* 3) but also implying 'perplexity' (*OED* sv *n* 2) and, possibly, 'wonder' (*OED* sv *n* 4). (Shakespeare is credited by *OED* with the first use of three of the four senses of the word.)

14 piteous pitiful, pitying.

There's no harm done.

MIRANDA   O, woe the day.

PROSPERO   No harm.   15

I have done nothing but in care of thee –
Of thee my dear one, thee my daughter – who
Art ignorant of what thou art, nought knowing
Of whence I am, nor that I am more better
Than Prospero, master of a full poor cell,   20
And thy no greater father.

MIRANDA   More to know
Did never meddle with my thoughts.

PROSPERO   'Tis time
I should inform thee farther. Lend thy hand
And pluck my magic garment from me – so –
[*Miranda assists Prospero; his cloak is laid aside*]
Lie there my art. Wipe thou thine eyes; have comfort.   25
The direful spectacle of the wrack which touched
The very virtue of compassion in thee,
I have with such provision in mine art
So safely ordered, that there is no soul,

---

19 more better] F; *more or better Rowe²*   24 SD *Miranda . . . aside*] *This edn; Lays down his mantle / Pope; Miranda helps him to disrobe / Orgel; not in* F   29 no soul,] F; *no soul lost, Rowe; no soil, Johnson; no soul – Steevens*

15 No harm Johnson gave the words 'No harm', uttered as a question, to Miranda.

16–17 I have . . . daughter The importance of Prospero's concern for his daughter as motivation for his actions is underlined by the parallelism and repetition in these lines. A rhetorically trained listener or reader might note the use of the figures of *anadiplosis* (repetition of the last words of a clause at the beginning of the next), *anaphora* (repetition of words at the beginning of successive clauses), *isocolon* (clauses of equal length) and *alliteratio*. Puttenham suggested that such rhetorical repetition 'doth much alter and affect the eare and also the mynde of the hearer, and therefore is counted a very brave figure both with the Poets and rhetoriciens' (p. 165).

19 more better of higher status. The double comparative is not uncommon in Shakespeare (Abbott 11).

20 full poor cell Very small, humble dwelling, but 'cell' carries strong overtones of the monastic, contemplative life. Compare the cave in which Belarius dwells in *Cym.* 3.3.1–4, where the implied stage direction, requiring the actors to 'stoop' as they enter, might suggest that this rocky cell was a physical property on stage, perhaps set before the central opening. In either play, however, such a prop would bring a number of practical problems with it.

21 no greater i.e. of no higher status than our circumstances indicate.

22 meddle with mingle, interfere with.

24 so F's punctuation attaches 'so' to the following clause; but it is possible to construe it as part of Prospero's request to Miranda to assist in removing the cloak, or acknowledgement of her help.

25 art Prospero's magic inheres at this point in his garment, as it does later in his staff, while to Caliban it seems to lie in his books. Fuller, *Holy State*, p. 257, recorded of Sir William Cecil that: 'when he put off his gown at night, he used to say, "Lie there, lord treasurer"' (cited by Steevens). The relationship of clothing to social status and political function is developed by Antonio in 2.1.268–70.

26 direful having dire consequences.

26 wrack This, the consistent spelling in F, is not just a spelling variant, but derives from an Old English root, rather than the Old Norse of 'wreck'.

27 virtue essence.

28 provision foresight, careful preparation.

29–30 soul . . . hair Syntactically awkward

No, not so much perdition as an hair   30
Betid to any creature in the vessel
Which thou heard'st cry, which thou saw'st sink. Sit down,
For thou must now know farther.
                              [*Miranda sits*]
MIRANDA   You have often
Begun to tell me what I am, but stopped
And left me to a bootless inquisition,   35
Concluding, 'Stay: not yet.'
PROSPERO   The hour's now come;
The very minute bids thee ope thine ear,
Obey, and be attentive. Canst thou remember
A time before we came unto this cell?
I do not think thou canst, for then thou wast not   40
Out three years old.
MIRANDA   Certainly, sir, I can.
PROSPERO By what? By any other house, or person?
Of any thing the image, tell me, that
Hath kept with thy remembrance.
MIRANDA   'Tis far off;
And rather like a dream, than an assurance   45

---

33 SD *Miranda sits*] *This edn; They sit / Orgel; not in* F   37 ear,] F; *ear; Johnson; ear. Orgel*   45 dream, than] F; *dream than Grant White*

though this is, the sense is clear enough: 'There is no soul lost – there isn't even a hair of the head missing.' (The changing of syntactical direction in the middle of a sentence is the rhetorical figure *anacoluthon*, and is characteristic of many of Prospero's speeches in this scene.) The lines play upon the double meaning of 'perdition' as 'damnation' and as 'loss'. Compare Acts 27.34, where Paul promises to those caught in a storm that 'there shall not an hair fall from the head of any of you'. Ariel confirms Prospero's statement later at 217.

31 Betid Befallen, happened.

32 Which . . . which The first clause describes the 'creature', the second the 'vessel'.

35 bootless inquisition useless or unrequited questioning. (This contradicts Miranda's earlier assertion that she was not curious about her past.)

37–8 ear, Obey Most modern editors place a full stop after 'ear', emphasising Prospero's commanding of his daughter, but F's comma makes Miranda obedient to the necessity of the moment rather than solely to her father.

41 Out . . . old Beyond your third year.

43–4 Of any thing . . . remembrance

Describe to me any pictures that have been retained in your memory. In classical and Renaissance thought the memory specifically stored 'images'.

45–6 And . . . warrants 'It is more like the uncertain picture of a dream than a secure image which my memory is able to guarantee.' F's comma after 'dream', omitted by all modern editors, is actually helpful to the understanding of these lines. The primary contrast Miranda makes is between dream and memory, not between dream and 'assurance'. In the allegory of the mind in Spenser's *Faerie Queene*, 2.9.51, 'devices, dreames, opinions unsound' belong in the foremost chamber of the brain controlled by Phantastes ('fantasy', 'imagination'), whereas in the rearward chamber of Eumnestes ('good memory') are laid up records of whatever had happened 'where they for ever incorrupted dweld' (stanza 56). Burton writes: 'Memory lays up all the species which the senses have brought in, and records them as a good register, that they may be forthcoming when they are called for . . . his seat and organ the back part of the brain' (1.1.2.7). Miranda's comment initiates the play's preoccupation with the trustworthiness of memory.

That my remembrance warrants. Had I not
Four or five women once, that tended me?
PROSPERO Thou hadst, and more, Miranda. But how is't
That this lives in thy mind? What seest thou else
In the dark backward and abysm of time?   50
If thou rememb'rest aught ere thou cam'st here,
How thou cam'st here thou mayst.
MIRANDA   But that I do not.
PROSPERO Twelve year since, Miranda, twelve year since,
Thy father was the Duke of Milan and
A prince of power –
MIRANDA   Sir, are not you my father?   55
PROSPERO Thy mother was a piece of virtue, and
She said thou wast my daughter; and thy father
Was Duke of Milan; and his only heir,
And princess, no worse issued.
MIRANDA   O the heavens!
What foul play had we, that we came from thence?   60
Or blessèd was't we did?
PROSPERO   Both, both, my girl.
By foul play, as thou say'st, were we heaved thence,
But blessedly holp hither.
MIRANDA   O, my heart bleeds

---

48 is't] *This edn;* is it F   50 dark backward] F3; dark-backward F   53 Twelve year . . . year] F; 'Tis twelve years . . . years *Pope*   58 and his] F; and thou his *Hanmer*   59 And princess] F; A princess *Pope*

48 **is't** The elision is for the metre.

50 backward There is no parallel for this use of 'backward' as a noun, though the habit of forming nouns from adjectives is frequent in Shakespeare. *OED* (sv *adv, adj, n* C2) cites only this and one later instance for the meaning 'the past portion of time'. F's original punctuation produces a strange compound, perhaps symptomatic of some scribal uncertainty as to what was meant. In the light of Miranda's previous speech, however, it might be possible to read this as 'back ward' or 'rear chamber', alluding to the place of memory in the brain (though I have found no unambiguous parallel for this idiom).

50 abysm abyss, chasm.

52 thou mayst i.e. you might remember (these two lines have a characteristic rhetorical balance).

53 year Used as plural.

54 Milan Must be accented on the first syllable rather than the second, though F's spelling 'Millaine' (customary in the period, and perhaps reflecting Italian stress-patterns) suggests an even weighting of the syllables, rather than the clipped pronunciation frequently adopted by modern actors.

56–7 Thy . . . daughter These lines have been taken to indicate that the same anxiety about paternity which Leontes feels in *WT* (1.2.119ff.) is present in Prospero's mind, but this is surely to misread the tone of the tribute he offers to his dead wife.

56 piece model, masterpiece.

58–9 heir, And princess Most modern editors have rejected Pope's tempting emendation to 'a princess'. They have also rejected F's comma after 'heir', but this comma, suggesting perhaps a brief pause, a look to Miranda as Prospero tells her of her sudden elevation, softens the awkwardness of the line as it stands.

59 no . . . issued of no less noble birth (than her father).

63 holp helped.

To think o'th'teen that I have turned you to,
Which is from my remembrance. Please you, farther.   65
PROSPERO My brother and thy uncle, called Antonio –
I pray thee mark me, that a brother should
Be so perfidious – he, whom next thyself
Of all the world I loved, and to him put
The manage of my state, as at that time   70
Through all the signories it was the first,
And Prospero the prime duke, being so reputed
In dignity, and for the liberal arts
Without a parallel; those being all my study,
The government I cast upon my brother,   75
And to my state grew stranger, being transported
And rapt in secret studies. Thy false uncle –
Dost thou attend me? –
MIRANDA   Sir, most heedfully.

---

77 studies. Thy] F4; studies, thy F

64 **teen** affliction, grief.
64 **I . . . to** I have caused you. Miranda speaks of the burden she feels herself to have been at the time of their expulsion.
65 **is . . . remembrance** I cannot remember ('from' = 'beyond').
67–8 **mark . . . perfidious** Prospero's insistence on the especial wickedness of brotherly treachery is a constant feature throughout the play, and had a proverbial status. Cf. Erasmus, *Adagia*, 1.2.50, *fratrum inter se irae sunt acerbissimae*: 'the bitterest quarrels are between brothers'. Orlando's resentment in the opening speech of *AYLI* at his treatment by his brother is a clear parallel.
70 **manage** administration.
71 **signories** lordships, territories (applied specifically to the Italian city-states).
71 **first** The primacy of Milan is borne out by Thomas's description: 'For though in name (being but a duchy) it should not seem great, yet in very deed, both for the wealth of the country and for the quantity, the thing hath been of as great reputation as some realms of Europe. Out of doubt there have been some Dukes of Milan much greater in territory, wealthier in revenues and treasure, more puissant in wars, and, finally, more honorable in peace than divers of them that had kingly titles' (Thomas, p. 112).
72 **prime** senior, highest in rank.
72–4 **being . . . parallel** The syntax here is ambiguous, since these qualities might apply to Prospero, or to Milan, or to both. The former is

more likely, since the dukedom's university at Pavia was not famous in England, though Thomas speaks of 'the fayre palace in Pavia, with that goodly librarie, that yet is seen there' (p. 194).
73 **liberal arts** 'Those "arts" or "sciences" that were worthy of a free man' (*OED* Art *n* 1); the subjects studied at universities.
76 **state** The dukedom – either the office or the country (Orgel).
76–7 **transported . . . rapt** Both words suggest an ecstatic, quasi-mystical experience.
77 **secret studies** (1) studies conducted in seclusion, (2) studies of the hidden secrets of magic. It is an open question whether Prospero's studies exceed the permissible 'liberal arts' of which he earlier spoke.
77 **studies. Thy** F's comma here leaves the syntax ambiguous. Though, since F4, it has been strengthened to a full stop, it would be possible, with no less plausibility, to place a full stop earlier after 'stranger', and retain F's comma here, suggesting an immediate causal relationship between Prospero's seclusion and Antonio's treachery.
78 **Dost thou attend me** The punctuation of Prospero's narrative with demands to Miranda to pay attention needs careful handling on stage. It should probably not be taken to indicate that she is actually bored by his speech, but rather to suggest the urgency of this narrative to Prospero himself, and his concern to repair Miranda's 'ignorance' – which is also that of the audience.

PROSPERO Being once pèrfected how to grant suits,
            How to deny them; who t'advance, and who   80
            To trash for over-topping; new created
            The creatures that were mine, I say, or changed 'em,
            Or else new formed 'em; having both the key
            Of officer, and office, set all hearts i'th'state
            To what tune pleased his ear, that now he was   85
            The ivy which had hid my princely trunk,
            And sucked my verdure out on't – thou attend'st not!
MIRANDA O good sir, I do.
PROSPERO   I pray thee mark me:
            I, thus neglecting worldly ends, all dedicated
            To closeness, and the bettering of my mind   90

---

84 i'th'state] F; *not in* Pope   89 dedicated] F; dedicate *Steevens*

79–87 Being . . . on't Prospero's anger is indicated by the complex syntactic and rhetorical structure of the speech, and his obsessive preoccupation
with his brother's treachery is emphasised by the
way all clauses depend upon 'thy false uncle' as
their subject. The parallelism of the opening
clauses (the rhetorical figure of *isocolon*, or *parison*)
is rendered more obvious by retaining F's semi-
colons.

79 Being . . . pèrfected Once he had mastered
(the political arts).

79 suits petitions or requests to those in
authority.

80–1 who . . . over-topping whom to check
for undue ambition. 'Trash' is a term from dog-
training, meaning 'to check by means of a cord';
'over-topping' means 'becoming excessive in size or
importance', with a specific derivation from forestry,
where a small tree growing underneath a canopy is
said to be 'overtopped' (*OED* Overtop *v* 3). (Compare *Ant.* 4.12.23–4, where Antony says of himself:
'this pine is bark'd / That overtopped them all'.)

82 creatures . . . mine those who owed their
position to me, those created by me.

82–3 or changed . . . formed 'em Antonio both
transformed the allegiance of existing officials and
created new honours as an instrument of political
control. The successive modifications in each clause
beginning with the word 'or' is the rhetorical figure
of *correctio*.

83–4 key . . . office Several significances
combine: (1) possession of actual keys (as of the
Privy Chamber, for example) was a badge of high
office; (2) more generally, Antonio acquired the
means of control over distribution of offices, and
the officers who held them; (3) it suggests a musical
'key', initiating the conceit of the next two lines; (4)

possibly, as suggested first by Hawkins, a 'tuning
key' for a keyboard instrument (Furness).

84–5 set . . . ear The conceit that the sovereign
had a quasi-musical power to control or direct his
subjects is frequently to be found in court entertainments. (Ben Jonson's *Pan's Anniversary*, lines
161–2, for example, reads: '[King James's] loud
music all your manners wrought, / And made your
commonwealth a harmony.') Antonio's metaphorically musical power is literalised in Prospero's
employment of music as a means of dictating action
throughout the play.

85 that so that.

86 ivy Prospero characterises the ivy as a
destructive parasite, though in much emblem literature ivy surrounding the elm or oak is used as a
positive image of mutuality, especially in marriage.
Antonio's perversion of proper mutual relationship
is emphasised in this double signification of the
emblem. William Cartwright, in *The Lady-errant* (c.
1628–38), 4.6, makes a similar point: 'But that doth
twine and wreath itself about / Our growing loves,
as Ivy 'bout the Oak; / We think it shelters, when
(alas!) we find / It weakens and destroys.'

87 verdure greenness, sap.

89–105 I, thus neglecting . . . growing In the
first sentence of this complicated speech Prospero
elaborates on the way his own conduct contributed
to the incitement of his brother's treason. The
second sentence focuses upon Antonio's self-
perception, as he grows to believe he is indeed the
Duke of Milan because he has been exercising all
the privileges of the role.

89 I . . . dedicated This is an unusually long line
of thirteen syllables – no doubt prompting
Steevens's emendation to 'dedicate'.

90 closeness retirement, secrecy.

With that which, but by being so retired,
O'er-prized all popular rate, in my false brother
Awaked an evil nature; and my trust,
Like a good parent, did beget of him
A falsehood, in its contrary as great   95
As my trust was – which had indeed no limit,
A confidence sans bound. He being thus lorded,
Not only with what my revènue yielded,
But what my power might else exact – like one
Who, having into truth by telling of it,   100
Made such a sinner of his memory

---

99 exact –] *Grant White;* exact. F   **100** into truth] F; unto truth *Warburton;* to untruth *Collier MS.*   **100** of it] F; oft *Warburton*

91–2 but ... rate (1) If 'but' is taken to mean 'except', then either (a) Prospero's studies, except that they made him so retired, were above general estimation, so valuable were they; or (b) Prospero himself valued his studies more than popular estimation, except for the retirement they compelled him to, which in turn enabled Antonio's rebellion. Both of these agree with the valuation of his books that Prospero makes in 73–4 above. (2) Taking it as 'merely', however, produces: 'by the very fact of its seclusion, my study placed itself beyond the comprehension of the people'. This is the sense favoured by Kermode and Orgel.

92 O'er-prized exceeded in value. (It could equally be modernised as 'o'erpriced'.)

92 rate estimation, consideration (*OED n* 2b).

93–5 trust ... falsehood An elaboration of the proverbial 'Trust is the mother of deceit' (Tilley T555). Prospero recognises that his excessive trust in Antonio raised an equal but contrary treachery in him.

94 Like ... parent The paradox that trust begets falsehood is couched in a simile 'alluding to the observation that a father above the common rate commonly has a son below it' (Johnson). See Erasmus, *Adagia,* 1.6.32, *Heroum filii noxae*: 'Great men have trouble from their children ... even today it remains current as a humorous saying, that the wisest fathers have most fools for their children.' This thought is extended in Miranda's comment at 120 below.

97 sans bound without limit.

97–105 He being ... prerogative The complex syntax of this, as of Prospero's other speeches in the narrative, may be taken to indicate his perturbation of mind. The syntax clearly puzzled Crane or the F

compositors, who placed a full stop after 'exact'. Rhetorically the sentence is controlled by the parallel phrases 'He being thus lorded' and 'he did believe / He was indeed the duke'. The repetition of 'he' is not grammatically necessary, but clarifies the pattern and the causal relationship between the two stages. The first part of the sentence elaborates the ways in which Antonio had all the appearance of the duke, and, through the parenthetical simile of 99–102, explains how he internalised his exercise of power. The latter part of the sentence then emphasises further the way in which his belief in his right to the dukedom rested on outward appearance.

97 lorded made a lord.

99–102 like ... lie Though the syntax is tortured, the general sense of the simile is plain – someone who lies persistently comes to believe their lie to be true, and conveniently forgets the real situation. (Furness cites many parallel instances of this idea.)

100 having into truth 'Into' is generally explained as 'unto' or 'against', so the syntax is 'having (against the truth) made a sinner of his memory'. The frequent efforts at emendation indicate the problem that this convoluted structure generates, but if there is corruption here, there is no obvious solution.

100 of it i.e. of the lie. The pronoun looks forward to 102, not back to 'truth'. 'Tell' perhaps carries something of the sense 'make public' (*OED* Tell *v* 3.2), which suggests that it is Antonio's public execution of Prospero's power which persuaded him to believe he was the duke. Warburton's emendation of 'of it' to 'oft' implies more strongly that it is the act of repetition which generates self-deceit.

To credit his own lie – he did believe
He was indeed the duke, out o'th'substitution
And executing th'outward face of royalty
With all prerogative. Hence his ambition growing –   105
Dost thou hear?

MIRANDA   Your tale, sir, would cure deafness.

PROSPERO To have no screen between this part he played,
And him he played it for, he needs will be
Absolute Milan. Me, poor man, my library
Was dukedom large enough. Of temporal royalties   110
He thinks me now incapable; confederates –
So dry he was for sway – wi'th'King of Naples
To give him annual tribute, do him homage,
Subject his coronet to his crown, and bend
The dukedom yet unbowed – alas, poor Milan –   115
To most ignoble stooping.

MIRANDA   O the heavens!

PROSPERO Mark his condition, and th'event, then tell me
If this might be a brother.

MIRANDA   I should sin
To think but nobly of my grandmother –

---

103 out o'th'substitution] F; from substitution *Pope*   112 wi'th'] *Rowe;* with F   116 most] F; much F2

---

102 To credit As to believe.

103 out o'th'substitution as a consequence of my having surrendered my place to him.

104 executing . . . royalty from his exercise of an apparent royal power.

105 prerogative The powers that pertain to a ruler.

107–8 To have . . . for One difficulty here is that the 'screen' refers (1) to the way in which Antonio as deputy plays the part of the duke and so screens Prospero from view, but (2) to the distinction between the brother's performance of the ducal role and the fully constituted identity of the duke which is Prospero's. A second problem lies in the phrase 'played it for' which means 'at whose will he played it' but also 'whose role he played'. Thus the sense is: 'He absolutely desired to remove that screen, the role of deputy (and with it the screen that separates playing the part from really being the duke).' Compare the Duke's choice of Angelo as deputy in *MM*, where the role, but not the substance, of the Duke is leased.

107 screen (1) something interposed so as to conceal from view (*OED* sv *n*¹ 3a), (2) anything which intervenes obstructively (*OED* sv *n*¹ 4a, citing this passage).

109 Absolute Unlimited, free from restraint, therefore having absolute power.

109 Me For me.

110 temporal royalties Those things that belong to the secular, practical exercise of royal power.

111 confederates makes an alliance.

112 dry . . . for sway thirsty for control, desperately eager to exercise power.

114 Subject . . . crown Place the dukedom (the 'coronet') under the control of the king (the 'crown'). During the sixteenth century both Milan and Naples were in fact subject to the Spanish crown.

115 yet thus far, hitherto.

117 condition (1) treaty (as below, 120), (2) character, moral nature.

117 event consequence, outcome.

118–20 I should sin . . . sons Prospero's suggestion that Antonio did not behave as a brother should is taken by Miranda to imply that he was the illegitimate product of adultery, a suggestion she refutes.

119 but otherwise than.

Good wombs have borne bad sons.

PROSPERO   Now the condition.   120
This King of Naples, being an enemy
To me inveterate, hearkens my brother's suit,
Which was, that he, in lieu o'th'premises
Of homage, and I know not how much tribute,
Should presently extirpate me and mine   125
Out of the dukedom, and confer fair Milan,
With all the honours, on my brother. Whereon,
A treacherous army levied, one midnight
Fated to th'purpose did Antonio open
The gates of Milan, and i'th'dead of darkness   130
The ministers for th'purpose hurried thence
Me, and thy crying self.

MIRANDA   Alack, for pity!
I, not remembering how I cried out then,
Will cry it o'er again; it is a hint
That wrings mine eyes to't.

PROSPERO   Hear a little further,   135
And then I'll bring thee to the present business
Which now's upon's; without the which, this story
Were most impertinent.

MIRANDA   Wherefore did they not
That hour destroy us?

PROSPERO   Well demanded, wench;

---

120 Good ... sons] F; *assigned to Prospero by Hanmer (Theobald conj.)*   131 ministers] F; minister *Rowe*   133 out] F; on't *Theobald*

120   **Good ... sons** Proverbial. Tilley cites 'Many a good cow has an ill calf' (c761) and 'A wise man hath commonly a fool to his heir' (m421) and see 94 n. above.

121–2   **Naples ... inveterate** There is no historical referent for this statement. During the fifteenth century the relationship between Milan and Naples was continually shifting between alliance and enmity.

122   **hearkens ... suit** listens positively to Antonio's petition.

123   **in lieu ... premises** In return for, or in consideration of, the agreed conditions. The language here is legalistic, and 'premises' may suggest specifically the details set out at the beginning of a legal document, though *OED* dates this usage a little later than the play (Premise *n* 3, first citation 1641).

125   **presently** immediately.

extirpate Literally 'to root up'; here 'to drive out' (*OED* sv *v* 3b).

129   **Fated to th'purpose** Destined as suitable for the project. The sense that 'Fate' played a part in Prospero's banishment links with his claim at 178–84 that Fortune now has turned in his favour.

131   **ministers** servants, agents, executants.

134   **hint** occasion, suggestion.

135   **wrings** forces, squeezes out (her tears).

137   **the which** i.e. the present business.

138   **impertinent** irrelevant.

139   **wench** 'A familiar or endearing form of address, used chiefly in addressing a daughter, wife or sweetheart' (*OED* sv *n* 1c). The term is here uncontaminated by other usages, which imply low social status, or loose morality (as in 1.1.41).

My tale provokes that question. Dear, they durst not,   140
So dear the love my people bore me; nor set
A mark so bloody on the business; but
With colours fairer painted their foul ends.
In few, they hurried us aboard a barque,
Bore us some leagues to sea, where they prepared   145
A rotten carcass of a butt, not rigged,
Nor tackle, sail, nor mast – the very rats
Instinctively have quit it. There they hoist us
To cry to th'sea, that roared to us; to sigh
To th'winds, whose pity sighing back again   150
Did us but loving wrong.

MIRANDA   Alack, what trouble
Was I then to you!

PROSPERO [*Sitting*]   O, a cherubin
Thou wast that did preserve me. Thou didst smile,
Infusèd with a fortitude from heaven,
When I have decked the sea with drops full salt,   155
Under my burden groaned; which raised in me
An undergoing stomach, to bear up

---

148 have] F; had *Rowe*   152 you!] *Capell;* you? F   152 SD *This edn; not in* F *(Oxford places the same direction at 135)*   152 cherubin] F; cherubim F4   155 decked] F; mock'd *Warburton;* flecked *Johnson conj.*

141–2 set . . . bloody give such a bloody signature to their work (the phrase 'set a mark' was used for the act of appending a cross to documents by those unable to write their name). It may also allude to the mark imprinted by God on Cain, as sign of his murder of his brother (Genesis 4.15: 'And the Lord set a mark upon Cain').

143 colours . . . painted The image draws upon the association of 'colours' with rhetorical figures, and of 'paint' with cosmetics, to intensify the sense of deceitful cover-up and false appearance. (See Introduction, pp. 76–7.)

144 In few In short.

barque a small boat (though Milan is not a seaport).

146 carcass skeleton.

146 butt tub or barrel. It is not elsewhere used as a term for a ship (unlike 'tub'). But the image is unsurprising enough not to need justification by invoking, as editors have done, the etymologically unrelated Italian *botto* (a sloop) or French *boute* (a leathern vessel).

147–8 rats . . . quit it The earliest instance which Tilley records of the proverb of mice or rats leaving a sinking ship is from the late sixteenth century (M1243).

148 hoist (1) bear away (*OED* sv *v* 3), (2) lifted up (into the derelict ship) (*OED* sv *v* 1).

149–51 cry . . . loving wrong To retain F's comma after 'sea' clarifies the way in which the different responses of the elements of sea and wind correspond to the 'cries' and 'sighs' of Prospero and Miranda, and emphasises the rhetorical parallelism which structures the sentence.

152 SD Prospero must sit at some point, so that he can rise at 169 (but see note below). This seems a 'natural' place, as he responds warmly to his daughter (and was the point at which Alec McCowen sat in the 1993 RSC production), though there are many other possibilities.

152 cherubin The Hebrew plural of 'cherub', but used as a singular form in English until the seventeenth century. Prospero likens Miranda to a guardian angel who 'preserved' him.

155 decked adorned. Earlier commentators explained this as 'covered' or 'flecked'. Kermode rightly suggests that their anxiety about the straightforward meaning is misplaced.

156 which i.e. Miranda's childish smiling.

157 undergoing stomach courage to endure. (Orgel sees a continuation of a metaphor of childbirth from the 'groaning' of the previous line.)

Against what should ensue.
MIRANDA How came we ashore?
PROSPERO   By providence divine.
Some food we had, and some fresh water, that   160
A noble Neapolitan, Gonzalo,
Out of his charity – who being then appointed
Master of this design – did give us, with
Rich garments, linens, stuffs, and necessaries
Which since have steaded much. So, of his gentleness,   165
Knowing I loved my books, he furnished me
From mine own library, with volumes that
I prize above my dukedom.
MIRANDA   Would I might
But ever see that man.
PROSPERO [*Standing*]   Now I arise,
Sit still, and hear the last of our sea-sorrow.   170
Here in this island we arrived, and here
Have I, thy schoolmaster, made thee more profit
Than other princes can, that have more time
For vainer hours, and tutors not so careful.
MIRANDA Heavens thank you for't. And now I pray you, sir –   175
For still 'tis beating in my mind – your reason

---

159 divine.] *Pope;* divine; F4; divine, F   **162** who] F; *om. Pope*   **169** SD *Standing*] *Orgel subst;* Resumes his mantle / *Dyce;*
not in F   **169** arise,] F; arise: *Pope;* arise. *Orgel*   **173** princes] *Rowe;* Princesse F; princess' *Dyce;* princesses *Cam.*

159 By . . . divine Like the majority of editors I
have strengthened F's comma at the end of the line
to a full stop, making thereby a clear distinction
between the providence that guided the boat and
the human offices which provided them with material goods. Orgel, adopting a semi-colon, suggests
that the phrase floats between the two.
163 design plan, purpose.
164 Rich garments See 5.1.84 n.
stuffs (1) household goods or utensils (cf.
3.2.88), (2) fabrics – including perhaps those which
are set out to catch the conspirators in Act 4.
165 steaded much been very useful.
165 So In the same way.
165 gentleness both of character and of social
class.
167 library To omit the comma, as most editors
do, shifts the emphasis firmly to the word 'volumes',
whereas to retain it might allow some suggestion of
Prospero's fond recollection of his former state.
167–8 volumes . . . dukedom The present tense
of this statement is important, indicating that the
feelings of 91–2 persist, and that, as Caliban recognises, his (magical) books are still of importance.

169 Now I arise The dominant meaning is the
obvious one that Prospero here stands up to begin
the next movement of the scene, and quickly
instructs Miranda to remain seated. To strengthen
F's comma, as editors have often done,
makes more plausible the suggestion that Prospero
is referring metaphorically to the rise in his fortunes, now 'in the ascendant' (Kermode, Orgel).
Prospero here may resume his cloak in preparation
for charming Miranda to sleep, as Dyce first
suggested.
172 made . . . profit enabled you better to
progress or improve (cf. *AYLI* 1.1.6: 'My brother
Jacques he keeps at school, and report speaks gold-
enly of his profit'). Prospero's care in educating his
daughter as thoroughly as male princes is a mark of
his humanist inclinations at a time when the education of girls was generally thought less important
than that of boys.
173 princes F's 'Princesse' is a Crane spelling.
'Prince' could be applied to royal children of either
sex.
174 careful Both 'caring' and 'meticulous'.

For raising this sea-storm?
PROSPERO   Know thus far forth:
By accident most strange, bountiful Fortune,
Now my dear lady, hath mine enemies
Brought to this shore; and by my prescience   180
I find my zenith doth depend upon
A most auspicious star, whose influence
If now I court not, but omit, my fortunes
Will ever after droop. Here cease more questions.
Thou art inclined to sleep. 'Tis a good dullness,   185
And give it way; I know thou canst not choose.
          [*Miranda sleeps*]
Come away, servant, come; I'm ready now.
Approach, my Ariel. Come!

                    Enter ARIEL

ARIEL All hail, great master, grave sir, hail! I come
To answer thy best pleasure; be't to fly,   190
To swim, to dive into the fire, to ride
On the curled clouds. To thy strong bidding task

---

186 SD *Theobald; not in* F   187 I'm] *Oxford conj.;* I am F   190 pleasure; be't] F; pleasure. Be't *Wilson*   192 clouds. To] *Ard3;* clouds, to *Kermode;* clowds: to F

180 prescience foreknowledge. The ability to make astrological prediction was a customary attribute of the magician. In this speech, however, the relationships of accident and plan, fate and fortune are blurred.

181–2 I find ... star 'Astrologers taught that God was the first cause, and defined the stars as secondary causes operating by divine permission. They argued that the stars inclined man's will without compelling it' (Bernard Capp, *Astrology and the Popular Press*, 1979, p. 17).

181 zenith Highest point of the heavens or of the orbit of a star; hence the achievement of Prospero's greatest good fortune.

182 influence astrological power.

183 omit neglect.

185 good dullness beneficent or timely drowsiness.

186 give it way give in to it.

186 thou canst not choose In performance this is usually taken to imply that Prospero charms Miranda to sleep either with a gesture or (by analogy with the lords in 2.1) through the introduction of music.

187 I'm Contraction for metre.

187 I'm ready now Orgel conjectured that Pros-

pero reassumed his magic robe here, as a sign of his 'readiness' to meet Ariel, but his comment need indicate no more than that his first task of informing Miranda of their past is now complete, and he is ready to move on to the next stage of his plan by instructing Ariel to bring Ferdinand to her (though execution of this instruction is much delayed).

188 SD There is a strong theatrical impulse to give Ariel a spectacular entrance, either flying or emerging from a trap-door, an impulse frequently indulged from the eighteenth century to the present. Either of these would have been possible in the seventeenth century. (The production at Shakespeare's Globe, 2000, flew Ariel in.)

190–2 pleasure ... clouds There are alternative possibilities for the punctuation of these lines. Wilson and Oxford choose to put a full stop after 'pleasure', and comma after 'clouds', so that the intervening phrases answer Prospero's 'bidding', rather than his 'best pleasure'.

192 curled The metaphorical adjective is widely used poetically to describe the eddies of water; to use it of clouds seems to be a Shakespearean coinage.

192 task assign work to (*OED* sv *v* 2a).

Ariel, and all his quality.

PROSPERO Hast thou, spirit, performed to point the tempest
          That I bade thee?

ARIEL   To every article.   195
          I boarded the king's ship. Now on the beak,
          Now in the waist, the deck, in every cabin,
          I flamed amazement. Sometime I'd divide
          And burn in many places; on the topmast,
          The yards and bowsprit, would I flame distinctly,   200
          Then meet and join. Jove's lightning, the precursors
          O'th'dreadful thunder-claps, more momentary
          And sight-outrunning were not; the fire and cracks
          Of sulphurous roaring the most mighty Neptune
          Seem to besiege, and make his bold waves tremble,   205
          Yea, his dread trident shake.

PROSPERO   My brave spirit!
          Who was so firm, so constant, that this coil
          Would not infect his reason?

ARIEL   Not a soul
          But felt a fever of the mad, and played

193–5 *This edn; Ariel . . . Qualitie. / Pro.* Hast . . . Spirit, / Performed . . . thee. / *Ar.* To . . . Article. F; *Ariel . . . spirit /
Performed . . . thee? / *Ar.* To . . . article. *Pope* 193 quality] F; qualities *Pope* 198 Sometime] F; Sometimes F2 200
bowsprit] F *(Bore-spritt)* 201 lightning] F; lightnings *Theobald* 205 Seem] F; Seem'd *Rowe* 209 mad] F; mind *Rowe²*

193–5 **Ariel . . . article** F's lineation generates
two irregular lines out of three. The relineation
here leaves a short line to complete Ariel's speech
(a common occurrence in the play) and follows this
with two regular lines, at the same time metrically
binding Ariel's answer to Prospero's question. (See
Textual Analysis, p. 239.)

193 **quality** Either (1) ability or (2) company (of
spirits). In a number of recent productions Ariel has
been accompanied on his first entrance by other
spirits dressed more or less identically to him.

194 **to point** exactly.

196 **beak** projection at the prow of the vessel.

197 **waist** in the middle of the vessel.

198 **flamed amazement** appeared as terrifying
fire. See Erasmus, 'Shipwreck', p. 139: 'Suddenly a
fiery ball appeared beside him – a very bad sign to
sailors when it's a single flame, lucky when it's
double. Antiquity believed these were Castor and
Pollux . . . Soon the blazing ball slid down the ropes
and rolled straight up to the skipper . . . After stopping there a moment, it rolled the whole way round
the ship, then dropped through the middle hatches

and disappeared.' It was perhaps this popular Col-
loquy which suggested the way Ariel 'divides'
himself. The double significance of St Elmo's fire is
particularly appropriate to this storm, which is both
a disaster and a means to a happy outcome. The
phenomenon is also described in the Strachey letter.
(See Introduction, p. 31.)

200 **yards** spars on which sails are set.

200 **bowsprit** boom to which the foremast stays
are fastened.

200 **distinctly** separately.

201 **Jove** One of the attributes of the king of the
gods was his control of the weather, especially
thunder and lightning. (See also 10 n. above.)

202 **momentary** lasting but a moment, transitory (*OED* sv *adj* 1).

203 **sight-outrunning** faster than the eye could
follow.

204 **Neptune** God of the sea, who carried a
three-pronged spear or 'trident'.

207 **coil** noisy disturbance.

209 **fever of the mad** a fever such as the mad
feel.

Some tricks of desperation. All but mariners   210
Plunged in the foaming brine and quit the vessel,
Then all a-fire with me; the king's son Ferdinand,
With hair up-staring – then like reeds, not hair –
Was the first man that leaped; cried 'Hell is empty,
And all the devils are here.'

PROSPERO   Why that's my spirit.   215
But was not this nigh shore?

ARIEL   Close by, my master.

PROSPERO But are they, Ariel, safe?

ARIEL   Not a hair perished;
On their sustaining garments not a blemish,
But fresher than before. And as thou bad'st me,
In troops I have dispersed them 'bout the isle.   220
The king's son have I landed by himself,
Whom I left cooling of the air with sighs
In an odd angle of the isle, and sitting,
His arms in this sad knot.

PROSPERO   Of the king's ship,
The mariners, say how thou hast disposed,   225

---

211 vessel,] *Rowe;* vessell; F   212 me;] *This edn;* me: *Rowe;* me, *Ard3;* me F   224 ship,] F; ship *Hanmer*

210 tricks characteristic acts (*OED* Trick *n* 7).

212 with me Most editors have added punctuation here, so that it is the vessel, rather than Ferdinand, which is 'a-fire', as F implies. Wilson and Ard3 choose to follow F. Either reading is possible.

213 up-staring standing on end. Halliwell, *Notes*, cites Johnson's *Famous History of the Seven Champions of Christendome* (1608): 'Ormondine the magician, with his haire staring on his head . . . as though legions of spirits had incompast him about', which might lend some support to the second reading of the previous line (and cf. Spenser, *Faerie Queene*, 1.9.22: 'curld uncombed heares / Upstaring stiffe, dismayd with uncouth dread').

214 Hell is empty Proverbial. Tilley H403: 'Hell is broke loose.'

215 devils, spirit Both words must be pronounced as monosyllables.

217 Not . . . perished Confirming Prospero's remarks to Miranda, above, 29–30 (cf. Luke 21.18, 'But there shall not an hair of your head perish').

218 sustaining garments Implies that air

trapped in their clothes held them up in the water, as Ophelia's dress is said to do : 'Her clothes spread wide, / And mermaid-like awhile they bore her up' (*Ham.* 5.1.175–6).

220 troops i.e. separate groups.

223 angle corner.

224 this . . . knot Ariel folds his arms, a conventional sign of melancholy, frequently found in paintings and miniatures. The frontispiece to Samuel Rowlands's satiric poem *The Melancholie Knight* (1615) depicts him with folded arms, and complaining, 'I crosse mine armes at crosses that arise.' It was also a pose associated with the lover, which Ferdinand becomes (see *LLL* 3.1.18–19 where Moth speaks of the lover 'with your arms crossed on your thin-bellied doublet like a rabbit on a spit').

224–5 Of . . . mariners F's comma suggests that Prospero asks first about the ship and then the mariners – and that is how Ariel replies. The decision of some editors to omit it produces an unnecessarily strained inversion.

And all the rest o'th'fleet?

ARIEL   Safely in harbour
Is the king's ship, in the deep nook, where once
Thou call'dst me up at midnight to fetch dew
From the still-vexed Bermudas, there she's hid;
The mariners all under hatches stowed,   230
Who, with a charm joined to their suffered labour,
I've left asleep. And for the rest o'th'fleet –
Which I dispersed – they all have met again,
And are upon the Mediterranean float
Bound sadly home for Naples,   235
Supposing that they saw the king's ship wracked,
And his great person perish.

PROSPERO   Ariel, thy charge
Exactly is performed; but there's more work.
What is the time o'th'day?

ARIEL   Past the mid-season.

PROSPERO At least two glasses. The time 'twixt six and now   240
Must by us both be spent most preciously.

---

229 Bermudas] *Theobald; Bermoothes* F   232 I've] *Pope; I have* F   240 SH PROSPERO] F *(subst.);* ARIEL *Warburton*

227 deep nook The phrase perhaps recalls the Virgilian description of the haven where Aeneas lands, after the storm in Book 1 of the *Aeneid*, described as *in secessu longo* ('in a deep inlet', line 159), translated by Stanyhurst as 'in a nook uplandish'.

228 dew Conventionally required for magic – associating Prospero with Sycorax's 'wicked dew' of 322.

229 still-vexed always angry.

229 Bermudas The storminess of the Bermudas was often alluded to. They were also associated with magic, as in Jourdain's *A Discovery of the Barmudas* (1610), where it is described as 'a most prodigious and inchanted place' (p. 8), though this notion was disappearing quickly, as the dedication of the reprint of Jourdain's treatise in 1613 made plain: 'Who did not thinke till within these foure yeares, but that those Ilands had been rather a habitation of Divells, then fit for men to dwell in?' (quoted in Gary Schmidgall, '*The Tempest* and *Primaeleon*: a new source', *SQ*, 37 (1986), 421–40; p. 437). Editors solemnly point out that it was also the name for a notorious district of London – but this is surely a context which would insulate most of the audience

from recalling it. It is the only reference to the Americas in the whole play.

230 under hatches below deck.

231 their suffered labour the toil they have endured (which, together with Ariel's charm, ensures that they will sleep).

232 I've The elision is for the metre.

234 float sea.

235 Bound . . . Naples This short line is considered 'effective' by Kermode. Medial short lines, though unusual, are not without precedent in Shakespeare's versification, particularly in the late plays.

237 charge commission, duty.

239 mid-season noon.

240 two glasses two hours measured by the hour-glass.

240 'twixt six and now Between now (2 p.m.) and six; that is, in four hours. The first scene places great emphasis upon timing and upon the urgency of seizing the moment, tying in with the play's exceptional observance of temporal unity.

241 preciously 'As a precious thing, as a thing of value' (*OED* sv *adv* 2, citing this passage).

ARIEL   Is there more toil? Since thou dost give me pains,
        Let me remember thee what thou hast promised,
        Which is not yet performed me.
PROSPERO   How now? Moody?
        What is't thou canst demand?
ARIEL   My liberty.   245
PROSPERO   Before the time be out? No more.
ARIEL   I prithee,
        Remember I have done thee worthy service,
        Told thee no lies, made no mistakings, served
        Without or grudge or grumblings. Thou did promise
        To bate me a full year.
PROSPERO   Dost thou forget   250
        From what a torment I did free thee?
ARIEL   No.
PROSPERO   Thou dost! And think'st it much to tread the ooze
        Of the salt deep,
        To run upon the sharp wind of the north,
        To do me business in the veins o'th'earth   255
        When it is baked with frost.
ARIEL   I do not, sir.
PROSPERO   Thou liest, malignant thing. Hast thou forgot

---

248 made no] *Rowe;* made thee no F

242 **give me pains** demand labours of me.
243 **remember** remind.
244 **Moody** The modern meaning, 'sullen, ill-humoured', is used elsewhere by Shakespeare, but here it seems too weak, and Prospero's rebuke seems to carry an older sense of 'stubborn, wilful, obstinate' (*OED* sv *adj* 2; last instance 1460). The anonymous *King Leir*, line 2193, speaks of 'moody fury', and something of that fierceness seems to be required. Many recent performances of the play have chosen to emphasise Ariel's 'moodiness'. (See Introduction, p. 62.)
246 **time be out** indentured period of service is finished. Prospero here and elsewhere uses the terminology of an apprenticeship to describe his relationship with Ariel, in a fashion quite distinct from his language to Caliban. (See Gurr, 'Industrious Ariel'.)
248 **no mistakings** F's 'made thee no mistakings' is both unmetrical and clumsy, and an easy error for scribe or compositor to make.
250 **bate** let me off, remit; again using the terminology of indentured service.

252 **dost** F's colon is usually reduced to a comma in modern editions. Stronger punctuation seems required to set up the pattern of emphatic contradiction that begins each of Prospero's next two speeches.
252 **ooze** wet mud of the sea-bed (cf. 3.3.100).
253 **Of . . . deep** This short line is seen as a sign of revision by Wilson, but though the previous line is very crowded in F there seems no obvious corruption of sense.
255 **veins** (1) underground streams, (2) seams of precious metal.
256 **baked** caked, hardened.
257 **malignant** Here used in the obsolete sense: 'disposed to rebel against God or against constituted authority; disaffected, malcontent' (*OED* sv *adj* 1), rather than 'characterised by . . . intense ill-will' (*OED* sv *adj* 4).
257 **forgot** As with the inquisition of Miranda, questions of remembering and forgetting are important here.

The foul witch Sycorax, who with age and envy
Was grown into a hoop? Hast thou forgot her?
ARIEL   No, sir.
PROSPERO   Thou hast. Where was she born? Speak. Tell me.   260
ARIEL   Sir, in Algiers.
PROSPERO   O, was she so? I must
Once in a month recount what thou hast been,
Which thou forget'st. This damned witch Sycorax,
For mischiefs manifold, and sorceries terrible
To enter human hearing, from Algiers   265
Thou know'st was banished. For one thing she did
They would not take her life. Is not this true?
ARIEL   Ay, sir.

---

261 Algiers] *Oxford; Argier* F   261 so?] *Pope; so – Orgel;* so: F

258 **Sycorax** The name has not been satisfactorily explained. It may derive from the Greek words
sus (pig) and *corax* (raven). The qualities attributed
to Caliban's mother fuse literary representations
(especially those deriving from Ovid's depiction of
Medea in *Metamorphoses*, 7, and from the figure of
Circe) with details from popular contemporary conceptions of the witch. Kermode suggested that
Circe's origins in Colchis, the district of the Coraxi
tribe, may have suggested her name, while Orgel
offers the possibility that her name sounds like an
epithet for Medea the 'Scythian raven'. Since Prospero can never have seen her, the source of his
knowledge is open to question.
258–9 **age . . . hoop** The stereotypical witch was
an old and ugly woman whose outward appearance
mirrored her inner malevolence. Harsnett wrote of
'the true Idaea of a Witch, an olde weather-beaten
Croane, having her chin & her knees meeting for
age' (*Declaration*, 136–7). Lyndal Roper suggests:
'Envy was the motor of witchcraft as seventeenth-
century people understood it'(*Oedipus and the Devil*,
1994, p. 214). The harm that witches were thought
to do was frequently represented as a response to a
refusal of their demands for charity, hence 'envy' in
a loose sense. In Ripa's *Iconologia* one representation of Envy (*Invidia*) is as an old, ugly woman,
'livid' of colouring (see below, 269 and n.) and with
serpents on her head and breast.
259–60 **Hast thou forgot . . . Tell me** Prospero's question, and his response to Ariel's answer,
suggested to Wilson that Prospero was 'about to
contradict Ariel but does not do so; and the text
leaves us in doubt as to the birthplace of Sycorax'.
Whilst it is possible that Ariel only became
Sycorax's servant on her arrival in the island and so
did not in fact know from whence she came, Pros-

pero himself can have only indirect information,
and his 'O, was she so' is more probably to be taken
as sarcastic confirmation of what they both already
believe. The exchange is for the benefit of the audience, and emphasises Sycorax's origin in North
Africa.
261 **Algiers** F's 'Argier' is the modern Algiers,
and consistency demands modernisation of that
spelling, though (as with Milan) an equal stress is
required, since here the emphasis falls on the first
syllable, but on the second at 265. Samuel C. Chew,
in *The Crescent and the Rose: Islam and England
during the Renaissance*, 1937, cites Purchas's
description of Algiers as 'the Whirlepoole of these
Seas, the Throne of Pyracie, the Sinke of Trade and
the Stinke of Slavery . . .' (p. 344), and Thomas
Monson claimed that 'the inhabitants consist principally of desperate rogues and renegadoes, that live
by rapine, theft and spoil, having renounced God
and all virtue and become reprobates to all the
Christian world' (Monson, III, 86).
261 **was she so** The customary use of a question
mark here should not exclude the possibility that
Prospero makes a weary statement of confirmation
rather than asks a question.
266 **For one thing she did** The usual explanation that Sycorax was reprieved because she was
pregnant is not convincing. The execution of pregnant women was indeed stayed, but was almost
always carried out once they had given birth (as
happened, for example, in the case of one of the
witches condemned at Chelmsford in 1589). The
sense here seems to be that she performed some
public service, but speculation as to its nature is
redundant; more significant is the parallel to, and
contrast with, Prospero's explanation to Miranda of
the reasons for his own survival (140–1).

PROSPERO This blue-eyed hag was hither brought with child,
　　　　　　　And here was left by th'sailors. Thou, my slave,　　　　270
　　　　　　　As thou report'st thyself, was then her servant;
　　　　　　　And for thou wast a spirit too delicate
　　　　　　　To act her earthy and abhorred commands,
　　　　　　　Refusing her grand hests, she did confine thee,
　　　　　　　By help of her more potent ministers,　　　　　　　　275
　　　　　　　And in her most unmitigable rage,
　　　　　　　Into a cloven pine, within which rift
　　　　　　　Imprisoned thou didst painfully remain
　　　　　　　A dozen years; within which space she died,
　　　　　　　And left thee there; where thou didst vent thy groans　　280
　　　　　　　As fast as mill-wheels strike. Then was this island –
　　　　　　　Save for the son that she did litter here,
　　　　　　　A freckled whelp, hag-born – not honoured with
　　　　　　　A human shape.
ARIEL　　　　　　　　　　　　Yes, Caliban her son.

---

269 blue-eyed] F; blear-eyed *Staunton*   282 she] *Rowe;* he F

269 **blue-eyed hag** 'Blue' could mean both 'sky-coloured' and 'livid', or else 'bleary'; 'eyes' could include eyelids and the area round the eye (as in the modern 'black eye'). This generates a series of possibilities and associations, which are not mutually exclusive: (1) blue eyelids were a sign of pregnancy, as in Davenant's *The Play-House to be Let* (1662), Act 5: 'Her eyes look blue; pray Heav'n she be not breeding', (2) at a time when the eyes of a beauty were most frequently characterised as grey or black, blue eyes were often seen as a mark of imperfection. They are associated with old and malevolent women, for example, in Chapman's *The Gentleman Usher*, 4.1: 'An old wive's eye / Is a blue crystal full of sorcery', (3) a 'livid' blue is associated with witches in Milton's *Comus*, line 434, 'Blue meagre hag', and with Envy in Ripa's *Iconologia*, (4) Scot wrote that 'One sort of such as are said to be witches are women which be commonly old, lame, blear-eyed, pale, foul and full of wrinkles', (5) Hakluyt refers to native women 'marked in the face with blewe streekes . . . round about the eyes' (VII, 209). See Leah Marcus, *Unediting the Renaissance*, 1996, ch. 1, for an extended discussion of this line which seeks to reinstate the straightforward modern meaning of blue eyes, remarkable in a North African figure, and Diane Purkiss, *The Witch in History*, 1996, ch. 10.

271 **As . . . thyself** 'As thou report'st thyself' is syntactically ambiguous. If it attaches to 'my slave', then Prospero comments ironically on Ariel's repre-sentation of their relationship as that of master and slave. But it could equally belong with the following clause, and therefore mean: 'You were then Sycorax's servant according to your own report.' Elsewhere Prospero contrasts his contractual bond with Ariel as servant with the master–slave relationship he has with Caliban, and only here does he address Ariel as 'slave'. It is just possible that the terms 'slave' and 'servant' have been transposed in the text.

272 **delicate** fine, exquisite in nature (*OED* sv *adj* 6b, citing this passage).

274 **grand hests** great or principal commands.

275 **more potent ministers** These 'more powerful' spirits are the 'ministers of Satan' or the familiars of a witch, rather than merely the 'agents' of 131.

276 **unmitigable** incapable of being assuaged.

279 **A dozen years** The twelve years of Ariel's imprisonment and the twelve years of Prospero's occupancy of the island mean that Caliban must be at least twenty-four years old at the time of the play.

280 **vent** emit.

281 **as mill-wheels strike** as the paddles of a mill-wheel strike the water.

282 **she** F's 'he' has, since Dryden and Davenant, been emended to 'she'.

282 **litter** A contemptuous use of a term associated with animal birth.

284 **human shape** It is significant that Prospero himself endows Caliban with the external appearance of humanity.

PROSPERO　Dull thing, I say so: he, that Caliban　　　　285
　　　　　Whom now I keep in service. Thou best know'st
　　　　　What torment I did find thee in. Thy groans
　　　　　Did make wolves howl, and penetrate the breasts
　　　　　Of ever-angry bears. It was a torment
　　　　　To lay upon the damned, which Sycorax　　　　290
　　　　　Could not again undo. It was mine art,
　　　　　When I arrived and heard thee, that made gape
　　　　　The pine, and let thee out.
ARIEL　　　　　　　　　　I thank thee, master.
PROSPERO　If thou more murmur'st, I will rend an oak
　　　　　And peg thee in his knotty entrails till　　　　295
　　　　　Thou hast howled away twelve winters.
ARIEL　　　　　　　　　　　　Pardon, master.
　　　　　I will be correspondent to command
　　　　　And do my spiriting gently.
PROSPERO　　　　　　　Do so;
　　　　　And after two days I will discharge thee.
ARIEL　That's my noble master! What shall I do?　　　　300
　　　　　Say what? What shall I do?
PROSPERO　　　　　　　　Go make thyself
　　　　　Like to a nymph o'th'sea. Be subject to

298–305 *This edn; for* F *see Textual Analysis*　298 spiriting] *Capell;* spriting F　302 Like to] F2; like F

285 **Dull thing** Either Prospero chides Ariel for
the literal-mindedness with which he finds it necessary to name Caliban after Prospero's circumlo-
cutory characterisation of him in the preceding
lines, or else he takes offence at Ariel's implied
mockery of his pomposity.
286 **now . . . service** The implication of 'now' is
consistent with Prospero's claim that he initially
treated Caliban differently (346–9).
287–9 **groans . . . bears** Ariel's groans provoked
a response in animal creation which is the inverse
of the soothing power music conventionally has to
quieten even savage beasts.
290–1 **Sycorax . . . undo** Either because she had
no power to do so, thus elevating Prospero's power
by contrast, or else simply because she had died.
292 **made gape** opened up.
294 **murmur'st** rebelliously complain. ' "Mur-
muring" . . . was the standard English term for
biblical reluctance toward God's commands; bib-
lically alert auditors would have noted this' (Strier,
'Politics', p. 20).
294 **oak** Prospero's threat is to imprison Ariel in
a hardwood tree from which it would be even more

difficult to free himself than from the softwood pine
in which Sycorax had confined him. The oak was
conventionally associated with Jove, the king of the
gods (as it is at 5.1.45).
296 **Thou hast** Should probably be elided to
'Thou'st' for the metre, thereby generating an effective emphasis on 'howled'.
297 **correspondent** responsive, answerable.
298–305 **And do . . . shape** See Textual Analysis, p. 241, for the lineation here.
299 **discharge** relieve of your duties.
302 **Like to** F2's emendation is perfectly plausible, though presumably entertained in order to
repair the metre of the short line in F's lineation;
'like' and 'like to' were interchangeable, but the
former occurred much more frequently, so perhaps
tempting the compositor into the omission. (Expansion of the elision 'o'th'sea' would similarly correct
the metre.)
302–3 **nymph . . . invisible** Editors have frequently worried that it is absurd for Ariel to transform himself if no-one except Prospero and he
could see what he was wearing, but his costume-
change is significant to the audience, visually

No sight but thine and mine, invisible
To every eye-ball else. Go take this shape
And hither come in't. Go! Hence with diligence.   305

                                        Exit [*Ariel*]

[*To Miranda*] Awake, dear heart, awake; thou hast slept well,
Awake.

MIRANDA   The strangeness of your story put
Heaviness in me.

PROSPERO   Shake it off. Come on,
We'll visit Caliban, my slave, who never
Yields us kind answer.

MIRANDA   'Tis a villain, sir,   310
I do not love to look on.

PROSPERO   But as 'tis
We cannot miss him. He does make our fire,
Fetch in our wood, and serves in offices
That profit us. What ho! Slave! Caliban!
Thou earth, thou! Speak!

CALIBAN (*Within*)   There's wood enough within.   315

PROSPERO Come forth, I say; there's other business for thee.
Come, thou tortoise, when?

                    Enter ARIEL *like a water-nymph*

---

303 thine and] *om. Rowe*   306 SD *Orgel; not in* F   310–11 *As Pope; one line in* F

demonstrating his metamorphic nature, and this
costume in particular is appropriate to his next
appearance, luring Ferdinand from the sea-shore.
The question of what exactly characters on stage
actually 'see' recurs throughout the play (especially
in 2.1 and 3.3), and at one level this is a remark
which clarifies matters for the audience. (Despite
this clear instruction a number of productions have
attempted to convey a sense that Ariel is invisible
also to Prospero.) Sturgess, pp. 85–7, suggests that
this becomes Ariel's principal costume, and itself
therefore an indication of invisibility, but Ariel
could equally well resume his original costume after
this scene. Orgel ingeniously (but unnecessarily)
suggests that something has been cut here, and that
it might be the spirits who 'bear the burden' of the
song later on who were to be 'invisible'.

308 **Heaviness** i.e. of the eyes, drowsiness.

310 **villain** Both 'evil' and 'low-born' (the latter
is the original sense of the word, usually spelled
'villein' in Modern English).

312 **miss** do without.

313 **offices** tasks.

314 **profit** benefit.

315 **earth** Emphasising Caliban's elemental
opposition to the fiery and airy Ariel.

315 SD This direction suggests that Caliban
speaks at stage level from behind one of the side
doors, though he might emerge through a trap-door
from under the stage. (It is conceivable, if unlikely,
that Caliban's 'hard rock' might have been a physical prop on stage.)

317 **tortoise** The primary sense here is of the
slowness of the tortoise. But, in view of Trinculo's
bemused question at 2.2.23, 'What have we here –
a man, or a fish?', it is relevant that the tortoise was
generally described as an amphibious creature, and
in Jonson's *Volpone* Sir Politic-Would-Be, disguised
as a tortoise, is called 'a fish' (5.2.65). Some productions have taken this as a cue to costume Caliban
as a giant turtle (see Vaughans, pp. 13, 76, 233–4).

317 **when** An exclamation of impatience (*OED*
sv *adv* 1b).

Fine apparition! My quaint Ariel,
Hark in thine ear.

[Whispers to Ariel]

ARIEL   My lord, it shall be done.   *Exit*

PROSPERO Thou poisonous slave, got by the devil himself   320
Upon thy wicked dam, come forth.

Enter CALIBAN

CALIBAN As wicked dew as e'er my mother brushed
With raven's feather from unwholesome fen
Drop on you both! A south-west blow on ye,
And blister you all o'er!   325

PROSPERO For this, be sure, tonight thou shalt have cramps,
Side-stitches that shall pen thy breath up; urchins
Shall, for that vast of night that they may work,
All exercise on thee; thou shalt be pinched
As thick as honeycomb, each pinch more stinging   330
Than bees that made 'em.

CALIBAN   I must eat my dinner.

---

319 SD *Orgel subst.; not in* F   328 Shall, for that vast of night that . . . work,] *Rowe²;* Shall forth at vast of night, that . . . work *Oxford (White conj.);* Shall for that vast of night, . . . worke F   328 vast] waste *Rowe*   330 honeycomb] F; honey- combs *Pope*

318 quaint Prospero may be praising Ariel's skill and ingenuity in general, or more specifically be commenting on the costume in which he appears. In the latter context, either 'elegance' or 'strange, outlandish fashion' might be implied.

319 Hark . . . ear Prospero finally gives the instruction to fetch Ferdinand, the task for which he was 'ready' at 187, and was about to ask Ariel to perform at 238.

320 got by the devil The notion that witches sealed their pact with the devil with sexual inter- course is a commonplace of 'learned' lore. The *Malleus Maleficarum* devotes a long section to proving that Incubi could have intercourse leading to pregnancy, though the seed with which they begat children was stolen from human males, so that the child was 'the son not of the devil, but of some man' (ed. Summers, 1948, p. 28). Such chil- dren are 'powerful and big in body' (p. 112). The whole idea of diabolical copulation was ridiculed in most English treatises on witchcraft, though found in fiction – see the extract from *The Mirrour of Knighthood* (1586) printed in Bullough, pp. 305–8, as an analogue to Prospero's account.

321 dam mother; usually used of animals, so continuing the denigration of Sycorax implied by 'litter' above.

322 wicked dew See 228 n. above.

323 raven's feather The raven as a bird of ill- omen is particularly associated with witchcraft.

324 south-west 'Southerly winds were associ- ated with warm, damp weather and considered unwholesome' (Orgel).

327 pen . . . up i.e. the pain will be so severe that it will prevent you breathing.

327 urchins Either (1) hedgehogs, (2) goblins or (3) spirits in the shape of hedgehogs.

328–9 for that vast . . . thee During the long hours of the night in which evil spirits are permit- ted to be abroad they will all exercise themselves on you. White's emendation to 'forth at vast', and acceptance of F's punctuation is endorsed by Oxford, Ard3, and others, giving the sense 'shall come out during the vast space of night, so that they might perform all discipline upon you'. 'Exercise' here is understood as a noun, meaning 'disciplinary suffering, trial' (*OED* Exercise *n* 6c). This seems strained.

329–30 pinched . . . honeycomb i.e. the marks of the pinches will be as numerous as the cells in a honeycomb. 'The image perhaps derives from the notion that bees mould their wax by pinching it into shape' (Orgel).

331 'em i.e. honeycombs.

331 I . . . dinner This reply might be taken in a number of ways: Caliban might complain that he

This island's mine by Sycorax my mother,
Which thou tak'st from me. When thou cam'st first
Thou strok'st me and made much of me; wouldst give me
Water with berries in't, and teach me how   335
To name the bigger light, and how the less,
That burn by day and night. And then I loved thee
And showed thee all the qualities o'th'isle,
The fresh springs, brine-pits, barren place and fertile –
Cursèd be I that did so! All the charms   340
Of Sycorax – toads, beetles, bats – light on you!
For I am all the subjects that you have,
Which first was mine own king; and here you sty me
In this hard rock, whiles you do keep from me
The rest o'th'island.

PROSPERO   Thou most lying slave,   345
Whom stripes may move, not kindness! I have used thee,
Filth as thou art, with humane care, and lodged thee

334 made] F; mad'st Rowe   340 Cursèd] This edn; Curs'd F   340 that . . . so] F; that I . . . so F2   347 humane] F; human F4

has been interrupted in his meal, and enter from his cell eating, or else he turns away from Prospero, in apparent indifference to his curses, to go back to his cell, or else he mutinously demands his food. (Each of these has been used in production.)

332 This has become one of the most potent lines in prompting a reading of Caliban's situation as that of the colonised native. See Introduction, p. 33 ff.

335 Water with berries In *Dyets Dry Dinner* (1599) there are a number of suggestions that different berries may be infused with wine, but none of a non-alcoholic cordial. This would indicate that the 'water' here is significant precisely because it is unusual, and therefore establishes a contrast between the sober drink that Prospero offered Caliban and the wine with which Stephano and Trinculo bemuse him. Jonathan Bate has argued, however, that the phrase is Caliban's best effort to find a name for something with which he is unfamiliar, and that it is 'grapes' which are implied, so that Prospero himself first wooed Caliban with alcohol brought with him from Milan, and long since finished (*The Genius of Shakespeare*, 1997, p. 246). Bate is anticipated by Jones, who simply glosses the phrase as 'some kind of wine'. The problem here is that Caliban gives no sign of recollection when he first drinks from Stephano's bottle, and Prospero specifically mentions 'fresh water', but not wine, at 160 above.

336 bigger . . . less Compare Genesis 1.16:

'God then made two great lights: the greater light to rule the day, and the less light to rule the night.'

339 brine-pits Caliban showed them both the positive and negative aspects of the island. The line is chiastically constructed, so that the contrast between springs and briny waters is reversed in barren and fertile places. F's semi-colon after 'brine-pits' makes this pattern clearer.

340 Cursèd F's 'Curs'd' produces a non-metrical line, which could equally be remedied by F2's emendation to 'Curs'd be I that I did so.'

340 charms spells.

341 toads . . . bats All of them were frequently invoked as witches' agents.

343 sty keep like a pig.

344–5 keep from me . . . island Since Caliban fetches wood, he must here be exaggerating the extent to which he is confined to his rocky prison.

346 stripes lashes of a whip. Whether or not servants should be beaten was a topic of debate in the period. (See Introduction, p. 57.)

347 humane F's spelling is frequently modernised to 'human'; either meaning is possible – the first emphasises Prospero's generosity, the second implies that he has treated Caliban the savage with the care appropriate to a human being (cf. 4.1.188–90).

347–8 lodged . . . cell Prospero has treated Caliban as a young household servant by this act. See 2.2.159 n. below.

In mine own cell, till thou didst seek to violate
The honour of my child.
CALIBAN   O ho, O ho! Would't had been done.
Thou didst prevent me – I had peopled else   350
This isle with Calibans.
MIRANDA   Abhorrèd slave,
Which any print of goodness wilt not take,
Being capable of all ill! I pitied thee,
Took pains to make thee speak, taught thee each hour
One thing or other. When thou didst not, savage,   355
Know thine own meaning, but wouldst gabble like
A thing most brutish, I endowed thy purposes
With words that made them known. But thy vile race –
Though thou didst learn – had that in't which good natures
Could not abide to be with; therefore wast thou   360
Deservedly confined into this rock,
Who hadst deserved more than a prison.

---

349 Would't had] F; I would it had *Pope*   351 SH F; *assigned to Prospero by Dryden, Theobald*

348–9 till . . . child We are not told how recent was this attempted rape.

349 O ho, O ho This exclamation appears in earlier drama as a characterisation of a villain or mischief-maker, and especially of Satan himself. See, for example, *Gammer Gurton's Needle*, 2.3.15: 'did not the devil cry "ho, ho, ho"', and Wager, *Enough is as Good as a Feast*, line 1428, where Satan enters crying, 'Oh, oh, oh, oh. All is mine, all is mine.' (This exclamation is not counted in the metre, though Pope's emendation would create a full verse line.)

350–1 peopled . . . Calibans Caliban's view of sexuality as primarily procreative, and a potential political weapon in populating the island, is reiterated at 3.2.97–8 when he offers Miranda to Stephano. It is his lack of shame or penitence at his action which exacerbates Prospero's anger.

351–62 From Davenant's adaptation through to the early twentieth century this speech was always given to Prospero, rather than Miranda. Theobald suggested that it 'would be . . . an Indecency in her to reply to what Caliban last was speaking of'. If the assumption that Miranda should not in her character of virtuous, virginal girl speak these strong words is less than appealing to a modern readership, the speech nonetheless raises significant questions as to who actually undertook the linguistic educa-

tion of Caliban. Dymkowski suggests that the first production to give the speech to Miranda was Lena Ashwell's in 1925, and notes that many more recent productions have continued to ascribe it to Prospero.

352 print imprint.

353 capable of (1) susceptible to, (2) having the capacity for.

357 purposes intentions, ideas; but also used as a plural of discourse, conversation (*OED* Purpose *n* 4b).

358 words . . . known Miranda implies that things are not 'known' until they have words to express them. (See Introduction, p. 41.)

358 race Often explained as 'natural or inherited disposition' (*OED* sv *n*² 7 citing this line). Though the modern sense of the word, implying specific ethnicity, did not, according to the *OED*, enter the language until the nineteenth century, its general sense in the period – of a grouping by descent or common characteristics – does not exclude the possibility of its carrying something of its current resonance.

362 more than a prison Miranda presumably means the death penalty, which was the punishment for rape, though 'attempted rape' was not a felony – it was precisely a defence against the charge that a man 'did not carnally know her' (Pulton, pp. 133–4).

CALIBAN   You taught me language, and my profit on't
    Is, I know how to curse. The red plague rid you
    For learning me your language!

PROSPERO   Hag-seed, hence!   365
    Fetch us in fuel; and be quick, thou'rt best,
    To answer other business. Shrug'st thou, malice?
    If thou neglect'st, or dost unwillingly
    What I command, I'll rack thee with old cramps,
    Fill all thy bones with aches, make thee roar,   370
    That beasts shall tremble at thy din.

CALIBAN   No, pray thee.
    [*Aside*] I must obey; his art is of such power,
    It would control my dam's god Setebos,
    And make a vassal of him.

PROSPERO   So, slave, hence.

              Exit Caliban

 Enter FERDINAND, *and* ARIEL *invisible, playing and singing*

        SONG
ARIEL   Come unto these yellow sands,   375
    And then take hands.

---

371 pray] *Orgel;* 'pray F 372 SD *Capell; not in* F 374 So] F; Go *Tannenbaum conj.*

363–4 You . . . curse A line significant to the postcolonial reading of the play (see Introduction, p. 40 ff.), but it may also signify Caliban's abuse of the gift of speech – cf. James 3.7–10: 'But the tongue can no man tame; it is an unruly evil, full of deadly poison. Therewith bless we God . . . and therewith curse we men . . . Out of the same mouth proceedeth blessing and cursing. My brethren, these things ought not to be.'
363 profit Compare the 'profit' Prospero has done Miranda, 172 above.
364 curse In the strong sense of a witch's curse.
364 red plague Either the red sores from the plague, or else typhus, which causes red skin eruptions (see Hoeniger, pp. 216–17).
rid destroy.
365 learning teaching. The use of 'learn' for 'teach' was not a mark of uneducated speech in Early Modern English, as it is often taken to be today.
365 Hag-seed Offspring of a witch.
366 thou'rt best thou wert best; it would be in your best interests.
367 answer other business to respond to other tasks. At 316 Prospero had explicitly called Caliban

for 'other business', which he seems to have forgotten in the meantime.
369 rack torment, as 'on the rack'.
369 old cramps the pains of the aged.
370 aches Pronounced 'aitches'.
370–1 roar . . . beasts A parallel to the effect of the torments of Sycorax on Ariel (287–9).
373 Setebos A 'great devil of the Patagonians' found in Eden's translation of Antonio Pigafetta's account of Magellan's expedition. 'By worshipping [Setebos] . . . Sycorax is identified with the most remote, God-forsaken and degenerate of sixteenth-century Amerindian types' (Gillies, *Geography*, p. 142).
374 SD.2 *playing* The most likely instrument is the lute, so that Ariel could accompany his own singing, the courtly instrument which brings Ferdinand on stage contrasting with the lower-class pipe which later leads Caliban, Stephano and Trinculo to the mire.
375 yellow sands Though the phrase is used in the period for the sea-shore, plainly the dominant meaning here (as it is in *MND* 2.1.126 where Titania speaks of 'Neptune's yellow sands'), the adjective more commonly appears associated with

Curtsied when you have, and kissed,
The wild waves whist.
Foot it featly here and there,
And sweet sprites the burden bear.   380
    Hark, hark
    The watch-dogs bark
    Bow wow, bow wow.
[*Spirits dispersedly echo the burden 'Bow wow'*]
Hark, hark! I hear
The strain of strutting Chanticleer,   385
    Cry cock-a-diddle-dow.

---

377 kissed,] *Dryden;* kist F   **379–86** *This edn; for* F *see Textual Analysis*   **380** the burden bear] *Pope, following Dryden²;* beare / the burthen F   **381–3** Hark . . . wow] *This edn;* Harke, harke, bowgh wawgh: the watch-Dogges barke, / bowgh waugh F   **383** SD *Spirits . . . wow'*] *This edn; Burthen dispersedly / at 380* F

the sands of rivers. There may, therefore, be a recollection of Aeneas' first sight of the yellow sands of the Tiber in *Aeneid*, 7.30–2.

377–8 kissed . . . whist Punctuation is crucial here. If a comma is added after 'kissed' then the phrase 'the wild waves whist' is parenthetical, meaning 'the wild waves being, or becoming, silent (= whist)'. Almost all settings of the song make a musical break after 'kissed', implying that the beginning of the dance coincides with, or causes, the cessation of the storm. Orgel, following Brissenden, objected that a kiss was not part of the customary courtesies at the beginning of a dance, and he chooses therefore to follow F's punctuation, implying that the waves themselves are kissed into silence. Barbara Ravelhofer and Lieven Baert, however, inform me that Italian and French treatises normally prescribed a kissing of one's own hand before taking that of the partner and beginning to dance. The sequence is not quite that of the song, in that the kiss preceded the curtsy, but they note that there was an 'elastic understanding in dance sources of the period of what exactly constitutes a reverence or curtsy–kiss routine'. There are no historical grounds, therefore, for refusing the addition of a comma which produces an altogether simpler sense, and a lyric more easily set to music.

379 featly with graceful agility, nimbly (*OED* sv *adv* 2b).

380–6 And sweet sprites . . . dow This lyric as presented in F (see Textual Analysis, p. 247) is clearly unsatisfactory in a number of ways. The instruction 'burden dispersedly' seems, as at 403 below, to be placed early (perhaps because this was the only line with space on which it could be set), and though F's additional speech heading for Ariel at 384 suggests that the burden is sung by off-stage spirits, what words they sing and when is not obvious. The parallel injunction to 'hark' to both

dogs and cock might further suggest that the spirits should echo also the last line, and it is this potential parallelism which prompts the radical 'solution' offered here, in which it is assumed that scribe or compositor misplaced the first 'Bow wow', and omitted a second instruction for a refrain at the end. Other possible solutions are presented in the Textual Analysis, pp. 248–9. In this song, and in 'Full fathom five' which follows, at least two spirits probably echoed words from Ariel's song, either moving about the curtained music-room, or else positioned above, behind and possibly below the stage to give a stereophonic effect.

380 burden (1) Repeated words at the end of a song, or at the end of each stanza, (2) Bass part, as in *Ado* 3.4.44–5 where Margaret's invitation to 'Clap's into "Light o'Love": that goes without a burden', clearly implies the absence of a male bass line, (3) More specifically a drone or bagpipe-like bass part. Depending on how a composer chooses to set the song, any of these might be possible, though the first seems most likely to be the dominant meaning.

385 strain song, tune.

385 strutting Chanticleer Chanticleer is most often poetically used as a name for the cock as herald of the morning, but the epithet 'strutting' recalls the boastful Chanticleer of Aesop's *Fables*, and Chaucer's *Nun's Priest's Tale*. In setting the burdens of dogs and cocks a composer might either provide a light-hearted imitation of farmyard sounds, or introduce a disturbing undertone to the song which might look forward to the dogs which later chase Caliban and his fellow-conspirators at 4.1.249–50. The imitation of animal or bird noises in song and madrigal was not unusual in the period; amongst many other instances a madrigal in Robert Jones's 1607 collection opens: 'Cock-a-doodle doo, thus I begin.'

[*Spirits dispersedly echo the burden 'cock-a-diddle-dow'*]

FERDINAND Where should this music be? I'th'air, or th'earth?
It sounds no more; and sure it waits upon
Some god o'th'island. Sitting on a bank,
Weeping again the king my father's wrack,   390
This music crept by me upon the waters,
Allaying both their fury and my passion
With its sweet air. Thence I have followed it –
Or it hath drawn me rather; but 'tis gone.
No, it begins again.   395

SONG

ARIEL Full fathom five thy father lies,
Of his bones are coral made;
Those are pearls that were his eyes;
Nothing of him that doth fade,
But doth suffer a sea-change   400
Into something rich and strange.
Sea-nymphs hourly ring his knell.
Hark, now I hear them, ding dong bell.

[*Spirits dispersedly echo the burden 'ding dong bell'*]

FERDINAND The ditty does remember my drowned father.

---

386 SD *Orgel subst.; not in* F   403 SD *Spirits . . . bell'*] *This edn; Sea . . . knell.* /Burthen: ding dong. / *Harke . . . bell.* F

387 **music** The sound of the music itself, but also possibly the group of musicians who perform it.

388 **waits** attends.

390 **again** over and over, continually.

392–3 **Allaying . . . air** The belief that earthly music, by its imitation of celestial harmony, could order both nature and the human passions was a commonplace in the period. Especially, as Burton comments, 'it is a sovereign remedy against despair and melancholy, and will drive away the devil himself' (2.2.4).

392 **passion** suffering; intense feeling; but also passionate outburst or lament.

394 **drawn me rather** Ferdinand, the first of the many characters we see being manipulated by music, emphasises its power to secure an involuntary response.

396 **Full fathom five** At least 9 metres (30 feet) deep (a fathom is the nautical measure of the depth of the sea, about 1.8 metres (6 feet)). The song is literally untrue, but represents the situation as Ferdinand believes it to be.

398 **pearls** Though the dominant sense is of pearls as gems of great price, other associations cluster about them. Tears are frequently characterised as 'pearls', and the word might be used also of the pupils of the eyes, and of the eye-disease of cataracts (*OED* Pearl *n*[1] 4a, 4b). Furthermore, most pearls in the period were imported from the Spanish American colonies. (I am grateful to B. J. Sokol for this information.)

399 **fade** decay.

400 **sea-change** A Shakespearean locution which has entered the language as a conventional phrase.

402 **knell** The tolling of a bell as a person lay dying.

403 **ding dong** As in the previous song, F's placing of 'Burthen: ding dong' in the margin before the final line of the lyric seems wrong. Johnson's setting enables an imitative 'ding dong bell' in the lower parts to extend the ending of the song, as is indicated in its later three-part arrangement. (See Textual Analysis, p. 248, and Appendix 1, p. 252.)

404 **ditty** the song's words.

404 **remember** recall, commemorate.

                    This is no mortal business, nor no sound   405
                    That the earth owes. I hear it now above me.
PROSPERO [*To Miranda*] The fringèd curtains of thine eye advance,
                    And say what thou seest yond.
MIRANDA   What is't? A spirit?
                    Lord, how it looks about! Believe me, sir,
                    It carries a brave form. But 'tis a spirit.   410
PROSPERO No, wench, it eats, and sleeps, and hath such senses
                    As we have, such. This gallant which thou seest
                    Was in the wrack; and but he's something stained
                    With grief – that's beauty's canker – thou might'st call him
                    A goodly person. He hath lost his fellows,   415
                    And strays about to find 'em.
MIRANDA   I might call him
                    A thing divine, for nothing natural
                    I ever saw so noble.
PROSPERO [*Aside*]   It goes on, I see,
                    As my soul prompts it. [*To Ariel*] Spirit, fine spirit, I'll free
                                   thee
                    Within two days for this.
FERDINAND [*Seeing Miranda*]   Most sure the goddess   420
                    On whom these airs attend. Vouchsafe my prayer
                    May know if you remain upon this island,
                    And that you will some good instruction give
                    How I may bear me here. My prime request,
                    Which I do last pronounce, is – O you wonder –   425

---

407 SD *Oxford; not in* F   408 What is't? A] *Capell;* What is't a F*;* What, is't a *Riv.;* What is't, a *Ard3*   418 SD *Pope; not in* F   419 SD *Orgel; not in* F   420 SD *Rann; not in* F

406 **owes** owns.
406 **above me** i.e. from the music-room above the stage.
407 **fringèd . . . eye** eyelids. Miranda's attention must have been focused elsewhere for Prospero's injunction to be necessary. The rhetorical periphrasis establishes that 'this will be a ritual, ceremonial first meeting' (Barton). Compare *Per.* 3.2.98–100 for a similar conceit in a ritual context.
407 **advance** raise, lift up.
408 **What . . . spirit** The line might, alternatively, be punctuated 'What? Is't a spirit?'
410 **brave** handsome, splendid.
412 **gallant** Fine fellow, ladies' man, often 'playful or semi ironical in tone' (*OED* sv *n* 2).
413 **but** except that.
414 **canker** 'Anything that frets, corrodes, cor-

rupts, or consumes slowly and secretly' (*OED* sv *n* 6); hence Ferdinand's beauty is marred by his weeping.
420 **goddess** Continuing the thought of 388–9. To mistake a heroine for a goddess is a commonplace of romance, but here there is specific recall of Aeneas' phrase on meeting with his mother Venus, disguised as a huntress: 'O dea certe' (*Aeneid,* 1.128).
421 **airs** songs.
421 **Vouchsafe** Grant, graciously permit (that).
422 **remain** live, dwell.
424 **bear me** conduct myself.
424 **prime** most important.
425 **wonder** Without knowing it, Ferdinand plays on the Latin derivation of Miranda's name from the verb *miror*: I wonder.

If you be maid, or no?

MIRANDA   No wonder, sir,
  But certainly a maid.

FERDINAND   My language? Heavens!
  I am the best of them that speak this speech,
  Were I but where 'tis spoken.

PROSPERO   How the best?
  What wert thou if the King of Naples heard thee?   430

FERDINAND A single thing, as I am now, that wonders
  To hear thee speak of Naples. He does hear me,
  And that he does, I weep. Myself am Naples,
  Who, with mine eyes, ne'er since at ebb, beheld
  The king my father wracked.

MIRANDA   Alack, for mercy!   435

FERDINAND Yes, faith, and all his lords, the Duke of Milan
  And his brave son being twain.

PROSPERO [*Aside*]   The Duke of Milan
  And his more braver daughter could control thee
  If now 'twere fit to do't. At the first sight
  They have changed eyes. [*To Ariel*] Delicate Ariel,   440
  I'll set thee free for this! [*To Ferdinand*] A word, good sir;

---

429 How the best?] *This edn;* How? The best? F; How! The best? *Collier*   434 ne'er] *Pope; neuer* F   437 SD *Dyce; not in* F   440 SD *Rann; not in* F   441 SD *Collier; not in* F

426 maid i.e. human, not divine (and see 446–7 n., below).

427 language Retaining F's question mark suggests a reaction of puzzlement rather than simply astonishment. It can be played as a brief comic moment, but, taken together with the earlier discussion of Caliban's learning of language and with Stephano's reaction to Caliban in 2.2.60–1, it is part of a significant thematic strand in the play.

429 How the best F's 'How? The best?' is possible – a surprised exclamation preceding the question – but 'In what way can you be the best?' is perhaps more pointed.

431 single thing solitary, without family.

432 He does hear me Because Ferdinand believes himself to be the king he therefore 'hears' himself.

434 ne'er . . . ebb i.e. the tide of tears has never ebbed.

434 ne'er The elision is for the metre.

437 brave son A 'ghost' character that it would

seem Shakespeare either simply forgot, or else cut for practical reasons of casting. (See Appendix 3, p. 261.)

438 braver Applied to Miranda the term suggests 'excellent worthiness', contrasting with the previous line where it implies 'valiant' or merely 'splendid'.

control contradict, rebuke.

439 At the first sight Compare *AYLI* 3.5.81–2: 'I find thy saw of might, "Who ever lov'd that lov'd not at first sight"', quoting Marlowe's *Hero and Leander*. It is a proverb well-enough established in the world of the love sonnet from Petrarch onwards for Sidney to contradict it playfully in *Astrophil and Stella*, 2: 'Not at first sight, nor with a dribbed shot / Love gave the wound.'

440 changed eyes interchanged looks, fallen in love. That love enters in at the eye was a commonplace of love theory and love poetry; cf. Donne, 'The Ecstasy', lines 7–8: 'Our eye-beams twisted, and did thread / Our eyes, upon one double string.'

440 Delicate Compare 272 n. above.

             I fear you have done yourself some wrong; a word.
MIRANDA [*Aside*] Why speaks my father so ungently? This
             Is the third man that e'er I saw; the first
             That e'er I sighed for. Pity move my father   445
             To be inclined my way.
FERDINAND   O, if a virgin,
             And your affection not gone forth, I'll make you
             The Queen of Naples.
PROSPERO   Soft, sir, one word more.
             [*Aside*] They are both in either's powers; but this swift
                 business
             I must uneasy make, lest too light winning   450
             Make the prize light. [*To Ferdinand*] One word more. I
                 charge thee
             That thou attend me! Thou dost here usurp
             The name thou ow'st not, and hast put thyself
             Upon this island as a spy, to win it
             From me, the lord on't.
FERDINAND   No, as I am a man.   455
MIRANDA There's nothing ill can dwell in such a temple.
             If the ill spirit have so fair a house,
             Good things will strive to dwell with't.
PROSPERO [*To Ferdinand*]   Follow me.
             [*To Miranda*] Speak not you for him: he's a traitor.
             [*To Ferdinand*] Come!

---

442 you have] F; you've *Pope* 443 SD *Capell; not in* F 449 SD *Aside*] *Johnson; not in* F 451 SD *Collier; not in* F
458 SD *Johnson; not in* F 459 SD *To Miranda*] *Johnson; not in* F 459 SD *To Ferdinand*] *Folger; not in* F

442 you have Probably should be elided to 'you've' for the metre.

442 done . . . wrong i.e. in claiming to be King of Naples; a politely ironic way of suggesting that Ferdinand is mistaken.

442 a word Prospero attempts to command Ferdinand's attention and take him aside, but his eyes remain fixed upon Miranda, and he responds to the fact of her speaking, though presumably he does not hear her words, as she, it seems, does not hear his response.

443 SD See Introduction, p. 72 n. 3.

444 third man Miranda later (3.1.51–3) excludes Caliban from her list of male acquaintance.

446–7 if a virgin . . . forth if you are unmarried, and have not bestowed your love elsewhere. Ferdinand is scrupulous and mannerly in paying court to Miranda, rather than (primarily, at least)

inquisitive about her chastity.

450 uneasy difficult.

450–1 light . . . light A quibble; the first 'light' means 'easy', the second 'of little value' with a suggestion of sexual lightness.

453 ow'st ownest.

456 Alluding to the biblical notion of the body as a temple of the holy spirit (1 Corinthians 6.19), and to the conventional neo-platonic view that beauty of outward appearance signified a beautiful spirit within.

457–8 Miranda counters the recognition that not all beautiful people are virtuous by suggesting that even if the devil ('ill spirit') tries to inhabit such a body, good will be attracted to it and, by implication, drive evil out.

459 traitor Either to Prospero or to the King of Naples, or both.

I'll manacle thy neck and feet together;   460
Sea water shalt thou drink; thy food shall be
The fresh-brook mussels, withered roots, and husks
Wherein the acorn cradled. Follow.

FERDINAND   No!
I will resist such entertainment, till
Mine enemy has more power.

He draws, and is charmed from moving

MIRANDA   O dear father,   465
Make not too rash a trial of him, for
He's gentle, and not fearful.

PROSPERO [*To Miranda*]   What, I say,
My foot my tutor? [*To Ferdinand*] Put thy sword up, traitor,
Who mak'st a show, but dar'st not strike, thy conscience
Is so possessed with guilt. Come from thy ward,   470
For I can here disarm thee with this stick,
And make thy weapon drop.

MIRANDA [*Kneeling*]   Beseech you, father!

PROSPERO Hence! Hang not on my garments.

MIRANDA   Sir, have pity;
I'll be his surety.

PROSPERO   Silence! One word more
Shall make me chide thee, if not hate thee. What,   475
An advocate for an impostor? Hush!
Thou think'st there is no more such shapes as he,
Having seen but him and Caliban. Foolish wench,
To th'most of men this is a Caliban,
And they to him are angels.

MIRANDA   My affections   480

---

467 SD *This edn; not in* F   468 SD *This edn; not in* F   469 mak'st] F; makes F2   472 SD *This edn; not in* F   477 is] F; are
Rowe

462 **fresh-brook mussels** They are inedible.
OED cites a 1603 source: 'the Ryver muskles are not
for meate' (Mussel *n* 1).

464 **entertainment** treatment, including the
diet he is threatened with.

466 **rash** hasty, impetuous.

467 **not fearful** (1) not a cause of fear, because
he is of gentle (or gentlemanly) disposition, (2) not
afraid, because he is noble.

468 **foot . . . tutor** Prospero rebukes Miranda
for her breach of hierarchy in attempting to tell her

father what to do, using a proverbial image of rebellion (cf. Tilley, 'Do not make the foot the head'
(F562)). In the *Homily against Disobedience and
Wilful Rebellion* (1570), for subjects to judge princes
would be 'as though the foot must judge of the
head'.

463 **Put . . . up** Sheathe your sword.

470 **Come . . . ward** Give up your defensive
posture, drop your sword.

479 **To** Compared to.

Are then most humble. I have no ambition
To see a goodlier man.
PROSPERO [*To Ferdinand*]   Come on, obey.
Thy nerves are in their infancy again
And have no vigour in them.
FERDINAND   So they are.
My spirits, as in a dream, are all bound up.   485
My father's loss, the weakness which I feel,
The wrack of all my friends, nor this man's threats,
To whom I am subdued, are but light to me,
Might I but through my prison once a day
Behold this maid. All corners else o'th'earth   490
Let liberty make use of; space enough
Have I in such a prison.
PROSPERO [*Aside*]   It works. [*To Ferdinand*] Come on!
[*To Ariel*] Thou hast done well, fine Ariel. [*To Ferdinand*]
Follow me.
[*To Ariel*] Hark what thou else shalt do me.
MIRANDA [*To Ferdinand*]   Be of comfort;
My father's of a better nature, sir,   495

---

482 SD *Johnson; not in* F   487 nor] F; *and* Rowe; *or* Capell   492 SD *Aside*] Capell; *not in* F   492 SD *To Ferdinand*] Collier;
not in F   493 SD *To Ariel*] Theobald; *not in* F   493 SD *To Ferdinand*] Cam.; *To Ferdinand and Miranda* / Steevens; *not in* F
494 SD *To Ariel*] Steevens; *not in* F

482 SD Though the whole of this speech seems most obviously to be addressed to Ferdinand, Dymkowski notes that in some productions 'Come on, obey' is addressed to Miranda before Prospero turns to Ferdinand.

483 **nerves** An imprecise term in Renaissance anatomy, probably here implying sinews, or that which controls movement.

485 **spirits** 'Subtle, highly-refined substances or fluids formerly supposed to permeate the blood and chief organs of the body' (*OED* Spirit *n* 16a). The animal, vital and natural spirits, deriving from the brain, heart and liver, were carried respectively through the body by the sinews (nerves), arteries and veins. The meaning here, as elsewhere in the play, is primarily physiological, and 'psychological' as a consequence of the bodily effect.

487 **nor** Though this introduces a syntactical ambiguity into the sentence, the clear implication is that neither his misfortunes nor Prospero's threats would be unbearable if he could only see Miranda.

489–90 **Might I . . . Behold** Echoing the plight of Palamon and Arcite in Chaucer's *Knight's Tale*, who saw Emilie through the window of their prison, and, in particular, Arcite's complaint when he has been released that he would rather be back in prison, since 'Thanne hadde I been in blisse, and nat in wo. Oonly the sighte of hire whom that I serve . . . Wold han suffised right ynough for me' (lines 1231–3). (Shakespeare, with Fletcher, dramatised the *Tale* in *Two Noble Kinsmen*.)

490–2 **All corners . . . prison** Freedom may wander through the whole world, but the enclosed space of the prison cell is sufficient for me.

492 **It works** Prospero refers to his intent to make Miranda valuable because hard to obtain (449–51), as well as continuing the self-congratulation of 418–19.

492–4 SDS This is not the only possible way of sorting out Prospero's speech – he might address the 'Follow me' to Ariel, or to Miranda, though the repetition of his coercion of Ferdinand seems the most obvious reading.

494 **Hark . . . me** Though Prospero is presumably sending Ariel on his errand to the lords, the precise commands he utters are deliberately concealed from the audience. He instructs Ariel during Miranda's speech.

Than he appears by speech. This is unwonted
Which now came from him.
PROSPERO [*To Ariel*]   Thou shalt be as free
As mountain winds; but then exactly do
All points of my command.
ARIEL   To th'syllable.
PROSPERO [*To Ferdinand*] Come follow. [*To Miranda*] Speak not for
him.   500

                                                         Exeunt

2.1 *Enter* ALONSO, SEBASTIAN, ANTONIO, GONZALO, ADRIAN,
FRANCISCO *and others*

GONZALO Beseech you, sir, be merry. You have cause –
So have we all – of joy; for our escape
Is much beyond our loss. Our hint of woe
Is common; every day some sailor's wife,
The masters of some merchant, and the merchant   5
Have just our theme of woe. But for the miracle –
I mean our preservation – few in millions
Can speak like us. Then wisely, good sir, weigh
Our sorrow with our comfort.
ALONSO   Prithee, peace.
SEBASTIAN [*Apart to Antonio*] He receives comfort like cold   10
porridge.

---

497 SD *Hanmer; not in* F   500 SD *To Ferdinand*] *Johnson; not in* F   500 Come follow] F; Come, follow *Johnson*   500 SD *To
Miranda*] *Johnson; not in* F   Act 2, Scene 1   2.1] *Actus Secundus. Scœna Prima* F   0 SD. 2 *and others*] F; *om. Oxford*   5
masters] F; master *Johnson*   6 of woe] *om. Steevens conj.*   10 SD *Apart to Antonio*] *This edn; Aside to Antonio / Wilson; To
Antonio / Oxford; not in* F

496 by Grey's conjecture 'by's' clarifies the sense,
though is not necessary to it.
496 unwonted unusual.
497–8 free . . . winds A commonplace expression; cf. *Cor.* 1.9.88–9: 'he should / Be free as is the
wind'.

Act 2, Scene 1
0 SD.2 *and others* Some editors remove this 'permissive' direction, by analogy with 5.1.57 where
no extras are called for, but at this point the actors
who played the Master and Boatswain, at the least,
would be available to fill out the retinue. (See
Appendix 3, pp. 257–61.)
2–3 escape . . . loss the good fortune of our
escape far outweighs the extent of our loss.
3 hint occasion.

5 The officers of a merchant ship and the merchant who owns it or its cargo. 'Master' is ambiguous in that it could mean a captain of the ship (as
in 1.1) or else the owner of it. 'Merchant' could
signify either the ship itself or a trader. Whilst it is
just possible that the second 'merchant' also refers
to the vessel, which is thereby personified as suffering in a shipwreck, the play on the two meanings
is much more likely.
6 theme of woe Kermode remarks that this is
an odd repetition of 3, noting Steevens's suggestion
that the hypermetrical 'of woe' in this line could be
a compositorial addition.
8–9 weigh . . . comfort balance our misfortune
against the comfort of having survived.
10 SD Throughout much of the first part of this
scene Antonio and Sebastian engage in conversa-

ANTONIO [*Apart to Sebastian*] The visitor will not give him o'er so.

SEBASTIAN Look, he's winding up the watch of his wit,
     By and by it will strike.

GONZALO [*To Alonso*] Sir, –   15

SEBASTIAN One: tell.

GONZALO   When every grief is entertained
          That's offered, comes to the entertainer –

SEBASTIAN A dollar.

GONZALO Dolour comes to him indeed; you have spoken truer than you
     purposed.   20

SEBASTIAN You have taken it wiselier than I meant you should.

GONZALO Therefore, my lord –

ANTONIO Fie, what a spendthrift is he of his tongue.

ALONSO I prithee, spare.

GONZALO Well, I have done. But yet –   25

SEBASTIAN He will be talking.

---

12 SD *Apart to Sebastian*] *This edn; Aside to Sebastian / Wilson; To Sebastian / Oxford; not in* F   13–14 *As* F; *as prose Pope*
15 SD *Oxford; not in* F   16 One] F; *On* F2   16–17 *As Pope;* When . . . entertaind, / That's . . . entertainer F; When . . .
offer'd, / Comes . . . entertainer *Kermode*

tion which comments on the actions and words of others on stage. The other characters at times seem not to hear them, or else make every effort to ignore them, only occasionally responding directly to their words. This suggests that Sebastian and Antonio stand to one side of the main group, which surrounds and attempts to comfort Alonso. On the problems of staging this scene, see Introduction, p. 55.

11 **porridge** pottage, soup of vegetables or meat. Sebastian puns on 'peace' interpreting it as 'pease' (used as both singular and plural of 'pea') from which porridge could be made. The first part of this scene is characterised by Sebastian and Antonio's relentless (and often feeble) punning. Pope argued that the bulk of this scene was made up of 'very impertinent stuff' which 'seems to have been interpolated (perhaps by the Players)'. But Peacham commented: 'For as much as this figure serveth to wittie allusions, and often to pleasant occasions of mirth: it may fall easily into excesse or untimely use, which follie and boldnesse do oft commit' (p. 57). The 'untimeliness' and 'excess' of Antonio and Sebastian's punning is therefore an indication of their characters. There is a purposeful contrast between their rhetoric here and in the later part of the scene.

12 Gonzalo is compared to a parish visitor of the sick, who will not give up attempting to give comfort so easily.

14 **strike** 'Striking or "repeating" watches were invented about the year 1510' (Kermode).

16 **One: tell** 'He has struck one; keep count.' T. W. Craik objects that though Sebastian 'counts' Gonzalo's 'Sir' as the first stroke of the watch, 'there are no further obvious strokes and no indication that Antonio counts any, so "Tell", in dramatic terms leads nowhere'. He suggests that 'Tell' was a stage direction in the imperative mood to explain Sebastian's 'One', mistakenly incorporated into the text by Crane (*N&Q*, 242 (1997), 514).

16–17 **When every . . . offered** If a person admits every cause of grief that comes his way.

17 **entertainer** Gonzalo means 'he who entertains grief'; Sebastian takes it as 'one who entertains, a performer' and offers payment.

18–20 **A dollar . . . purposed.** The alternation between prose and verse in this scene is erratic. It would, however, be possible to arrange this exchange as verse. (See Textual Analysis, p. 236.)

18 **dollar** Literally either a German or a Spanish silver coin, here used by Italians for the purposes of the pun.

19 **Dolour** Grief, sadness.

23 **spendthrift** one who employs or uses something lavishly or profusely; a prodigal . . . waster of something (*OED* sv *n* 2, citing this passage).

24 'I pray you, stop.' Alonso either addresses Gonzalo specifically, or else reacts more generally to the verbal sparring between the lords.

ANTONIO Which, of he or Adrian, for a good wager, first begins to
    crow?

SEBASTIAN The old cock.

ANTONIO The cockerel.   30

SEBASTIAN Done. The wager?

ANTONIO A laughter.

SEBASTIAN A match!

ADRIAN Though this island seem to be desert –

ANTONIO Ha, ha, ha!   35

SEBASTIAN So: you're paid.

ADRIAN Uninhabitable, and almost inaccessible –

SEBASTIAN Yet –

ADRIAN Yet –

ANTONIO He could not miss't.   40

ADRIAN It   must   needs   be   of   subtle,   tender   and   delicate
    temperance.

ANTONIO Temperance was a delicate wench.

SEBASTIAN Ay, and a subtle, as he most learnedly delivered.

ADRIAN The air breathes upon us here most sweetly.   45

SEBASTIAN As if it had lungs, and rotten ones.

ANTONIO Or as 'twere perfumed by a fen.

GONZALO Here is everything advantageous to life.

ANTONIO True, save means to live.

SEBASTIAN Of that there's none, or little.   50

---

35 SH ANTONIO] *Grant White; Seb.* F   36 SH SEBASTIAN] *Grant White; Ant.* F

27 good wager good subject for a bet (*OED* Wager *n* 4).

29–30 old cock . . . cockerel Proverbial: 'the young cock crows as he the old hears' (Tilley C491). Adrian is the young cock who simply imitates Gonzalo.

31 Agreed. What's the prize? (*OED* Wager *n* 2b).

32 laughter Alluding to the proverb, 'He laughs that wins' (Tilley L93). Some commentators have pointed out that a 'laughter' is also a clutch of eggs (*OED* sv *n²* 2), and suggested a strained continuation of the 'cock . . . cockerel' exchange.

34 desert uninhabited.

35–6 F gives 35 to Sebastian, 36 to Antonio, but as Adrian speaks first, Antonio wins the bet; and since laughter is the prize, most editors have transposed the speeches.

36 you're paid i.e. by your laughter you have claimed the prize.

40 'He was bound to say that.'

41 subtle rarefied (*OED* sv *adj* 1).

42 temperance mildness of weather or climate (*OED* sv *n* 4, citing this passage). John Gillies notes that the temperateness of the climate of Virginia was frequently used in propaganda for the colonial enterprise. (Gillies, 'Masque', pp. 678–70). Montaigne's Essay, 'Of the Cannibals', from which some later details of this scene are taken, states: 'they live in a country of so exceeding pleasant and temperate situation' (vol. 1, no. 30).

43 Antonio takes 'Temperance' as a name (it was so used in the period) and uses 'delicate' ironically to suggest a woman given to pleasure.

44 subtle Sebastian continues the quibbling by implying 'crafty, cunning, sly' (*OED* sv *adj* 10), and thereby mocking Adrian's 'subtle' learning.

47 fen marshland; cf. 2.2.1–2 n. for the association with disease.

49 save except.

GONZALO How lush and lusty the grass looks! How green!

ANTONIO The ground indeed is tawny.

SEBASTIAN With an eye of green in't.

ANTONIO He misses not much.

SEBASTIAN No, he doth but mistake the truth totally.   55

GONZALO But the rarity of it is, which is indeed almost beyond
    credit –

SEBASTIAN As many vouched rarities are.

GONZALO That our garments being, as they were, drenched in the sea,
    hold notwithstanding their freshness and glosses, being rather new-   60
    dyed than stained with salt water.

ANTONIO If but one of his pockets could speak, would it not say he
    lies?

SEBASTIAN Ay, or very falsely pocket up his report.

GONZALO Methinks our garments are now as fresh as when we put   65
    them on first in Afric, at the marriage of the king's fair daughter
    Claribel to the King of Tunis.

SEBASTIAN 'Twas a sweet marriage, and we prosper well in our
    return.

ADRIAN Tunis was never graced before with such a paragon to their   70
    queen.

GONZALO Not since widow Dido's time.

---

60 glosses] F; gloss *Dyce;* gloss, *as Wilson*

---

51 lush tender. *OED* (sv *adj* a¹ 2a) gives the sense 'luxuriant' specifically to this passage, and to subsequent uses deriving from it. Orgel suggests that this is anachronistic.

51 lusty of vigorous growth (*OED* sv *adj* 5a).

52 tawny The main point of the exchange is to emphasise that what characters 'see' reflects upon themselves rather than upon objective reality, yet there might be reference to the actual stage, strewn with green rushes (at the Globe), or covered with a green cloth (at Blackfriars or at court).

53 eye 'slight shade, tinge' (*OED* sv *n*¹ 9a), or else 'spot' (*OED* sv *n*¹ 12).

54 (1) He is only slightly in error (spoken ironically), (2) He sees even the smallest token of greenness.

55 he doth . . . totally he gets it completely wrong. Sebastian picks up the first implication of Antonio's speech and exaggerates Gonzalo's error further.

56 rarity exceptional nature.

57 credit belief.

58 vouched rarities acknowledged, accepted strange phenomena.

60 glosses lustre. Another case where scribe or compositor may have added a final 's'.

60–1 being . . . water Gonzalo's comment confirms, and is confirmed by, Ariel's remark at 1.2.218–19.

62–3 Antonio suggests that the pockets of Gonzalo's garments would contradict the evidence of outward appearance, having retained water inside them.

64 very falsely . . . report If the pocket were not to speak it would then be falsely concealing Gonzalo's error. 'Pocket up' means conceal, suppress or ignore, particularly in the context of failing to respond to an insult or injury (see Tilley 170), and 'report' refers to Gonzalo's narrative.

65 Methinks It seems to me.

68 we prosper well Sebastian's ironic comment is the first example of the resentment that boils over at 118 below.

72–4 widow Dido Dido was the widow of Sychaeus, and fled from Tyre after his murder by her brother Pygmalion, arriving finally in Africa to found the city of Carthage. Gonzalo's characterisa-

ANTONIO Widow? A pox o'that! How came that 'widow' in? Widow
  Dido!

SEBASTIAN What if he had said 'widower Aeneas' too?　75

ANTONIO Good Lord, how you take it!

ADRIAN [*To Gonzalo*] Widow Dido, said you? You make me study of
  that. She was of Carthage, not of Tunis.

GONZALO This Tunis, sir, was Carthage.

ADRIAN Carthage?　80

GONZALO I assure you, Carthage.

ANTONIO His word is more than the miraculous harp.

SEBASTIAN He hath raised the wall, and houses too.

ANTONIO What impossible matter will he make easy next?

SEBASTIAN I think he will carry this island home in his pocket, and give　85
  it his son for an apple.

---

73 'widow'] *This edn; punctuation not in* F　76 SH ANTONIO] *This edn (Craik conj.); not in* F　77 SD *To Gonzalo*]
Bevington; not in F

tion of her is, therefore, accurate. As Orgel pointed
out, the subsequent exchange turns on the fact that
there were two alternative myths of the story of
Dido, in the older of which she finally committed
suicide to avoid a forced marriage, and was a heroic
image of chastity. But Antonio and Sebastian take
Gonzalo's description of her as a 'widow' as an
attempt to gloss over her illicit relationship with
Aeneas as narrated in Virgil's *Aeneid*, the more
famous story of her fate. The historical truth of
Virgil's account was often questioned in the period
– Sandys, for example, writes 'this was meerely a
fiction of Virgil's . . . for it is more than probable
that Dido arrived in Africa, two hundred and eighty
nine yeares after the destruction of Troy' (p. 476).
It is possible that Antonio bestows an obscene
meaning on the name in 74 – 'dido' was a term both
for the male or female sexual parts and for a dildo
(Williams, 'dido').

　73 'widow' To punctuate as here emphasises that
Antonio is questioning Gonzalo's characterisation
of her, rather than denying the parallel between
Dido and Claribel.

　75 'widower Aeneas' This characterisation is,
again, accurate, in that Aeneas' wife Creusa had
died in the sack of Troy. Sebastian extends the
ridicule of Gonzalo by suggesting how inappropriate the title is to the man who abandoned Dido, and
may also be making a vulgar pun on 'any ass' or 'any
arse'. (See Dekker and Middleton's *The Roaring
Girl*, 3.2.59–60: 'though Aeneas made an ass of
Dido, I will die to thee', for an analogous playing
with these names.)

　76 how you take it T. W. Craik's suggestion to

me that, since this remark appears on a separate line
in F, the compositor may have omitted a speech
heading assigning it to Antonio, is very persuasive.
It could be read either as an approving comment on
Sebastian's sarcastic question, as mock-priggish
comment on obscene wordplay, or even as further
continuation of it, since 'take' could mean 'receive
sexually' (Williams, 'take'). (See Textual Analysis,
p. 237).

　77 make me study give me to think.

　78 Carthage . . . Tunis After the sack of
Carthage, the city of Tunis, some 14.5 or 16km (9
or 10 miles) distant from its site, took over its political and mercantile functions. The two places were
elided in Renaissance cartographic and political
writing, so that 'the debate was apparently not as
clear-cut as Sebastian and Adrian suggest' (Brotton,
p. 40, n. 22). John Gillies notes: 'Gonzalo's point is
not that modern Tunis occupies the same piece of
land as ancient Carthage . . . modern Tunis reca-
pitulates ancient Carthage in moral–geographical
terms' (Gillies, *Geography*, p. 48). He suggests that
this encourages an ironic juxtaposition of Claribel's
marriage to the ill-starred relationship of Dido and
Aeneas. The laboriousness and obscurity of lines
70–81 has frequently led to their being cut in production. (See Introduction, p. 55.)

　82–3 Gonzalo's words are more powerful than
the mythical harp of Amphion, in that his music
summoned the stones to build only the walls of
Thebes, not the whole city which Gonzalo's words
have constructed.

　85–8 carry . . . islands Commentators cite the
analogous passage in *Ant.* 5.2.91–2: 'Realms and

ANTONIO And sowing the kernels of it in the sea, bring forth more
islands.

GONZALO Ay.

ANTONIO Why, in good time.   90

GONZALO [*To Alonso*] Sir, we were talking, that our garments seem
now as fresh as when we were at Tunis at the marriage of your
daughter, who is now queen.

ANTONIO And the rarest that e'er came there.

SEBASTIAN Bate, I beseech you, widow Dido.   95

ANTONIO O widow Dido? Ay, widow Dido.

GONZALO Is not, sir, my doublet as fresh as the first day I wore it – I
mean, in a sort –

ANTONIO That sort was well fished for.

GONZALO – when I wore it at your daughter's marriage?   100

ALONSO You cram these words into mine ears, against
The stomach of my sense: would I had never
Married my daughter there. For coming thence
My son is lost, and, in my rate, she too,
Who is so far from Italy removed   105
I ne'er again shall see her. O thou mine heir
Of Naples and of Milan, what strange fish
Hath made his meal on thee?

FRANCISCO   Sir, he may live.

89 Ay] *Rowe;* Ay? *Capell;* I F   91 SD *Orgel; not in* F   97 sir, my doublet] F; my doublet, Sir F2   97–8 wore it . . . sort –]
This edn; wore it? I mean in a sort. F   108 SH FRANCISCO] F; GONZALO *Rann conj.*

islands were / As plates dropped from his pocket',
but where that image magnifies Antony's status this
quasi-mythological picture is intended to ridicule
Gonzalo.

89 Ay F's 'I' has almost always been modernised
as 'Ay', and taken as Gonzalo's further confirmation
of his assertion in line 81. There is, however, a
relatively long gap between his speeches, and
Johnson's suggestion that Gonzalo is about to begin
a new sentence, 'I', only to be again interrupted, is
a theatrically viable alternative reading.

90 in good time at last. Antonio's ironic
response echoes Sebastian's first derisory comment
at 10–11 on Gonzalo's ponderousness.

94 Tannenbaum gave this line to Adrian,
presumably feeling that it does not accord well
with Antonio's habitually dismissive attitude. But
Antonio is ironically recalling Adrian's claim in
70–1.

95 Bate Except.

97–100 F's question mark after 'wore it' and full
stop after 'sort' break up what can perhaps better

be taken as a continuous sentence, restarted firmly
by Gonzalo after Antonio's interruption.

97 doublet close-fitting jacket.

98 in a sort after a fashion, comparatively.

99 'He did well to add that qualification', or 'He
struggled to dredge up that qualification.' These are
the most straightforward readings, continuing
Antonio's scepticism.

101–2 cram . . . sense The image is of being
force-fed with words against his will. 'Stomach' can
mean 'appetite' or 'relish' (*OED* Stomach *n* 5a, b)
but also 'disposition, state of feeling' (*OED* sv *n* 7a).

104 rate opinion, judgement. Alonso's sense
that his daughter, like his son, is effectively lost,
prepares the ground for Antonio's persuasion of
Sebastian in 242–50 below.

106–7 heir . . . Milan This suggests that
Antonio gained Alonso's support by ceding the title
to Alonso's heirs.

108–17 This is Francisco's only significant
speech, and some editors have conjectured that it
should be given to Gonzalo, on the grounds that

> I saw him beat the surges under him,
> And ride upon their backs; he trod the water   110
> Whose enmity he flung aside, and breasted
> The surge most swol'n that met him. His bold head
> 'Bove the contentious waves he kept, and oared
> Himself with his good arms in lusty stroke
> To th'shore, that o'er his wave-worn basis bowed,   115
> As stooping to relieve him. I not doubt
> He came alive to land.

ALONSO   No, no, he's gone.

SEBASTIAN Sir, you may thank yourself for this great loss,
> That would not bless our Europe with your daughter,
> But rather lose her to an African,   120
> Where she, at least, is banished from your eye,
> Who hath cause to wet the grief on't.

ALONSO   Prithee, peace.

SEBASTIAN You were kneeled to and impòrtuned otherwise
> By all of us; and the fair soul herself
> Weighed between loathness and obedience, at   125
> Which end o'th'beam should bow. We have lost your son,

---

114 stroke] F; strokes F4   120 lose] Rowe; loose F   126 o'th'beam] F; the beam *Rowe*   126 should bow] F; she'd bow *Capell*   126 We have] F; We've *Pope*

---

these are the only words that could explain Antonio's comment at 227–34 below. Donna Hamilton suggests that Shakespeare draws upon *Aeneid*, 2.203–8 (*Virgil and 'The Tempest'*, 1990, pp. 22–3, see Appendix 2 and Introduction, pp. 74–5).

113 contentious quarrelsome (continuing the idea of the sea's 'enmity').

114 lusty strong, powerful.

115–16 shore . . . relieve him The waves have eroded the bottom of the cliffs so that the land appears to bend down towards him to make landfall easier. The conceit may derive from *Aeneid*, 1.166, describing the haven where Aeneas landed: *fronte sub adversa scopulis pendentibus antrum* ('Under the brow of the fronting cliff is a cave of hanging rock').

116 I not doubt I doubt not (Abbott 305).

120 rather . . . African In Sebastian's speech the opposition between Europe and Africa moves Claribel from the literary connection with Dido into the world of current politics, where Tunis was part of the Ottoman Empire, so that her marriage might be seen as a politically dangerous mismatch of both race and religion. (Nabil Matar observes, however, that English–Muslim marriages were 'possible if not desirable' in the period. *Turks, Moors and Englishmen in the Age of Discovery*, 1999, p. 40.)

120 lose A case where a modernised spelling has to choose between alternatives: F's 'loose' was the normal contemporary spelling for 'lose', but 'loose' or 'release' is also possible, in that Alonso as father gives up his authority over his daughter as he hands her to her husband.

121 at least at the least.

122 Who hath cause . . . grief on't 'Who' may refer to Alonso, who has good cause to weep at the situation, but it could also refer specifically to his eye, which has reason to express grief through tears.

123 impòrtuned begged – stressed on the second syllable.

125–6 Weighed . . . bow 'Weigh' is used in the sense 'to balance in the mind with a view to choice or preference' (*OED* Weigh *v*¹ 12a), or simply 'ponder, consider' (*OED v*¹ 14b). Claribel hesitated between her distaste for her proposed husband and her duty to her father, considering which should weigh more heavily with her, and thus 'bow' or bend one side of the scales of her judgement, before finally accepting the marriage. (On the significance of her marriage, and the contrast with Miranda's situation see Introduction, pp. 70–1.)

126 We have Should probably be elided to 'We've' for the metre, as Pope suggested.

        I fear for ever. Milan and Naples have
        More widows in them of this business' making
        Than we bring men to comfort them. The fault's
        Your own.
ALONSO   So is the dearest of the loss.   130
GONZALO   My lord Sebastian,
        The truth you speak doth lack some gentleness,
        And time to speak it in; you rub the sore,
        When you should bring the plaster.
SEBASTIAN   Very well.
ANTONIO   And most chirurgeonly.   135
GONZALO   [*To Alonso*] It is foul weather in us all, good sir,
        When you are cloudy.
SEBASTIAN   Foul weather?
ANTONIO   Very foul.
GONZALO   Had I plantation of this isle, my lord –   140
ANTONIO   He'd sow't with nettle-seed.
SEBASTIAN   Or docks, or mallows.
GONZALO   – And were the king on't, what would I do?
SEBASTIAN   'Scape being drunk, for want of wine.

129–31 *This edn;* Then . . . them / The fault's . . . owne / So . . . losse / My . . . Sebastian/ F; Then . . . them / The fault's . . . loss / My . . . Sebastian/ *Hanmer;* Then . . . them / The fault's . . . own / So . . . Sebastian/ *Ard3*   **130** dearest of the loss] *Steevens;* deer'st oth' losse F   **134–5** *As Steevens;* When . . . plaister. / Very . . . chirurgeonly / F   **137–9** *This edn;* When . . . cloudy. / Fowle . . . foule F; When . . . Foul . . . foul *Malone*   **138–9** Foul . . . foul] F3; Fowle . . . foule F

128–9 More . . . comfort them Sebastian assumes that the other ships are lost, but, seemingly, that they themselves will be able to return home.

129–30 The fault's . . . loss F's lineation is unsatisfactory, and though no totally regular solution is possible, the relineation suggested here seems the best available. (See Textual Analysis, pp. 240–1.)

130 dearest Both 'most severe, heavy, grievous' (*OED* Dear *adj²* 2) and 'most precious in significance' (*OED* Dear *adj¹* 4b).

133 time appropriate time.

133 rub the sore Proverbial (Tilley s64 'to rip up [rub] old sores'). Erasmus comments: 'We speak also of rubbing up the memory, which means administering a mild reminder, but nearly always with an intent to annoy' (*Adagia*, 1.6.80).

134 plaster Specifically a dressing for a wound, more generally a healing measure (*OED* sv *n* 1a, b).

135 chirurgeonly like a surgeon.

137 cloudy 'darkened by misfortune . . . gloomy' (*OED* sv *adj* 6).

138–9 F's spelling 'fowle . . . foule' suggests that some sort of pun is intended, perhaps, remembering the description of Gonzalo as a 'cock' earlier, on 'fowl'. Antonio then might 'mimic a fowl' (Orgel), a gesture I have seen used on stage. Even given the quality of punning so far in this scene, this seems particularly desperate. Though it is possible to see Sebastian and Antonio's lines as completing an (irregular) line of verse, it seems better to take them as disruptive prose interjections.

140 plantation The rights of colonisation or settling (as in the 'plantation' of Ulster with Scots and English being undertaken at the time of the play) but taken by Sebastian and Antonio in its literal horticultural sense.

141 docks . . . mallows Both are weeds, but the leaves of the dock have always been used to soothe nettle stings, and the mallow could also be made into a soothing ointment. See William Turner, *A New Herball* (1551): 'Mallowes are good to be laid to against the stingings of wasps and bees' (ed. Chapman and Tweddle, 1989, 2 vols.) II, 435.

142 on't of it.

143 want lack.

GONZALO I'th'commonwealth I would by contraries
            Exècute all things. For no kind of traffic   145
            Would I admit; no name of magistrate;
            Letters should not be known; riches, poverty,
            And use of service, none; contract, succession,
            Bourn, bound of land, tilth, vineyard, none;
            No use of metal, corn, or wine, or oil;   150
            No occupation, all men idle, all;
            And women too, but innocent and pure;
            No sovereignty –
SEBASTIAN   Yet he would be king on't.
ANTONIO The latter end of his commonwealth forgets the begin-
            ning.   155
GONZALO All things in common nature should produce
            Without sweat or endeavour. Treason, felony,

---

147 riches, poverty] F; poverty, riches *Capell*

144–61 Gonzalo's speech is closely based on a
portion of Montaigne's Essay 'Of Cannibals', but
Montaigne himself was drawing on the classics, and
in particular on Ovid. The classical myth of the first
age of the world as a Golden Age was blended with
the biblical paradise of Adam and Eve, and endlessly reimagined in the Renaissance. The Indians
of America were often seen as Golden Age inno-
cents. Richard Eden, for example, translating Peter
Martyr, writes: 'Mine and Thine, the seeds of all
mischief, have no place with them . . . they seem to
live in the Golden World, without toil . . . They
deal truly with one another, without laws, without
books, without judges' (quoted in H. C. Porter, *The
Inconstant Savage*, 1979, p. 24). 'Though recogniz-
ably derived from New World accounts, this ideal
commonwealth appears to be peopled by Europeans
and modeled on Ovidian and Virgilian descriptions
of the Golden Age' (Halpern, p. 268).
   144 by contraries in opposition to that which is
customary. The orator was directed to find appropriate materials for a speech by turning to 'topics'
or 'commonplaces', and here Gonzalo composes his
miniature oration through the exploration of 'contraries' – one of the topics set out by Aristotle,
Cicero and subsequent rhetorical teachers.
   145 Exècute Stressed on the second syllable.
   145 traffic trade, business.
   146 magistrate A civil officer charged with the
administration of the laws.
   147 Letters Learning, literature.
   148 use of service (1) employment of servants,
(2) custom or practice of servitude.
   148 succession inheritance.

149 Bourn, bound of land Both meaning
'boundary'. The increasing enclosure of common
land was a particular source of social tension in the
sixteenth and seventeenth centuries.
   149 tilth husbandry, raising of crops.
   150 corn . . . oil Echoing Coverdale's translation
of Psalm 4.8: 'the time that their corn, and wine,
and oil, increased'. This was the version authorised
for use in church services (and retained in the 1662
Book of Common Prayer). The Bishops' Bible (and
Authorised Version) have only 'corn' and 'wine'.
   151 occupation employment.
   151 idle Idleness was customarily seen as the
nurse of lechery, as in Dod and Cleaver's *Plaine and
Familiar Exposition of the Ten Commandments*: 'For
idlenesse is the mother of foul lusts' (1630 edn, p.
249, and see below, 163). Hence Gonzalo rapidly
emphasises the innocence and purity of his ideal
society. The idleness of the first Virginian colonists,
and their need to be replaced by hard workers if the
settlement was to survive, however, was a frequent
topic in the colonial propaganda of 1609–12, and
further complicates our response to his idealised
picture.
   154–5 Pointing out that the end of Gonzalo's
speech contradicts its opening proposition of being
'king' of the island. As T. W. Baldwin observes:
'Gonzalo would found his commonwealth on contraries, and is caught up on a contrary' (*Shakespere's
Small Latine and Less Greeke*, 1944, 2 vols., II,
115–16).
   156 in common for communal use.
   157 Without . . . endeavour Genesis 3.19 gives
as one of the consequences of the Fall: 'In the sweat

Sword, pike, knife, gun, or need of any engine
Would I not have; but nature should bring forth
Of it own kind, all foison, all abundance   160
To feed my innocent people.

SEBASTIAN No marrying 'mong his subjects?

ANTONIO None, man, all idle; whores and knaves.

GONZALO I would with such perfection govern, sir,
          T'excel the Golden Age.   165

SEBASTIAN 'Save his majesty!

ANTONIO Long live Gonzalo!

GONZALO And – do you mark me, sir?

ALONSO Prithee, no more; thou dost talk nothing to me.

GONZALO I do well believe your highness, and did it to minister occa-   170
sion to these gentlemen, who are of such sensible and nimble lungs,
that they always use to laugh at nothing.

ANTONIO 'Twas you we laughed at.

GONZALO Who, in this kind of merry fooling, am nothing to you; so
you may continue, and laugh at nothing still.   175

---

160 it] F; it's F3; its F4   165–8 *As Orgel;* T'Excell . . . Age. / 'Saue . . . Gonzalo/ And . . . sir / F; T'excel . . . Majesty /
Long . . . sir? / *Steevens*   168 And – do] *Dyce;* And do F

of thy face shalt thou eat bread', and this was taken
to imply that until they fell, Adam and Eve did not
need to toil.

158 engine machine, especially one used in
warfare.

159–60 nature . . . abundance This amplifies
156–7, suggesting that food will be provided by
what grows naturally, without cultivation. Fraunce
expresses the same idea: 'Fruytefull ground
vntorne, vntucht, was free fro the plough share, /
And self-sufficient, of her owne selfe yeelded
aboundance' (sig. a4ᵛ).

160 it 'The form its, adopted by F3 and F4, was
in use in Shakespeare's time, but the regular genitive of "it" was "his", and often the earlier genitive
"it" was used also. See Abbott 228' (Kermode).
Nonetheless it could easily be a compositorial error.

160 kind nature. It applies either to Nature itself,
or else to the specific varieties of food that nature
produces.

160 foison plenty.

161 innocent As in the time of paradise, before
Adam and Eve ate of the tree of knowledge.

162 No marrying Sebastian responds with
mock horror to what is implicit in the absence of
'contract' and in the holding of things in common
in Gonzalo's commonwealth. Sexual freedom as a
feature of the Golden Age was, according to Harry

Levin, 'left for the Renaissance to develop' (*The
Myth of the Golden Age in the Renaissance*, 1970, p.
24.) It becomes commonplace in the period, for
example in the Garden of Adonis in Spenser's
Faerie Queene, 3.6.41, where 'franckly each para-
mour his leman knowes'.

165 Golden Age The association of the ideal
ruler with the return of the Golden Age was made
by Virgil in his praise of Augustus in the 'Fourth
Eclogue'. The idea was frequently invoked in
praises of Elizabeth and James, notably, for
example, in Ben Jonson's masque, *The Golden Age
Restor'd* (1616).

166–8 In F Sebastian and Antonio's exclamations
are arranged as a single line. Most modern editors
make Sebastian's speech complete Gonzalo's
line, with the succeeding two speeches making
one imperfect line. But at this point verse gives
way to prose, and since no arrangement is completely satisfactory it seems best to take Sebastian
and Antonio's ironic salutations as prose interruptions.

166 'Save Abbreviation of 'God save' – perhaps
in response to the Act forbidding oaths on stage.

170–1 minister occasion provide the
opportunity.

171 sensible sensitive.

172 use to are accustomed to.

ANTONIO What a blow was there given!

SEBASTIAN And it had not fall'n flat-long.

GONZALO You are gentlemen of brave mettle; you would lift the moon
out of her sphere, if she would continue in it five weeks without
changing.   180

Enter ARIEL [*invisible*] *playing solemn music*

SEBASTIAN We would so, and then go a-batfowling.

ANTONIO Nay, good my lord, be not angry.

GONZALO No, I warrant you, I will not adventure my discretion so
weakly. Will you laugh me asleep, for I am very heavy?

ANTONIO Go sleep, and hear us.   185

[*All sleep except Alonso, Sebastian and Antonio*]

ALONSO What, all so soon asleep? I wish mine eyes
Would with themselves shut up my thoughts; I find
They are inclined to do so.

SEBASTIAN   Please you, sir,

---

178 mettle] F *(*mettal*)*   180 SD *invisible*] *Malone; not in* F   185 SD *Capell subst.; not in* F   187–8 *As Pope;* Would . . .
thoughts, / I . . . so/ F

176 blow A verbal insult or riposte, but Sebastian takes it as a physical blow.

177 And If.

177 fall'n flat-long Struck with the flat of the
blade, not the edge – Gonzalo's attempt at wit is
condemned as ineffective.

178 mettle spirit.

178–9 lift . . . her sphere In the Ptolemaic universe each of the planets occupied a 'sphere' revolv-
ing round the earth, the moon's being closest to it.
Gonzalo suggests that the lords aspire to rip the
moon from its sphere, but could only do so if it
would stay still for an extra week, thus mocking
their arrogance and impotent vanity.

180 SD *invisible* Ariel must be invisible here.
Whilst he might still wear the costume he donned
at Prospero's bidding in 1.2, he could equally well
have changed, perhaps into something like the 'robe
for to goo invisibell' listed in Henslowe's papers as
belonging to the Lord Admiral's Men – though
what this robe looked like is a matter for conjecture.

180 SD *solemn music* (1) a slow-moving, stately
piece, (2) referring to the instrument on which Ariel
plays. The stage direction *solemn music* is found in
Shakespeare only in *Cym.* 4.2.186, where it indicates the sounding of Belarius' (unspecified) 'ingenious instrument', and in 5.4.29 where it initiates the
vision of Leonatus, and in *H8* 4.2.81 where *sad and
solemn music* is provided for the dying Queen
Katherine. It is, however, frequent elsewhere in
masques and plays, in a context either of ceremo-

nial, or of melancholy. As a description of particular instruments it is often associated with recorders,
or with the organ, both of which would have been
available at Blackfriars. That Antonio and Sebastian appear not to hear the music can be taken symbolically to indicate their wickedness (cf. *MV*
5.1.83–8: 'The man that hath no music in himself,
/ Nor is not moved with concord of sweet sounds,
/ Is fit for treasons, stratagems and spoils; . . . Let
no such man be trusted.') In some productions,
however, Ariel is made to charm individual lords to
sleep with a gesture, thus enforcing a reading of this
part of the scene as deliberately planned by Prospero.

181 Indeed we would, and then use the moon as
a lantern to catch birds by. 'Batfowling' means 'the
catching of birds at night when at roost, beating
them with clubs or "bats"' (*OED* sv *n*).

182 Sebastian's words engender a hostile reaction
from Gonzalo, whom Antonio then patronisingly
appeases.

183 warrant you promise you.

183–4 adventure my discretion so weakly
hazard my good judgement (by becoming angry) on
such feeble grounds as you give me.

184 heavy sleepy (Gonzalo is beginning to
respond to Ariel's music).

185 Go to sleep and we will indeed laugh (as you
requested).

186–7 eyes . . . thoughts I wish that shutting
my eyes would still my thoughts.

> Do not omit the heavy offer of it.
> It seldom visits sorrow; when it doth,   190
> It is a comforter.

ANTONIO   We two, my lord,
> Will guard your person while you take your rest,
> And watch your safety.

ALONSO   Thank you. Wondrous heavy.

[Alonso sleeps.]   *[Exit Ariel]*

SEBASTIAN   What a strange drowsiness possesses them?

ANTONIO   It is the quality o'th'climate.

SEBASTIAN   Why   195
> Doth it not then our eyelids sink? I find
> Not myself disposed to sleep.

ANTONIO   Nor I; my spirits are nimble.
> They fell together all, as by consent
> They dropped, as by a thunder-stroke. What might,   200
> Worthy Sebastian, O, what might? – No more.
> And yet, methinks I see it in thy face,
> What thou shouldst be. Th'occasion speaks thee, and
> My strong imagination sees a crown
> Dropping upon thy head.

SEBASTIAN   What? Art thou waking?   205

190–1 *As Rowe*] One line in F   191–3 *As Rowe*] We two . . . person / While . . . safety/ F   193 SD *Alonso sleeps*] Capell; *Exit Ariel*] Malone; not in F   197–8 *As* F; *as one line* Steevens   199–200 consent / They] F; consent, / They *Pope;* consent; / They *Cam.*   202–3 face, . . . be.] F *(*face . . . be:*); *face. / What . . . be *Oxford*

189 **omit** neglect, ignore.

189 **heavy offer** The chance of sleep that is proffered.

190–1 **It seldom . . . comforter** The sorrowful person rarely sleeps, but is comforted when sleep finally comes. The paradox that sleep is the cure for sorrow, but sorrow drives out sleep is commonplace in the poetry and songs of the period. (cf. Sonnet 28, lines 3–4: 'When day's oppression is not eased by night, / But day by night and night by day oppressed'.)

195–8 Little seems possible to regularise lineation here. Antonio's 'Nor I' can be taken to complete Sebastian's line, but it might be better to regard these as two short lines.

198 **spirits** See 1.2.485 n. above.

199 **consent** agreement.

200 **dropped** Most modern editors insert a strong stop after 'consent', whereas the lack of punctuation in F produces a nicely parallel construction with each clause introduced by 'as' (the rhetorical figure of *anaphora*).

200–1 **What . . . might** Antonio lures Sebastian by breaking off his sentence – the rhetorical figure of *aposiopesis*. The invitation it offers for the hearer to fill out what is implied is one which is characteristically deployed by schemers such as Edmund in *Lear* 1.2.27 ff. and Iago in *Oth.* 4.1.31 ff. It entices the person to whom it is addressed, but also allows the speaker to test the ground without committing himself. (See Brian Vickers, *In Defence of Rhetoric*, 1988, pp. 336–7.)

202 **yet** F's comma is often deleted by modern editors, but it might suggest a pause which continues Antonio's building up of his persuasion through mock hesitation.

203 **Th'occasion . . . thee** The opportunity calls out to you. Commentators since Coleridge have pointed to the resemblance between this scene and *Mac.* 1.3. Oxford punctuates with a full stop after 'face' and no stop after 'be' in 202–3, producing the meaning : 'This opportunity reveals to you what you should be.'

205 **waking** awake.

ANTONIO Do you not hear me speak?

SEBASTIAN   I do, and surely
It is a sleepy language, and thou speak'st
Out of thy sleep. What is it thou didst say?
This is a strange repose, to be asleep
With eyes wide open; standing, speaking, moving,   210
And yet so fast asleep.

ANTONIO   Noble Sebastian,
Thou let'st thy fortune sleep – die rather; wink'st
Whiles thou art waking.

SEBASTIAN   Thou dost snore distinctly;
There's meaning in thy snores.

ANTONIO I am more serious than my custom. You   215
Must be so too, if heed me; which to do,
Trebles thee o'er.

SEBASTIAN   Well: I am standing water.

ANTONIO I'll teach you how to flow.

SEBASTIAN   Do so – to ebb
Hereditary sloth instructs me.

ANTONIO   O!
If you but knew how you the purpose cherish   220
Whiles thus you mock it; how in stripping it
You more invest it. Ebbing men, indeed,

216 if heed] F; if you heed *Rowe*

212–13 wink'st . . . waking Shut your eyes (to your opportunity) even though you are awake.

213 distinctly 'so as to be clearly understood' (*OED* sv *adv* 2). (The reading 'you're obviously snoring', sometimes implied on the modern stage, is anachronistic.)

214 Elaborates the previous line.

216 if heed me if you are to heed me.

217 Trebles thee o'er Makes you three times greater. C. J. Sisson suggests that this is an image from the game of draughts (checkers) where to 'treble' is to jump three pieces in one move. Sebastian would 'leap over' Alonso, Ferdinand and Claribel in assuming the throne (*New Readings in Shakespeare*, 1955, p. 48 – though he suggests that Antonio, rather than Claribel, is the third over whom Sebastian would jump by becoming a king).

217 standing water Neither ebbing nor flowing, hence poised to move backwards or forwards.

218–19 to ebb . . . instructs me (1) natural laziness prompts me to draw back, (2) the idleness imposed on me by my hereditary position as

younger brother has taught me to do little. 'Antonio's reply dwells on the implications of (2), and ends with a reproach aimed at the indolence confessed in (1)' (Kermode).

220–1 If . . . mock it If only you could see that in mocking your own indolence you actually indicate how acutely you desire to overcome it through the plan ('purpose') I hint at.

221–2 stripping . . . invest it Antonio repeats the same idea as in the previous lines. 'Stripping' carries first the sense of satirical attack or mockery, a development of *OED* strip *v*¹ 2c, 'to expose the nature of (a person or thing)'. Antonio then puns on the literal meaning of the word, and suggests that, far from 'stripping' the idea, Sebastian actually 'invests', or 'clothes' it. 'Invests' carries a strong suggestion of a ceremonial robing, as at an investiture.

222 Ebbing men Men whose fortunes are in decline. In the Renaissance court world, jockeying for place and position was endemic, and observers had a keen sense of whose fortunes were rising and

Most often do so near the bottom run
By their own fear, or sloth.

SEBASTIAN   Prithee say on.
The setting of thine eye and cheek proclaim   225
A matter from thee; and a birth, indeed,
Which throes thee much to yield.

ANTONIO   Thus, sir:
Although this lord of weak remembrance, this,
Who shall be of as little memory
When he is earthed, hath here almost persuaded –   230
For he's a spirit of persuasion, only
Professes to persuade – the king his son's alive,
'Tis as impossible that he's undrowned
As he that sleeps here, swims.

SEBASTIAN   I have no hope
That he's undrowned.

ANTONIO   O, out of that 'no hope'   235
What great hope have you! No hope that way is
Another way so high a hope that even
Ambition cannot pierce a wink beyond,
But doubt discovery there. Will you grant with me

---

239 doubt] F; doubts *Capell;* douts *Wilson (Nicholson conj.)*

whose falling. See Lear's 'and hear poor rogues /
Talk of court news … who's in, who's out'
(5.3.13–15).

225 setting fixed, determined look.

226 matter something of importance.

227 throes … yield causes you much pain in
uttering it. 'Throes' as a verb is unusual (though
Shakespeare uses it as such in *Ant.* 3.7.80), but the
throes of childbirth are often used as a metaphor for
bringing forth a literary composition (as in Sidney's
Astrophil and Stella, Sonnet 1, line 12: 'Thus great
with child to speak, and helpless in my throes').

228 weak remembrance feeble memory;
perhaps 'as demonstrated in the Tunis/Carthage
confusion' (Barton).

229 as little memory as little remembered.

230 earthed buried.

231 a spirit of persuasion the quintessence of
persuasion. Antonio and Sebastian's emphasis on
Gonzalo as a rhetorician is not simply an ironically
dismissive one – it is presumably his persuasiveness
as well as his integrity that they fear.

231–2 only … persuade his only function (as a
councillor) is to persuade.

234–7 hope … hope The multi-layered rhetor-

ical patterning of 'hope … no hope' in Antonio's
speech intensifies his persuasive effort.

236 that way i.e. of Ferdinand's safety.

238–9 Ambition … there The precise sense is
difficult to ascertain, though the general drift seems
to be that the hope which is offered to Sebastian (i.e.
of the crown) is so high that there is nothing beyond
it which ambition could aspire to. The problem,
however, is adequately to explain the words 'But
doubt', which seem to imply uncertainty, rather
than the sure promise that Antonio holds out, and
editors have struggled to find a satisfactory paraphrase. Kittredge suggests: 'The eye of ambition
can reach no higher summit of aspiration, but must
even doubt the reality of what it discerns there, so
magnificent is the prospect.' Emendation to 'douts'
(= extinguishes), produces the meaning: 'Even
Ambition cannot look beyond a crown, but there
puts out her torch of discovery' (Kermode), but
this, too is somewhat strained. Perhaps a line has
dropped out (see Textual Analysis, p. 230). It is possible to take refuge in Orgel's suggestion that the
confused syntax expresses 'conflict and anxiety' in
Antonio's mind, or Ard3's proposal that it is a
'deliberate obfuscation of the murder' – but these

That Ferdinand is drowned?

SEBASTIAN   He's gone.

ANTONIO   Then tell me,   240
Who's the next heir of Naples?

SEBASTIAN   Claribel.

ANTONIO She that is Queen of Tunis; she that dwells
Ten leagues beyond man's life; she that from Naples
Can have no note, unless the sun were post –
The man i'th'moon's too slow – till new-born chins   245
Be rough and razorable; she that from whom
We all were sea-swallowed, though some cast again –
And by that destiny, to perform an act
Whereof what's past is prologue; what to come
In yours and my discharge.   250

SEBASTIAN What stuff is this? How say you?
'Tis true my brother's daughter's Queen of Tunis,
So is she heir of Naples, 'twixt which regions

240–1 *As Pope;* He's gone. / Then ... Naples F   246 she that from whom] F; she from whom *Rowe;* she for whom *Pope*
248 And by that destiny, to] F; May by that *Pope;* And that by destiny. To *Johnson*   250 In] F; Is *Pope*

are not qualities otherwise in evidence in his solicitation of Sebastian.

243 Ten ... life Way beyond a lifetime's
journey. A 'league' was primarily a poetic term of
indeterminate distance, suiting Antonio's extrava-
gant hyperbole. The distance from Naples to Tunis
was actually about 483 km (300 miles), a voyage
often made in the way of trade, and one, after all,
successfully completed by the lords themselves in
their journey to the marriage.

244 note information.

244 post messenger.

245 too slow Since it takes the moon a month to
complete its cycle, compared with the sun's single
day.

246 she that from whom she in coming from
whom. The parallel beginnings to the series of
assertions Antonio makes, in a crescendo of exaggeration, produce in this last instance a rather
strained syntax. This persuaded Malone that 'the
compositor's eye probably glanced on a preceding
line'. But whether one takes 'from' as having 'the
force of a verb of motion' (Kermode), or simply
regards it as an ellipsis for 'coming from', the over-
riding sense of rhetorical excitement generated by
the repetition of 'she that' (the figure of *anaphora*)
is worth the awkwardness.

247 cast Cast up, but also 'vomited', continuing
the image of 'sea-swallowed'. Some editors have
seen it as implying the sense 'cast theatrically', but

the verb was only used in this sense from the eighteenth century onwards, and 'cast' as a noun is not
used in a theatrical sense anywhere in Shakespeare.

248 And ... destiny Antonio's suggestion that
Fate has provided them with an opportunity they
must seize recalls Prospero's sense that his opportunity for revenge has been given by a Fate he must
obey (1.2.181–4). F brackets these words, suggesting that they are to be taken as an appositional
phrase. If this is accepted, then Johnson's emendation (adopted by Kermode), to 'that by destiny', is
attractive, giving the sense 'what has happened so
far has been fated; the next step we may take as free
agents'.

249 what's past i.e. the storm which has made
possible the action Antonio proposes. Many editors
reduce F's semi-colon to a comma, but the stronger
punctuation might suggest an effective rhetorical
pause here.

250 For the two of us to perform. Orgel cites
Bottom's claim that he 'will discharge' the role of
Pyramus in *MND* 1.2.93 for the theatrical connota-
tions of the verb.

251 stuff May be taken neutrally as 'matter',
but the word was beginning at this time to acquire
its now customary negative connotations (as in
'stuff and nonsense'). Either reading is possible,
depending on the degree to which an actor feels
Sebastian is beginning to fall in with Antonio's
plan.

There is some space.

ANTONIO   A space, whose ev'ry cubit
Seems to cry out, 'How shall that Claribel   255
Measure us back to Naples? Keep in Tunis,
And let Sebastian wake.' Say this were death
That now hath seized them, why, they were no worse
Than now they are. There be that can rule Naples
As well as he that sleeps; lords that can prate   260
As amply and unnecessarily
As this Gonzalo; I myself could make
A chough of as deep chat. O, that you bore
The mind that I do! What a sleep were this
For your advancement! Do you understand me?   265

SEBASTIAN Methinks I do.

ANTONIO   And how does your content
Tender your own good fortune?

SEBASTIAN   I remember
You did supplant your brother Prospero.

ANTONIO   True;
And look how well my garments sit upon me,
Much feater than before. My brother's servants   270

255–7 'How . . . wake.'] *Grant White;* 'How . . . Naples'. Keep . . . wake. *Capell; no quotation marks in* F   256 Keep] F;
Sleep *Johnson conj.*

254 cubit A measure 'varying at different times and places, but usually about 45–55 cm (18–22 inches)' (*OED* sv *n* 2), but here used in a vague sense.

255–7 'How shall . . . wake' Conventionally all three lines are taken to be the 'cry' of the cubit. It is equally possible, however, as older editors suggested, that the cubit's 'speech' ends at 'Naples', and Antonio in his own voice contemptuously addresses Claribel: 'Keep in Tunis . . .'

256 Measure us back Traverse us (it is the cubits that 'speak').

256 Keep Stay (addressed to Claribel).

258–9 no worse . . . are i.e. 'in their present circumstances they are as good as dead', or 'in their sleep they imitate death'. That sleep is the image of death was a poetical commonplace.

259 There be There are those that.

262–3 I myself . . . chat I could teach a jackdaw (chough) to prattle as profoundly as Gonzalo.

264 that I do Oxford and Orgel weaken F's semicolon to a comma, making the 'what' clause conditional – 'if only you thought as I, then . . .'. I

follow Kermode and others in strengthening it in order to make two parallel assertions, but either reading is possible.

266 content acquiescence (*OED* sv *n²* 2) but also 'liking'.

267 Tender Regard with either favour or fear (*OED* sv *v²* 3b, e), but also 'foster . . . look after' (3d). Antonio leads Sebastian on from merely understanding his meaning to thinking of its implications for his own conduct.

269 well . . . upon me Clothing in the period was tied to rank and status, but the potential gap between the outward appearance and the inner reality was frequently explored and exploited. See, for example, Lear's bitter cry, 'Robes and furred gowns hide all' (4.6.165), or the comment on Macbeth's ill-fitting robes (*Mac.* 5.2.20–2), and Introduction, p. 57.

270 feater more neatly, with better fit. Antonio claims that this indicates his suitability to the role of duke, exhibiting the habit of mind that Prospero described in 1.2.97–105.

Were then my fellows, now they are my men.
SEBASTIAN But for your conscience?
ANTONIO Ay, sir: where lies that? If it were a kibe
            'Twould put me to my slipper; but I feel not
            This deity in my bosom. Twenty consciences   275
            That stand 'twixt me and Milan, candied be they,
            And melt ere they molest. Here lies your brother,
            No better than the earth he lies upon,
            If he were that which now he's like – that's dead;
            Whom I with this obedient steel, three inches of it,   280
            Can lay to bed for ever: whiles you doing thus,
            To the perpetual wink for aye might put
            This ancient morsel, this Sir Prudence, who
            Should not upbraid our course. For all the rest,
            They'll take suggestion as a cat laps milk;   285
            They'll tell the clock to any business that
            We say befits the hour.
SEBASTIAN   Thy case, dear friend,
            Shall be my precedent. As thou got'st Milan,

---

273 it were] *Steevens;* 'twere F

271 **fellows** equals, companions.

272 **But what about your conscience?** F has no question mark, and without it Sebastian is saying 'except for your feelings of guilt', delivering a rebuke to Antonio which 'tersely answers the implied "I'm better off than before"' (Kermode). But turning it into a question hints that Sebastian is beginning to respond more positively to Antonio's suggestion, though worrying about any burden of guilt he might carry if he were to go through with it.

273–5 **If . . . bosom** If conscience were a chilblain ('kibe') on my foot, then it would make me wear a slipper, but I do not feel any guilt ('this deity') inwardly. Antonio's indifference is maintained to the end of the play, where Prospero attributes 'inward pinches' of remorse to Sebastian, but not to Antonio (5.1.74–8).

273 **it were** F's elision ''twere' produces an unnecessarily unmetrical line.

276 **candied** Either 'frozen into ice' or 'coated with sugar'. Shakespeare uses both meanings elsewhere, the icy in *Tim.* 4.3.226 and the sweet in *Ant.* 4.12.22. The second meaning is much more common in the period, though the first more naturally leads to the next line.

277 **molest** interfere.

280 **steel . . . inches** The measurement suggests a dagger rather than a sword.

281 **doing thus** (1) by doing the same, (2) Antonio mimes the action of stabbing. Most modern editors add a comma after 'you', which decisively tilts towards the second possible meaning.

282 **perpetual wink** everlasting sleep of death.

283 **morsel** (1) a scrap, small piece (often contemptuous), (2) a choice dish, or portion of food – 'applied jocularly to a person' (*OED* sv *n* 2), usually a desirable woman. Given Antonio's characteristic attitude, the first meaning is more likely. (Compare *John* 4.3.143: 'this morsel of dead royalty'.)

284 **Should not upbraid** i.e. if he is dead he will not be able to criticise.

285 **suggestion** Prompting, often with the implication 'to evil' (cf. *Mac.* 1.3.134–5: 'that suggestion / Whose horrid image doth unfix my hair').

286–7 **tell the clock . . . hour** agree with our judgement that the time is appropriate for whatever action we propose. A compressed metaphor, continuing the previous line's assertion about the docility of the attendant lords. Antonio's confidence in being able to command allegiance recollects Prospero's account of his success in setting all hearts 'To what tune pleased his ear' (1.2.85).

   I'll come by Naples. Draw thy sword; one stroke
   Shall free thee from the tribute which thou payest,   290
   And I the king shall love thee.
ANTONIO   Draw together:
   And when I rear my hand, do you the like
   To fall it on Gonzalo.
SEBASTIAN   O, but one word.

       [They talk apart]

   Enter ARIEL *[invisible] with music*

ARIEL My master through his art foresees the danger
   That you, his friend, are in, and sends me forth –   295
   For else his project dies – to keep them living.
      Sings in Gonzalo's ear
   While you here do snoring lie,
   Open-eyed conspiracy
    His time doth take.
   If of life you keep a care,   300
   Shake off slumber and beware.
    Awake, awake.

---

293 SD.1 *They talk apart*] *Capell; not in* F 293 SD.2 *invisible*] *Capell; not in* F 293 SD.2 *with music*] *Oxford; with Musicke and Song.* F; *Music. Re-enter Ariel invisible Collier* 295 you, his friend] F *(subst.)*; these, his friends *Johnson*; you, his friends *Grant White* 296 them] F; you *Hanmer*; thee *Halliwell* 303 SD *This edn; not in* F 304 SD *Waking*] *Wilson; not in* F 304 SD *He shakes Alonso*] *Kittredge subst; They wake / Rowe; not in* F 305–6] F; *see Commentary*

290 tribute . . . payest An aspect of Antonio's bargain with Alonso which particularly affronted Prospero (1.2.124).

293 but one word Whilst this remark causes no difficulty to the reader, this contrived halting of the action to allow Ariel's re-entry poses a problem for the actor playing Sebastian in implying to the audience a convincing reason for the delay. Some clue to his hesitation may be found in the sequence wherein Sebastian's request to Antonio to 'Draw *thy* sword' is followed by Antonio's emphatic 'Draw *together*', which insists on Sebastian playing his part. After the temporary halt Antonio returns insisting 'let us *both* be sudden'. This pattern suggests Sebastian's continued reluctance to act for himself. (As Dymkowski notes, some performances have evaded the problem by making Ariel prevent the conspirators from proceeding with a magic charm.)

293 SD.2 For invisibility see above, 180 SD. *With music* could mean either that Ariel is playing an instrument as he enters, or possibly that he is accompanied by other instrumentalists (a *music*). F's *and Song* is redundant, since Ariel does not sing immediately, but it is a characteristic Cranean anticipation of action to come.

294–6 Though this speech is ostensibly addressed to Gonzalo, it is principally for the audience's information. Gonzalo only hears a 'humming' rather than the words of the song, and clearly is not aware of Prospero's presence on the island. Ariel's comment nonetheless leaves open the question whether Prospero foresaw the conspiracy before he put the lords to sleep.

295–6 friend . . . them Ariel makes a clear distinction between Prospero's two aims: first to preserve his friend, secondly to keep all the lords alive so that his larger purposes may be secured. The lack of grammatical agreement, however, persuaded earlier editors to emend one or other of the terms.

296 project Both 'plan' and 'purpose'; it is also a term for alchemical experiment (cf. 5.1.1).

299 time . . . take seizes its opportunity.

ANTONIO   Then let us both be sudden.
                    [*Antonio and Sebastian draw their swords*]
GONZALO   [*Waking*] Now, good angels preserve the king.
                    [*He shakes Alonso*]
ALONSO   Why, how now? ho! Awake? Why are you drawn?   305
              Wherefore this ghastly looking?
GONZALO   What's the matter?
SEBASTIAN   Whiles we stood here securing your repose,
              Even now, we heard a hollow burst of bellowing,
              Like bulls, or rather lions; did't not wake you?
              It struck mine ear most terribly.
ALONSO   I heard nothing.   310
ANTONIO   O, 'twas a din to fright a monster's ear,
              To make an earthquake. Sure it was the roar
              Of a whole herd of lions.
ALONSO   Heard you this, Gonzalo?
GONZALO   Upon mine honour, sir, I heard a humming,   315
              And that a strange one too, which did awake me.
              I shaked you, sir, and cried. As mine eyes opened,
              I saw their weapons drawn. There was a noise,
              That's verily. 'Tis best we stand upon our guard,
              Or that we quit this place. Let's draw our weapons.   320
ALONSO   Lead off this ground, and let's make further search
              For my poor son.
GONZALO   Heavens keep him from these beasts:
              For he is sure i'th'island.
ALONSO   Lead away.

314 Gonzalo] F; *om. Pope*

303 SD The conspirators may, of course, have
first drawn their swords earlier, at 291; but they
must be drawn here to account for Gonzalo's
response.
305–6 Editors from Staunton and Dyce onwards
have reassigned parts of this speech to Gonzalo, so
that, for example, 'Why, how now?' is addressed by
him to Sebastian and Antonio, 'ho! Awake' to
Alonso, and the king begins his speech either at
'Why are you drawn?' or takes over Gonzalo's
'What's the matter'. But Alonso's fragmented
speech as he wakes and looks round to see the drawn
swords makes sense as it stands.
306 ghastly (1) causing terror, (2) full of fear
(*OED* sv *adj* 1a, 3). Either of these meanings is possible here. Sebastian and Antonio may appear
threatening to Alonso, or may be simulating fear in
themselves to bolster their story.

307 securing your repose guarding you while
you slept.
308 hollow The adjective was used to describe
natural sounds, as in Drayton, *Nimphidia*, line 425
'the whirlewindes hollow sound', or the hoarse
groaning of human or wild beast, or the sound of
(particularly brass) instruments: 'Wanting body;
not full-toned; sepulchral' (*OED* sv *adj* 4). The
same term is used at 4.1.142 SD.2.
309 bulls . . . lions cf. Psalm 22. 12–13: 'bulls of
Basan close me in on every side . . . as it were a
ramping and a roaring lion'. The roar of lions
would not be totally unfamiliar to a seventeenth-
century audience; they were kept at the Tower of
London, and subjected periodically to baiting.
315 humming i.e. Ariel's music and song.
317 cried called out.
319 verily the truth.

ARIEL　Prospero my lord shall know what I have done.
　　　　So, king, go safely on to seek thy son.　　　　　　　325

　　　　　　　　　　　　　　　　　　　　Exeunt

2.2　*Enter* CALIBAN, *with a burden of wood. A noise of thunder heard*

CALIBAN　All the infections that the sun sucks up
　　　　　From bogs, fens, flats, on Prosper fall, and make him
　　　　　By inch-meal a disease. His spirits hear me,
　　　　　And yet I needs must curse. But they'll nor pinch,
　　　　　Fright me with urchin-shows, pitch me i'th'mire,　　　5
　　　　　Nor lead me like a firebrand in the dark
　　　　　Out of my way, unless he bid 'em; but
　　　　　For every trifle are they set upon me,
　　　　　Sometime like apes, that mow and chatter at me
　　　　　And after bite me; then like hedgehogs, which　　　10
　　　　　Lie tumbling in my barefoot way and mount
　　　　　Their pricks at my footfall; sometime am I
　　　　　All wound with adders, who with cloven tongues
　　　　　Do hiss me into madness.

　　　　　　　　　　　　Enter TRINCULO

Act 2, Scene 2　2.2] *Scœna Secunda* F　0 SD *A noise . . . heard*] F; *Orgel moves the phrase after line 3* disease　4 nor] F; not F3　12 sometime] F; *sometimes Theobald*

324–5 The use of rhyming couplets to close a scene, common in Shakespeare's earlier work, is comparatively rare in the late plays.

Act 2, Scene 2

0 SD *thunder* The scene may open with thunder, though since it seems to be required at line 3, its early placement may be a scribal alteration.

1–3 All . . . disease As Dymkowski notes: 'Many Calibans treat the first $2\frac{1}{2}$ lines as a formal curse or an attempt to cast a spell.'

1–2 infections . . . flats Infections were thought to derive from 'poisonous air', of which a foul smell was an indication. See, for example, Dekker, writing of the plague in *Newes From Graves-ende*: 'From Bogges; from ranck and dampish Fenns, / From Moorish breaths, and nasty Denns, / The Sun drawes up contagious Fumes, / Which falling downe burst into Rhewmes, / And thousand maladies beside' (F. P. Wilson, ed., *The Plague Pamphlets of Thomas Dekker*, 1925, p. 83).

2 flats flatlands, swamps (*OED* Flat *n*[3] c 5b).

3 inch-meal inch by inch.

3 His . . . hear me Caliban presumably responds to a clap of thunder, which he takes as a sign of Prospero's response to his curse. To delay thunder to this point would certainly be dramatically more effective than placing it at the beginning. (Though in some productions it is an off-stage noise or shout from the approaching Trinculo which prompts Caliban's fear.)

4 curse Picking up his comment at 1.2.363–4.

5 urchin-shows goblin-shows.

6 firebrand Literally a piece of wood kindled at the fire. Though not elsewhere used as a term for the *ignis fatuus*, the 'will-o'-the-wisp' seems to be implied.

9 mow make grimaces.

11 mount raise.

13 wound with entwined by.

Lo, now lo!
Here comes a spirit of his, and to torment me   15
For bringing wood in slowly. I'll fall flat,
Perchance he will not mind me.
[*He lies down, and covers himself with a cloak*]
TRINCULO Here's neither bush nor shrub to bear off any weather at all,
and another storm brewing – I hear it sing i'th'wind. Yond same
black cloud, yond huge one, looks like a foul bombard that would   20
shed his liquor. If it should thunder as it did before, I know not
where to hide my head. Yond same cloud cannot choose but fall by
pailfuls. [*Sees Caliban*] What have we here – a man, or a fish? Dead
or alive? A fish, he smells like a fish; a very ancient and fishlike
smell; a kind of, not-of-the-newest poor-John. A strange fish. Were   25
I in England now – as once I was – and had but this fish painted,
not a holiday-fool there but would give a piece of silver. There
would this monster make a man; any strange beast there makes a
man. When they will not give a doit to relieve a lame beggar, they
will lay out ten to see a dead Indian. Legged like a man – and his   30
fins like arms. Warm, o'my troth! I do now let loose my opinion,
hold it no longer: this is no fish, but an islander, that hath lately
suffered by a thunderbolt. [*Thunder*] Alas, the storm is come again.

15 and] F; *sent Dryden; now Pope*   17 SD *Orgel; not in* F   23 SD *Capell subst.; not in* F   33 SD *Capell; not in* F

15 spirit Caliban's misperception of Trinculo as
a spirit echoes Ferdinand and Miranda's first reaction to each other in 1.2, and is picked up again at
98 below.

17 mind notice.

18 bear off ward off.

19 sing i'th'wind Trinculo hears the impending
storm in the sound of the wind. cf. Fletcher and
Massinger, *Sir John van Olden Barnavelt* (1619),
4.3.91–3: 'what so confident Sailor, that heares the
sea rore, / The winds sing lowd, and dreadfull . . .
but he will cry a storme.'

20 bombard Originally a cannon, thence 'a
leather jug or bottle for liquor . . . probably from
some resemblance to the early cannons' (*OED* sv *n*
3). Trinculo seems to have both senses in mind.

25 poor-John dried, salted hake, a common food
of the poor.

26 in England now The joke is that the 'Italian'
Trinculo is 'now' on an English stage.

26 painted i.e. depicted on a sign hung outside
a booth at a fair to attract custom. (Kittredge com-
pares *Mac.* 5.8.25–6, where Macduff threatens:
'We'll have thee, as our rarer monsters are, /
Painted upon a pole.')

27 holiday-fool Monsters and curious prodigies

were prominent attractions at holiday fairs; the
gullibility of those attending such gatherings is the
basis of Ben Jonson's play, *Bartholomew Fair*. (See
Mark Thornton Burnett, '"Strange and woonderfull syghts": *The Tempest* and the discourses of
monstrosity', *S. Sur.*, 50 (1997), 187–99, for discussion of the fairground and the monstrous.)

28–9 make a man . . . makes a man make(s) a
man's fortune. Trinculo mocks English gullibility.
The second phrase may possibly be taken to mean
'is considered a man', implying a more pointed jibe
at the English.

29 doit Small coin of little value, originally half
a farthing.

30 dead Indian The display of natives from the
New World was common across Europe in the sixteenth century. See Alden T. Vaughan, 'Trinculo's
Indian: American natives in Shakespeare's England', in Hulme and Sherman, pp. 49–59.

30–1 Legged . . . arms Trinculo establishes that
Caliban is not the fish he first thought him to be –
though he later insults him again as 'half a fish'
(3.2.26) and Antonio, at 5.1.265 sees him as 'a plain
fish'.

31 Warm Therefore not a cold-blooded fish.

33 suffered by been killed by.

My best way is to creep under his gaberdine; there is no other
shelter hereabout. Misery acquaints a man with strange bedfellows. 35
I will here shroud till the dregs of the storm be past.

[*He hides under Caliban's cloak*]

Enter STEPHANO [*carrying a bottle and*] *singing*

STEPHANO   I shall no more to sea, to sea,
            Here shall I die ashore.
This is a very scurvy tune to sing at a man's funeral. Well, here's
my comfort. (*Drinks*)   40
(*Sings*) The master, the swabber, the boatswain and I,
            The gunner and his mate,
         Loved Mall, Meg and Marian, and Margery,
            But none of us cared for Kate.
         For she had a tongue with a tang,   45
         Would cry to a sailor, 'Go hang!'
         She loved not the savour of tar nor of pitch,
         Yet a tailor might scratch her where'er she did itch.
         Then to sea, boys, and let her go hang!

---

36 SD.1 *He . . . cloak*] Kittredge subst.; not in F   36 SD.2 *carrying a bottle*] Capell subst.; not in F   37–8 *As Capell; one line in* F

---

34 gaberdine 'The coarse frock or outward garment of a peasant' (Malone, quoting Steevens). The long cloak Caliban wears may, however, carry further connotations. The mantles of the Irish were seen as a symbol of, and cover for, their dangerous deceitfulness, and were compared, in the travel literature, to the cloaks of Native Americans. Powhatan's dress, for example, was described as 'a faire Robe of skins as large as an Irish mantle' (quoted from John Smith's *Works* in Barbara Fuchs, 'Conquering islands: contextualizing *The Tempest*', *SQ*, 48 (1997), 45–62; p. 51). Shylock's 'Jewish gaberdine', *MV* 1.3.112, is less relevant here, though it emphasises the way in which the garment was significantly connected with 'outsiders'. The potential for comic business as Trinculo creeps under the gaberdine can be much exploited in stage performance.

35 Misery . . . bedfellows Proverbial (Dent B197.1), but also a reality in the period, when sharing beds was common. Actors, addressing the audience directly, have extracted various kinds of comedy or salacious innuendo from the line.

36 shroud take shelter (*OED* sv *v*¹ 2c).

36 dregs the last remains, but also continuing the metaphor of the cloud as a bottle of liquor from 20.

39 scurvy 'sorry, worthless' (*OED* sv *adj* 2); a general term of dismissive abuse.

39 man's funeral i.e. his own funeral rites.

41 swabber Seaman whose job is to clean the decks, the lowliest of ranks (cf. Viola's dismissal of Maria as 'good swabber', *TN* 1.5.203).

43–4 Mall . . . Kate Patricia Gartenberg suggests that the first three names refer to notorious women of the period, Moll Cutpurse, Long Meg of Westminster and Marian Umbree, and that the sharp-tongued Kate may recollect the heroine of *Shr.* (*N&Q*, 225, NS 27 (1980), 174–5). The names, however, are probably to be taken simply as characteristic nicknames for prostitutes. 'Margery' is to be prononounced to rhyme with 'I', and stressed on the first and final syllables.

45 tang stinging effect (*OED* sv *n*¹ 5c) but perhaps also 'a sound of unpleasant tone' (*OED* sv *n*²).

47 savour smell.

47 tar . . . pitch Both are strong-smelling substances used in ship-building, the first as a wood preservative, the second in stopping up the seams.

48 tailor The woman's tailor, from the intimate proximity to his clients which his job afforded him, was often characterised as either lecherous or else unmanly.

48 where'er she did itch Sexual desire in both male and female was frequently characterised as a genital 'itch'.

49 go hang go to the devil.

This is a scurvy tune too; but here's my comfort. (*Drinks*)   50
CALIBAN Do not torment me! O!
STEPHANO What's the matter? Have we devils here? Do you put tricks
upon's with savages and men of Ind? Ha? I have not 'scaped drowning to be afeared now of your four legs. For it hath been said, 'As
proper a man as ever went on four legs, cannot make him give   55
ground'; and it shall be said so again, while Stephano breathes at'
nostrils.
CALIBAN The spirit torments me! O!
STEPHANO This is some monster of the isle, with four legs, who hath
got, as I take it, an ague. Where the devil should he learn our lan-   60
guage? I will give him some relief if it be but for that. If I can
recover him, and keep him tame, and get to Naples with him, he's
a present for any emperor that ever trod on neat's leather.
CALIBAN Do not torment me, prithee! I'll bring my wood home faster.
STEPHANO He's in his fit now, and does not talk after the wisest. He   65
shall taste of my bottle. If he have never drunk wine afore, it will
go near to remove his fit. If I can recover him, and keep him tame,

---

56–7 at' nostrils] F; at nostrils F3; at his nostrils *Rowe;* at's nostrils *Grant White*

52–3 put tricks upon's cf. *AWW* 4.5.60, 'If I
put any tricks upon 'em', which Dent PP18, classes
as proverbial. Tilley's 'Do not put tricks upon travellers' (T521) seems to postdate the play.
53 men of Ind (West) Indian natives. (Though
it is possible that East Indian natives might be
meant – as in *LLL* 4.3.218.) Noble (p. 250) notes
that the expression appears in the Bishops' Bible
translation of Jeremiah 13. 23: 'May a man of Ind
change his skin?' (The Geneva Bible reads 'can the
black Moor change his skin'.)
54–5 As proper . . . four legs 'As good a man as
ever went on two legs' is the common saying (Tilley
M66) which Stephano adapts – perhaps with comic
hesitation – to the apparently four-legged monster
he sees. Though Caliban and Trinculo lie so that
there is a head at each end, Siamese twins were frequently invoked as a type of monstrous birth – in
Montaigne's Essay 'On a Monstrous Child' (vol. II,
no. 30), or in broadside ballads. (See David Cressy,
*Travesties and Transgressions in Tudor and Stuart
England*, Oxford, 2000, ch. 2.)
56–7 at' nostrils cf. *JC* 1.2.253, 'he foamed . . .
at mouth'. It was an accepted idiom (see Abbott
143), and the apostrophe, suggesting an elision of
'at the nostrils', may be a hypercorrection by Crane.
58 The spirit torments me Caliban here is

either reacting to Stephano's voice, or else Stephano
prods him, or else he responds to Trinculo, who,
hiding under the gaberdine, begins to shake with
fear. There must be some visible trembling here,
from Caliban, Trinculo or both, to explain
Stephano's comment at 60.
59 isle F's comma, usually omitted by modern
editors, usefully suggests an incredulous pause as
Stephano examines what is in front of him.
60 ague 'A common term for any kind of acute
illness accompanied by pain' (Hoeniger, p. 218), but
usually describing a malarial fever, and particularly
the shivering or shaking associated with its second
stage.
60–1 Where . . . language Where could he have
learnt our language? Stephano's reaction echoes
Ferdinand's response to Miranda at 1.2.427.
61 for that i.e. for speaking our language.
62 recover restore, cure.
63 present . . . emperor Where Trinculo imagines profiting from Caliban by exhibiting him at a
popular fair, Stephano thinks of royal reward.
63 trod . . . leather A variant of the proverb at
54–5: 'As good a man as ever trod on shoe (neat's)
leather' (Tilley M66).
63 neat's leather cowhide.
65 after the wisest in the wisest fashion.

I will not take too much for him; he shall pay for him that hath him,
and that soundly.

CALIBAN Thou dost me yet but little hurt; thou wilt anon, I know it by   70
thy trembling. Now Prosper works upon thee.

STEPHANO Come on your ways. Open your mouth; here is that which
will give language to you, cat. Open your mouth; this will shake
your shaking, I can tell you, and that soundly.
                    [*Caliban drinks and spits it out*]
You cannot tell who's your friend: open your chops again.   75
                    [*Caliban drinks again*]

TRINCULO I should know that voice. It should be – but he is drowned,
and these are devils. O defend me!

STEPHANO Four legs and two voices; a most delicate monster! His
forward voice now is to speak well of his friend; his backward voice
is to utter foul speeches, and to detract. If all the wine in my bottle   80
will recover him, I will help his ague. Come.
                        [*Caliban drinks*]
Amen. I will pour some in thy other mouth.

TRINCULO Stephano.

STEPHANO Doth thy other mouth call me? Mercy, mercy! This is a
devil, and no monster. I will leave him; I have no long spoon.   85

TRINCULO Stephano! If thou beest Stephano, touch me, and speak to
me; for I am Trinculo – be not afeared – thy good friend Trinculo.

---

74 SD *Caliban . . . out*] *This edn; Gives Caliban drink / Kittredge; not in* F   75 SD *This edn; not in* F   81 SD *Wilson subst.;
not in* F

68 **I will not . . . him** It is impossible for me to
sell him too dear (Malone).

68–9 **he shall pay . . . soundly** anyone who
wants him will have to pay a good price.

70 **anon** soon, straightway.

71 **thy trembling** It is presumably Trinculo's
'trembling' that Caliban feels, and thinks he is one
of Prospero's tormenting spirits.

72 **Come . . . your ways** Come here. *OED* notes
that in rustic speech the phrase is used specifically
of animals or children (Way *n*¹ 23b).

72–3 **here . . . cat** Alluding to the proverb: 'Ale
will make a cat speak' (Tilley A99).

74 SD **spits it out** Caliban must have some reaction to the first offer of a drink which explains
Stephano's next comment. To spit out the wine is a
common device in production, and fits with
Stephano's subsequent request for him to open his
mouth 'again', but it could simply be that he rejects

the drink stubbornly or, as in one production, bites
Stephano's hand.

75 **chops** jaws, mouth.

75 SD **drinks again** Usually Caliban responds
more positively here, and enthusiastically by 82.

78 **delicate** the same term as Prospero applied
to Ariel at 1.2.272, here an ironic paradox or
oxymoron.

80 **detract** speak disparagingly (*OED* sv *v* 3b).

81 **help** cure.

82 **Amen** That's enough, that's the end.

85 **long spoon** proverbial. 'He must have a long
spoon that will eat with the devil' (Tilley S771) cf.
Err. 4.3.63 ff.

86 **touch me** i.e. if he touches him he will find
he is real, not a devil. In an analogous fashion Prospero later embraces Alonso to reassure him of his
bodily reality (5.1.108–9).

STEPHANO If thou beest Trinculo, come forth! I'll pull thee by the lesser legs. If any be Trinculo's legs, these are they.

[Pulls him out]

Thou art very Trinculo indeed! How cam'st thou to be the siege of   90
this moon-calf? Can he vent Trinculos?

TRINCULO I took him to be killed with a thunder-stroke. But art thou not drowned, Stephano? I hope now thou art not drowned. Is the storm over-blown? I hid me under the dead moon-calf's gaberdine for fear of the storm. And art thou living, Stephano? O Stephano,   95
two Neapolitans 'scaped!

[Embraces Stephano]

STEPHANO Prithee do not turn me about, my stomach is not constant.

CALIBAN [*Aside*] These be fine things, and if they be not sprites. That's a brave god, and bears celestial liquor. I will kneel to him.

STEPHANO How didst thou 'scape? How cam'st thou hither? Swear by   100
this bottle how thou cam'st hither. I escaped upon a butt of sack which the sailors heaved o'erboard, by this bottle – which I made of the bark of a tree, with mine own hands, since I was cast ashore.

CALIBAN I'll swear upon that bottle to be thy true subject, for the liquor is not earthly.   105

STEPHANO Here. Swear then how thou escap'dst.

TRINCULO Swum ashore, man, like a duck. I can swim like a duck, I'll be sworn.

---

89 SD *Oxford subst.; not in* F   96 SD *Embraces Stephano*] *This edn; He capers with Stephano* / *Bevington; not in* F   98 SD *Dyce; not in* F   98–9 *As* F; These . . . sprites; / That's . . . liquor. / I . . . him *Johnson*

90 **very** the real.

90 **siege** excrement – Stephano pulls Trinculo from between Caliban's legs.

91 **moon-calf** Monstrosity, imperfectly formed through the influence of the moon at the time of birth. Also, more generally 'an idiot'. In Jonson's *Bartholomew Fair* (1614) the tapster to Ursula the pig-woman is named Mooncalf, perhaps a deliberate recollection of Shakespeare's characterisation of Caliban. (And see 3.2.2 n. below.).

91 **vent** evacuate, defecate.

93 **I hope . . . drowned** Otherwise Trinculo fears he must be seeing a ghost.

96 SD In order to explain Stephano's next comment Trinculo here must embrace, or else attempt to dance with him.

97 **constant** settled, steady (*OED* sv *adj* 7).

98 **fine things** Compare 15 above.

99 **kneel** A mark of reverence to a divinity, but also of subservience to a monarch (see 3.2.35 and n.).

101 **butt** cask (cf. 1.2.146).

101 **sack** White wine from Spain or the Canaries.

106 **Here** Addressed probably to Trinculo, gesturing with the bottle, though it could be interpreted as offering Caliban another drink in response to his previous offer to 'swear'.

107 **Swum . . . duck** No explanation is needed for Trinculo's boast, but in Erasmus, 'The Shipwreck', an account is given of one who resisted the waves by 'putting his head under water as divers and ducks do' (p. 146).

STEPHANO [*Gives bottle to Trinculo*] Here, kiss the book. Though thou
    canst swim like a duck, thou art made like a goose.   110
TRINCULO O Stephano, hast any more of this?
STEPHANO The whole butt, man. My cellar is in a rock by the sea-side,
    where my wine is hid. [*To Caliban*] How now, moon-calf, how does
    thine ague?
CALIBAN Hast thou not dropped from heaven?   115
STEPHANO Out o'th'moon I do assure thee. I was the man i'th'moon,
    when time was.
CALIBAN I have seen thee in her; and I do adore thee. My mistress
    showed me thee, and thy dog, and thy bush.
STEPHANO Come, swear to that! [*Giving him the bottle*] Kiss the book   120
    – I will furnish it anon with new contents. Swear.
                    [*Caliban drinks*]
TRINCULO [*Aside*] By this good light, this is a very shallow monster. I
    afeared of him? A very weak monster. The man i'th'moon? A most
    poor, credulous monster. Well drawn, monster, in good sooth.
CALIBAN I'll show thee every fertile inch o'th'island. And I will kiss thy 125
    foot – I prithee be my god.

---

109 SD *Orgel subst.; not in* F   113 SD *This edn; not in* F   120 SD *This edn; not in* F   121 SD *Barton; not in* F   122 SD *Kittredge; not in* F   125 island] F; isle F2

109 kiss the book (1) take a drink ('kiss the cup'
was proverbial: Tilley C909), (2) alluding to the
kissing of the Bible to confirm an oath. Stephano's
repeated characterisation of the bottle as a 'book'
associates the alcohol through which he enslaves
Caliban with the book which Caliban himself sees
as the instrument of Prospero's mastery over him.
110 goose Generally used for a simpleton or silly
fellow, but possibly here suggesting either ridicule
of Trinculo's build, or else that in sticking out his
neck to take the drink he looks like a goose, with the
bottle as a beak.
116 Out o'th'moon 'Stephano's claim to be
descended from the moon was commonly made by
unscrupulous voyagers who seized the chance of
turning to account the polytheism of the Indians'
(Kermode).
117 when time was once upon a time.
118 My mistress Miranda. This might
confirm the ascription of the speech at 1.2.351–62
to her, though at 1.2.335–7 Caliban says that it is
Prospero who taught him how to name the sun and
moon.
119 dog . . . bush 'The man, according to the
folktale, was banished to the moon, variously for

stealing a bundle of kindling, or for gathering kindling on the Sabbath' (Orgel). For a literal-minded,
comic presentation of this image see *MND*
3.1.59–60, and 5.1.257–9, where Starveling, representing Moonshine, observes crossly to the nobles
who have been ridiculing his performance: 'All I
have to say is to tell you that the lanthorn is the
moon, I the man i'th'moon, this thorn-bush my
thorn-bush, and this dog my dog.' Caliban's adop-
tion of this popular superstition is to be taken as an
indication of his simple-mindedness, as is suggested by Trinculo's mocking comments at 123–4.
122 SD Trinculo's alienation from the growing
combination of Stephano and Caliban begins here,
and it makes theatrical sense for him to speak from
this point onwards either to himself or directly to
the audience.
122 this good light i.e. the sun.
122 shallow 'wanting in depth of mind, feeling
or character' (*OED* sv *adj* 6c).
124 credulous over-ready to believe.
124 Well drawn Trinculo comments, probably
ironically, on the huge gulp Caliban takes from the
bottle.
124 in good sooth truly.

TRINCULO [*Aside*] By this light, a most perfidious and drunken monster
   – when's god's asleep he'll rob his bottle.
CALIBAN I'll kiss thy foot; I'll swear myself thy subject.
STEPHANO Come on then: down and swear.   130
TRINCULO [*Aside*] I shall laugh myself to death at this puppy-headed
   monster. A most scurvy monster. I could find in my heart to beat
   him –
STEPHANO [*To Caliban*] Come, kiss.
TRINCULO – but that the poor monster's in drink. An abominable   135
   monster.
CALIBAN I'll show thee the best springs; I'll pluck thee berries;
   I'll fish for thee, and get thee wood enough.
   A plague upon the tyrant that I serve!
   I'll bear him no more sticks, but follow thee,   140
   Thou wondrous man.
TRINCULO [*Aside*] A most ridiculous monster, to make a wonder of a
   poor drunkard.
CALIBAN I prithee let me bring thee where crabs grow;

127, 131, 134, 142 SDS *This edn; not in* F   137–41 *As Pope; as prose in* F   144–9 *As Pope; as prose in* F

127 perfidious treacherous.

129 kiss thy foot A sign of servility. The kissing
of the Pope's foot was frequently invoked in anti-
Catholic propaganda.

131 puppy-headed Generally taken to mean
'stupid' rather than as a description of his appearance. Though it has been argued that Trinculo's
epithet reflects a legend, founded on an etymology
which derived 'cannibal' from the Latin *canis*
('dog'), which represented them as men with dog's
heads, the tone of his remark does not seem obviously to invoke this menacing image. (See E. C.
Brown, 'Caliban, Columbus and canines in *The
Tempest*', *N&Q*, 47 (2000), 92–4; Mario Klarer,
'Cannibalism and the carnivalesque: incorporation
as Utopia in the early image of America', *NLH*, 30
(1999), 389–410; p. 391, reproduces an early sixteenth-century image of dog-headed men enthusiastically butchering and eating a human body.)

133–5 him . . . but Trinculo's speech continues
round Stephano's interruption.

135 in drink drunk.

135 abominable F's 'abhominable' was the customary spelling in the period, and it suggested a
false derivation of the word from the Latin 'ab
homine', signifying 'away from men, inhuman,
beastly' (*OED* etymology). This is the implication
in Trinculo's use of the term.

137–49 Caliban's speeches are printed as prose in

F, but from Pope onwards editors have lineated as
verse.

137–8 The fact that Caliban exchanges one servitude for another is emphasised by the way in which
he here replicates his behaviour to the newly arrived
Prospero (1.2.337–9), and also by the contrast
between his willingness now to 'get wood' and his
angry rejection of the task at 1.2.315.

141 wondrous man A further comic recollection of Ferdinand's reaction to Miranda at 1.2.425.

142 wonder In Trinculo's ironic comment
'wonder' edges towards its other common meaning
of 'strange prodigy'.

144–9 I prithee . . . rock As will appear by the
following notes, Caliban's list of promised delica-
cies is distinctly odd. Whilst the temptation is to try
to make sense of his various offerings in terms of
their desirability as food, the very strangeness of the
list underlines the exotic nature of the island.

144 crabs Usually taken to mean 'crab-apples'
(small, wild apples), but these are sour-tasting
and eaten only when preserved in sugar as a jelly.
Their bitterness, indeed, is proverbial (Tilley
C783). It is the verb 'grow' which has persuaded
editors that the shellfish is not meant here, but,
as Orgel observes, this is not a conclusive argument, and it is quite possible that Caliban is pro-
mising to find edible crustaceans rather than
inedible fruit.

And I with my long nails will dig thee pig-nuts,   145
Show thee a jay's nest, and instruct thee how
To snare the nimble marmoset. I'll bring thee
To clust'ring filberts, and sometimes I'll get thee
Young scamels from the rock. Wilt thou go with me?

STEPHANO   I prithee, now lead the way without any more talking. Trin-   150
culo, the king and all our company else being drowned, we will
inherit here. [*To Caliban*] Here; bear my bottle. Fellow Trinculo,
we'll fill him by and by again.

CALIBAN   (*Sings drunkenly*) Farewell, master; farewell, farewell.

TRINCULO   A howling monster; a drunken monster.   155

CALIBAN   [*Singing*] No more dams I'll make for fish,
         Nor fetch in firing
         At requiring,

---

149 scamels] F; shamois *Theobald;* sea-mels *Malone;* staniels *Theobald conj.;* seamews *Oxford (Jackson conj.)*   152 SD *Orgel; not in* F

145 pig-nuts An edible wild tuber, also called 'earth-nuts' and other names.

146 jay An odd species to offer, since the jay was prized for its plumage, rather than as food. Since Caliban offers to show them the nest, he may be thinking of eggs rather than the bird – but again there is no record of the eggs being considered a delicacy.

147 marmoset A small monkey. Harcourt, in *A Relation of a Voyage to Guiana* (1613), calls it 'good meate' (Kermode).

148 filberts hazelnuts.

149 scamels This unique word has provoked endless discussion, and elicited much editorial ingenuity – though Malone's comment: 'It is no Matter which of the Readings we embrace, so we take a Word signifying the Name of something in Nature', remains eminently reasonable. Though the most obvious sense would seem to be some kind of mollusc, the most plausible emendation orthographically is to 'sea-mels', a variant of sea-mew (a gull). The suggestion is supported by the fact that Strachey gives an account of catching sea-birds 'of the bigness of an English . . . Sea-Mewe', but contradicted by Tobias Venner, in *Via Recta ad Vitam Longam* (1637), who says that 'The Seagull or Meaw . . . is of a very ill juyce, and is not only unpleasant, but also very offensive to the stomach' (p. 84). It is not impossible that Shakespeare here preserves a now lost dialect word (Malone records that 'Mr Holt asserted that limpets are in some places called scams').

150 prithee F has no comma here. It could equally be placed after 'now'.

151 our company else the rest of our companions.

152 inherit Stephano seems not yet fully to have grasped the presence of Prospero on the island, since he sees his succession as an unproblematic consequence of the death of the Neapolitans. At the same time, however, he casually repeats Prospero's disinheritance of Caliban, this time (unlike at 1.2.332) without any answering protest.

Here . . . bottle This remark is most probably addressed to Caliban, who thus performs an act of service, in a parody of the role of cup-bearer to the monarch, though the instruction could be directed to Trinculo with a comma after 'bottle'.

153 him i.e. the bottle.

153 by and by soon, or immediately.

154 SD F's SD may be misplaced here, anticipating the actual song which follows.

156 dams . . . fish i.e. dams creating pools in which fish could be trapped. Possibly alluding to the artificial fish weirs created by the Virginians, mentioned by Ralph Lane: 'wee had no weares of fish, neither coulde our men skill of the making of them' (Hakluyt, VIII, 334–6). But Ard3 points out that the practice was common in England too (and see 4.1.64 n.).

157 firing firewood.

158 At requiring On request.

Nor scrape trencher, nor wash dish,
Ban, ban, Ca-caliban   160
Has a new master – get a new man.
Freedom, high-day, high-day freedom, freedom high-day, freedom.
STEPHANO O brave monster, lead the way!

Exeunt

3.1 *Enter* FERDINAND, *bearing a log*

FERDINAND [*Sets down the log*] There be some sports are painful, and
         their labour
    Delight in them sets off. Some kinds of baseness

---

159 trencher] *Pope;* trenchering F   Act 3, Scene 1   3.1] *Actus Tertius. Scœna Prima* F   1 SD *This edn; not in* F   1 and]
F; *but Pope*   2 sets] *Rowe;* set F

---

159 Caliban disowns the standard mealtime
duties of a household servant. Meals were served in
large communal 'dishes' from which individuals
helped themselves, placing food on 'trenchers',
which were originally of bread. Between courses, as
Hugh Rhodes advised, the servant removed 'the
Morsels that they doe leave on their Trenchours.
Then with your Trenchour knyfe take off such
fragments . . . and sette them down cleane agayne'
(*The booke of Nurture, or Schoole of Good Maners for
Men, Servants and Children* (1577), sig. A5ᵛ). It is
this action to which Caliban alludes in the verb
'scrape'. The point here is precisely the typical
nature of these duties – we may doubt whether
Prospero and Miranda managed formal meals, or
whether Caliban, banished from the cell, in reality
waited at table.

159 trencher Most editions gloss as 'wooden
plate' (*OED* sv *n*¹ 2), but bread was still also used as
a plate in this period (though *OED* wrongly gives
the last use for this meaning as 1513). F's 'trenchering' is the only example cited by *OED*, and may be
explained by the influence on the compositor of
'firing' and 'requiring' in the previous line.

160 Ban . . . Ca-caliban Caliban makes a nonsense refrain out of his own name. 'Ca-caliban'
might represent a drunken hiccup.

161 get a new man Addressed to Prospero, who
must find a new servant.

162 Freedom . . . freedom In F this line is
clearly set off from the song, but Caliban could (and
in performance often does) continue in a repetitive,
rhythmic chant.

162 high-day holiday, feast day. Martin W.
Walsh notes the connection of drunken revelry with
changing of masters at the feast of Martinmas
(*Cahiers Elisabéthains*, 43 (1993), 57–60).

Act 3, Scene 1
1 SD Ferdinand speaks directly to the audience,
and in virtually every performance does in fact stop
working in order to speak. The addition of a stage
direction assists in clarifying the problematic line 15
below.

1–2 There be . . . sets off 'The pleasure we take
in some recreations cancels out, or else is height-
ened by, the labour involved in them.' The notion
has a quasi-proverbial status (cf. *Mac.* 2.3.42: 'The
labour we delight in physics pain'; Tilley D407:
'What we do willingly is easy'). Ferdinand's speech
is constructed out of a series of paradoxical propositions – and it is important here that the metrical
stress falls upon 'be', 'sports' and 'painful', rather
than upon 'some', heightening the oxymoronic
nature of the statement.

1 sports Recreations or diversions in general,
rather than the modern meaning of 'physical
games'.

1 painful Difficult, laborious, as well as the more
obvious modern sense.

2 sets off (1) removes (*OED* Set *v*¹ 147a (a)), (2)
acts as a foil to, sets in relief (*OED* Set *v*¹ 147e (a)).
If it is understood in the first sense, then 'Delight'
is its subject, producing the meaning 'pleasure
cancels the pain'; if in the second, 'labour' is the
subject, producing the meaning 'toil heightens the
pleasure by contrast'. Rowe's emendation of F's 'set'
has generally been accepted, though, as Orgel
points out, the labour of sports could be considered
a plural subject.

2–3 baseness . . . nobly Ferdinand's next
paradox derives from social class: 'to undergo social
degradation (by working with the hands) may
sometimes be a noble thing to do'. In 1587 a gentleman is defined as one who 'can live without

Are nobly undergone; and most poor matters
Point to rich ends. This my mean task would be
As heavy to me as odious, but   5
The mistress which I serve quickens what's dead,
And makes my labours pleasures. O, she is
Ten times more gentle than her father's crabbed –
And he's composed of harshness. I must remove
Some thousands of these logs, and pile them up,   10
Upon a sore injunction. My sweet mistress
Weeps when she sees me work, and says such baseness
Had never like executor. I forget. [*Picks up the log*]
But these sweet thoughts do even refresh my labours,
Most busy, least when I do it.   15

Enter MIRANDA, *and* PROSPERO [*following at a distance*]

MIRANDA   Alas, now pray you
Work not so hard. I would the lightning had
Burnt up those logs that you are enjoined to pile.

4–5 *As Pope;* Point . . . Taske / Would . . . but F   **5** as odious] F; as 'tis odious *Pope*   **9** remove] F; move *Pope*   **13** SD *This edn; not in* F   **15** busy, least] F2 (busie least); busie lest, F; busiest *Grant White* (*Holt White conj.*); busy-less *Theobald;* busilest *Kermode (Bulloch conj.);* busy left *Hirst*   **15** SD *following at a distance*] *Rowe* (subst.); *not in* F   **18** you are] F; thou art F2; thou'rt *Rowe;* you're *Hanmer*

---

manual labour' (Harrison, p. 114). This recollects of the lords' unwillingness to 'work' in 1.1.

3–4 poor . . . rich Compare Proverbs 3.17: 'there is that maketh himself poor, yet hath great riches'.

4–5 Point . . . but Pope's relineation here seems persuasive, with, as Malone pointed out, the word 'odious' pronounced as a trisyllable.

5 heavy wearisome.

5 but except that.

6 which Originally used of persons, as in the Lord's Prayer: 'Our Father, which art . . .'

quickens brings to life.

8 crabbed sour-tempered, peevish (by association with the fruit of the crab-apple – cf. 2.2.144 n.).

11 sore injunction harsh command (with legal overtones).

12–13 baseness . . . executor such a demeaning task was never performed by one such as I.

13 I forget i.e. to work at my task, hence suggesting that he immediately returns to it. Miranda's comment at 19 indicates that he is again carrying the logs, and her speech is more convincing if he has recommenced before she enters.

14 even To be pronounced 'e'en' for the metre.

14–15 Such thoughts as these are a refreshment to the work I must undertake, and they are most active when I cease from toil. These lines have been much discussed as they appear to contradict Ferdinand's earlier suggestion that thinking of Miranda makes the work itself pleasurable. Kermode therefore conjectures that the line should read 'most busilest [i.e. 'busiliest' = most busy] when I do it', glossing it thus: 'Ferdinand is perfectly cheerful, and returns to his task knowing that his sweet thoughts, so far from being present only when he idles, will attend him even more assiduously when he works.' But this misses the importance of the words 'I forget', with their implied cue to Ferdinand to resume his task, and their suggestion of a feeling of guilt at having temporarily abandoned it. The speech we have just heard is, precisely, an example of his thoughts working busily when he ceases from his labour, and these final lines act as an apology and justification for his taking time off from toil to express the consolation that he receives from Miranda's tender weeping over him. It is not contradictory to argue that whilst the thoughts of Miranda always assist him in his work, they crowd in upon him even more pleasurably when he takes a break from it.

15 SD Prospero might enter 'above' (as at 3.3.17).

18 you are Hanmer's elision to 'you're' preserves metrical regularity.

enjoined ordered.

Pray set it down, and rest you. When this burns
'Twill weep for having wearied you. My father   20
Is hard at study; pray now, rest yourself –
He's safe for these three hours.

FERDINAND   O most dear mistress,
The sun will set before I shall discharge
What I must strive to do.

MIRANDA   If you'll sit down
I'll bear your logs the while. Pray give me that;   25
I'll carry it to the pile.

FERDINAND   No, precious creature,
I'd rather crack my sinews, break my back,
Than you should such dishonour undergo,
While I sit lazy by.

MIRANDA   It would become me
As well as it does you; and I should do it   30
With much more ease, for my good will is to it,
And yours it is against.

PROSPERO [*Aside*]   Poor worm, thou art infected;
This visitation shows it.

MIRANDA   You look wearily.

FERDINAND No, noble mistress, 'tis fresh morning with me
When you are by at night. I do beseech you   35

---

27 I'd] *This edn;* I'ad *Pope;* I had F   32 it is against] F; against *Steevens*   32 SD *Capell; not in* F   35–6 beseech you /
Chiefly,] F; beseech you, / Chiefly *Rowe*

---

19 Pray . . . rest you For the audience there is
comedy in Miranda's concern, since we have only
just observed Ferdinand taking a rest.
  this i.e. the log.
  19–20 When . . . weep Miranda coins an elegant
conceit from the way wood exudes drops of resin as
it burns, which she imagines as tears.
  22 safe 'not likely to come out, intervene or do
hurt' (*OED* sv *adj* 10).
  23 discharge fulfil, complete (continuing the
legal overtones of 11, above).
  28 dishonour Both because of her class and her
gender.
  31–2 my good will . . . against I am well disposed to the task, whereas it offends you.
  32–3 Poor . . . wearily The conventional lineation here produces two very long lines. It might
be better to consider Prospero's interjection as two
short lines.
  32 Poor worm . . . infected Poor thing, you
have caught the disease (of love). 'Worm' is here
used 'with qualification expressing tenderness'

(*OED* sv *n* 10c) as an affectionate diminutive for
Miranda. The idea that love is an 'infection' is commonplace in the period; for a less benign version,
see Sonnet 147: 'My love is as a fever, longing still
/ For that which longer nurseth the disease.'
  33 visitation visit. The word carries overtones
of 'inspection for charitable purposes' (cf. 2.1.12).
  34–5 'tis fresh . . . night A conventional poetic
hyperbole. Malone cites Tibullus, Lib. iv, Elegy xiii:
'tu nocte vel atra lumen' (you are light even in
night's darkness). Ferdinand employs it though he
has not yet spent a night on the island, giving the
'illusion that he has loved Miranda for longer than
in fact he has' (Barton).
  35 by nearby.
  35–6 beseech . . . Chiefly I make my principal
request. All modern editors remove F's comma so
that this line becomes an explanatory parenthesis –
'my reason for asking is principally so that I may
add your name to my prayers'. Either reading is
possible.

Chiefly, that I might set it in my prayers,
What is your name?
MIRANDA   Miranda. – O my father,
I have broke your hest to say so.
FERDINAND   Admired Miranda,
Indeed the top of admiration, worth
What's dearest to the world. Full many a lady   40
I have eyed with best regard, and many a time
Th'harmony of their tongues hath into bondage
Brought my too diligent ear. For several virtues
Have I liked several women, never any
With so full soul but some defect in her   45
Did quarrel with the noblest grace she owed,
And put it to the soil. But you, O you,
So perfect and so peerless, are created
Of every creature's best.
MIRANDA   I do not know
One of my sex; no woman's face remember,   50

---

41 I have] F; I've *Pope*   47 soil] *This edn;* foile F   48 peerless] F2; peetlesse F

38 hest behest, command.

38–9 Admired Miranda . . . admiration Punning on the Latin meaning of her name, and intensifying the compliment by use of the rhetorical figure of *polyptoton* (repetition of words from the same root but with different endings). Ferdinand in this speech moves into a self-consciously elegant and rhetorical linguistic register.

40 dearest most valuable.

40–7 Full many . . . soil Ferdinand's amatory experience is turned into a carefully worked praise of Miranda. Donne uses the same technique more pithily in 'The Good Morrow': 'If any beauty I did see / Which I desir'd and got / 'Twas but a dream of thee.'

41 I have Possibly to be elided to 'I've'.

41 regard Both 'look' and 'estimation'.

43 diligent attentive.

43–4 several . . . several There is a probable play on the two meanings of the word: first 'different' and then 'a number of' (the rhetorical figure of *antistasis*).

45 With . . . soul The phrase probably refers to the quality of Ferdinand's affection – he loved none 'with such total passion' (*OED* Full *adj* 9a, citing this passage); but it could describe the quality of the women themselves who have not a completeness of moral virtue.

46 quarrel with stand in opposition to, challenge.

47 put . . . soil Her imperfections besmirched her noblest grace. For discussion of the reasons for emending F's 'foile' see Textual Analysis, p. 229.

47 you, O you Technically the rhetorical figure of *diacope* (repetition of a word with one or more words in between), used to express strong emotion, and here leading to the climax of Ferdinand's speech.

48–9 created . . . best Made as a composite of the best features of every creature (= 'created being'). Orlando, in his poem in *AYLI* 3.2.140–52, extravagantly praises Rosalind with an elaboration of the same conceit, which may, as Johnson suggested, derive ultimately from the story of the creation of a statue of Venus by Apelles as a synthesis of all the most beautiful women he could find. In *Ado* 2.3.28–9 Benedick, affirming his intention not to fall in love, varies the same idea: 'till all graces be in one woman, one woman shall not come in my grace'.

49–58 I do not . . . like of Miranda's speech is an equally formal response to Ferdinand's protestations, but where he founds his compliment on his previous experience with women, she derives her praise of him from her contrasting ignorance of men.

50 no . . . remember Whilst this line, together with 52, seems to contradict 1.2.443–4, it is pedantic to object to the inconsistency, since the purpose here is primarily to make the maximum contrast

Save from my glass, mine own. Nor have I seen
More that I may call men than you, good friend,
And my dear father. How features are abroad
I am skilless of; but by my modesty,
The jewel in my dower, I would not wish   55
Any companion in the world but you;
Nor can imagination form a shape
Besides yourself, to like of. But I prattle
Something too wildly, and my father's precepts
I therein do forget.   60

FERDINAND   I am in my condition
A prince, Miranda; I do think a king –
I would not so – and would no more endure
This wooden slavery than to suffer
The flesh-fly blow my mouth. Hear my soul speak.   65
The very instant that I saw you, did
My heart fly to your service, there resides
To make me slave to it, and for your sake
Am I this patient log-man.

MIRANDA   Do you love me?

FERDINAND   O heaven, O earth, bear witness to this sound,   70
And crown what I profess with kind event
If I speak true; if hollowly, invert

---

54 I am] F; I'm *Theobald*   **60–1** *As* F; *as one line / Steevens*   **60** therein do forget] F; do forget *Pope;* therein forget *Steevens*
64 wooden] F2; wodden F   **64** to] F; I would *Pope*

with Ferdinand's speech.

51 glass mirror, looking-glass.

53–4 How features . . . of I have no knowledge of what people elsewhere might look like.

54 modesty 'Womanly propriety of behaviour' (*OED* sv *n* 3a), including specifically her chastity.

54–5 modesty . . . dower That Miranda should characterise 'modesty' as the most important quality she could bring to her future husband in her 'dower' (dowry) indicates that she has fully internalised the standard Renaissance prescriptions for feminine virtue.

58–60 prattle . . . forget Prospero has clearly instructed her also in the conventional view that women should be sparing in their speech. Thomas Becon, for example, asserted: 'There is nothing that doth so much commend, advance, set forth, adorn, deck, trim, and garnish a maid as silence' (quoted in Katherine Usher Henderson and Barbara F. McManus, *Half Humankind*, 1985, p. 54).

60–1 These two lines are frequently represented as a single split line, but their unmetricality makes this less than persuasive.

61 condition rank, social status.

63 would not so wish it were not the case.

64 suffer endure; permit.

65 flesh-fly Fly that lays its eggs in dead flesh.

65 blow my mouth deposit its eggs in my mouth.

67 there resides The poetic conceit of the heart of a lover physically 'residing' in the beloved is commonplace. Cf. Donne, 'The Message', line 9: 'Send home my harmless heart again.'

68 to it i.e. to her service.

69 patient (1) long-suffering (*OED* sv *adj* 1b), (2) diligent, unwearied (*OED* sv *adj* 1d).

70 sound In the restricted sense 'utterance, speech' (*OED* sv *n*³ 4a). Ferdinand is either calling the heavens to witness what he is about to say, or responding to Miranda's speech.

71 kind event favourable outcome.

72 hollowly insincerely.

72–3 invert . . . mischief turn the very best that is promised me to evil or misfortune.

What best is boded me to mischief. I,
Beyond all limit of what else i'th'world,
Do love, prize, honour you.

MIRANDA   I am a fool   75
To weep at what I'm glad of.

PROSPERO [*Aside*]   Fair encounter
Of two most rare affections. Heavens rain grace
On that which breeds between 'em.

FERDINAND   Wherefore weep you?

MIRANDA At mine unworthiness, that dare not offer
What I desire to give, and much less take   80
What I shall die to want. But this is trifling,
And all the more it seeks to hide itself
The bigger bulk it shows. Hence, bashful cunning,
And prompt me, plain and holy innocence.
I am your wife, if you will marry me;   85
If not, I'll die your maid. To be your fellow
You may deny me, but I'll be your servant
Whether you will or no.

FERDINAND [*Kneeling*]   My mistress, dearest,

---

76 SD *Capell; not in* F   88 SD *Orgel subst.; not in* F   88–90 *As Orgel;* dearest / And ... then?/ *Steevens*

---

74 what whatever.

74 world F has no comma here – perhaps appropriately for the rush of Ferdinand's feelings.

75 love ... honour Echoing, but overgoing, the husband's promise to his wife in the marriage service, that he will 'love her, comfort her, honour and keep her'.

78 that ... 'em Prospero is referring principally to the growth of their mutual affection, but his words may also look forward to children from their marriage.

79–80 dare not ... give Miranda feels that her 'unworthiness' prevents her from offering herself to Ferdinand. Orgel suggests that the offer is 'unconsciously sexual'; but Miranda is perfectly conscious of the significance of her virginity, and of the social constraints that forbid her articulating her sexual desire, even if she is only imperfectly aware or in control of the potential double entendres of her speech. The tendency in recent productions to give Miranda a more openly sexual nature than was customary in the past is not as anachronistic as it might seem – unambiguously virtuous women in many Renaissance plays acknowledge their desires, though usually only when alone, or in the company of other women. Sophonisba in Marston's *The Wonder of Women, or the Tragedy of Sophonisba*, 1.2.47, however, says

to her husband: 'What I dare think I boldly speak.'

81 die to want die if I lack it. (The commonplace double entendre of 'die' as 'experience orgasm' is barely repressed, though not intended by Miranda.)

81 trifling prattling (with the implication of evasive euphemism). The clauses in Miranda's first sentence are actually rhetorically balanced repetitions of the same syntactical pattern (the figure of *isocolon*).

82–3 all the more ... it shows 'The imagery here is of secret pregnancy' (Barton).

83 bashful cunning i.e. the euphemism she has adopted out of (deceitful) modesty.

85 I am your wife The shock of Miranda's statement derives from its blunt contrast to the rhetorical elaboration which has preceded it, as well as from its transgression of conventional female 'modesty'. (See Introduction, p. 75.) The present tense of her statement is significant – see below 91–2 n.

86 maid Both 'virgin' and 'servant'.

86 fellow (1) bedfellow, wife, (*OED* sv *n* 4) (2) companion, social equal (*OED* sv *n* 5).

88 mistress i.e. 'a woman who has command over a man's heart' (*OED* sv *n* 10), emphatically not 'an illicit lover'.

And I thus humble ever.
MIRANDA My husband then?
FERDINAND   Aye, with a heart as willing   90
As bondage e'er of freedom. Here's my hand.
MIRANDA And mine, with my heart in't; and now farewell
—Till half an hour hence.
FERDINAND   A thousand thousand.

Exeunt [Ferdinand and Miranda separately]

PROSPERO So glad of this as they I cannot be,
Who are surprised with all; but my rejoicing   95
At nothing can be more. I'll to my book,
For yet ere supper-time must I perform
Much business appertaining.   *Exit*

3.2 *Enter* CALIBAN, STEPHANO *and* TRINCULO

STEPHANO Tell not me. When the butt is out we will drink water, not
a drop before; therefore bear up, and board 'em. Servant monster,
drink to me.

---

90 as] F; so F2   93 SD *Exeunt . . . separately*] *Capell subst; Exeunt* F   Act 3, Scene 2   3.2.] *Scæna Secunda* F   1 Tell not
me.] *Orgel;* Tell not me, F

---

89 thus humble Indicating that he kneels or makes a low bow to her.

90–1 as willing . . . freedom as desirous ('willing') as ever the slave is to be free (a particularly loaded image in this play).

91–2 Here's . . . And mine In England at this time, as Martin Ingram points out, 'the essential requisite for a legally binding union was not the formal solemnisation of marriage in church but a *contract* – called, in popular usage, "spousals", "making sure" or "handfasting" – by which the couple took each other as husband and wife using words of the present tense (*per verba de praesenti*)' (*Church Courts, Sex and Marriage in England, 1570–1640*, 1987, pp. 189–90). This Ferdinand and Miranda have done (85, 90–2). Strenuous efforts were being made during the sixteenth and seventeenth centuries to enforce the celebration of marriages in church and to require parental consent, but though they might be disapproved of, contracts such as these were still regarded as binding – and frequently led to consummation before any public ceremony was enacted. It is in this context that Prospero's later anxiety about the sexual restraint of the couple (4.1.15–23, 51–4) must be seen, since he knows, from overseeing this meeting, that their union is in effect already achieved. (This is a central

issue in *MM*, and in *AYLI* the mock 'marriage' of Rosalind-as-Ganymede with Orlando supervised by Celia in 4.1 flirts comically with the same situation.)

92 with . . . in't Proverbial. 'With heart and hand' (Tilley H339).

93 thousand thousand i.e. a million farewells.

95 surprised (1) taken unawares, (2) amazed.

95 with all (1) with everything that has happened, (2) 'withal'; therewith.

98 appertaining related to this.

Act 3, Scene 2

1 Tell not me Stephano enters in the middle of a conversation, and might be addressing either Trinculo or Caliban. It is most likely, however, that he is imagined as responding to criticism from Trinculo of his excessive drinking, with 'tell' carrying the meaning 'to direct the attention to a fault by way of admonition' (*OED* Tell *v* 8a), and so is saying, 'Don't criticise me.'

1 butt is out the cask is finished.

2 bear up . . . board 'em approach and attack. These terms from naval warfare are here used for an assault on the bottle. F's comma suggests that Stephano might separate the two parts of the statement – 'lift the bottle, then drink'.

2 Servant monster Often, following Theobald,

TRINCULO [*Aside*] Servant monster? The folly of this island! They say
there's but five upon this isle; we are three of them – if th'other   5
two be brained like us, the state totters.

STEPHANO Drink, servant monster, when I bid thee; thy eyes are
almost set in thy head.

TRINCULO Where should they be set else? He were a brave monster
indeed if they were set in his tail.   10

STEPHANO My man-monster hath drowned his tongue in sack. For my
part, the sea cannot drown me – I swam, ere I could recover the
shore, five and thirty leagues off and on. By this light, thou shalt
be my lieutenant, monster, or my standard.

TRINCULO Your lieutenant if you list; he's no standard.   15

STEPHANO We'll not run, monsieur monster.

TRINCULO Nor go neither; but you'll lie like dogs, and yet say nothing
neither.

STEPHANO Moon-calf, speak once in thy life, if thou beest a good
moon-calf.   20

---

4 SD *This edn; not in* F   13 off and on. By] *Cam.;* off and on; by *Rowe;* off and on, by F   13 light, thou] *Theobald;* light
thou F; light. Thou *Capell*   14 lieutenant, monster] *Rowe;* Lieutenant Monster F

hyphenated. The collocation seems to have been
sufficiently striking for it to be picked up by Jonson
in the Induction to *Bartholomew Fair*, where the
Scrivener sets out articles of agreement between
author and audience, and includes mocking allusion
to Shakespeare's late plays: 'If there be never a
servant-monster i'the Fair, who can help it? he
says: nor a nest of antics? He is loth to make
Nature afraid in his plays, like those that beget
Tales, Tempests, and such-like drolleries.' (And see
2.2.91 n.)

4 SD Throughout the early part of this scene
Trinculo is peripheral to the exchanges of Caliban
and Stephano, and his words seem to be directed
primarily to the audience until he is drawn into a
quarrel at line 23. It is, however, possible that he
argues directly with Stephano.

4 **Servant monster?** F's question mark has often
been changed to an exclamation mark, but Trinculo's incredulity at the absurd paradox is perhaps
better indicated by retaining it.

4 **folly** Either Trinculo makes a general comment
on the madness that has overtaken them on the
island, or else redefines Caliban as a 'freak', in
answer to his own question (the term was regularly
used in this sense).

6 **brained like us** have brains in the drunken
condition of ours.

6 **totters** is in a precarious condition, about to
collapse (*OED* Totter *v* 3b). The sense of 'totter' as
'walk unsteadily' was relatively recent at the time of
the play (*OED* sv *v* 4, 1602 as first instance), but is
clearly also invoked here.

8 **set** drunkenly fixed.

9 **set** placed. Trinculo's punning is, of course,
characteristic of the role of a jester.

9 **brave** splendid (ironic).

13 **five . . . leagues** Stephano exaggerates
distance (he claims to have swum about 160 km
(100 miles)).

13 **off and on** (1) one way or another, (2) by fits
and starts.

13 **By this light** F has a comma after 'on', and
the oath could equally well belong to the previous
sentence.

14 **standard** standard-bearer.

15 **list** like.

15 **no standard** i.e. he's reeling drunk. On stage
Caliban frequently falls over at this point.

16 **run** take flight.

17 **go** walk. Cf. 'He may ill run that cannot go'
(Tilley R208).

lie . . . say nothing Trinculo puns on 'lie down'
and 'tell lies' (Dent D510.2 'to lie like a dog').

CALIBAN How does thy honour? Let me lick thy shoe. I'll not serve
him, he is not valiant.

TRINCULO Thou liest, most ignorant monster; I am in case to jostle a
constable. Why, thou deboshed fish thou, was there ever man a
coward that hath drunk so much sack as I today? Wilt thou tell   25
a monstrous lie, being but half a fish, and half a monster?

CALIBAN Lo, how he mocks me. Wilt thou let him, my lord?

TRINCULO 'Lord', quoth he? That a monster should be such a natural!

CALIBAN Lo, lo again! Bite him to death, I prithee.

STEPHANO Trinculo, keep a good tongue in your head. If you prove a   30
mutineer, the next tree. The poor monster's my subject, and he shall
not suffer indignity.

CALIBAN I thank my noble lord. Wilt thou be pleased to hearken once
again to the suit I made to thee?

STEPHANO Marry will I. Kneel, and repeat it. I will stand, and so shall 35
Trinculo.

25–6 tell a] F; tell me a F2   34 to . . . thee] F; the suit I made thee *Steevens*

21–2 Caliban's speech as printed in F could be
understood as two pentameter lines – the ghost of
verse can often be heard in Caliban's words – but it
seems best to lineate as prose until 46. (See Textual
Analysis, p. 233.)

21 lick . . . shoe The idiom 'to *lick* someone's
boots (shoes)' is much less common in the period
that to '*kiss* someone's shoe' which is used earlier by
Caliban (2.2.138) and, for example, by Pistol in *H5*
4.1.47. (*OED* Foot *n* 35a gives only this example
from before the nineteenth century.) That Caliban
offers to 'lick' rather than 'kiss' Stephano's shoe,
therefore, makes his servility even more excessive.

22 not valiant Caliban may be remembering
Trinculo's fear at the beginning of 2.2.

23–4 in case . . . constable in a fit state to push
or shove an officer of the peace (as evidence of his
'valour').

24 deboshed fish 'Deboshed' is a form of
'debauched'. Its primary meaning in the period was
'one seduced from proper duty of obedience', but
it also could include drunkenness as part of its
implication (and perhaps particularly so in the collocation with 'fish', since 'to drink like a fish' was a
common phrase then as now). This spelling, the
commoner in the period, and revived in the nineteenth century, is perhaps worth retaining, since in
modern usage the word 'debauched' has come to
carry predominantly a sense of sexual licence,
which is not relevant here.

26 monstrous lie (1) an enormous untruth, (2)
a lie told by a monster.

26 half a fish . . . monster Trinculo insults

Caliban by suggesting that he cannot tell a truly
'monstrous' lie, since he is only half a monster.
(The line returns to Trinculo's earlier perception of
Caliban at 2.2.23 ff.). There are many mythological
beasts made up of two different animal elements.

28 natural simpleton. A paradox, since a
monster, by definition, is 'unnatural'. The distinction between a 'natural fool' and the 'fool artificial',
who consciously adopted the function of jester, is a
significant one in the period – and important to the
trading of insults between Caliban and Trinculo in
this scene (see below, 57).

30 keep a good tongue i.e. speak civilly. 'To
keep a good tongue in one's head' is proverbial
(Tilley T 402).

31 next tree i.e. he will hang Trinculo from the
nearest tree.

32 indignity Treatment unworthy of his status
as Stephano's subject.

33–4 These lines, set as prose in F, were lineated
as verse by Pope, dividing at 'pleased', and the
metre 'improved' by Steevens.

34 suit 'Petition made to prince or other high
personage' (*OED* sv *n* 11a). Stephano and Caliban
play out the rituals of a mock royal court.

35 Marry Abbreviation of 'by the Virgin Mary';
a mild oath.

35 Kneel . . . stand Stephano again constructs a
quasi-courtly ritual. Smith quotes Leopold von
Wedel's report of Queen Elizabeth calling a
courtier to her to converse, and 'when she does
so, he has to kneel until she orders him to rise'
(p. 83).

Enter ARIEL *invisible*

CALIBAN As I told thee before, I am subject to a tyrant, a sorcerer, that
    by his cunning hath cheated me of the island.

ARIEL Thou liest.

CALIBAN [*To Trinculo*] Thou liest, thou jesting monkey thou. I would   40
    my valiant master would destroy thee. I do not lie.

STEPHANO Trinculo, if you trouble him any more in's tale, by this
    hand, I will supplant some of your teeth.

TRINCULO Why, I said nothing.

STEPHANO Mum then, and no more. [*To Caliban*] Proceed.   45

CALIBAN I say by sorcery he got this isle;
    From me he got it. If thy greatness will
    Revenge it on him – for I know thou dar'st,
    But this thing dare not –

STEPHANO That's most certain.   50

CALIBAN Thou shalt be lord of it, and I'll serve thee.

STEPHANO How now shall this be compassed? Canst thou bring me to
    the party?

CALIBAN Yea, yea, my lord, I'll yield him thee asleep,
    Where thou mayst knock a nail into his head.   55

ARIEL Thou liest, thou canst not.

37–8 *As Pope;* As . . . Tirant, / A . . . me / Of . . . Island F; As . . . tyrant, / A . . . hath / Cheated *Steevens* **40** SD *Orgel;*
not in F **40–1** *As Orgel;* Thou . . . thou: / I . . . thee. / I . . . lye. F **45** SD *Johnson; not in* F

36 SD *invisible* See note on 2.1.180 SD above.
Kermode suggests that the scene which follows is
'perhaps a variation on the ancient echo-scene,
which was popular at this period. It is found in
commedia dell'arte'. Orgel points to the parallels
with Puck in *MND* 3.2.354 ff. and the tricks
played on the Pope in Marlowe's *Doctor Faustus*,
7.50 ff.
37 subject to a tyrant By characterising
Prospero as a 'tyrant' Caliban brings into play the
much-debated question of justified rebellion. See
Introduction, p. 56.
38 cunning The older meaning 'knowledge,
learning' is perhaps the dominant one here, though
combined with the sense of 'trickery'.
39 Thou liest Ariel echoes Trinculo's earlier
accusation at 23, and in performance usually imitates Trinculo's voice. Though in most productions
Trinculo reacts with astonishment to Ariel's words,
in others his bemusement at the accusations levelled
at him suggests that he himself does not hear Ariel.
40–1 Lineated as verse in F, this seems a marginal
case, and is therefore perhaps better taken as prose.

41 valiant master i.e. Stephano.
43 supplant uproot, remove. The term in this
sense is usually applied to plants or trees, but in this
play carries a political resonance, which may affect
its connotations here.
45 Mum Keep quiet ('I will say nothing but
mum' is proverbial, Tilley N279).
49 this thing i.e. Trinculo (continuing the claim
that Trinculo is 'not valiant').
51 thee Caliban's speech has now moved decisively into verse, and, as Orgel notes, reading this as
a pentameter line produces an appropriate stress on
'thee', emphasising Caliban's rejection of Prospero.
52 compassed brought about.
53 party person concerned.
54 asleep Replicating the threat to the sleeping
Alonso in 2.1.
55 knock a nail The sleeping Sisera is murdered
by Jael in this fashion in the biblical story (Judges
4.21). In Jonson's *Oberon* (1610), in a clearly comic
environment, a Satyr suggests that sleeping Silvans
might be woken with 'a good nail / Through their
temples' (lines 185–6).

CALIBAN   What a pied ninny's this? [*To Trinculo*] Thou scurvy patch!
[*To Stephano*] I do beseech thy greatness give him blows,
And take his bottle from him. When that's gone,
He shall drink nought but brine, for I'll not show him   60
Where the quick freshes are.

STEPHANO   Trinculo, run into no further danger. Interrupt the monster
one word further, and by this hand, I'll turn my mercy out o'doors,
and make a stockfish of thee.

TRINCULO   Why, what did I? I did nothing. I'll go farther off.   65

STEPHANO   Didst thou not say he lied?

ARIEL   Thou liest.

STEPHANO   Do I so?

[*Strikes Trinculo*]

Take thou that! As you like this, give me the lie another time.

TRINCULO   I did not give the lie. Out o'your wits, and hearing too? A   70
pox o'your bottle! This can sack and drinking do. A murrain on
your monster, and the devil take your fingers!

CALIBAN   Ha, ha, ha!

STEPHANO   Now forward with your tale. [*To Trinculo*] Prithee stand
further off.   75

CALIBAN   Beat him enough; after a little time
I'll beat him too.

STEPHANO   Stand farther. [*To Caliban*] Come, proceed.

---

57 SD *This edn; not in* F   58 SD *This edn; not in* F   65 *As Pope; Why, . . . nothing: /* Ile F   65 go farther] F; go no further
F2   68 SD *Rowe subst.; not in* F   70 give the lie] F; give thee the lie F4   74 SD *Orgel; not in* F   78 SD *Oxford; not in* F

57 **pied ninny** parti-coloured fool. Trinculo is
clad in the jester's motley (though modern productions frequently reject the invitation to dress him
thus). There may be something of an *ad personam*
joke here, in that the actor thought likely to have
played either Trinculo or Caliban, Robert Armin,
had recently published a collection of stories entitled *A Nest of Ninnies* (1608), most of which
concern 'natural' fools.

57 **patch** jester, fool. Probably an anglicised form
of Italian *pazzo*, a fool, though derived in the period
from 'the nickname of Cardinal Wolsey's fool'
(*OED* Patch *n*² etymology), or else referring again
to the 'patched' costume of the jester (cf. 'a patched
fool' in *MND* 4.1.209).

61 **quick freshes** flowing springs of fresh water
(cf. 1.2.339).

64 **stockfish** Salted fish, beaten to tenderise it
before cooking. 'To beat like a stockfish' is proverbial (Tilley s867).

69 **give me the lie** call me a liar. To suggest that
someone was lying was considered grounds for a
challenge to a duel; Touchstone comically elaborates an anatomy of lies in *AYLI* 5.4.85–103.

70 **give the lie** F4's reading, 'give thee the lie',
adopted by many editors, is a plausible emendation
– it would be an easy compositorial error to omit the
pronoun, particularly if, as Kermode suggests, it
was spelt 'the' in the copy.

71 **murrain** plague.

72 **devil . . . fingers** Trinculo curses the hand
that has just struck him.

74 SD It is just possible, as Furness and others
suggest, that Stephano is affronted by Caliban's
smell and urges him, not Trinculo, to stand clear.

78 Stephano's line can be taken as completing
Caliban's verse. Though it seems best to preserve
Stephano as a prose-speaker, here as elsewhere he is
attracted by the rhythms of Caliban's poetry. (See
Textual Analysis, p. 233.)

CALIBAN Why, as I told thee, 'tis a custom with him
    I'th'afternoon to sleep. There thou mayst brain him,   80
    Having first seized his books; or with a log
    Batter his skull, or paunch him with a stake,
    Or cut his wezand with thy knife. Remember
    First to possess his books; for without them
    He's but a sot, as I am, nor hath not   85
    One spirit to command – they all do hate him
    As rootedly as I. Burn but his books;
    He has brave ùtensils – for so he calls them –
    Which when he has a house, he'll deck withal.
    And that most deeply to consider, is   90
    The beauty of his daughter. He himself
    Calls her a nonpareil. I never saw a woman
    But only Sycorax my dam, and she;
    But she as far surpasseth Sycorax
    As great'st does least.   95
STEPHANO Is it so brave a lass?
CALIBAN Ay, lord, she will become thy bed, I warrant,
    And bring thee forth brave brood.
STEPHANO Monster, I will kill this man. His daughter and I will be

---

80 There] F; then *Collier MS.* 92 never saw a woman] F; never saw woman *Pope;* ne'er saw woman *Theobald*

79–80 custom . . . sleep cf. Old Hamlet, whose afternoon sleep also provides opportunity for murder (*Ham* 1.5.59–60).

80 There Then (Abbott 70), but the sense of place is also present.

82 paunch stab in the belly, disembowel; a term used both of killing in warfare and in the contexts of hunting or butchery.

83 wezand throat, wind-pipe.

83 Remember Be mindful, do not forget.

85 sot fool.

87 rootedly groundedly, firmly (*OED* sv *adv* gives this as the first instance of the term).

87 Burn but (1) Burn only his books (since other things he possesses will be useful), (2) Only be certain to burn his books. F's punctuation, a comma after 'books', leans towards the first of these readings. Caliban's insistence on the significance of Prospero's books as the source of his power is borne out by Prospero's later decision to drown his book as a sign of giving up his magic.

88 ùtensils The term could be applied specifically to vessels, pots and pans, or more generally to household stuff. This meaning suits with sense (1) for the previous line. It is possible that Caliban means magic paraphernalia, which he has heard Prospero half-jokingly call his 'utensils', but it seems more likely that, having established the priority of the destruction of the books, he now persuades Stephano to agree to the conspiracy first by the promise of material 'bravery', and then by offering him Miranda as a prize. Accented on the first syllable.

90 that that which it is.

92 nonpareil without equal.

92–3 I never . . . Sycorax Parallels Miranda's comments at 3.1.51–3.

96 Another example of an apparent completion of Caliban's half-line.

97 become thy bed be suitable to, give grace to, your bed.

98 bring . . . brood As in his comment on his own attempted rape (1.2.349–51), Caliban sees Miranda as a fertile breeder rather than simply as a source of sexual pleasure.

king and queen – 'save our graces! – and Trinculo and thyself shall   100
be viceroys. Dost thou like the plot, Trinculo?
TRINCULO Excellent.
STEPHANO Give me thy hand. I am sorry I beat thee. But while thou
liv'st, keep a good tongue in thy head.
CALIBAN Within this half hour will he be asleep,   105
   Wilt thou destroy him then?
STEPHANO Ay, on mine honour.
ARIEL This will I tell my master.
CALIBAN Thou mak'st me merry. I am full of pleasure,
   Let us be jocund. Will you troll the catch   110
   You taught me but whilere?
STEPHANO At thy request, monster, I will do reason, any reason. Come
on, Trinculo, let us sing.
   [*They sing*] Flout 'em, and scout 'em
       And scout 'em, and flout 'em.   115
       Thought is free.
CALIBAN That's not the tune.

---

114 SD *They sing*] Orgel; *Sings* F 114 scout] Rowe; *cout* F 115 scout] *skowt* F

100 'save God save.
101 viceroys The authorised deputies of a king.
The term is usually used of the governor of an out-
lying province or part of an empire, and thus is
wildly inappropriate to the island which Stephano
intends to rule.
101 plot Used in the modern sense, though
Kermode suggests it might also imply the obsolete
sense of 'a skeleton programme giving a synopsis of
a masque or entertainment'.
102 Excellent 'Uttered, presumably, in a sulky
tone of voice, which prompts Stephano's subsequent attempt to make amends' (Barton).
104 good tongue Compare 30, above.
108 Suggesting that this is a conspiracy which,
unlike that of Sebastian and Antonio in 2.1, Prospero does not foresee.
110 jocund cheerful.
110 troll sing.
110 catch A musical composition in the form of
a round, where each singer takes up the same tune
in sequence (as in 'Three blind mice' or 'Frère
Jacques'). See *TN* 2.3.58–72 for a similar drunken
catch and an analogous suggestion of subversive
companionship in the musical combination.
111 but whilere only recently.
112 do reason do anything reasonable.
114 SD There are a number of possible ways to
stage this episode. Stephano specifically invites

Trinculo to sing, but since he has just taught
Caliban the tune, it is possible that Caliban also
joins in.
 Flout Mock.
 scout deride (*OED* sv *v*² 1). Orgel objects to
Rowe's emendation of F's 'cout', that 'the similarity between the two words exists only in a modernised text: F reads "cout" and "skowt"'. But since
OED records 'cout' only as a variant of 'colt' and
'coot', explanations have been forced to resort to the
possibility of it being a 'nonce word or unrecorded
slang'. By contrast, the chiastic repetition of the
two lines, as emended, seems much more likely as
the lyric for a rhythmical popular catch.
 116 Proverbial (Tilley T244); cf. Maria in *TN*
1.3.69. In the context of this conspiracy, however,
an audience might remember that treason was identified as 'imagining' the death of the sovereign, and
recall the biblical words: 'Wish the king no evil in
thy thought, nor speak no hurt of him in thy privy
chamber' (Ecclesiastes 10.20). Annabel Patterson
points out that conspiratorial optimism is undercut
by Ariel's surveillance (*Shakespeare and the Popular
Voice*, 1989, p. 161).
 117 That's not the tune Caliban could refer
either to the catch itself or to the tune Ariel plays.
If it is the first then either (1) Stephano and Trinculo sing a tune Caliban does not recognise as the
one he has been taught; or (2) their performance

Ariel plays the tune on a tabor and pipe

STEPHANO What is this same?

TRINCULO This is the tune of our catch, played by the picture of
Nobody.   120

STEPHANO If thou beest a man, show thyself in thy likeness: if thou
beest a devil, take't as thou list.

TRINCULO O, forgive me my sins!

STEPHANO He that dies pays all debts! I defy thee! Mercy upon us!

CALIBAN Art thou afeared?   125

STEPHANO No, monster, not I.

CALIBAN Be not afeared; the isle is full of noises,
          Sounds, and sweet airs, that give delight and hurt not.
          Sometimes a thousand twangling instruments
          Will hum about mine ears; and sometime voices,   130
          That if I then had waked after long sleep,

---

129 Sometimes] F; Sometime *Dyce*   129 twangling] F; twanging *Pope*   130 sometime] F; sometimes F2

(perhaps including Caliban) falls apart as, in their
cups, they lose their musical way. If it applies to
Ariel's playing then (3) he begins to play before
Caliban speaks, eliciting a comment on the strangeness of the music. Any of these is possible in performance, though since Trinculo states that Ariel
plays the transmuted tune of their catch, (2) is the
most likely.

117 SD *tabor and pipe* A small drum hanging at
the side and played simultaneously with a three-
hole whistle held in one hand. The combination was
associated with popular festivity, and with the professional clown (as with Feste in *TN* 3.1.1–10 and
famously with William Kemp and Richard Tar-
leton). In Alciati's *Emblemata* (1614), a drunken
Bacchus plays these instruments (illustration 8).

119–20 picture of Nobody This may be a topical
allusion. Furness noted an anonymous comedy of
1606 entitled *Nobody and Somebody* which has a
picture on its title page of a man with head and limbs
but no body, and that its publisher, John Trundle,
used the sign of Nobody over his shop.

121–2 The implication of this speech is not
obvious. Stephano may first issue a challenge: 'If
you are a real man and not a coward, come out
so that we can see you', but then suddenly think
that it might be a devil, and fearfully backtrack,
crying 'take my words as you like'. On the other
hand 'take it as you list' can itself be an aggres-
sive phrase, and Orgel cites Kittredge's suggestion
that 'Stephano in his drunkenness has mixed his
terms up: it is the devil who should be asked to
appear in his true shape, the man who should

be invited to take Stephano's challenge any way he
pleases.'

124 He . . . debts A proverb (Tilley D148), used
several times by Shakespeare in variant forms, e.g.
1H4 3.2.157.

127 noises Though nothing more than 'an agree-
able or melodious sound' (*OED* Noise *n* 5a) may be
implied, the word 'noise' could also be used of a
company of musicians or a musical ensemble (*OED*
Noise *n* 5b), suggesting that the sounds of which
Caliban speaks are not natural, but played by Ariel
and his fellow-sprites.

128 Sounds F's comma, omitted by many editors,
yet makes a distinction between the different kinds
of noise Caliban reports upon.

128 airs Though most often used of a vocal song,
an 'air' could indicate any tune, instrumental or sung.

129 twangling instruments The adjective is
most frequently used of the sound of plucked string
instruments, such as the lute or harp. Often used
pejoratively (as, for example, in Katherine's insult-
ing of the lute-teacher Hortensio as a 'twangling
jack', *Shr.* 2.1.158), it could also have a more positive connotation, as in Francis Quarles's version of
Psalm 137: 'The sprightly Twang of the melodious
lute'. In court masques twenty or more lutes of different sizes might play together, and it is perhaps
this opulent sound that Caliban's words suggested
to some of the seventeenth-century audience.

130 hum The verb (used also by Gonzalo in 2.1)
is not the most obvious verb for 'twangling' instruments. It is presumably the idea of 'continuous
noise' that is uppermost.

Will make me sleep again; and then in dreaming,
The clouds methought would open, and show riches
Ready to drop upon me, that when I waked
I cried to dream again.   135

STEPHANO   This will prove a brave kingdom to me, where I shall have
my music for nothing.

CALIBAN   When Prospero is destroyed.

STEPHANO   That shall be by and by: I remember the story.

[Exit Ariel, playing music]

TRINCULO   The sound is going away; let's follow it, and after do our   140
work.

STEPHANO   Lead, monster, we'll follow. I would I could see this taborer,
he lays it on.

TRINCULO   [*To Caliban*] Wilt come? I'll follow Stephano.

Exeunt

3.3   *Enter* ALONSO, SEBASTIAN, ANTONIO, GONZALO, ADRIAN,
FRANCISCO *and others*

GONZALO   By'r lakin, I can go no further, sir,
My old bones aches. Here's a maze trod indeed

139 SD *This edn; not in* F   144 SD *To Caliban*] *Orgel; not in* F   144 Wilt come?] F; *ascribed to Stephano / Grey conj.*   144
I'll follow Stephano] F; *I'll follow, Stephano Steevens;* STEPH. *I'll follow Capell*   Act 3, Scene 3   3.3] *Scena Tertia* F
0 SD. 2 *and others*] &c F; *om. Oxford*   2 aches] F; *ache* F2

135 cried . . . dream again cf. Sidney, *Astrophil
and Stella*, line 38, where the poet wakes from a
dream of his beloved and: 'seeing better sights in
sight's decay, / Called it anew, and wooed sleep
again'.
136 brave splendid.
136–7 have . . . nothing Orgel suspects a topical
allusion to the increasing expense of the musicians
at court, particularly in the performances of the
masque, but this is not necessary for the apprecia-
tion of the reductiveness of Stephano's reaction to
Caliban's poetry.
139 by and by The phrase (like the word
'presently') was, in the period, slipping from
meaning 'immediately' to indicating 'soon'. Here it
seems as if Stephano means the latter, as he puts
Caliban off, being for the moment more fascinated
by the music he hears. (It becomes, then a proleptic moment, anticipating the way in which Prospero
easily diverts the conspiracy later.)
139 SD Ariel leads them about the island as he had
earlier led Ferdinand.
143 lays it on bangs the drum enthusiastically.
144 Wilt come . . . Stephano This is the

reading implied by F's punctuation, with Trinculo
repeating Stephano's invitation to Caliban to lead
them off and himself offering to bring up the rear.
But it is equally possible that (1) he speaks to
Stephano, in which case a comma (as given by many
editors) is required after 'follow', or (2) that
Stephano, despite his invitation to Caliban to lead,
has himself set off in pursuit of the music, leaving
the others to tag along behind. Some editors have
assigned 'Wilt come?' to Stephano.

Act 3, Scene 3

0 SD.2 *and others* F's '*etc.*' is expanded by analogy
with 2.2.1. For the availability of actors to swell the
retinue in this scene, see Appendix 3, pp. 257–61.
1 By'r lakin A mild oath, an abbreviation of 'By
our Ladykin', a diminutive for 'Our Lady' (the
Virgin Mary).
2 aches Another possible scribal/compositorial
final 's' error – though a singular verb with plural
subject is a permissible construction. (See Textual
Analysis, pp. 227–8.)
maze The literary maze, from the legend of the
Minotaur onwards, involves the possibility of

Through forth-rights and meanders. By your patience,
I needs must rest me.
ALONSO   Old lord, I cannot blame thee,
Who am myself attached with weariness   5
To th'dulling of my spirits. Sit down, and rest.
Even here I will put off my hope, and keep it
No longer for my flatterer. He is drowned
Whom thus we stray to find, and the sea mocks
Our frustrate search on land. Well, let him go.   10
ANTONIO [*Drawing Sebastian aside*] I am right glad that he's so out of
hope.
Do not for one repulse forgo the purpose
That you resolved t'effect.
SEBASTIAN [*To Antonio*]   The next advantage
Will we take throughly.
ANTONIO   Let it be tonight;
For now they are oppressed with travail, they   15
Will not, nor cannot use such vigilance
As when they're fresh.
SEBASTIAN   I say tonight: no more.

---

11 SD *Drawing . . . aside*] Hanmer *(Aside to Seb.); not in* F   13 SD *To Antonio*] Capell *(Aside to Ant.); not in* F   13–14 *As*
Pope; *The next . . . throughly/* F   15 travail] F; *travel* F3

wrong turnings and false choices, but actual mazes
until the later seventeenth century were 'unicursal'
or single winding paths which might be cut in turf,
or bordered by hedges, and were to be found in
gardens, public places and in or near churches,
when they were used as part of a popular rite,
'treading the maze' (see Penelope Reed Doob, *The
Idea of the Labyrinth*, 1990). In emblem literature
either kind of maze might be used as a symbol of
the tribulations of life in the world (see illustration
23) and the image here carries that symbolic weight.
  3 forth-rights and meanders straight and
winding paths (as in a maze).
  3 By your patience With your permission.
  5 attached seized (*OED* attach *v.* 3). This is a
transferred sense from the original 'arrested'.
  6 To th'dulling . . . spirits The fatigue he
endures has a physiological effect in 'dulling' the
circulation of the spirits (see 1.2.485), and consequently induces a feeling of hopelessness.
  7 put off abandon.
  7–8 keep . . . flatterer The 'hope' which Alonso
abandons is figuratively represented as a courtly
sycophant who tells the monarch what he wishes to
hear.
  10 frustrate vain, defeated.
  11 SD Antonio and Sebastian begin this scene as

they did 2.2, setting themselves apart from their
companions.
  12 for one repulse because of one setback.
  14 throughly thoroughly, perfectly.
  15 now now that, since (cf. Epilogue 3n.).
  15 travail (1) labour, (2) journeying. The spellings
of 'travail' and 'travel' were interchangeable in the
period, and either or both meanings may apply here.
  17 they're The elision of F's 'they are' regularises the metre.
  17 SD *Solemn and strange music* For 'solemn'
music see 2.1.180 n. above. The epithet 'strange' is
frequently applied to the music which accompanied
antimasques at court – for example, to the dance of
witches in Jonson's *Masque of Queenes* (1609), and
to the masque of *frantics* in Campion's *The Lords'
Masque* (1613), though it could also signify simply
'otherworldly', as in the *strange and heavenly music*
called for in Dekker and Middleton's *The Magnificent Entertainment* (1604). The 'strangeness' of such
music might lie in its instrumentation (as in
Jonson's *Love Freed from Ignorance and Folly*, which
opens with *a strange Musique of wilde Instruments*),
or in the irregular rhythms or phrase structures
which are characteristic of some surviving antimasque music. If the direction is Crane's elaboration it is a felicitous one, for the combination of

Solemn and strange music, and [enter] PROSPERO *on the top, invisible*

ALONSO   What harmony is this? my good friends, hark!
GONZALO   Marvellous sweet music.

*Enter several strange shapes, bringing in a banquet, and dance about it
with gentle actions of salutations, and inviting the king, etc. to eat, they
depart*

ALONSO   Give us kind keepers, heavens! What were these?   20
SEBASTIAN   A living drollery! Now I will believe
          That there are unicorns; that in Arabia
          There is one tree, the phoenix' throne, one phoenix
          At this hour reigning there.
ANTONIO   I'll believe both;
          And what does else want credit, come to me   25
          And I'll be sworn 'tis true. Travellers ne'er did lie,
          Though fools at home condemn 'em.
GONZALO   If in Naples

17 SD *Solemn . . . invisible*] *After* fresh *in* F   19 SD *Enter . . . depart*] *Wilson; continuous with* 17 SD *in* F; *Folger place* 'inviting . . . depart' *after 39*   20 were] F; are F4

adjectives (which seems to be unique to this text) draws attention to the ambiguity of the 'shapes'.

17 SD *on the top, invisible* Prospero enters above, and it has been suggested that 'the top' is a term for a level above the musicians' gallery, and thus 'the highest point possible on the Jacobean stage' (Orgel). In *1H6* 3.2.25 Pucelle appears 'on the top' with a burning torch. At the Globe this might have been from the hut from which the trumpet sounded to announce the play. Sturgess notes a direction in Fletcher's Blackfriars play *The Double Marriage* for *a boy atop*, and a reference in Jonson's *Hymenaei* to a statue of Jupiter *in the top figuring the heavens* (p. 91). But Andrew Gurr points out to me that there is no evidence for a third level in the Black-friars *frons scenae*, and he doubts whether anything more than an entry on the gallery is meant. It is not impossible that the term owes more to Crane than to theatrical accuracy. For a highly conjectural reconstruction of the staging of this scene see J. C. Adams, *The Globe Playhouse*, 1954, pp. 319–22, and 'The staging of *The Tempest*, 3.3', *Review of English Studies*, 14 (1938), 404–19. More measured is Sturgess, pp. 90–2.

19 SD In F this stage direction runs continuously on from the preceding one. Some editors have further divided it, placing *inviting . . . they depart* after 39. It was Crane's habit to roll directions together, and there is perhaps some gain in having the lords respond first to the music, then to the sight

of the shapes. But Alonso's past tense at 20 suggests that the shapes do indeed leave at this point. If this, again, is Crane's elaboration of a simpler original stage direction, then he may have derived its com-bination of strangeness and gentleness from Gonzalo's reaction in 30–4 below.

19 SD.2 *salutations* greetings.

20 kind keepers benevolent guardian angels.

21 living drollery (1) a comic picture brought to life, (2) a comic entertainment, (3) a puppet show. The word 'drollery' was only just coming into the language – *OED* gives 1597 as the first instance of (1), and *The Tempest* as the first for (3). It is perhaps the novelty of the term, as well as the nature of the action, that Jonson was mocking in the Induction to *Bartholomew Fair*, when referring to 'those that beget *Tales*, *Tempests*, and such-like drolleries' (see 3.2.2–3 n.).

22–4 Arabia . . . reigning there The phoenix was a mythical Arabian bird, of which only one was said to exist at any one time, and to reproduce by dying in flames, resurrecting itself every 500 years.

25 what does . . . credit whatever else lacks credibility.

26 Travellers . . . lie 'Contradicting the proverb, "A traveller may lie with authority" (Tilley, T746)' (Kermode). The truthfulness of travellers' tales is debated by Montaigne in the Essay, 'Of the Cannibals' (vol. I, no. 30).

I should report this now, would they believe me?
If I should say I saw such islanders –
For certes, these are people of the island –   30
Who though they are of monstrous shape, yet note
Their manners are more gentle, kind, than of
Our human generation you shall find
Many, nay almost any.
PROSPERO [*Aside*]   Honest lord,
Thou hast said well – for some of you there present   35
Are worse than devils.
ALONSO   I cannot too much muse,
Such shapes, such gesture, and such sound, expressing –
Although they want the use of tongue – a kind
Of excellent dumb discourse.
PROSPERO [*Aside*]   Praise in departing.
FRANCISCO They vanished strangely.
SEBASTIAN   No matter, since they   40
Have left their viands behind; for we have stomachs.
Wilt please you taste of what is here?
ALONSO   Not I.
GONZALO Faith, sir, you need not fear. When we were boys,
Who would believe that there were mountaineers,
Dewlapped like bulls, whose throats had hanging at 'em   45
Wallets of flesh? Or that there were such men

---

29 islanders] F2; Islands F   32 gentle, kind] F; gentle-kind *Theobald*   34 SD *Capell; not in* F   36 muse,] F4; muse F; muse;
Capell   39 SD *Capell; not in* F   40–1 *This edn;* No . . . since / They . . . stomacks. F

30 certes certainly (by Shakespeare's time
already an archaic and poetic form).

32 gentle, kind F's comma can be interpreted as
equivalent to a modern hyphen, in which case
'gentle-kind' (adopted by Orgel) would be a compound word meaning 'of more noble nature', but,
as Kermode observes, 'F is quite satisfactory, with
kind reinforcing the recurring word *gentle.*'

33 human generation human race.

36 muse gaze meditatively or with wonder (*OED*
Muse *v* 4). F has no comma here, which would give
the transitive sense 'to marvel at', and this reading,
endorsed by *OED* (Muse *v* 10), has been adopted
by the majority of recent editors. Shakespeare,
however, does not elsewhere use the verb transitively, and that usage is much less frequent in the
period than the various intransitive senses.

39 Praise in departing Prospero, knowing what
is to come, warns 'Keep your praise till the end',
echoing the proverb (Tilley P83).

40 They . . . strangely Francisco's only line
apart from 2.1.108–17.

40–1 They . . . Have Moving 'have' to the next
line makes both lines regular.

41 viands food.

41 stomachs appetites.

44 mountaineers those who live in the mountains. This word seems to be a Shakespearean
coinage, first used in *Cym.* 4.2.71, 100 and 120,
where, however, it is used by Cloten with an insult-
ing implication.

45–6 Dewlapped . . . flesh A 'dewlap' is the flap
of skin hanging from the throats of cows and other
animals, which is expanded in the 'wallets' or 'pro-
tuberant nodules of flesh'. Kittredge suggests that
it might allude to the goitre suffered by Swiss
mountain people.

Whose heads stood in their breasts? Which now we find
Each putter-out of five for one will bring us
Good warrant of.

ALONSO   I will stand to, and feed,
Although my last, no matter, since I feel   50
The best is past. Brother, my lord the duke,
Stand to and do as we.

Thunder and lightning. Enter ARIEL, *like a harpy, claps his wings upon
the table, and with a quaint device the banquet vanishes*

---

47 heads .... breasts These are the blemyae,
who figure in Pliny, and in many bestiaries from the
Middle Ages onwards. They are referred to in *Oth.*
1.3. 144–5: 'men whose heads / Do grow beneath
their shoulders'. A closely analogous comment is
to be found in Walter Raleigh, *The Discoverie of
Guiana* (1596), where he writes of 'a nation of
people, whose heades appeare not above their shoulders, which though it may be thought a meere fable,
yet for mine owne part I am resolved it is true' (pp.
69–70). (See illustration 15.)

48 Each . . . one London brokers accepted a sum
deposited by a traveller before setting out on a
journey, and if he returned with proof that he had
reached his destination repaid him fivefold. The
'putter-out' here could be either the traveller, who
brings back evidence of his success, or the broker.
(Kermode cites Jonson, *Every Man Out of His
Humour*, 2.3.244, where Puntarvolo engages in this
transaction.)

49 Good warrant Secure proof.

49–51 I will . . . past The buried regular couplet
in these lines might suggest relineation to bring it
to the fore, but F's lineation is also regular as it
stands, and there is therefore no good reason to alter
it.

51 The best is past Proverbial (Tilley B318).

52 Stand to 'To set to work, fall to; esp. to begin
eating' (*OED* Stand *n* 101b).

52 SD.1 lightning See note to 1.1.0 SD.

52 SD.1 Enter ARIEL Ariel may have been flown
in, as Juno perhaps is later in 4.1. Jowett, 'Directions', p. 119, argues that such a descent would be
appropriate to a visitor to the 'lower world' and to
Ariel's winged costume. He suggests that after
being lowered to the table to cause the disappear-
ance of the banquet Ariel would have been raised to
an intermediate position to deliver his speech.
Thunder could have been provided at his entrance,
as it is at his exit. The SD may, however, anticipate
the moment at which he finally makes the banquet
disappear, so that the first part of the speech might

be spoken as he descends, as seems to be the case
with Jupiter's speech in *Cym.* 93 ff. But descents
were slow and noisy, and since it is the element of
shock and surprise which most seems to be required
here, entrance through a trap-door under or behind
the table, or concealment under the table as it is
brought in, is perhaps more likely. (The production
at Shakespeare's Globe, 2000, though Ariel had
flown in earlier, chose the last of these alternatives.)

52 SD.1 harpy A mythical creature with the face
and breasts of a woman, the body and wings of a
bird, and talons for hands. This episode is based on
Aeneid, 3.225 ff., where Aeneas and his companions
take refuge in the islands called the Strophades but
have their meals devoured by the harpies who
inhabit there, and are warned to leave for Italy by
their leader Celaeno. (See Appendix 2.) The harpies
were allegorised as the punishers of human sins of
avarice and greed. They appear as such in Henry
Peacham's *Minerva Britanna* (1612) (illustration
10), and Sandys, pp. 251–2, sums up the allegorising tradition when he represents them as 'the ministers of [Jupiter's] wrath upon the covetous, who
are ever their own tormentors', and specifically of
'prodigal Sycophants, and greedy Officers, who
consume the treasure, and pollute the fame of miserable Princes, abused in their trust, and blinded in
their understandings'. The harpy is therefore a
specifically appropriate agent of Prospero's
vengeance on the 'three men of sin'.

52 SD.1 claps his wings Suggested by *Aeneid*,
3.226: *magnis quatiunt clangoribus alas* ('with loud
clanging shake their wings').

52 SD.2 quaint device. . . . vanishes by an ingenious contrivance the banquet is made to disappear.
The expression of this SD has generally been seen
as characteristic of Crane's elaboration, and it is
impossible to specify exactly how the banquet was
made to vanish – though a reversible table-top
which flips over as Ariel covers the banquet with his
wings is as practical a suggestion as any. (See illustration 6.)

ARIEL You are three men of sin, whom Destiny –
      That hath to instrument this lower world,
      And what is in't – the never-surfeited sea   55
      Hath caused to belch up you. And on this island,
      Where man doth not inhabit – you 'mongst men
      Being most unfit to live – I have made you mad;
      And even with suchlike valour men hang and drown
      Their proper selves.
      [*Alonso, Sebastian, Antonio draw their swords*]
                 You fools! I and my fellows   60
      Are ministers of Fate. The elements

---

56 belch up you] F; belch you up F4; belch up *Theobald*; belch up; yea *Hudson*   56 you.] *This edn*; you; F; you, *Orgel*   58 live –] *Ard3*; liue: F; live. *Kermode*   58 I have] F; I've *Dyce*   60 SD *Alonso . . . swords*] *Bevington*; *Seeing Alonso, Sebastian &c draw* / *Hanmer*; *not in* F

53 You . . . sin Exactly who is imagined as hearing and seeing the vision of Ariel is not clear. Kermode suggests that Gonzalo's response at the end of the scene indicates that the speech is 'heard' only by the three to whom it is addressed, though this is not straightforward to bring off in the theatre.

53 Destiny Prospero has scripted Ariel's speech, as he says at 85 below, and the invocation of Destiny recalls 1.2.177–84.

53–6 Destiny . . . you Destiny has caused the sea to belch you up.

54 hath to instrument has as its instrument (for working out its purposes). Destiny rules the world beneath God.

54 lower world i.e. the earth, the realm below the moon's sphere.

55 never-surfeited never satisfied or overfed, always greedy.

56 belch up Compare 2.1.247.

56–8 you . . . mad F's punctuation leaves the relationship between the successive clauses ambiguous. Adopting a full stop after 'you', but weakening F's colon after 'live' (where most editors strengthen to a full stop) has two consequences. First, it means that the syntactically unnecessary 'you' in line 56 becomes an emphatic closing repetition of the 'you' with which Ariel begins his castigation of the lords in line 53 (the rhetorical figure of *epanalepsis*). Secondly, and more importantly, it clarifies and emphasises the sequence of events: Fate causes them to be shipwrecked, then the avenging spirit of the island, represented by Ariel, maddens them (cf. Ariel's account of the tempest in 1.2 where they 'felt a fever of the mad'). Other arrangements of the punctuation are, however, possible.

57 man doth not inhabit Ariel's comment is, strictly, untrue. But, like the earlier untruth embod-

ied in the song 'Full fathom five', it represents the situation as those to whom he speaks understand it.

57–8 you . . . unfit to live Because of their sin they do not deserve human company. Given the fact that Antonio's sin, and the sin to which he encourages Sebastian, is fratricide, there may be a recollection of the punishment of Cain, who murdered his brother Abel: 'a fugitive and a vagabond shalt thou be in the earth' (Genesis 4.13).

58 I have Though Dyce's elision to 'I've' makes the line regular, this is an example where one might not want to lose the emphasis on the first-person pronoun.

59 suchlike valour bravery of the insane kind that leads men to desperate acts.

60 proper selves themselves i.e. this mad and perverted valour leads to suicide. Compare Burton 1.2.1.2: 'as when a desperate man makes away himself, which by hanging or drowning they frequently do'.

60 SD It is presumably only the three guilty men to whom the speech is addressed who actually respond by drawing their swords.

60 fellows In mythological narratives there are generally three harpies, and, with 65 below, this might suggest that Ariel is accompanied by additional spirits, although they are not mentioned in the stage direction. It would, however, have been difficult to provide additional actors (see Appendix 3, p. 260), and Ariel probably refers to the *shapes* who brought in and carry out the banquet.

61 ministers agents.

61–2 elements . . . tempered The steel of which the swords are made is 'tempered', i.e. brought 'to a suitable degree of hardness and elasticity or resiliency by heating it to the required temperature and immersing it, while hot, in some liquid, usually cold water'(*OED* Temper *v* 14a).

Of whom your swords are tempered may as well
Wound the loud winds, or with bemocked-at stabs
Kill the still-closing waters, as diminish
One dowl that's in my plume. My fellow ministers   65
Are like invulnerable. If you could hurt,
Your swords are now too massy for your strengths,
And will not be uplifted. But remember –
For that's my business to you – that you three
From Milan did supplant good Prospero;   70
Exposed unto the sea – which hath requit it –
Him, and his innocent child; for which foul deed,
The powers, delaying, not forgetting, have
Incensed the seas and shores, yea, all the creatures
Against your peace. Thee of thy son, Alonso,   75
They have bereft; and do pronounce by me
Ling'ring perdition – worse than any death
Can be at once – shall step by step attend
You, and your ways; whose wraths to guard you from –
Which here, in this most desolate isle, else falls   80

---

65 plume] *Rowe;* plumbe F   67 strengths] F; strength F4   79 wraths] F; wrath *Theobald*

62 whom which (Abbott).

64 still-closing that always close up again.

65 dowl . . . plume the smallest feather in my plumage. Ariel, as a harpy, is clad in a feathered costume, though 'plume' might apply specifically to a headdress.

66 like similarly.

66 invulnerable Compare *Aeneid*, 3.242, where the harpies are invulnerable to the swords of Aeneas and his companions, who attempted to ambush them.

67 massy heavy (and recalling Prospero's treatment of Ferdinand at 1.2.468, 483–5).

69 business errand, purpose.

71 Exposed Begins a parallel clause, demanding that they recall both the crime of usurpation and their subsequent treatment of Prospero and his daughter.

71 requit it Appropriately repaid their crime of abandoning Prospero and Miranda to the sea.

73 delaying . . . forgetting The notion that God's justice would ultimately prevail is pervasive in the period, invoked repeatedly in legal proceedings and in religious discourse alike. The message was encapsulated in the proverb: 'God stays long but strikes at last' (Tilley G224), and many other similar proverbs. Luther in his commentary on the story of Cain and Abel remarks that 'this judgement

of Cain did not take place on the first day, but there was a lapse of some time. God is by nature long-suffering because He anxiously desires sinners to return to Him. But He does not for this reason postpone punishment indefinitely' (*Works*, vol. i, ed. Pelikan, p. 259).

74 creatures natural creation.

75 Against your peace To destroy your peace of mind.

76 bereft robbed, deprived.

77 Ling'ring perdition Slow ruin and destruction. The sense of 'perdition' as 'damnation' is also present here, suggesting religious connotations that are reinforced at the end of this speech. As punctuated in F (and here) this phrase can be understood as both the object of 'pronounce' and the subject of 'shall attend', but it is possible to assume an implied 'that', or an omitted colon, at the end of line 76, which permits 'ling'ring perdition' to be taken as the formal 'sentence' which Ariel pronounces.

77–8 death . . . once i.e. any immediate death-sentence.

79–82 whose . . . ensuing In quasi-theological terms the 'three men of sin' are told that only repentance and amendment of life will prevent their punishment in the desolation of the island.

79 whose wraths i.e. the anger of the 'powers'.

80 desolate In this context the frequent biblical

Upon your heads – is nothing but heart's sorrow,
And a clear life ensuing.

He vanishes in thunder; then, to soft music, enter the shapes again, and
dance, with mocks and mows, and [then depart] carrying out the table

PROSPERO Bravely the figure of this harpy hast thou
    Performed, my Ariel; a grace it had devouring.
    Of my instruction hast thou nothing bated   85
    In what thou hadst to say. So, with good life
    And observation strange, my meaner ministers
    Their several kinds have done. My high charms work,
    And these, mine enemies, are all knit up
    In their distractions. They now are in my power;   90
    And in these fits I leave them, while I visit
    Young Ferdinand, whom they suppose is drowned,
    And his and mine loved darling.   *[Exit]*
GONZALO I'th'name of something holy, sir, why stand you
    In this strange stare?
ALONSO   O, it is monstrous: monstrous!   95

---

81 heart's sorrow] F (*hearts-sorrow*); heart-sorrow *Cam.*   82 SD. 2 *then depart*] *Orgel subst; not in* F   90 now] F; *om. Pope*
93 mine] F; my *Rowe*   93 SD *Exit*] *Theobald (subst.); not in* F

association of 'desolation' with punishment for sin is suggested. See, for example, Isaiah 59.10, Ezekiel 27.20.

81 is nothing but there is no alternative.

81 heart's sorrow repentance, grief. The idea that a broken, sorrowful heart is an essential prelude to forgiveness and salvation is central to Christian thinking. See, for example, 2 Corinthians 7.10: 'For godly sorrow causeth repentance to salvation not to be repented of'.

82 clear life ensuing future life free from moral taint. The intention not to sin again is requisite for forgiveness. Frye cites Luther: 'the proverb is true . . . which says "To sin no more is the highest form of repentance"'.

82 SD.1 vanishes in thunder Either by descending through the trap, or, possibly, by being flown up.

82 SD.2 mocks and mows mocking grimaces.

84 a grace . . . devouring it (i.e. the harpy) was graceful even as the food was apparently 'devoured' or spirited away. Prospero explicitly distinguishes Ariel from the unpleasantness of the classical harpies, who had 'a disgusting outflow from their bellies' and 'befoul' as well as devour the Trojans' food.

85 bated omitted. As always, Prospero is checking on the faithfulness with which Ariel carries out his orders.

86 So In the same way.

86 good life (1) with great liveliness, (2) with a life-like performance.

87 observation strange amazingly observant care (*OED* sv *n* 4, citing this passage), a further commendation from Prospero of Ariel's precision in carrying out instructions. It is just possible, however, that 'observation' may be used with the sense 'the fact of being noticed' (*OED* sv *n* 5a) and Prospero be commenting on the intense reaction of the nobles as Ariel's audience.

87 meaner ministers lesser spirits.

88 several kinds distinct, separate roles.

90 distractions mental conflicts or disturbance.

91 fits paroxysms, or 'sudden and transitory states of activity or inaction' (*OED* Fit *n²* 4a).

92 whom for 'who'.

93 mine for 'my'. 'The use of the form before a consonant, while unusual, is not unique in Shakespeare' (Orgel).

95 stare state of amazement indicated by staring.

Methought the billows spoke and told me of it,
The winds did sing it to me, and the thunder,
That deep and dreadful organ-pipe, pronounced
The name of Prosper. It did bass my trespass;
Therefore my son i'th'ooze is bedded; and   100
I'll seek him deeper than e'er plummet sounded,
And with him there lie mudded.   *Exit*

SEBASTIAN   But one fiend at a time, I'll fight their legions o'er.
ANTONIO   I'll be thy second.

                          Exeunt [Sebastian and Antonio]

GONZALO   All three of them are desperate. Their great guilt,   105
Like poison given to work a great time after,
Now 'gins to bite the spirits. I do beseech you,
That are of suppler joints, follow them swiftly,

---

99 bass] *Johnson;* base F   **102–4** *This edn;* And . . . mudded / But . . . time, / Ile . . . ore. / Ile . . . Second F; And . . .
time, / I'll . . . second/ *Steevens;* And . . . mudded / But . . . time, / I'll . . . second/ *Folger*   **104** SD *Sebastian and Antonio*]
Malone; not in F

96–7 billows . . . sing it to me Compare Prospero's account of the seas and winds responding to
him and Miranda, 1.2.148–51.

96 it i.e. the 'trespass', or perhaps the name of
Prospero.

98 dreadful inspiring fear.

98 organ-pipe Alonso draws on the image of the
cosmos as a huge organ (cf. Milton 'On the
Morning of Christ's Nativity', line 130: 'And let the
base of heaven's deep organ blow'). The organ itself
in Elizabethan times had none of the low pedal
notes that might now be associated with this image,
though the 'great pipe' of the organ of St Paul's
seems to have been especially noted, and is referred
to in Samuel Rowlands, *The Letting of Humours
Blood in the Head-Vaine* (1600), Satire 6, and
Heywood's *The Royall King and the Loyal Subject*
(1637), Act 1.

99 bass my trespass (1) proclaimed my guilt in
a bass voice (the only use cited in *OED* Bass v^2), (2)
'provide a (musical) ground or basis for the revela-
tion of my guilt' (Orgel). The word 'trespass', with
its resonances of the Lord's Prayer, maintains the
religious undertones of the latter part of Ariel's
speech.

100 Therefore For that.

101 plummet lead weight (used, when lowered
on a line, to measure the depth of water).

103–4 But . . . second In most editions Sebastian's first half-line is taken to complete the half-line
at the end of Alonso's speech, and his second to be
completed by Antonio's short line. But this generates an unsatisfactory thirteen-syllable line. It seems

better to assume that the compositors broke Sebastian's line to waste space at the bottom of a page,
and print as here.

103 If only the devils come one at a time, I'll fight
them all.

103 legions Folger cites the response of the
demoniac to Christ in Mark 5.9. 'My name is
Legion; for we are many.'

104 second supporter, assistant.

105 desperate (1) despairing, (2) reckless or
infuriated from despair (*OED* sv *adj* 4). Joseph Hall
observed that 'Consciences that are without
remorse are not without horror; wickedness makes
men desperate' (*Works*, ed. Philip Wynter, 1863, 1,
20).

106 poison . . . after Gonzalo sees their present
frenzy as a long-delayed consequence of their sins,
echoing Ariel's message of the delayed justice of
the Fates. His image is drawn from the widespread
contemporary fear of poison, and belief in the
possibility of its delayed action, which was to be
dramatically exhibited in the Overbury murder
trials of 1615–16, and is manifested in many plays
of the period, especially those set in Italy (cf. *WT*
1.2.319–20, where Camillo speaks of 'a ling'ring
dram'; Webster, *Duchess of Malfi*, 5.2.265–6: 'a
ling'ring poison may chance lie / Spread in thy
veins and kill thee seven year hence'). But he also
reflects the commonly held religious belief that sin-
fulness will always torment the impenitent. See
Introduction, pp. 50–1.

107 'gins begins.

107 spirits see 1.2.485 n.

> And hinder them from what this ecstasy
> May now provoke them to.

ADRIAN   Follow, I pray you.   110

Exeunt

4.1 *Enter* PROSPERO, FERDINAND *and* MIRANDA

PROSPERO [*To Ferdinand*] If I have too austerely punished you
> Your compensation makes amends, for I
> Have given you here a third of mine own life,
> Or that for which I live; who once again
> I tender to thy hand. All thy vexations   5
> Were but my trials of thy love, and thou
> Hast strangely stood the test. Here, afore heaven,
> I ratify this my rich gift. O Ferdinand,
> Do not smile at me, that I boast her of,
> For thou shalt find she will outstrip all praise   10

Act 4, Scene 1   4.1] *Actus Quartus. Scena Prima* F   1 SD *Orgel; not in* F   3 third] F; thread *Theobald*   4 who] F; whom
Pope   9 her of] F; her off F2; hereof *Wilson;* of her *Orgel*

109 ecstasy madness, transport.

110 Follow . . . you Adrian's remark is addressed either to Gonzalo, or to Francisco and the *others*.

Act 4, Scene 1
1 austerely harshly.
1 punished made you suffer. Orgel sees Prospero as maintaining the fiction that he has been punishing Ferdinand for the 'crimes' of which he accused him in 1.2, but 'punish' need not imply retribution.
3 third . . . life i.e. Miranda. What exactly Prospero implies here is not clear. The other two thirds have variously been explained as his own life, his dukedom or his dead wife. With greater strain, the phrase has been taken to imply that the upbringing of Miranda has occupied a third of his life-time. Orgel's suggestion that 'a third merely signifies a very important part, as it clearly does in Prospero's later declaration that "Every third thought shall be my grave"' is, however, eminently sensible.
4 Or that . . . I live Using the rhetorical figure of *correctio* to redefine his first statement, Prospero recalls his opening comment to Miranda, 'I have done nothing but in care of thee.'
4 who for 'whom', Abbott 274.
4 once again We have not, in fact, seen Prospero offer Miranda to Ferdinand before. It is possible

that we are to imagine this scene as a formal recapitulation and confirmation of an off-stage event, as is implied by the past tense of 3.
5 tender offer. Prospero combines the actions of the bride's father and the priest in the Prayer Book marriage service, where 'The Minister, receiving the Woman at her father's or friend's hands, shall cause the Man with his right hand to take the Woman by her right hand.'
5 thy vexations the physical efforts to which I have put you (*OED* Vexation *n* 1).
6 trials tests.
7 strangely marvellously, wonderfully.
8 ratify 'confirm or make valid by giving assent' (*OED* sv *v* 1).
8 rich gift That a woman was the property of the father to bestow in marriage was standard legal thinking at the time, embodied in the Minister's question in the marriage service, 'Who giveth this woman to be married to this man?'
9 boast her of boast of her. Some recent editors treat this as a compositor's transposition, and emend to 'boast of her'. F2 emended to 'boast her off', i.e. 'cry up her praises' (Kermode), though there are no parallels in Shakespeare for this usage. See Textual Analysis, p. 227.
10 outstrip all praise exceed the best that could be said of her (a conventional hyperbole).

And make it halt behind her.

FERDINAND I do believe it against an oracle.

PROSPERO Then, as my gift, and thine own acquisition
Worthily purchased, take my daughter. But
If thou dost break her virgin-knot before   15
All sanctimonious ceremonies may
With full and holy rite be ministered,
No sweet aspersion shall the heavens let fall
To make this contract grow; but barren hate,
Sour-eyed disdain and discord shall bestrew   20
The union of your bed with weeds so loathly
That you shall hate it both. Therefore take heed,
As Hymen's lamps shall light you.

FERDINAND   As I hope
For quiet days, fair issue, and long life,

12 *This edn;* I . . . it / Against . . . oracle F   12 do] F; *om. Pope*   13 gift] *Rowe;* guest F   14 But] F; *om.* F2   17 rite] *Rowe;*
right F   18 aspersion] F; *aspersions* F4   23 lamps] F; *lamp Wilson (Elze conj.)*

11 **halt** limp, stumble.

12 The lineation adopted here gives Ferdinand a
complete verse line, rather than completing the final
line of Prospero's first speech with a short line. This
conforms to Shakespeare's preferred practice. (The
metre could be regularised by eliding 'believ't'.)

12 **against an oracle** even if an oracle should
deny it. Ferdinand's hyperbole, as Orgel points out,
seems somewhat foolhardy in the light of Leontes'
ill fortunes in *WT*, which are linked to his denying
the truth of an oracle's pronouncement.

13 **gift** Rowe's emendation of F's 'guest' has been
universally accepted, and gains some support from
the fact that 'guift', Crane's normal spelling of the
word, and so printed by F at 8 above, could be
misread by a compositor as 'guest'.

14 **purchased** won, 'bought' by the efforts he has
undergone.

15 **virgin-knot** In Roman marriage rites the
virgin bride wore a knotted girdle (see Catullus,
3.27). Jonson's gloss in his 1605 masque *Hymenaei*
(which may have provided a number of suggestions
for this scene) reads 'That was *Nodus Herculeanus*
[Hercules' knot], which the husband, at night,
untied in sign of good fortune, that he might be
happie in propagation of issue, as Hercules was'
(line 194 n.). Orgel suggests that the violence of the
verb 'break' indicates that the physical act of taking
Miranda's virginity is strongly present in Prospero's injunction.

16 **sanctimonious** holy, sacred (without the
modern implication of hypocrisy).

17 **holy rite** See 3.1.91–2 n. The religious
celebration of a marriage was not required by law
in the period.

18 **aspersion** Literally a sprinkling of water,
with strong connotations of a religious rite, and
without the negative resonances that the word most
usually carried then, as now. Here it links with the
'refreshing showers' that promise fertility.

19 **contract grow** In the marriage service the
Minister prays that God may 'sow the seed of
eternal life in their hearts', and this, as well as
the more obvious implication that their marriage
should 'grow' through the begetting of children,
may be suggested here.

20–1 **bestrew . . . weeds** The marriage-bed was
(in literary convention if not always in reality) customarily strewn with flowers (see the Epithalamion
at the end of *Hymenaei*: 'Whole showers of roses
flow; / And violets seeme to grow, / Strew'd in the
chamber there').

21 **loathly** loathsome.

22 **take heed** be attentive (to my command).

23 **Hymen's lamps** Hymen, the Roman god of
marriage, was conventionally represented as carrying a single torch, but in *Hymenaei* other lamps are
mentioned, and afforded symbolic significance.
Kittredge noted that the clear burning of the lamps
was a good omen, but bad if they were smoky, so
that Prospero is here warning Ferdinand and
Miranda to behave properly in order that the lamps
may burn brightly.

24 **issue** children.

With such love as 'tis now, the murkiest den,   25
The most oppòrtune place, the strong'st suggestion
Our worser genius can, shall never melt
Mine honour into lust, to take away
The edge of that day's celebration,
When I shall think or Phoebus' steeds are foundered,   30
Or night kept chained below.
PROSPERO   Fairly spoke.
Sit then, and talk with her, she is thine own.
What, Ariel! My industrious servant Ariel!

Enter ARIEL

ARIEL What would my potent master? Here I am.
PROSPERO Thou and thy meaner fellows your last service   35
Did worthily perform; and I must use you
In such another trick. Go bring the rabble –

28 lust, to] F; lust to *Folger*

25 such love . . . now i.e. with a love sustained
at its present intensity.

25 murkiest den darkest hiding place. Recalling
the cave in which Dido and Aeneas consummated
their illicit love; Kermode notes that Virgil's
'*speluncam*' is translated by Stanyhurst as 'den'.

26 oppòrtune convenient. Stressed on the
second syllable.

26 suggestion temptation, as earlier at 2.1.285.

27 worser genius Alluding to the belief that a
good and bad angel compete for the soul of the individual (an idea employed in Sonnet 144, and dramatised in the Good and Bad Angels of Marlowe's
Doctor Faustus).

27 can i.e. can make.

28 to take so as to take. Folger and Ard3 remove
F's comma after 'lust', so that the desire is to anticipate the marriage night, but this seems to underplay the opposition between 'honour' and 'lust'.

29 edge keenness of appetite or anticipation.

29 that day i.e. the wedding day itself.

30–1 When I shall . . . below Ferdinand's sense
that the celebrations of the marriage will go on so
late that he will frequently think the wedding night will never
come is frequently echoed in the conclusions to
Jacobean marriage masques. See, for example, the
dialogue song in Campion's *Lord Hay's Masque*
(1607):

2. Love Bridegroomes revels?
1.   But for fashion.
2. And why?   1. They hinder wisht occasion.
2. Longing hearts and new delights.
Love short dayes and long nights.

At the same time, however, Ferdinand's comments
underline the fact that the entertainment Prospero
is about to present is a celebration of betrothal, not,
as it is often carelessly described, a 'marriage
masque'.

30 or either.

30 Phoebus' steeds The horses which pulled
the chariot of the sun in classical mythology.

30 foundered gone lame, so preventing nightfall.

34 potent powerful.

35 meaner fellows Compare the 'meaner
ministers' of 3.3.87.

35 last service i.e. the disappearing banquet of
the previous scene.

37 trick Though the word can mean 'ingenious
artifice' and be used specifically of a theatrical
device, the dominant implication in the period was
rather more negative, as it is in Modern English.
Here, and in the lines which follow, Prospero seems
to be belittling both the pageant of the harpy just
past and the show he is now setting up. This
dismissive attitude could be seen as preparing the
ground for the sentiments of 'our revels now are
ended', but, particularly in view of the serious
moral purposes of Prospero's shows, it can equally
be taken as an example of the rhetorical figure
of *meiosis* (understatement) which Puttenham said
might be used 'for modesties sake, and to avoide the
opinion of arrogance'.

37 rabble The 'crowd' of meaner ministers, a
term almost always used negatively in the period.

O'er whom I give thee power – here, to this place.
Incite them to quick motion, for I must
Bestow upon the eyes of this young couple   40
Some vanity of mine art. It is my promise,
And they expect it from me.

ARIEL   Presently?

PROSPERO Ay: with a twink.

ARIEL Before you can say 'come' and 'go',
And breathe twice, and cry 'so, so',   45
Each one tripping on his toe,
Will be here with mop and mow.
Do you love me master? No?

PROSPERO Dearly, my delicate Ariel. Do not approach
Till thou dost hear me call.

ARIEL   Well; I conceive.   *Exit* 50

PROSPERO [*To Ferdinand*] Look thou be true! Do not give dalliance
Too much the rein. The strongest oaths are straw
To th'fire i'th'blood. Be more abstemious,
Or else good night your vow.

FERDINAND   I warrant you, sir,
The white cold virgin snow upon my heart   55

---

51 SD *Wilson subst.; not in* F   52 rein] F4; raigne F   53 abstemious] F2; abstenious F

38 **O'er . . . power** This phrase is bracketed in F, and though this is a characteristic of Crane's punctuation, it might suggest that Prospero is conferring on Ariel power of command for this occasion only, whereas to remove the parentheses implies that he always has such authority. Either sense is possible, but on balance perhaps the first is to be preferred. If this is allowed, then it suggests that Ariel himself is imagined as organising, perhaps even devising, the masque (see 50 below).

41 **vanity** 'That which is of no value or profit . . . vain, idle or worthless thing' (*OED* sv *n* 4a).

42 **Presently** Immediately.

43 **twink** The time it takes to wink an eye.

44–7 **Before . . . mow** Sometimes set as a song, especially in eighteenth- and nineteenth-century performances.

47 **mop and mow** grimaces (see 3.3.82 SD.2).

50 **conceive** (1) understand (*OED* sv *v* 9), (2) plan, devise, formulate an idea (*OED* sv *v* 7).

51 SD Prospero is presumably rebuking Ferdinand for some real (or imagined) flirtation or physical contact with Miranda which threatens to undermine the earlier promise of chaste conduct.

51 **true** Both 'honourable' and 'true to your word'.

51 **dalliance** amorous conversation or flirtation.

52 **Too much the rein** Too much freedom or scope. The proper management of the horse was frequently used as an allegory of the control of the affections and desires (cf. Adonis' 'brave courser' who 'breaketh his rein' in *Venus and Adonis*, line 264).

52 **straw** 'With reference to its ready inflammability' (*OED* sv *n*¹ 1b).

53 **abstemious** 'abstinent, refraining, sparing (with regard to other things than food)' (*OED* sv *adj* 2); a rare usage.

54 **Or else . . . vow** Or else you can say 'good night' to your promise.

54 **warrant** guarantee, promise.

55–6 **The white cold . . . liver** Ferdinand – perhaps somewhat tendentiously – argues that Miranda's chastity (understood as cold) moderates the fiery heat of his passion. He may be referring to her physical body pressed against his in an embrace (the occasion of Prospero's anxiety), or be elaborating the familiar poetic topos of the image of the beloved as fixed in the heart, and therefore cooling

Abates the ardour of my liver.
PROSPERO   Well.
Now come, my Ariel – bring a corollary,
Rather than want a spirit; appear, and pertly.
                        Soft music
No tongue! All eyes! Be silent!

                        Enter IRIS

IRIS Ceres, most bounteous lady, thy rich leas   60
        Of wheat, rye, barley, vetches, oats and peas;
        Thy turfy mountains, where live nibbling sheep,
        And flat meads thatched with stover, them to keep;
        Thy banks with pionèd and twillèd brims,

---

60 bounteous] F; beauteous *Rowe²*   61 vetches] *Capell*; fetches F   64 pionèd] F; peonied *Steevens*   64 twillèd] F; tulip'd
Rowe; tilled *Capell*; lilied *Steevens*

---

its heat. In Renaissance physiology the precise seat
of love and desire was much debated; Burton cites
one authority who 'will have this passion sited in the
liver, and to keep residence in the liver and heart'
(3.2.1.2), and there is often a division between the
liver as the source of lust, the heart as the seat of
love. The relationship of female 'coldness' and male
'heat' is important throughout the masque which
follows.

56 Well Prospero either commends Ferdinand's
answer – 'You have said well' – or is more ironical,
implying 'Make sure you act as you promise.'

57 a corollary an extra, one too many.

58 want lack.

58 pertly 'promptly, readily' (*OED* pert *adj* 3).

58 SD A technical term. Peter Walls comments:
'"soft music" need not necessarily be quiet, the
adjective . . . is probably intended to indicate something about sophistication and quality rather than
volume' (*Music in the English Courtly Masque*, 1996,
p. 152). It is likely, however, that this music would
be performed by bowed or plucked strings,
recorders or flutes, rather than the louder wind
instruments (which were conventionally used at
court for the entry of the main masquers). The SD
is placed in the right margin in F next to 58 and
above the direction *Enter Iris*. It could, therefore
equally follow 59, but probably the beginning of the
music functions as a cue for Prospero's subsequent
command.

59 Prospero's command is more than simply an
order to the audience to be quiet. As Johnson was
the first to point out, silence was required in the
presence of magical operations, and these injunc-
tions to Ferdinand and Miranda both underline the

quasi-magical effect of the masque and demand
attention to its visual dimension. (See also 126–7
below.)

60 IRIS The rainbow, hence the mediator
between heaven and earth; the messenger of Juno
as Mercury is of Jupiter.

60 Ceres The goddess of the earth and of harvest.

60 bounteous lady Echoing the Virgilian
epithet *alma Ceres* (*Georgics*, 1.7).

60 eas pasture, arable land.

61 vetches bean-producing plant for animal
feed.

62 turfy covered with turf, grassy.

63 meads meadows.

63 thatched covered as with a thatch.

63 stover winter food for animals. The word may
have been suggested by Golding's *Metamorphoses*,
5.116: 'Dame Ceres . . . made corne and stover soft
to grow upon the ground.'

63 them to keep To feed the sheep when they
came down from the mountains.

64 banks . . . brims One of the most contentious phrases in the play in editorial tradition. (1)
If the phrase is left unemended, then 'pionèd'
means dug out or excavated, either by erosion or
human action, and 'twillèd', literally meaning
'woven or plaited', describes plaited branches
supporting the banks. (Gervase Markham in *Maison
Rustique or the Countrey Farmer* (1616), pp. 505–6,
gives instruction for digging out fish-pools which
includes first driving in piles, then putting 'faggotts
and bundells of wood' between them.) The problem
with this reading is that nowhere else does the form
'pioned' exist as a derivative of the verb 'pion', nor
does *OED* cite 'twilled' as used of anything but

Which spongy April at thy hest betrims   65
To make cold nymphs chaste crowns; and thy broom-groves,
Whose shadow the dismissèd bachelor loves,
Being lass-lorn; thy pole-clipped vineyard,
And thy sea-marge, sterile and rocky-hard,
Where thou thyself dost air: the queen o'th'sky,   70
Whose watery arch and messenger am I,
Bids thee leave these, and with her sovereign grace,
Here on this grass-plot, in this very place

---

66 broom-groves] F; brown groves *Hanmer conj.*   68 pole-clipped] F *(pole-clipt);* poll-clipped *Kermode*   72 F *has 'Iuno descends' in the right margin next to this and the next line; transposed to 101 by Theobald*

cloth. (2) Those who wish to emend have sought to make 'pionèd and twillèd' refer to flowers, modernising the first word to 'peonied' (of which it is an available spelling in the period), and emending the second, less plausibly, to 'tuliped', 'lillied', etc. The problem here is that 'brims' is a word used specifically (and in topographical contexts exclusively) of the edges of lakes or streams, whilst peonies are not waterside flowers, but garden plants which were cultivated both for their flowers and for the medicinal qualities of the roots. (This watery meaning for 'brims' also excludes C. O. Fox's otherwise attractive suggestion cited in Kermode that the 'banks' are hedges, planted on built-up mounds and then made dense by being layered.)

65 spongy wet ('April showers' are proverbial).

65 betrims adorns. The syntactical ambiguity of the verb contributes to the controversy surrounding 64: as an intransitive verb, it suggests that April adorns the bank with unspecified vegetation to make the crowns for the nymphs in 66; but taken transitively it indicates that is is precisely with 'pionèd and twillèd brims' that April adorns the banks. F's punctuation does not help to decide the matter.

66 cold nymphs Their coldness is a sign of their chastity.

66 chaste crowns Looking forward to the 'sedged crowns' bedecking the nymphs in the dance at 129 below.

66 broom-groves Broom is a yellow-flowering bush, and editors have worried that it cannot therefore be described as growing in 'groves', which imply more substantial trees. It is probably best understood as figurative. Orgel cites W. P. Mustard's suggestion that there is an allusion to Virgil's shepherds resting in the shade of the broom in *Georgics*, 2.434, and Grigson's claim that 'the

plant's amorous and magical properties were highly regarded' and that it figured 'in magic spells designed to ensure the success of love affairs'.

67 dismissèd bachelor rejected suitor, and therefore still single.

68 lass-lorn bereft of a woman.

68 pole-clipped Another contentious term. If unemended it signifies a 'vineyard with vines embracing, twined around their supporting poles' (Norton), or, possibly, a vineyard surrounded by poles. The 'clasping vine' is a poetical commonplace, and 'embrace' is a standard meaning for 'clip' (*OED* Clip *v*¹ 1a). If modernised as 'poll-clipped', however, it means pollarded or pruned. The second meaning is more straightforward, and gardening manuals make frequent reference to the necessity of careful pruning of vines. Though this is the meaning more frequently endorsed by recent editors, the expression is tautologous (either 'polled' or 'clipped' would be sufficient on its own).

69 sea-marge sea-shore.

70 air take the air.

70 queen o'th'sky Juno, queen of the gods, was specifically associated with the element of air, ruling the element below the sphere of fire which was the territory of her husband, Jupiter.

71 watery arch rainbow.

72 these i.e. her rich meadows. In F the marginal stage direction *Juno descends* sits beside 72 and 73. Where and how Juno appears has been the subject of much scholarly debate. The evidence is problematic, and is considered in the Textual Analysis, pp. 245–7. For reasons given there, I have chosen to follow the frequent earlier practice of transposing this stage direction to 101. This, however, is emphatically not to exclude the possibility of other stagings.

To come and sport. Her peacocks fly amain.
Approach, rich Ceres, her to entertain.   75

                          Enter CERES

CERES Hail, many-coloured messenger, that ne'er
        Dost disobey the wife of Jupiter;
        Who, with thy saffron wings, upon my flowers
        Diffusest honey drops, refreshing showers,
        And with each end of thy blue bow dost crown   80
        My bosky acres, and my unshrubbed down,
        Rich scarf to my proud earth. Why hath thy queen
        Summoned me hither, to this short-grazed green?

IRIS A contract of true love to celebrate,
        And some donation freely to estate   85
        On the blest lovers.

CERES   Tell me, heavenly bow,
        If Venus or her son, as thou dost know,
        Do now attend the queen? Since they did plot

---

74 Her] *Rowe;* Here F   83 short-grazed] *Collier;* short gras'd F; short grass'd F2; short-grass *Rowe²*

---

74 sport engage in recreation.

74 Her F's 'here' has, since Rowe, been modernised as 'her'. It is, however, possible, if Juno's descent were to begin here, that she might have entered as in *Hymenaei*, 'sitting in a Throne, supported by two beautiful Peacockes'; and that Iris might therefore gesture to this apparition – though the fact that she makes no further reference to the descending Juno is part of the problem with accepting the goddess's entry here.

74 peacocks The peacock was sacred to Juno, symbolically appropriate to her as goddess of riches, 'which are as glorious in shew, and as transitorie in truth, as the Peacockes spotted trayne, and make men as prowd and insolent, as a Peacocke' (Fraunce, p. 15).

74 amain speedily.

75 entertain greet as a guest.

76–7 ne'er Dost disobey In a play where dutiful service is a central issue, this phrase has particular emphasis.

78 saffron wings Perhaps alluding directly to *Aeneid*, 4.700, where Iris comes *croceis pinnis*, 'on saffron-coloured wings'.

81 bosky bushy.

81 down 'treeless land, serving as pasturage' (*OED* sv *n¹* 2).

83 short-grazed green Since F2, F's 'short-

grasd' has generally been modernised as 'short-grassed', but it is at least possible that the grass is imagined as being kept short by the grazing of animals upon it. Bacon, in 'Of Gardens' (*Essays* (1625), no. 46), wrote that 'nothing is more pleasant to the eye than green grass kept finely shorn'.

84 contract Again emphasising that this is a celebration of a betrothal.

85 estate bestow (usually with a sense of a gift of property).

87 Venus . . . son Venus, the goddess of love, and Cupid, her son. In Renaissance allegorisations of classical myth they each could be seen as types either of a 'good' celestial love, or of an earthly lust. Whereas Venus does not appear in Jonson's *Hymenaei*, she presides over the marriage celebrated in his *Haddington Masque* (1608). Here it is clearly the negative implication of both deities which is invoked. Their banishment chimes with Prospero's anxiety about the sexual continence of Ferdinand and Miranda, and is appropriate to a celebration of betrothal, rather than marriage.

87 as as far as.

88–9 plot . . . got According to Ovid, it was Venus and Cupid who inspired the love of Pluto for Ceres' daughter Proserpina, which led him to abduct her and take her to the underworld. Because Proserpina ate six seeds of the pomegranate she

The means that dusky Dis my daughter got,
Her and her blind boy's scandalled company   90
I have forsworn.
IRIS   Of her society
Be not afraid. I met her deity
Cutting the clouds towards Paphos, and her son
Dove-drawn with her. Here thought they to have done
Some wanton charm upon this man and maid,   95
Whose vows are, that no bed-right shall be paid
Till Hymen's torch be lighted – but in vain.
Mars's hot minion is returned again;
Her waspish-headed son has broke his arrows,
Swears he will shoot no more, but play with sparrows, 100
And be a boy right out.
                    [JUNO *descends*]
                              Highest queen of state,
Great Juno comes, I know her by her gait.

96 bed-right] F; bed-rite *Steevens*   101 SD *Transposed from 72 by Theobald; not in* F   101 Highest] F; High *Pope;* High'st *Capell*   102 gait] F *(gate)*

could not be released, but had to spend a part of every year in the underworld. This myth was often allegorised as the cause of seasonal change, and it is appropriate that it should be recalled only to be banished from a masque which celebrates a world without winter. It also explains why, within the mythological narrative of this masque, where Ceres has a central symbolic role, her 'enemies', the gods of love, need to be excluded.

89 dusky Dis The name is the Latin version of the Greek Pluto, god of the underworld (hence 'dusky') and also of riches.

90 blind boy Cupid was traditionally depicted as blind, betokening the arbitrariness of love.

90 scandalled 'disgraced, shameful' (*OED* sv *adj* 1, citing only this instance).

91 society company.

93 Cutting the clouds Cutting through, parting the clouds.

93 Paphos A city in Cyprus, a resort of the goddess and the centre of her cult.

94 Dove-drawn Doves, thought to be 'most abundantly inclined to procreation' (Lynche, *Fountaine of Ancient Fiction* (1599), sig. cciii), were sacred to Venus and, sometimes with swans, drew her chariot (see *Venus and Adonis*, lines 1190–4).

94–5 done . . . wanton charm cast a spell to incite the couple to lechery.

96 no bed-right . . . paid They will not have sexual intercourse. In canon law, and in the

marriage manuals of the period, sexual intercourse was a duty and obligation for both husband and wife, and for each of them, therefore, both a 'right' and a 'debt' which must be paid. Since Steevens, many editors have modernised to 'bed-rite', which is to misinterpret the dominant meaning, even though the subsidiary sense of 'ceremonial' may be present.

98 Mars's hot minion Venus, married to Vulcan, was the lover ('minion') of Mars, the god of war, a myth allegorised in the Renaissance either as a sign of the dangers of female lust, or else as a benign tempering of male bellicosity by the bonds of love – it is clearly the first that is in Iris's mind.

98 returned turned back.

99 waspish-headed Refers both to Cupid's personality, and to the arrows with which he inflicted the wound of love. In the first application, 'waspish' means 'petulantly spiteful', in the second it alludes to the 'sting' of love with which his arrows are tipped.

100 sparrows Conventionally considered as lecherous, and therefore associated with Venus.

101 be . . . out behave simply as a boy, not a deity.

102 gait bearing or carriage. The phrase derives, directly or indirectly, from Virgil's description of Venus in *Aeneid*, 1.405: *vera incessu patuit dea* ('in her step she was revealed as a true goddess'). Orgel, following Jowett, claims that the term does not necessarily indicate that she walks on stage, but all the

JUNO How does my bounteous sister? Go with me
         To bless this twain, that they may prosperous be,
         And honoured in their issue.   105
         [*Singing*] Honour, riches, marriage-blessing,
                      Long continuance, and increasing,
                      Hourly joys be still upon you,
                      Juno sings her blessings on you.
[CERES] [*Singing*] Earth's increase, and foison plenty,   110
                      Barns and garners never empty,
                      Vines, with clust'ring bunches growing,
                      Plants, with goodly burden bowing;
                      Spring come to you at the farthest,
                      In the very end of harvest.   115
                      Scarcity and want shall shun you,
                      Ceres' blessing so is on you.
FERDINAND This is a most majestic vision, and
         Harmonious charmingly. May I be bold

---

106 SD *Singing*] *This edn; They sing* F (*opposite* 105)   **106** marriage-blessing] *Theobald;* marriage, blessing F   **110** SH CERES]
Theobald; not in F   **110** SD *This edn; not in* F   **110** and] F2; *not in* F

senses given in *OED* (Gait *n*¹) occur in contexts
which imply movement, reinforcing the probability
that Juno either enters on foot, or here leaves her
carriage and walks forward to join Ceres. (See
Textual Analysis, pp. 245–7.)
  103 Go with me The straightforward implication of this phrase – that Juno and Ceres step
forward to sing their blessing – is one which is
resisted in Oxford and Orgel, who imagine Ceres
joining Juno in her carriage, and then being elevated
before singing.
  105 honoured . . . issue their children may be
an honour to them.
  106–9 This blessing mixes Christian and pagan,
so that the words of the Roman goddesses carry
echoes of the final prayer in the marriage service:
'Almighty God . . . pour upon you the riches of his
grace, sanctify and bless you, that ye may please him
both in body and soul, and live together in holy love
unto your lives' end.'
  106 The line brings together the mythographical
attributes of Juno as both the goddess of riches and
honour, and patroness of marriage and childbirth.
This stanza is therefore specifically adapted to the
singer. Though Shakespeare's masque does not
carry the ostentatious learning of Jonson's productions, his deployment of the classical gods is
precisely located. (See Introduction, p. 13.)
  107 Long continuance Both a long life together,
and long-sustained love between them.

107 increasing (1) children, (2) growing love.
108 still always.
110 and Oxford adopts this reading from F2 and
BL Egerton MS. 2421. It is persuasive in view of
the metrical regularity of the rest of this song.
110 foison plentiful harvest.
111–12 Iris first blesses them with plentiful grain
(for bread), then with wine. Her blessing resonates
with the frequent biblical collocation of corn and
wine as the staples of life, found, for example, in
Isaac's blessing of Jacob: 'Therefore God give thee
of the dew of heaven, and the fatness of the earth,
and plenty of corn and wine' (Genesis 27.28).
111 garners granaries.
114–15 This prayer, that spring will return
straight after harvest, thus excluding winter, is a
version of the Golden Age myth also invoked by
Gonzalo at 2.1.140ff. There are many literary
precedents and analogues, classical (Virgil, *Eclogues*,
4, and Ovid, *Metamorphoses*, 1), biblical (Leviticus
26), and contemporaneous (as, for example,
Spenser's Garden of Adonis in *Faerie Queene*,
3.6.42).
119 Harmonious charmingly A 'charm' is
both a magic spell and a song, and Ferdinand's
praise of the masque suggests that it, like the music
which first led him to Prospero and Miranda, has a
power beyond the mere delighting of the senses,
reflecting instead a divine, cosmic harmony.
119 May I be bold Would I be right.

To think these spirits?

PROSPERO   Spirits, which by mine art   120
I have from their confines called to enact
My present fancies.

FERDINAND   Let me live here ever;
So rare a wondered father, and a wife,
Makes this place paradise.

Juno and Ceres whisper, and send Iris on employment

PROSPERO   Sweet now, silence.
Juno and Ceres whisper seriously,   125
There's something else to do. Hush, and be mute,
Or else our spell is marred.

IRIS You nymphs called naiads of the windring brooks,
With your sedged crowns, and ever-harmless looks,
Leave your crisp channels, and on this green land   130
Answer your summons, Juno does command.

---

121 from their] F; from all their F2   123 wife] F2; wise F   124 Makes] F; Make *Pope*   124 SD *Capell; after 127 in* F   128
windring] F; winding *Rowe;* wandring *Steevens*

---

121 **confines** (1) region or territory where they
dwell (*OED* Confine *n²* 1), but also (2) with a sense
of 'place of confinement' (*OED* Confine *n²* 5).

122 **fancies** In origin a shortened form of
'fantasies' and applied to the workings of the
imagination. 'Fancy' could also carry, as it now
does predominantly, the sense of something light or
capricious, and so recall Prospero's earlier apparent
denigration of his masque. The ambiguity of
implication is apparent in Milton's description of
Shakespeare as 'fancy's child' in *L'Allegro*, line 133.

123 **wondered** (1) wonderful, (2) to be wondered
at, (3) performing such rare wonders. Any or all of
these senses may be suggested here.

123 **wife** For discussion of this much-debated
crux see Textual Analysis, pp. 229–30. Whether one
reads 'wife' or 'wise', Ferdinand's hyperbole is analogous to Miranda's 'brave new world' at 5.1.183–4,
and parallel to Gonzalo's Golden Age musings in 2.1.

124 SD *Juno . . . employment* This stage direction looks like an elaboration by Crane – one which,
like many others, specifies action clearly implied in
the text.

124–5 **Sweet** 'Sweet' could be used in the period
in address to a male, so that Prospero most probably speaks to Ferdinand. T. W. Craik ingeniously
suggests to me that the line might have read 'Sweet
son, now,' which would both mend the metre and
return the compliment of Ferdinand to his 'father'
in the previous line. Prospero could, however, be
addressing his warning to Miranda, who might
have seemed to be about to respond to Ferdinand's

speech. It has also been suggested that this line
should be given to Miranda (Wright).

126 **to do** to be done.

126–7 **Hush . . . marred** Prospero repeats and
strengthens the injunction of 58, intensifying the
sense of this as a quasi-magical performance.

128 **nymphs called naiads** 'Nymph' is the
generic title of female spirits who in classical
mythology peopled the countryside, woods and
streams. 'Naiads' is the name of those specifically
associated with water, and they were thought to
incarnate the divinity of the spring or stream that
they inhabited. Naiads appeared in Samuel Daniel's
masque, *Tethys Festival* (1610), and again in
Beaumont's *Masque of Gray's Inn and the Inner
Temple* (1613).

128 **windring** *OED* cites only this instance of
the word, considering it a misprint for 'winding'. As
Orgel observes, 'if it is a misprint, it is a peculiarly
felicitous one', and it can be taken as a 'blending' or
'portmanteau word' fusing together 'winding' and
'wandering'.

129 **sedged crowns** crowns woven of sedge, a
riverside plant (*OED* cites only this passage for the
'rare' use of 'sedged', and it could be a compositorial error for 'sedge'). In Beaumont's masque they
wore 'on their heads garlands of water-lilies'.

129 **harmless** innocent (but also suggesting that
the gaze of the nymphs does not have the power to
inspire lustful desire).

130 **crisp** 'Having a surface curled or fretted with
minute waves' (*OED* sv *adj* 2).

Come, temperate nymphs, and help to celebrate
A contract of true love. Be not too late.

Enter certain nymphs

You sun-burned sicklemen of August weary,
Come hither from the furrow, and be merry,   135
Make holiday; your rye-straw hats put on,
And these fresh nymphs encounter every one
In country footing.

*Enter certain reapers, properly habited. They join with the nymphs, in a
graceful dance, towards the end whereof Prospero starts suddenly and
speaks*

PROSPERO *[Aside]* I had forgot that foul conspiracy
Of the beast Caliban and his confederates   140
Against my life. The minute of their plot
Is almost come. *[To the spirits]* Well done! Avoid! No more.
To a strange, hollow and confused noise [the spirits] heavily vanish

134 sicklemen of] F; sicklemen, of F4   138 SD *Enter . . . speaks*] Oxford; F *continues with the direction placed after 142*   139
SD *Johnson; not in* F   142 SD.1 *To the spirits*] Johnson; not in F   142 SD.2 *To . . . vanish*] Oxford (subst.); *After which to a
strange hollow and confused noyse, they heavily vanish* F

132 **temperate** Suggesting modesty and sexual
continence, as well as a contrast to the 'sun-burned'
complexion of the sicklemen.
134 **sicklemen** i.e. workers engaged in
harvesting.
134 **of August weary** Many editors supply a
comma before this phrase, suggesting that the
reapers are made tired by the month's demands on
them. F's punctuation allows the possibility that 'of
August' qualifies the 'sicklemen', implying that they
are tired by their work, rather than by the month.
135 **furrow** 'used loosely for arable land . . . the
cornfields' (*OED* sv *n* 1c).
136 **rye-straw hats** 'The straw hat does not
seem to have been worn by any except country
folk during Shakespeare's age' (M. Channing
Linthicum, *Costume in the Drama of Shakespeare
and His Contemporaries*, 1936, p. 231).
137 **fresh** untainted, pure.
137 **encounter** meet, join.
138 **country footing** rustic dancing. In the court
masque 'country' dances were generally associated
with the antimasque, rather than with the dances of
the courtly masquers, though 'set' dances might
form part of the general revels, and were certainly
danced at court.
138 SD.1 *properly* fittingly, appropriately.
138 SD.1 *habited* dressed.

138 SD.2 *graceful dance* Suggesting that this,
though a 'country' dance, is elegantly performed,
and therefore free from the frequent association of
rural festivity with licence and riot.
141 **minute** appointed time.
142 **Avoid** Depart.
142 SD.2 *hollow . . . noise* In F this SD runs continuously on from the previous direction. This con-
flation is a characteristic habit of Crane's, and I
follow Oxford in splitting the direction. At this
point Juno's chariot withdraws into the heavens – if
it had not been raised earlier – either with or
without Juno in it. The slowness of the ascent and
the noise of the winch would have been covered by
the commotion. For the associations of *hollow* see
above, 2.1.308. The *noise* might have been made
vocally by the actors, but the strong suggestion is
that some kind of instrumental sounds contributed
to it. In Jonson's *Masque of Queenes*, '*These Witches,
with a kind of hollow and infernall musicque, came
forth from thence . . . All with spindells, timbrels,
rattles, or other veneficall instruments, making a confused noyse.*'
142 SD.2 *heavily* (1) 'With sorrow, grief, displea-
sure or anger' (*OED* sv *adv* 3), (2) laboriously. The
adjective is quite possibly Crane's addition, and in
the theatre it would seem that the first of these
senses would be more appropriate.

FERDINAND　This is strange. Your father's in some passion
　　　　That works him strongly.
MIRANDA　　　　　　　　　　　　　Never till this day
　　　　Saw I him touched with anger so distempered.　　　　　145
PROSPERO　You do look, my son, in a movèd sort,
　　　　As if you were dismayed. Be cheerful, sir,
　　　　Our revels now are ended; these our actors,
　　　　As I foretold you, were all spirits, and
　　　　Are melted into air, into thin air;　　　　　　　　　　150
　　　　And like the baseless fabric of this vision,
　　　　The cloud-capped towers, the gorgeous palaces,

---

145 anger so] *Theobald;* anger, so F　**146** You do look] F; Why, you do look *Hanmer;* You look *Pope*　**146** movèd] *This edn;* mou'd F　**151** And] F; And – *Ard3*　**151** this] their F2　**151** vision,] F; vision – *Ard3*

143 passion vehement emotion (often used specifically of anger, but applicable to other states as well (cf. 1.2.392)).

144 works works on, stirs, agitates.

144–5 Since Miranda has obviously seen her father angry before (in 1.2), the meaning must be that on this occasion Prospero's anger seems to her particularly unbalanced or 'distempered'. F's comma after 'anger', however, would imply, as Kermode suggested, that the two phrases are appositional, meaning Prospero is *both* angry *and* distempered.

145 distempered unbalanced, extreme. It was believed that violent feeling derived from imbalance between the four humours; like other mental states described in the play, Prospero's anger has a physiological origin.

146 movèd sort disquieted state. (F's 'mou'd' generates an unmetrical line.) Critics have perhaps unnecessarily worried at the fact that Prospero, himself in an agitated frame of mind, should turn to comfort Ferdinand. If the masque has carried its full celebratory weight in performance, Ferdinand's dismay, both at Prospero's anger and the disruption of the vision, is shared by the audience, and Prospero speaks to them as well as to Ferdinand. It is a formal, set-piece speech, meditating on the implications of the vanishing of the masque, and is bracketed by Prospero's sense of anger at Caliban's conspiracy. Its sentiments are, at the same time, consistent with Prospero's awareness of mortality evident in his later comment that in Milan 'Every third thought shall be my grave' (5.1.309).

147 cheerful It is perhaps this word which is most surprising in the dramatic context. Prospero seems to be encouraging Ferdinand to accept the fragility of the masque in a positive spirit, and to turn the fleeting nature of the masque to educative

purpose. (Note the parallel injunction to Alonso at 5.1.250–1.)

148 revels A term used generally of entertainments, more specifically of dancing (often with a negative connotation of unruliness), but here most strongly suggesting the social dances with which the court masque concluded, customarily described as 'the revels'. (This suggestion is even stronger in performances where Ferdinand and Miranda themselves join in the dance of nymphs and reapers.) The speech which follows has many parallels. T. W. Baldwin noted a parallel in Palingenius, adapted by Barnabe Googe; Kermode suggested Chrysostom and Job 20.6–8; Steevens noted a close analogue in William Alexander, Earl of Stirling, *The Tragedy of Darius* (1603). More generally, the ephemerality of the court masque was a central topos in the debate about the genre's ambition and moral purpose conducted between Ben Jonson and Samuel Daniel (see Introduction, p. 15).

149 foretold told you earlier (not 'prophesied').

151–6 And like ... behind Prospero's meditation is highly organised rhetorically, though deliberately elusive syntactically. It is an example of the rhetorical technique of 'amplification' – an elaboration of the simple proposition that 'everything decays'. Its first part is organised by two similes, each introduced by the phrase 'and like', and is built upon a sequence of parallel phrases (the figure of *isocolon*) juxtaposed without a connective (the figure of *asyndeton*). Then, in 156–8, the lesson of transitoriness is applied to the life of the individual.

151 baseless fabric structure without foundation. 'Fabric', meaning 'product of skilled workmanship', was frequently used to describe the 'universal fabric' of the world and the heavens, created by God.

152–3 The cloud-capped ... temples Pros-

The solemn temples, the great globe itself,
Yea, all which it inherit, shall dissolve,
And like this insubstantial pageant faded   155
Leave not a rack behind. We are such stuff
As dreams are made on; and our little life
Is rounded with a sleep. Sir, I am vexed.
Bear with my weakness, my old brain is troubled.
Be not disturbed with my infirmity.   160
If you be pleased, retire into my cell,
And there repose. A turn or two I'll walk
To still my beating mind.
FERDINAND *and* MIRANDA   We wish your peace
                               Exeunt [*Ferdinand and Miranda*]

---

163 your] F; you F4   163 SD *Exeunt . . . Miranda*] *This edn; Exeunt* / Theobald; *Exit* F

pero here speaks of the glories of the 'real' world, comparing them to the 'baseless' vision we have just seen. At the same time, however, his vocabulary recalls the elaborate settings and painted backdrops of the court masque designed by Inigo Jones, which frequently depicted such buildings. This double application is intensified by the syntactic ambiguity that means we are unclear where the simile ends. At first we can hear the series of phrases beginning 'The cloud-capped towers' as further *instances* of the 'baseless fabric of this vision', rather than as that which is being compared to it. To attempt to clarify and disambiguate the syntax, by, for example, bracketing off 'like . . . vision' as Ard3 does, seems to me mistaken. Not all critics, however, are willing to accept the cross-over between the terminology of masque and reality, pointing out that there are no such scenic illusions in the masque we have actually witnessed.

153 great globe The world, but also perhaps recalling both the Globe theatre and the globes on a turning machine which figured in Jones's designs for *Hymenaei* and *The Haddington Masque*.

154 all . . . it inherit all those who subsequently occupy the earth. The phrase is coloured by biblical language, in particular, perhaps, by the frequent reference in the Old Testament to the Jews 'inheriting' the land of Israel, and Matthew 5.5 where 'the meek shall inherit the earth'.

154 shall dissolve See 2 Peter 3.12: 'Seeing therefore that all these things must be dissolved'. In the King James Bible the same verb is used in verse 10, whereas the Geneva Bible reads: 'But the day of the Lorde will come as a thiefe in the night, in the which the heavens shall passe away with a noyse.'

155 insubstantial without material substance (a recapitulation of, and rhetorical parallel to, 151).

155 pageant The term might refer, technically, both to a scene acted upon a stage and to the stage on which it is performed. Prospero's pageant is 'insubstantial' because its performers are spirits rather than the actors or the 'real' courtiers who took part in court entertainments, but he also suggests the transitoriness of the elaborate illusionist settings for all court masques, taken down at the end of the single performance.

155 faded The word could apply either to the 'pageant' which has just evaporated, or to the world and all its inhabitants which will fade in the future, or to both.

156 rack cloud or mist (*OED* sv *n*¹ 3, 3b). It was also a variant spelling of 'wrack', and in this play above all others the homophone resonates.

157 on of.

158 rounded (1) surrounded, suggesting that we come from and return to sleep, (2) completed, rounded off. The latter sense, though the one adopted by *OED* (Round *v*¹ 4) seems to postdate the play, whereas the first is common in Shakespeare in both literal and metaphoric senses.

158–60 vexed . . . infirmity In presenting his anger as a 'weakness' and an 'infirmity' Prospero uses terms which cross between the moral and the physical. They point up the apparent contradiction between what Miranda notes as an excessive anger, and the elegiac containment of the speech which we have just heard.

163 beating disturbed, agitated.

PROSPERO [*Summoning Ariel*] Come with a thought! – [*To Ferdinand*
   and Miranda] I thank thee. – Ariel, come!

Enter ARIEL

ARIEL Thy thoughts I cleave to. What's thy pleasure?
PROSPERO   Spirit,   165
  We must prepare to meet with Caliban.
ARIEL Ay, my commander. When I presented Ceres
  I thought t'have told thee of it, but I feared
  Lest I might anger thee.
PROSPERO Say again, where didst thou leave these varlets?   170
ARIEL I told you, sir, they were red-hot with drinking,
  So full of valour that they smote the air

---

164 SD. 1 *Summoning Ariel*] *This edn; not in* F 164 SD. 1–2 *To . . . Miranda*] *This edn; not in* F 164 I thank thee. – Ariel,
come] *Kermode;* I thank thee *Ariell:* come F; I thank you: Ariel, come *Theobald;* I think thee, Ariel: come *Wilson* 165–6
As Theobald; Thy . . . pleasure? / Spirit . . . Caliban F 168 t'have] *This edn;* to have F 169 Lest] F4; Least F

164 with a thought as soon as I think of you (cf. the proverb 'as swift as thought', Tilley T240).

164 I thank thee Though the line has frequently been punctuated (as here) in a fashion which suggests that Prospero's thanks are a response to the departing Ferdinand and Miranda's good wishes (the singular form, 'thee', could be used in a plural address), F's punctuation, implying that this is part of Prospero's conjuration of Ariel, produces perfectly acceptable sense, and is preferred by some modern editors and performers. Either reading is possible.

165 cleave to adhere closely to.

165 Spirit The relineation here produces two regular lines. In F there is no space for the word at the end of the line, and 'We' is capitalised, which suggests that the exigencies of space forced the compositor's hand.

166 meet with encounter (a stronger sense than implied in Modern English).

167 I presented Ceres (1) when I acted ('represented') the part of Ceres, (2) when I produced the masque of Ceres, (3) when I introduced Ceres (whilst playing the part of Iris) (Kermode). The word 'presented' is a technical, theatrical term which could sustain any of these meanings. The most likely is the first, for, as the discussion of casting indicates (Appendix 3, pp. 257–61), to provide three boys to act the parts of the goddessess as well as (at least) two to dance as nymphs would have been difficult. Kermode's suggestion that Ariel, the play's principal musician, should be required to perform as Iris, the one deity who does not sing, seems odd, especially since there is no

Shakespearean precedent for having three boy singers in a single play.

168 t'have The elision is for the metre.

170 Say again Though Wilson used these words as part of his argument that the play had been cut, we can imagine that at some time between the end of 3.2 and the beginning of 4.1 Ariel (as he promised at 3.2.108) had reported back to Prospero, and that Prospero had temporarily forgotten this report of the conspiracy. But, like the 'once again' of 4 above, this is something that does not trouble an audience in the theatre, and is simply a device to allow Ariel to launch into his witty set-piece description of the drunken conspirators.

170 varlets Originally a term for a servant, by this time it had come to refer to a rogue or villain, and was used as 'an abusive form of address' (*OED* Varlet 1, 5a, 5b).

171 red-hot (1) highly inflamed or excited (*OED* sv *adj* 2a, citing this passage), 'fired up', (2) Alluding to the physiological effects of alcohol, thought to 'heat' the blood, and generate a fiery face (as demonstrated by the burning nose of Bardolph in *H4* and *H5*).

172–4 smote . . . feet The rhetorically parallel images translate the waving arms and falling over of the drunkards into comically absurd images of false valour. In each case there is a resonance with earlier moments in the play. At 3.3.63 Ariel had taunted the lords with the futility of attempting to 'Wound the loud winds'; in 2.2 Caliban's kissing of Stephano's foot had been a sign of servitude. There may also be a conscious recollection and parody of St Paul's words 'I therefore so run, not as uncer-

For breathing in their faces, beat the ground
For kissing of their feet; yet always bending
Towards their project. Then I beat my tabor,   175
At which like unbacked colts they pricked their ears,
Advanced their eyelids, lifted up their noses
As they smelt music. So I charmed their ears
That calf-like they my lowing followed, through
Toothed briars, sharp furzes, pricking gorse and thorns,   180
Which entered their frail shins. At last I left them
I'th'filthy mantled pool beyond your cell,
There dancing up to th'chins, that the foul lake
O'er-stunk their feet.

PROSPERO   This was well done, my bird!
Thy shape invisible retain thou still.   185
The trumpery in my house, go bring it hither
For stale to catch these thieves.

ARIEL   I go, I go.   *Exit*

---

tainly: so fight I, not as one that beateth the air.' (I
Corinthians 9.26).

174 bending aiming (*OED* Bend *v* 17), but
perhaps also continuing the mockery of their
drunken gait.

175 tabor See 3.2.117 SD n.

176–8 like unbacked colts ... music The
belief that animals could be influenced by the
harmony of music was a standard ingredient of
musical theory in the period. In *MV* 5.1.71–9,
where Lorenzo expatiates to Jessica on the power of
music, the same image is used, of 'youthful and
unhandled colts', which 'If they but hear perchance
a trumpet sound, / Or any air of music touch their
ears' are charmed 'by the sweet power of music'.
Here the emphasis is less upon the power of music
than it is upon the belittling of the conspirators as
animals.

176 unbacked never ridden, hence unbroken.

177 Advanced their eyelids A periphrasis for
'opened their eyes' (cf. 1.2.407). The self-
consciously poetic phrase exaggerates the absurdity
of the conspirators.

178 As As if.

178 smelt music The comic simile is an example
of *catachresis*, a deliberately strained metaphor.

179 lowing mooing (of the mother cow).

180 furzes, gorse Variant names for the same
spiny plant.

182 mantled covered (with scum) as if by a
mantle. This foul, standing pond contrasts with the

'quick freshes' which Caliban had made known to
Prospero as a source of drinking-water. Most
modern editions hyphenate filthy-mantled, but the
adjectives need not be compounded in this way.

184 O'er-stunk their feet By stirring up the
filthy pool they released a stink that was even worse-
smelling than their feet.

184 bird Prospero is no doubt primarily thinking of Ariel's ability to fly (Heather James, in
Shakespeare's Troy, 1998, p. 191, suggests an
allusion to Mercury as *avis Jovis*, 'the bird of Jove').
'Bird', however could mean 'child, youngster or
son' (though *OED*, Bird *n* 1c, gives the last date
for this use as 1571). Perhaps this older meaning
still resonates in Prospero's tone of affection, as
towards a child. (See 'chick' at 5.1.314, and compare
Cym. 4.2.197–8 where Arviragus says, of the apparently dead Fidele, 'The bird is dead / That we have
made so much on.' *OED* cites this as the last
example of the older meaning of 'bird' as 'young
woman', but at this point Innogen's female identity
is disguised.)

185 shape invisible Another reminder to the
audience of Ariel's invisibility – but not necessarily
indicating that he has returned to the sea-nymph
costume.

186 trumpery worthless stuff (but also perhaps
carrying something of the etymological sense of
'deceit').

187 stale Originally a live or stuffed bird used as
a decoy in hunting, more generally a trap.

PROSPERO A devil, a born devil, on whose nature
　　　　　Nurture can never stick; on whom my pains
　　　　　Humanely taken, all, all lost, quite lost;   190
　　　　　And, as with age his body uglier grows,
　　　　　So his mind cankers. I will plague them all,
　　　　　Even to roaring.

　　　　Enter ARIEL, *laden with glistering apparel, etc.*

　　　　　　Come, hang them on this line.
　　　　　[*Prospero and Ariel stand apart*]

　　　　Enter CALIBAN, STEPHANO *and* TRINCULO, *all wet*

CALIBAN Pray you tread softly, that the blind mole may not hear a foot
　　　fall. We now are near his cell.   195
STEPHANO Monster, your fairy, which you say is a harmless fairy, has
　　　done little better than played the jack with us.

---

193 SD. 1 *Enter . . . etc.*] *Capell; after* line *in* F   **193** them on] *Rowe;* on them F   **193** line] F; lime *Oxford*   **193** SD. 2 *Prospero . . . apart*] *This edn; Prospero and Ariel remain, invisible / Capell*   **194–5** *As* F; Pray . . . may / Not . . . cell. *Pope*   **196–201** *As Pope;* Monster . . . Fairy, / Has . . . vs. / *Trin.* Monster . . . which/ My . . . indignation. */Ste.* So . . . should / Take . . . you F

188–9 nature Nurture The relationship between what is inborn, and what is learnt was a frequent topic of discussion in the period, as now.

191–2 as with age . . . cankers The connection of bodily and moral deformity was a commonplace in the period; compare Prospero's characterisation of Caliban's mother as progressively deformed by age at 1.2.258–9.

192 cankers A 'canker' is a sore or ulcer (and originally a variant of 'cancer'), also a disease of plants. The verb figuratively means 'festers' or 'corrupts'.

193 Even to roaring To the point where they cry out loud.

193 line Though in almost every modern performance a clothes-line of some sort is reeled out on which the clothes are displayed, and though such a theatrical realisation makes more straightforward the laboured jokes below, commentators generally assume that 'line' refers to the linden or lime tree, of which it is a variant form. Property trees were available, and washing was indeed usually laid out to dry on hedgerows or bushes during the period (cf. *1H4* 4.2.47–8, and *WT* 4.3.5), though the stickiness of the lime tree does not suggest it as a particularly sensible choice of clothes-horse. In support of the reading of it as a clothes-line, however, it may be noted, contrary to Orgel's assertion that 'there are no contemporary references to

clothes-lines', that clothes in wardrobes were hung on ropes for storage and airing, as Janet Arnold's *Queen Elizabeth's Wardrobe*, 1988, p. 232, makes clear: 'pairs of staples were set opposite each other, embedded in the walls, with ropes stretched taut between them to take the weight of garments, which . . . would have been considerable'. This suits well with Trinculo's subsequent characterisation of the garments as a 'wardrobe'. (I owe this reference to Barbara Ravelhofer.)

193 SD.2 Capell suggested '*Prospero and Ariel remain, invisible.*' But, strictly speaking, only Ariel is 'invisible', and so I have adopted this form. F gives no direction for their exit, but it is possible, as Oxford suggest, for Prospero and Ariel to leave the stage here, returning with the dogs at 250.

194–5 Pray . . . cell Though printed as approximate verse by Pope and most subsequent editors, and though Caliban's later speeches are in verse, prose seems more convincing here.

194 blind mole Topsell, *The Historie of Fourefooted Beasts* (1607), writes, 'These Moles have no eares, and yet they heare in the earth more nimbly and perfectly than men can above the same' (p. 499). The mole is 'blind' in that it lives underground.

197 played the jack 'play the knave, do a mean trick' (*OED* Jack n¹ 2b). The meaning of this proverbial phrase (see Tilley J8) may derive from the 'jack' or 'knave' in a deck of cards.

TRINCULO Monster, I do smell all horse-piss, at which my nose is in
    great indignation.

STEPHANO So is mine. Do you hear, monster? If I should take a   200
    displeasure against you, look you –

TRINCULO Thou wert but a lost monster.

CALIBAN Good my lord, give me thy favour still.
        Be patient, for the prize I'll bring thee to
        Shall hoodwink this mischance. Therefore speak softly –   205
        All's hushed as midnight yet.

TRINCULO Ay, but to lose our bottles in the pool!

STEPHANO There is not only disgrace and dishonour in that, monster,
    but an infinite loss.

TRINCULO That's more to me than my wetting. Yet this is your   210
    harmless fairy, monster.

STEPHANO I will fetch off my bottle, though I be o'er ears for my
    labour.

CALIBAN Prithee, my king, be quiet. Seest thou here,
        This is the mouth o'th'cell. No noise, and enter.   215
        Do that good mischief which may make this island
        Thine own for ever, and I, thy Caliban,
        For aye thy foot-licker.

STEPHANO Give me thy hand. I do begin to have bloody thoughts.

TRINCULO O King Stephano, O peer, O worthy Stephano! Look what   220
    a wardrobe here is for thee.

CALIBAN Let it alone, thou fool, it is but trash.

208–13 *As Pope; Ste.* There . . . that / Monster . . . losse. / *Tr.* That's . . . wetting: / Yet . . . Monster. / *Ste.* I . . . bottle, / Though . . . labour. F   219–21 *As Pope; Ste.* Giue . . . hand, / I . . . thoughts. / *Trin.* O . . . *Stephano,* / Looke . . . thee. F

198 smell Either Trinculo smells, or himself stinks of, horse-piss.

198–9 in great indignation irritated. The inappropriately inflated language (the rhetorical figure of *bomphiologia*) might be taken as a sign of Trinculo's intoxication.

202 lost ruined, damned.

205 hoodwink . . . mischance 'Hoodwink' is a term from falconry, describing the placing of a hood over the head of the bird to render it immobile and harmless; hence Caliban suggests metaphorically that once the prize is achieved it will cover over, and consign to the past, the misfortune they have suffered.

206 hushed as midnight Proverbial (Dent M919.1).

212 fetch off search for and recover.

212 though . . . o'er ears i.e. even if I have to dive for it in the pool (which has been described as 'up to th'chins', 183).

216 good mischief A paradox, or *oxymoron*; the harm they do will bring them good fortune.

218 aye ever.

218 foot-licker Continues the dramatic image of 2.2.138.

220 King Stephano The circumstance suggests to Trinculo the popular ballad (also sung by Iago in *Oth.* 2.3.89 ff.), 'King Stephen was and-a worthy peer / His breeches cost him but a crown', which similarly associates king and clothing.

TRINCULO O ho, monster! We know what belongs to a frippery.
[*Puts on a garment*] O King Stephano!

STEPHANO Put off that gown, Trinculo! By this hand I'll have that   225
gown.

TRINCULO Thy grace shall have it.

CALIBAN The dropsy drown this fool! What do you mean
            To dote thus on such luggage? Let't alone,
            And do the murder first. If he awake,   230
            From toe to crown he'll fill our skins with pinches,
            Make us strange stuff.

STEPHANO Be you quiet, monster! Mistress line, is not this my jerkin?
[*He takes down the garment*] Now is the jerkin under the line. Now,
jerkin, you are like to lose your hair, and prove a bald jerkin.   235

TRINCULO Do, do; we steal by line and level, and't like your grace.

STEPHANO I thank thee for that jest; here's a garment for't. Wit shall
            not go unrewarded while I am king of this country. 'Steal by line
            and level' is an excellent pass of pate: there's another garment for't.

TRINCULO Monster, come put some lime upon your fingers, and away   240
with the rest.

---

224 SD *Puts . . . garment*] *This edn; He takes a robe from the tree and puts it on / Orgel; not in* F   229 Let't alone] *Rann;* let's
alone F; Let's along *Theobald;* let's all on *Wilson conj.*   234 SD *He . . . garment*] *This edn; Removes it from the tree / Orgel;
not in* F   234 line] F; lime *Oxford*

223 **frippery** second-hand clothes shop (*OED* sv
n 3). Trinculo implies that this is not junk (and,
indeed, it is difficult to think why and how Prospero
might have collected worthless clothing, even
though he describes it as 'trumpery' above, 186). In
production the clothing may be rich, even regal.
(See Introduction, p. 57).

225 **Put off** Remove. Trinculo has donned a
gown that Stephano claims for his own.

228 **dropsy** A disease 'characterised by the
accumulation of watery fluid' (*OED* sv *n* 1).

229 **luggage** baggage. Literally 'that which must
be lugged about', but often associated with trash or
rubbish.

229 **Let't alone** Leave it where it is.

233 **Mistress line** Referring to the rope (or tree).

234 **jerkin** Jacket, often of leather and fur and
usually sleeveless.

234–5 **Now . . . bald jerkin** Stephano clearly
intends a joke. 'Under the line' means 'at the
equator' (whereas we now draw the imaginary line
of the equator on the sea, and 'cross' it, in this
period the equinoctial line was imagined as drawn
in the heavens). A causal relationship is implied
between the jerkin being 'under the line' and its
consequent baldness, which might derive from
fevers contracted on long equatorial voyages. Orgel
claims a connection 'with having one's head shaved

in the shipboard horseplay traditionally consequent
on crossing the equator'. Losing one's hair was,
however, associated specifically with sexual disease
and its treatment – as it is in Donne's pithy
epigram, 'A Licentious Person': 'Thy sins and hairs
let no man equal call, / For, as thy sins increase, thy
hairs do fall.' The heat of the equator might then
be a metaphor for sexual heat, which causes the loss
of hair. Levin extended this further by suggesting
that 'under the line' should be understood anatomi-
cally as 'below the waist' ('Anatomical geography
in *The Tempest*, IV.i.235–8', *N&Q*, 11 (1964),
142–6).

236 **Do, do** An expression of approval, either of
the jerkin or the joke.

236 **by . . . level** according to the rule, precisely,
craftily. The proverbial phrase alludes to a plumb
line and a carpenter's level (cf. Tilley L305).

236 **and't like** if it please.

239 **pass of pate** 'A sally of wit: a witty thrust
or stroke' (*OED* Pass *n²* 9b). A metaphor derived
from a lunge, or 'pass', in fencing. The 'pate' is the
head, hence the source of wit.

240 **lime** birdlime, a sticky substance painted on
trees to trap birds, made, according to *A Iewell for
Gentrie* (1614), from the bark of the holly tree. Used
metaphorically and proverbially of the 'sticky
fingers' of a thief (cf. Tilley F236).

CALIBAN I will have none on't. We shall lose our time,
　　　　And all be turned to barnacles, or to apes
　　　　With foreheads villainous low.
STEPHANO Monster, lay to your fingers. Help to bear this away where   245
　　　　my hogshead of wine is, or I'll turn you out of my kingdom.
　　　　[*Loading Caliban with garments*] Go to, carry this.
TRINCULO And this.
STEPHANO Ay, and this.

A noise of hunters heard. Enter diverse spirits in shape of dogs and hounds,
　　　hunting them about, Prospero and Ariel setting them on

PROSPERO Hey, Mountain, hey!
ARIEL　　　　　　　　　　Silver! There it goes, Silver.   250
PROSPERO Fury, Fury! There, Tyrant, there! Hark, hark!
　　　　[*Exeunt Caliban, Stephano and Trinculo, pursued by spirits*]
　　　　[*To Ariel*] Go, charge my goblins that they grind their joints
　　　　With dry convulsions, shorten up their sinews
　　　　With agèd cramps, and more pinch-spotted make them,

---

243 to apes] F; apes *Pope* 247 SD *This edn; not in* F ; 251 SD *Exeunt . . . spirits*] *This edn; Calib. Steph and Trinc. driven out,*
roaring / *Theobald; not in* F 252 SD *This edn; not in* F

242 lose . . . time miss our opportunity by delay.
243 barnacles The barnacle goose was supposed to derive from the shellfish, which dropped into the water and were metamorphosed to birds. Orgel cites Gerard's *Herbal* (1597): 'There are . . . in the north parts of Scotland . . . certain trees, whereon do grow certain shell-fishes . . . which falling into the water, do become fowls, whom we call barnacles.' It is the bird which is implied here.
244 foreheads . . . low A low forehead was taken as a sign of stupidity; cf. Thomas Hill, *A Pleasant History Declaring the Whole Arte of Physiognomy* (1613): 'The forehead little and narrow, dooth indicate such a person to bee foolish, and a small likelyhoode in him to be taught' (p. 32).
244 villainous 'Villainously, vilely' (*OED* sv *adj* 5b). The implication of low birth and servile status is perhaps uppermost here.
245 lay to put to work.
246 hogshead large cask for liquor.
249 SD.1 *noise of hunters* The noise would almost certainly include the sound of the hunting horn, as well as cries of hunters and imitations of the barking of hounds (cf. *MND* 4.1.137).
249 SD.1 *diverse* several. The names called out by Ariel and Prospero suggest that four hounds are required.
249 SD.2 *setting them on* urging the animals to attack (*OED* Set *v*¹ 148c(a)). The customary term

in the hunting manuals for unleashing the hounds, however, is 'casting off'.
250–1 Mountain . . . Tyrant No specific origin for these names has been found, though a 'Silver' appears in *Shr.* 1.1.19. Prospero and Ariel imitate the standard cries of hunters encouraging hounds. In Turberville's *The Noble Arte of Venerie* (1575), a hunter is encouraged to 'blow his horne, and afterwards halow unto that hounde, naming him, as to say *Hyke a Talbot*, or *Hyke a Beaumont*, Hyke, Hyke, to him, to him, etc.'. Sandys points out that the harpies were 'called Jupiter's dogs' (p. 251), which offers a subterranean link between the punishment of these conspirators and Ariel's earlier appearance as a harpy to chastise the lords in 3.3.
252 charge command.
252–4 grind . . . cramps These are variations on a single idea. A 'convulsion' is 'A shrinking, or pulling together of the sinews, a cramp, a pang' (John Bullokar, *An English Expositor* (1616)). The sinews were the conduits which conveyed the animal spirits from the brain through the body, and so partook of the qualities of both 'nerves' and 'tendons', and were involved with (and sometimes used as synonyms for) both. They were imagined as 'moist'; hence to 'dry' them would produce the convulsion or cramp that Prospero commands.
254 agèd of the elderly.
254 pinch-spotted bruised by pinches.

Than pard, or cat-o'-mountain.

ARIEL   Hark, they roar.   255

PROSPERO Let them be hunted soundly. At this hour

Lies at my mercy all mine enemies.

Shortly shall all my labours end, and thou

Shalt have the air at freedom. For a little

Follow, and do me service.   260

Exeunt

5.1 *Enter* PROSPERO *in his magic robes, and* ARIEL

PROSPERO Now does my project gather to a head.

My charms crack not, my spirits obey, and Time

Goes upright with his carriage. How's the day?

ARIEL On the sixth hour; at which time, my lord,

You said our work should cease.

PROSPERO   I did say so,   5

When first I raised the tempest. Say, my spirit,

How fares the king and's followers?

ARIEL   Confined together

In the same fashion as you gave in charge,

Just as you left them; all prisoners, sir,

Act 5, Scene 1   5.1] *Actus quintus: Scœna Prima* F   7 together] F; *om. Pope*   9 all] F; all your *Pope*

255 pard leopard.

255 cat-o'-mountain Another term for leopard, or for any wild cat.

257 Lies For singular verb with plural subject see Abbott 335 (though, as so often, a possible compositorial error).

260 SD That Prospero and Ariel leave before re-entering immediately at the beginning of the next act is an indication that, at Blackfriars at least, act divisions were observed (see Introduction). Some modern productions have rearranged the dialogue across the act division to make continuous playing easier.

Act 5, Scene 1

0 SD *magic robes* This may well be a scribal addition – though it is a perfectly sensible one.

1 project scheme, design. Together with other terms in this speech the word can carry the suggestion of alchemical experiment, where 'projection' is the 'casting of the powder of philosopher's stone

... upon a metal in fusion to effect its transmutation into gold or silver' (*OED* sv *n* 2a).

1 gather ... head come to a climax. *OED* (Gather *v* 19b) cites it as a figurative use of 'to accumulate and come to a head as purulent matter in a body', and it could also refer to the boiling of ingredients in an alchemical experiment.

2 crack collapse, fail. In Jonson's *Alchemist*, 4.5.56, as Kermode points out, the term is used for the explosion of retorts which brings Epicure Mammon's alchemical adventure to an end.

2–3 Time ... carriage In this rather laboured personification Time is imagined as now able to 'walk' more uprightly as his burden (his 'carriage') becomes less.

3 How's the day? What's the time?

4 sixth hour compare 1.2.240.

5 You said At 1.2.299 Prospero had promised that Ariel would be free 'after two days'.

8 you ... charge you instructed me (though we heard no such instructions at the end of 3.3).

In the line-grove which weather-fends your cell;   10
They cannot budge till your release. The king,
His brother, and yours, abide all three distracted,
And the remainder mourning over them,
Brim full of sorrow and dismay; but chiefly
Him that you termed, sir, the good old lord Gonzalo.   15
His tears runs down his beard like winter's drops
From eaves of reeds. Your charm so strongly works 'em
That if you now beheld them, your affections
Would become tender.

PROSPERO   Dost thou think so, spirit?

ARIEL Mine would, sir, were I human.

PROSPERO   And mine shall.   20
Hast thou, which art but air, a touch, a feeling
Of their afflictions, and shall not myself,
One of their kind, that relish all as sharply
Passion as they, be kindlier moved than thou art?
Though with their high wrongs I am struck to th'quick,   25

---

10 line-grove] F; lime-grove *Dryden*   11 your] F; you F3   15 Him that you] F; Him you *Kermode*   15 sir] F; *om. Pope*
16 runs] F; run F2   16 winter's] F; winter F4   20 human] *Rowe*; humane F   23 sharply] F3; sharpely, F

10 **line-grove** grove of linden or lime trees.

10 **weather-fends** acts as a wind-break and defence against the weather.

11 **till your release** until you release them.

12 **distracted** mad, out of their wits (etymologically 'pulled apart').

14 **Brim full** Full to overflowing.

16 **tears runs** Another case of possible scribal/compositorial error.

17 **eaves of reeds** thatched roofs (the 'eaves' are the edge of the roof that overhangs the wall).

17 **works** works on, agitates, stirs (cf. 4.1.144).

18 **affections** feelings (the word can imply both negative and positive emotions).

20 **And mine shall** It is remarkable that Prospero's assertion of his intention to forgive his enemies, which can be seen as a crucial turning-point in the play, is contained within a half-line that, in reading, almost casually seems to complete Ariel's speech. This might be taken to indicate that Prospero had always intended forgiveness – but in performance it is possible for actors to make much of the moment. (See Introduction, p. 47.)

21 **touch** (1) sense, influence (*OED* sv *n* 13b), (2) a small amount (*OED* sv *n* 19).

23 **kind** species, genus (i.e. human, as Ariel is not).

23–4 **relish . . . they** feel suffering every bit as

strongly as they do. F's punctuation, with a comma after 'sharply', generates a different syntax, where the two clauses become parallel statements, with 'all' as an adverb and 'Passion' as a verb. The sense then would be 'I experience everything as keenly as they do; I suffer like them.' Either reading is possible.

24 **kindlier moved** (1) moved to act in a more human way, (2) stirred to a greater generosity. Both meanings are perhaps present, but the first is perhaps the stronger, both because it varies the noun 'kind' in the previous line (the rhetorical figure of *polyptoton*), and, crucially, because it defines Prospero's decision to forgive as more truly human. (See Introduction, p. 51.)

25–7 **Though . . . part** The formulation of Prospero's change of heart may derive from Montaigne's Essay, 'Of Crueltie' (vol. II, no. 11), as Eleanor Prosser first suggested ('Shakespeare, Montaigne and the "rarer action"', *S.St.*, 1 (1961), 261–6), though the idea itself is a commonplace, embodied in the proverb 'To be able to do harm and not do it is noble' (Tilley H170), and echoed also in Sonnet 94: 'They that have power to hurt and will do none . . . rightly do inherit heaven's graces.'

25 **high wrongs** grave, serious crimes (the phrase suggests 'high treason').

Yet, with my nobler reason, 'gainst my fury
Do I take part. The rarer action is
In virtue, than in vengeance. They being penitent,
The sole drift of my purpose doth extend
Not a frown further. Go, release them, Ariel.   30
My charms I'll break, their senses I'll restore,
And they shall be themselves.

ARIEL   I'll fetch them, sir.   *Exit*

PROSPERO Ye elves of hills, brooks, standing lakes, and groves,
And ye that on the sands with printless foot
Do chase the ebbing Neptune, and do fly him   35
When he comes back; you demi-puppets, that
By moon-shine do the green sour ringlets make,
Whereof the ewe not bites; and you, whose pastime
Is to make midnight mushrooms, that rejoice

---

26 Yet, . . . reason,] F Yet . . . reason *Kittredge*

26–7 Yet . . . part Most modern editors remove
F's punctuation in the first of these lines, so that the
sense of the whole phrase is 'I side with reason
against fury'; but the commas suggest a slightly
different possibility, that Prospero claims 'by the
exercise of my reason I am able to oppose my fury'.
Since both 'take part with' and 'take part against'
were available phrases, and since the verb could be
used both transitively and intransitively, either
reading is possible.

26 nobler reason In the hierarchy of the human
body it was believed that the rational faculty was the
highest, and that it ought to rule and control the
passions.

27 rarer 'of uncommon excellence or merit'
(*OED* Rare *adj*[1] 6a).

28 They being penitent The formula Prospero
uses recalls the priest's words in the absolution at
Morning and Evening Prayer: 'Almighty God . . .
hath given power and commandment to his ministers, to declare and pronounce to his people, being
penitent, the absolution and remission of their sins.'
In the event Prospero forgives even the impenitent
Antonio and Sebastian. (See Introduction, p. 52.)

29 sole drift only object.

33–50 Ye elves . . . art A close paraphrase of
Medea's incantation in Ovid, *Metamorphoses*,
7.197–209, mediated through Golding's translation. On the significance of the adaptation see

Introduction, pp. 28–9. For the original texts see
Appendix 2, pp. 255–6.

33 standing still, not flowing (but often with the
implication 'stagnant').

34 with printless foot leaving no footprint.

35 Neptune God of the sea (not mentioned in
the Ovidian original).

35 fly fly from (the rising tide).

36 demi-puppets half-sized or dwarf puppets.

37 green . . . make N. F. Blake suggests that
'make' should be taken as a 'ditransitive verb, one
with two objects', so that 'green' is taken as a noun,
and the sense is 'transform the succulent green
grass into sour ringlets'. ('"Do the green sour
ringlets make": *The Tempest* v.i.37', *N&Q* 238, NS
40 (1993), 201–2). But the reading of 'green' as an
adjective qualifying the sour ringlets is perfectly
possible, as the parallel in *Wiv.* 5.5.69–72, and the
following note, indicate.

37 sour ringlets Still called 'fairy rings'. Burton
writes of 'terrestrial devils': 'These are they that
dance on heaths and greens . . . and . . . leave that
green circle, which we commonly find in plain
fields, which others hold to proceed from a meteor
falling, or some accidental rankness of the ground'
(1.2.1.2).

39 midnight mushrooms i.e. mushrooms that
spring up in the night.

To hear the solemn curfew; by whose aid –　　　　　　　40
Weak masters though ye be – I have bedimmed
The noontide sun, called forth the mutinous winds,
And 'twixt the green sea and the azured vault
Set roaring war. To the dread rattling thunder
Have I given fire, and rifted Jove's stout oak　　　　　45
With his own bolt; the strong-based promontory
Have I made shake, and by the spurs plucked up
The pine and cedar; graves at my command
Have waked their sleepers, oped, and let 'em forth
By my so potent art. But this rough magic　　　　　　50
I here abjure. And when I have required
Some heavenly music – which even now I do –
To work mine end upon their senses that
This airy charm is for, I'll break my staff,
Bury it certain fathoms in the earth,　　　　　　　　55
And deeper than did ever plummet sound
I'll drown my book.

40 curfew The evening bell, rung at nine o'clock in Shakespeare's time (and to this day by the bell of Christ Church College, Oxford). Originally a signal to damp down fires, it does not generally in this period carry the sense of an injunction for the population to stay indoors. After this time spirits were said to be free to roam (cf. 1.2.328–9 and *Lear* 3.4.115–16 where the 'foul fiend . . . begins at curfew, and walks till the first cock').

41 masters ministers. Kermode cites Spenser, *Faerie Queene* 3.7.4: 'She was wont her sprites to entertain, / The masters of her art.' By calling them 'weak' Prospero diminishes the claims that he makes, and the phrase can be compared with Sycorax's 'more potent ministers' who imprisoned Ariel (1.2.275).

42–4 called . . . war Compare Miranda's description in 1.2.1 ff.

43 azured vault blue sky (possibly alluding to the canopy over the stage).

45 fire lightning.

45 Jove's . . . oak The oak was specifically associated with the king of the gods.

46 bolt thunderbolt. Jupiter was god of thunder.

47 spurs roots.

48 pine and cedar The loftiness of both trees emphasises Prospero's power in uprooting them.

48–9 graves . . . forth It was part of popular

superstition that the dead walked at midnight (cf. *MND* 5.1.379–81: 'Now it is the time of night / When the graves, all gaping wide / Every one lets forth his sprite'), and so the lines continue the narrative of the doings of the night that runs through the speech. That Prospero, following Ovid's Medea, claims the waking of the dead as the direct consequence of his own actions, however, introduces a potentially blasphemous element into his magic.

50 rough violent, harsh, cruel in its consequences; but also crude, unsubtle.

51 abjure renounce, recant upon oath. (A term with strong religious and legal resonance.)

51 required demanded, asked for.

52 heavenly music music as of the heavens, with the curative power thought to derive from it.

53 work . . . end achieve my aim.

53–4 their . . . for the senses of those for whom the charm is intended.

54 airy charm i.e. the music, sounding in the air, which works a magic spell.

56 plummet Instrument for measuring the depth of water, cf. 3.3.101.

57 This, one of the most powerful of short-line endings to a speech in the play, may be a deliberate echo of Faustus's unfulfilled cry at the very end of Marlowe's play: 'Ugly hell, gape not. Come not Lucifer! / I'll burn my books. Ah Mephostophilis!'

Solemn music. [*Prospero traces out a circle on the stage.*] *Here enters*
ARIEL *before; then* ALONSO *with a frantic gesture, attended by*
GONZALO; SEBASTIAN *and* ANTONIO *in like manner attended by*
ADRIAN *and* FRANCISCO. *They all enter the circle which Prospero had*
made, and there stand charmed; which Prospero observing, speaks

> A solemn air, and the best comforter
> To an unsettled fancy, cure thy brains,
> Now useless, boiled within thy skull. There stand,   60
> For you are spell-stopped.
> Holy Gonzalo, honourable man,
> Mine eyes, ev'n sociable to the show of thine,
> Fall fellowly drops. The charm dissolves apace,
> And as the morning steals upon the night,   65
> Melting the darkness, so their rising senses
> Begin to chase the ignorant fumes that mantle

57 SD.1 *Prospero . . . stage*] *This edn; Wilson places substantively the same direction before 33; not in* F   60 boiled] *Rowe;* boile
F   63 ev'n] F; ever *Wilson conj.*   64 drops.] F; *Bevington adds Aside*

57 SD.1 *Solemn music* See 2.1.180 SD n.

57 SD.1 *Prospero . . . stage* F's SD suggests that a circle is required for the lords to enter. Many editors indicate that the circle is traced earlier, at 33, so that Prospero himself stands inside a magic ring as he recounts his performance as a conjuror, but this is a matter for individual decision in production. So too, though editors have often specified that the circle is traced 'with his staff', other options are open – including scattering magic dust, as in the 1993 RSC production. F's wording, *They all enter the circle which Prospero had made*, is unusual in dramatic texts in describing an already completed action, and is almost certainly the product of scribal sophistication. Nonetheless, because nothing in the text itself specifically indicates the presence of a circle, it is very likely either that some such indication was present in the original manuscript, or that it is evidence of Crane's having witnessed performances of the play.

57 SD.2 *frantic gesture* gesture of the mad.

57 SD.2 *attended by* The SD makes a distinction between the 'three men of sin' who are 'frantic' and the lords who attend them, but the guiltless too must be 'knit up', even if not 'distracted', so that they do not respond to Prospero's presence or hear his subsequent speech.

58 *air* melody, not necessarily sung.

58 *and* i.e. 'which is'.

best comforter Alluding again to the belief that music was a cure for mental distress or distraction.

59 **unsettled fancy** disturbed imagination (a stronger sense than in Modern English).

59 **thy** The singular pronoun may suggest that Prospero speaks directly to Alonso, though plural address is possible.

60 **boiled** Most editors have accepted Rowe's emendation of 'boile' to 'boiled', though Orgel objects that the 'boiling' is still going on. As in 75 below, the uncertainty may derive from Crane's manuscript, since it would not be difficult to read his 'e' as 'd' and vice versa.

61 **spell-stopped** Once they have entered the circle they are prevented by magic from moving further. The short line seems particularly appropriate to the sense here.

62 **Holy** Used here in the general sense: 'of high and reverend excellence' (*OED sv adj* 3c).

63 **sociable** showing a human sympathy for.

63 **show** appearance (Gonzalo's eyes show that he is weeping).

64 **Fall** Let fall, weep.

64 **fellowly** companionable, sympathetic.

65 **as . . . night** A conventional poetic periphrasis for 'as dawn comes'.

66 **rising senses** Sunrise becomes an image of the lords' returning ability to perceive through their senses.

67 **ignorant fumes** the vapours that cause their ignorance. Again there is a physiological basis to this image, in that the clouding of the reasonable faculty is explained as a consequence of fumes or vapours which have risen to the brain and therefore befuddled its functioning.

67 **mantle** cover, cloud.

Their clearer reason. O good Gonzalo –
My true preserver, and a loyal sir
To him thou follow'st – I will pay thy graces   70
Home both in word and deed. Most cruelly
Didst thou, Alonso, use me, and my daughter.
Thy brother was a furtherer in the act –
Th'art pinched for't now, Sebastian. Flesh and blood,
You, brother mine, that entertained ambition,   75
Expelled remorse and nature, who, with Sebastian –
Whose inward pinches therefore are most strong –
Would here have killed your king; I do forgive thee,
Unnatural though thou art. Their understanding
Begins to swell, and the approaching tide   80
Will shortly fill the reasonable shore
That now lies foul and muddy. Not one of them
That yet looks on me, or would know me. Ariel,

---

72 Didst] F *Catchword on B2ʳ;* Did F *B3*   74 Th'art] *This edn;* Thou art F   75 entertained] F2; entertaine F   76 who]
Rowe; whom F   81–2 shore . . . lies] F3; shore . . . ly F; shores . . . lie *Malone*

68 clearer reason rational faculty.

69 true (1) loyal, (2) actual, real.

69 sir gentleman.

70–1 pay . . . Home Proverbial (Dent H535.1), meaning 'repay a debt completely'.

70 graces Both Gonzalo's virtues and the services he performed for Prospero at the time of his banishment.

71 word and deed Either indicating that Prospero himself will reward Gonzalo both in word and in deed when he returns to Milan, or, possibly, describing Gonzalo's 'graces' as both of speech and action.

73 brother . . . act Sebastian is here directly implicated as an assistant ('furtherer') in Prospero's banishment from Milan, confirming Ariel's accusation at 3.3.69–70, although he was not mentioned in the initial narrative in 1.2.

74 Th'art The contraction is required for the metre.

74 pinched tormented.

74 Flesh and blood As Prospero turns to the consideration of his brother, so his syntax recaptures some of the repetitive convolutedness it has in 1.2.

75 entertained harboured, gave way to. Like 'boiled' above, F's present tense has almost always been changed to the past, though Prospero may be underlining the fact that Antonio still entertains ambitions in the present.

76 remorse pity, compassion (*OED* sv *n* 3a).

76 nature natural feelings, here especially brotherly feelings.

76 who F's reading, 'whom', has often been retained in modern editions, though, as Orgel points out, if it is 'evidence of anything other than an error, it is not of normal Shakespearian syntax'.

77 Whose This seems to refer only to Sebastian, suggesting a difference between him and Antonio in their response to their guilt.

77 inward pinches torments of conscience.

80 swell (1) grow, increase, (2) rise up like a river, or the tide.

80–2 approaching . . . muddy This image varies 65–8, also drawing on the belief that the mind is controlled by the circulation of vapours and fumes in the body. Here the waves of understanding are gradually clearing the imagined detritus left by the 'ignorant fumes' which had clogged their reason.

81 reasonable shore edges of reason.

82 lies Generally, since F3, F's 'lie' has been brought into agreement, though Malone emended to 'shores / That now lie'.

83 yet looks The sense of sight is imagined as being 'stopped' by the spell.

83 would know me The lords would not recognise him because he is not wearing appropriate dress, rather than simply because they have not seen him for twelve years. It is dramatic convention that changes of clothes make a character unrecognisable.

Fetch me the hat and rapier in my cell.

[Exit Ariel]

I will discase me, and myself present   85
As I was sometime Milan. Quickly, spirit,
Thou shalt ere long be free.

ARIEL *[returns with hat and rapier,] sings, and helps to attire him*

[ARIEL] Where the bee sucks, there suck I;
          In a cowslip's bell I lie;
          There I couch when owls do cry;   90
          On the bat's back I do fly
          After summer merrily.
          Merrily, merrily, shall I live now,
          Under the blossom that hangs on the bough.
PROSPERO Why that's my dainty Ariel. I shall miss thee,   95
          But yet thou shalt have freedom. *[Arranging his attire]* So, so
          so.
          To the king's ship, invisible as thou art;

84 SD *Exit Ariel*] Steevens; *Exit Ariel and returns immediately* / *Theobald; not in* F   87 SD *returns . . . rapier*] *This edn; Re-enter Ariel* / *Capell; not in* F   88 suck] F; *lurk Theobald*   90 couch] F *(cowch);* crouch *(crowch)* F3   92 summer] F; *sunset Theobald*   95–6 *As* F2; misse / Thee F   96 SD *Orgel; not in* F

84 SD Theobald suggested that Ariel went and returned immediately, but Prospero's instruction, 'Quickly, spirit' at 86 can equally well be addressed to an off-stage Ariel.

84 **hat and rapier** Though they are conventional marks of gentlemanly rank, these seem rather basic signs of ducal authority, and often in production Ariel returns with a more substantial change of clothes, the 'Rich garments', perhaps, which Gonzalo had supplied (1.2.164).

85 **discase me** undress, take off my magic robe.

86 **As . . . Milan** As when I was the Duke of Milan.

88–94 Ariel's song – the first he has sung which is not scripted by Prospero, and an analogue to Caliban's song of freedom in 2.2 – has, in theatrical history, on occasion been moved to other places in the text. (See Introduction, pp. 20–2.)

88 **sucks . . . suck** Theobald changed the second 'suck to 'lurk', arguing: 'Could Ariel, a Spirit of a refin'd aetherial essence, be intended to want Food?' Though generally not accepted by more recent editors, this is the reading adopted in earlier settings of the song, including that of Thomas Arne, used in stage productions for more than a century.

90 **couch** (1) 'To lie at rest or sleep; to repose' (*OED* sv *v*¹ 16), (2) crouch, lie close (*OED* sv *v*¹ 2). Though F3's change to 'crowch' might support the latter sense, the first seems more consonant with the

next line's reference to the night-time flight of bats. The emphasis upon Ariel's future diminutiveness – and the evident disparity between the actor on stage and the fairy in a cowslip – returns to the world of the fairies in *MND* in its teasing of the audience's perspective.

90 **when owls . . . cry** i.e. at night.

91 **bat** The bat as a nocturnal animal, like the owl, was conventionally a creature of ill-omen, and linked to witches. How far these associations should be allowed to darken Ariel's song of freedom is an open question.

92 **After summer** i.e. he will migrate in pursuit of summer, living in a world without winter (though bats do not in fact migrate, which persuaded Theobald to emend to 'after sunset').

93–4 **Merrily . . . bough** The metre of the lyric moves clearly into a dactylic rhythm. A triple-time final section was common in songs of the period, and the metrical cue is accepted in Johnson's setting. (See Appendix 1, p. 253.)

95 **dainty** Prospero may either be commending Ariel as being 'of delicate beauty or grace' (*OED* sv *adj* 4), or else be commenting approvingly on the delicacy of the song he has sung.

96 **So, so, so** Prospero arranges his ducal attire (cf. 1.2.24).

97 **invisible** Yet another reminder to the audience.

There shalt thou find the mariners asleep
Under the hatches. The master and the boatswain
Being awake, enforce them to this place;   100
And presently, I prithee.

ARIEL I drink the air before me, and return
       Or ere your pulse twice beat.   *Exit*

GONZALO All torment, trouble, wonder and amazement
         Inhabits here. Some heavenly power guide us   105
         Out of this fearful country!

PROSPERO   Behold, sir king,
The wrongèd Duke of Milan, Prospero.
For more assurance that a living prince
Does now speak to thee, I embrace thy body,
And to thee, and thy company, I bid   110
A hearty welcome.
                  [*He embraces Alonso*]
ALONSO   Whether thou beest he or no,
Or some enchanted trifle to abuse me,
As late I have been, I not know. Thy pulse
Beats as of flesh and blood; and since I saw thee,
Th'affliction of my mind amends, with which   115
I fear a madness held me. This must crave,
And if this be at all, a most strange story.
Thy dukedom I resign, and do entreat

---

111 SD *Bevington; Orgel places after 109; not in* F   111 Whether] *Cam.;* Where F; Whe'er *Capell*

---

99 master . . . boatswain It is for practical reasons of the availability of actors that only these two are to be summoned. (See Appendix 3, pp. 257–61.)

100 enforce compel.

101 presently immediately.

102 drink the air The Latin expression *viam vorare* (to devour the road) is adapted to the motion of Ariel through the air. The same idea is used in *2H4* 1.1.47: 'He seem'd in running to devour the way.'

103 Or ere Before.

104–6 Gonzalo speaks in a virtual aside.

105 Inhabits The singular verb conflates the different aspects of the island of which Gonzalo speaks into a collective subject.

106 Behold, sir king Prospero ignores Gonzalo, and speaks first to the highest-ranking person, and the one who has in fact repented of his transgression.

108–9 For more assurance . . . body To make

it more certain that I am indeed a 'real' man (and not an apparition or a ghost) I embrace you. Trinculo asks Stephano to reassure him in the same way at 2.2.86.

111 SD Orgel places this direction immediately after 109 – but whether Prospero completes the speech before the embrace or not is open.

111 Whether F's 'Where' has often been modernised as 'Whe'er', but the disyllable produces a smoother line.

112 enchanted trifle magical hallucination.

112 abuse Both 'harm' and 'deceive'.

115 amends recovers, as from illness (*OED* Amend *v* 6b, citing this passage).

116 crave demand, call for.

117 if . . . all if this is really happening.

118 Thy dukedom I resign Alonso immediately performs the act of reparation (or 'satisfaction') which is a sign of true penitence (see Introduction, p. 51). The tribute he has accepted from Antonio placed Milan within his power, so that he has

Thou pardon me my wrongs. But how should Prospero
Be living, and be here?
PROSPERO [*To Gonzalo*]   First, noble friend,   120
Let me embrace thine age, whose honour cannot
Be measured or confined.
                    [*Embraces Gonzalo*]
GONZALO   Whether this be,
Or be not, I'll not swear.
PROSPERO   You do yet taste
Some subtleties o'th'isle, that will not let you
Believe things certain. Welcome, my friends all.   125
[*Aside to Sebastian and Antonio*] But you, my brace of lords,
        were I so minded
I here could pluck his highness' frown upon you
And justify you traitors. At this time
I will tell no tales.
SEBASTIAN   The devil speaks in him!
PROSPERO   No.
For you, most wicked sir, whom to call brother   130
Would even infect my mouth, I do forgive
Thy rankest fault – all of them – and require

---

120 SD *Wilson; not in* F   122 SD *Orgel; not in* F   126 SD *Johnson; not in* F   129 I will] F; I'll *Pope*   132 fault] F; faults F4

legitimate claim to control the dukedom and the
succession to it. He may, however, imply no more
than that he releases Prospero from the payment of
tribute.
  119 **my wrongs** i.e. wrongs done to you.
  121 **thine age** i.e. his aged body.
  121–2 **honour . . . confined** The respect due to
Gonzalo is beyond limit.
  122 **this** Gonzalo is either referring specifically
to Prospero's reappearance, or to the whole situation, including Alonso's restoration of Milan.
  123–4 **taste . . . subtleties** you are still affected
by the strange illusions. The metaphor derives
from the elaborate confections of sugar, marzipan
or pastry, set out before and after each course in a
banquet, known as 'subtleties'. Their designs were
often of allegorical figures and scenes, making a
kind of edible masque.
  126 **brace** pair. The term is almost always used
of animals, and here indicates Prospero's contempt.
  127 **pluck** bring down.
  128 **justify** satisfactorily prove.
  129 **I will** Elision would be metrically smoother,
but an emphasis on 'I' seems desirable.
  129 **devil . . . No** Sebastian is amazed that Pros-

pero apparently knows of their conspiracy. The line
is often marked as an *aside*, but this demands that
Prospero's 'No' be understood as 'a repetition of
his determination to tell no tales' (Orgel) rather
than as a contemptuous dismissal of Sebastian's
perception.
  129 **No** This is printed as a single line in F. Sebastian should probably contract 'devil' to a single syllable so that Prospero's derisive comment completes
the verse line with the same peremptory contradiction as in Ariel's retort at 1.2.251, or Ferdinand's at
1.2.463.
  130–1 **whom . . . mouth** Antonio has so abused
the ideal of brotherliness that for Prospero to call
him brother would pollute his mouth as he utters
the word.
  131 **even** To be elided to 'e'en' for the metre.
  132 **fault . . . them** 'Fault' has often been
emended to 'faults' (and it is certainly a possible
error) but as it stands the sequence is that Prospero
first forgives his most serious offence of usurpation,
then, with an effort of generosity, forgives him also
his subsequent crimes, including the plotting of
Alonso's death.
  132 **require** demand as a right (*OED sv v* 5a).

My dukedom of thee, which perforce I know
Thou must restore.

ALONSO   If thou beest Prospero,
Give us particulars of thy preservation,   135
How thou hast met us here, who three hours since
Were wracked upon this shore; where I have lost –
How sharp the point of this remembrance is –
My dear son Ferdinand.

PROSPERO   I am woe for't, sir.

ALONSO Irreparable is the loss, and Patience   140
Says it is past her cure.

PROSPERO   I rather think
You have not sought her help, of whose soft grace
For the like loss, I have her sovereign aid,
And rest myself content.

ALONSO   You the like loss?

PROSPERO As great to me, as late; and supportable   145
To make the dear loss have I means much weaker
Than you may call to comfort you; for I
Have lost my daughter.

ALONSO   A daughter?
O heavens, that they were living both in Naples,
The king and queen there! That they were, I wish   150

136 who] F2; whom F   139 I am] F; I'm *Pope*   145 supportable] F; insupportable F3; portable *Steevens*

133–4 perforce . . . restore Antonio, forestalled by Alonso, is in a position where he must give the dukedom back.

136 who By analogy with 76 above, F2's correction of F's 'whom' has been accepted.

138 point The memory is imagined as a stab of recollection.

139 woe i.e. woeful.

140 Patience The quality of endurance is personified. ('Patience' has a stronger meaning in the period than it customarily has now.)

141 past her cure beyond her ability to heal.

142 soft merciful, compassionate.

143 sovereign supreme. The word was frequently used in medicinal contexts of healing (see *OED* sv *adj* 3).

145 As great . . . late As heavy and as recent as your loss.

146 dear heavy, grievous.

146 much weaker Prospero contrasts his isolation with the fact that Alonso still has a daughter in Claribel, and is surrounded with courtiers who, as we have seen, attempt to comfort him.

147 you; for If, as in all recent editions, F's semi-colon after 'you' is weakened to a comma, then it suggests that the loss of a daughter is more insupportable than that of a son. Though this accords with the importance Prospero has placed upon his relationship with Miranda throughout the play, it would have seemed surprising in the seventeenth century, where the loss of a son and heir would be considered more devastating. Retaining F's punctuation permits the intervening clause from 'and supportable' to 'comfort you' to be taken as a parenthetical elaboration, before Prospero makes explicit the 'likeness' of his loss to Alonso's.

148 A daughter It is unnecessary to worry whether this indicates that Alonso did not know, or had forgotten, that Prospero had a daughter at the time of his banishment. It is the emotional power of the present moment rather than a novelistic consistency which matters.

150 That they were In order to make it possible that they might be. The metrical stress on 'that' clarifies the variation on the same phrase in the previous line.

Myself were mudded in that oozy bed
Where my son lies. When did you lose your daughter?
PROSPERO In this last tempest. I perceive these lords
        At this encounter do so much admire
        That they devour their reason, and scarce think   155
        Their eyes do offices of truth; these words
        Are natural breath. But howsoe'er you have
        Been jostled from your senses, know for certain
        That I am Prospero, and that very duke
        Which was thrust forth of Milan, who most strangely   160
        Upon this shore, where you were wracked, was landed
        To be the lord on't. No more yet of this,
        For 'tis a chronicle of day by day,
        Not a relation for a breakfast, nor
        Befitting this first meeting. Welcome, sir;   165
        This cell's my court. Here have I few attendants,
        And subjects none abroad. Pray you look in.
        My dukedom since you have given me again,
        I will requite you with as good a thing,
        At least bring forth a wonder, to content ye   170
        As much as me my dukedom.

Here Prospero discovers FERDINAND *and* MIRANDA, *playing at chess*

---

156 truth; these] *Capell;* Truth: Their F   **168** you have] F; you've *Pope*

---

151 mudded . . . bed Compare 3.3.100–2.

154 encounter meeting.

154 admire wonder, marvel.

155 devour their reason Wonder has caused them to lose the capacity for reason (perhaps implying an open-mouthed stare).

156 do . . . truth perform their function truthfully.

156 these words Capell's emendation is persuasive. Prospero is drawing the attention of Alonso precisely to those other lords who have not yet spoken but gape disbelievingly at what they see. In the same way that he had earlier been at pains to reassure Alonso that he himself was no phantasm, Prospero here underlines that his words also are the product of 'natural breath'. In short, he remarks that the lords believe neither their eyes nor their ears. This is an altogether more satisfactory sense than that produced by retaining the F reading and weakening its colon to a comma. (See Textual Analysis, pp. 228–9.)

158 jostled . . . senses driven from your reason.

160 strangely wonderfully, surprisingly.

162 To be . . . on't The phrase might, but need

not, suggest a causative relationship, a predestined sequence of events.

163 chronicle . . . by day (1) a history which requires much circumstantial detail of daily occurrences, (2) a chronicle which will take many days to relate.

164 relation narrative, story, report.

164 breakfast Used metaphorically of this first meeting.

167 abroad elsewhere on the island.

168 you have Whilst one might elide these words (as 'you've') to preserve the metre, some contrastive stress on 'you' and 'I' in the next line might be preferred.

169 requite repay.

170 wonder Prospero is, perhaps, punning on the name of the daughter who is to be revealed as a masque-like marvel.

171 SD *discovers* reveals (by pulling aside a curtain at the back of the stage in front of the central entrance).

171 SD *playing at chess* Chess was an aristocratic game, and often in literary tradition is associated

MIRANDA Sweet lord, you play me false.

FERDINAND No, my dearest love, I would not for the world.

MIRANDA Yes, for a score of kingdoms you should wrangle,
　　　And I would call it fair play.

ALONSO　　　　　　　　　　If this prove   175
　　　A vision of the island, one dear son
　　　Shall I twice lose.

SEBASTIAN　　　　　　　A most high miracle.

FERDINAND Though the seas threaten, they are merciful;
　　　I've cursed them without cause.
　　　　　　　[*He kneels before Alonso*]

ALONSO　　　　　　　　　　Now all the blessings
　　　Of a glad father compass thee about.   180
　　　Arise, and say how thou cam'st here.

MIRANDA　　　　　　　　　　O wonder!
　　　How many goodly creatures are there here!
　　　How beauteous mankind is! O brave new world

172–3 *This edn; Mir.* Sweet . . . false./ *Fer.* . . . loue/ I . . . world F   173 dearest] F; dear *Pope;* dear'st *Capell*   174 kingdoms you] F4; Kingdomes, you F; kingdoms. You *Johnson*   179 I've] *Pope;* I have F   179 SD *Theobald subst.; not in* F

with love. There has been considerable temptation
to read a good deal of ambiguity into the significance of this game, particularly perhaps under the
influence of the menace it carries in the famous
scene in Middleton's *Women Beware Women*, where
it acts as a metaphor for the off-stage rape of Bianca
by the Duke, and of the way it is used as political
allegory in his *The Game at Chess*. But to do so is
probably to over-interpret the visual emblem of the
young couple. (See Bryan Loughrey and Neil
Taylor, 'Ferdinand and Miranda at chess', *S.Sur.*,
35 (1982), 113–18.)
　172 **play me false** deceive me, are cheating me.
How earnestly this accusation is to be taken will
depend crucially on the way it is played on stage,
though it is difficult not to see it as a deflation of
the 'wonder' that Prospero reveals. (See Introduction, p. 79, for the significance of this challenge.)
　173 This speech is split between two lines in F.
The lineation here preserves Miranda's accusation
as a single short line, to be followed by regular
pentameters. (See Textual Analysis, p. 239.)
　174–5 **Yes . . . play** 'If twenty kingdoms were
actually at stake you certainly would dispute with
me – but I would still call it fair play.' Miranda takes
Ferdinand's empty hyperbole 'not for the world'
literally and teases him with its implication,
but then turns it into a confirmation of her love for
him.

174 **wrangle** contend, argue.
　175–7 **If . . . twice lose** If this is just another
deceitful illusion that this island produces, I will
lose my son a second time.
　177 **most . . . miracle** The actor playing Sebastian can adopt a wide range of possible tones, from
ironic disappointment to a genuinely wondering
response. He certainly has the most to lose by the
recovery of Alonso's heir.
　179 **I've** The elision is for the metre.
　179–80 **blessings . . . father** This carried a
stronger weight in the period, where parents, and
especially fathers, were advised to make the blessing of their children a daily ritual.
　180 **compass thee about** surround you.
　182 **goodly** handsome, worthy.
　182 **creatures** people (the word was not in the
period confined to animals).
　183 **mankind** humankind in general. In some
recent productions Miranda has emphasised with
evident delight the 'man' in 'mankind', thereby
confirming Prospero's comment on her lack of
experience at 1.2.477–80 (and unsettling the probability of her future happiness with Ferdinand).
To read it in this way, however, reflects a modern
sensitivity to the exclusion of women when
'mankind' is used in a general sense, rather than the
likely implication at its original performance.
　183 **brave** splendid.

That has such people in't!

PROSPERO   'Tis new to thee.

ALONSO [*To Ferdinand*] What is this maid with whom thou wast at
    play?   185
    Your eld'st acquaintance cannot be three hours.
    Is she the goddess that hath severed us,
    And brought us thus together?

FERDINAND   Sir, she is mortal;
    But by immortal providence, she's mine.
    I chose her when I could not ask my father   190
    For his advice, nor thought I had one. She
    Is daughter to this famous Duke of Milan,
    Of whom so often I have heard renown,
    But never saw before; of whom I have
    Received a second life; and second father   195
    This lady makes him to me.

ALONSO   I am hers.
    But O, how oddly will it sound, that I
    Must ask my child forgiveness!

PROSPERO   There, sir, stop.
    Let us not burden our remembrances with
    A heaviness that's gone.

GONZALO   I have inly wept,   200
    Or should have spoke ere this. Look down, you gods,
    And on this couple drop a blessèd crown;
    For it is you that have chalked forth the way

---

185 SD *Folger; not in* F   199 remembrances] F; remembrance *Rowe*   199–200 *As* F; remembrances / With . . . I've inly wept/ *Malone*   200 I have] F; I've *Pope*

186 **eld'st** longest; literally 'oldest'.

187 **goddess** Alonso makes the same assumption that Ferdinand had done at 1.2.420–1.

190–1 **ask . . . advice** Children were insistently urged to take the advice of their parents in their choice of marriage partner, even though not required to do so (see 3.1.91–2 n.).

193 **renown** report (implying celebrity or fame). Ferdinand's remark goes some way to confirm Prospero's claim about his status in his people's affections (1.2.140–1), and though it is pedantic to ask from whom Ferdinand would have heard such favourable reports, Gonzalo is the most likely source.

195 **second life** i.e. after his near-drowning.

195 **second father** i.e. father-in-law.

196 **I am hers** I am her father (-in-law).

199 **remembrances** memories, recollections. Often emended to a singular, for the sake of the metre, but, as Orgel points out, the plural is customary elsewhere in Shakespeare with a plural subject. Here it emphasises that both Alonso and Prospero have reason to bury the grief of the past in forgetful forgiveness.

200 **heaviness** grief, sadness.

200 **I have** Could be elided to 'I've' for the metre, though, again, an unmetrical emphasis on the first-person pronoun might be more effective here.

200 **inly** inwardly, in the heart.

202 **drop . . . crown** Compare 2.1.204–5.

203 **chalked forth** marked out 'as a course to be followed' (*OED* Chalk *v* 4c).

  Which brought us hither.

ALONSO   I say 'amen', Gonzalo.

GONZALO Was Milan thrust from Milan, that his issue   205
  Should become kings of Naples? O rejoice
  Beyond a common joy, and set it down
  With gold on lasting pillars: in one voyage
  Did Claribel her husband find at Tunis,
  And Ferdinand her brother found a wife   210
  Where he himself was lost; Prospero, his dukedom
  In a poor isle, and all of us ourselves,
  When no man was his own.

ALONSO [*To Ferdinand and Miranda*] Give me your hands:
  Let grief and sorrow still embrace his heart
  That doth not wish you joy.

GONZALO   Be it so, amen.   215

Enter ARIEL, *with the* MASTER *and* BOATSWAIN *amazedly following*

  O look, sir, look, sir, here is more of us!
  I prophesied, if a gallows were on land
  This fellow could not drown. [*To Boatswain*] Now,
    blasphemy,
  That swear'st grace o'erboard – not an oath on shore?

---

213 SD *Hanmer; not in* F 216 is] F; are *Pope* 218 SD *Orgel; not in* F

204 amen so be it; Alonso responds to Gonzalo's prayer to the gods.

205–13 As Gonzalo moves into a formal celebratory mode he begins with a rhetorical question, which Peacham suggests is employed when 'we would thereby make our speech more sharpe and vehement' (p. 105). The 'vehemency' continues with the 'O' at the beginning of the next sentence (the figure of *ecphonesis*), and the rhetorically trained listener would also note, amongst other things, the way his emphasis on the miraculous effects of the 'one' voyage is underlined by the use of *zeugma*, whereby the final clauses all depend on the single verb 'found'.

205 Milan . . . Milan The first is the duke, the second the place.

205 issue i.e. the children of Miranda.

207–8 set . . . pillars Gonzalo suggests that the events should be recorded on a permanent memorial. He seems to have in mind monuments such as Trajan's column in Rome, 'all of white marble, so well and finely graven with the stories of all Trajan's

wars and victories that it should seem impossible to paint a thing better' (Thomas, p. 39). Dennis Kay suggests that there is a reference here to the columns of Hercules, employed as the imperial emblem of Charles V of Spain, but though this was an extremely well-known symbol of expansionist ambition it has little to do with the record of past events which Gonzalo's lines require. ('Gonzalo's "lasting pillars": *The Tempest*, v.i.208', *SQ*, 25 (1984), 322–4.)

213 When . . . own When we had all lost our sense of our own identities.

213 Give . . . hands As Prospero had done earlier in Act 4, Alonso here performs a ritual action reminiscent of the wedding service.

214 still for ever.

215 SD *amazedly* in a bewildered fashion.

217 I prophesied Gonzalo recalls 1.1.25–8.

218 blasphemy i.e. blasphemer. See 1.1.35–6 n.

219 swear'st grace o'erboard By his swearing the Boatswain drives God's grace from the ship.

Hast thou no mouth by land? What is the news?   220
BOATSWAIN The best news is, that we have safely found
    Our king and company. The next, our ship,
    Which but three glasses since we gave out split,
    Is tight and yare and bravely rigged as when
    We first put out to sea.
ARIEL [*To Prospero*]   Sir, all this service   225
    Have I done since I went.
PROSPERO [*To Ariel*]   My tricksy spirit.
ALONSO These are not natural events, they strengthen
    From strange, to stranger. Say, how came you hither?
BOATSWAIN If I did think, sir, I were well awake,
    I'd strive to tell you. We were dead of sleep,   230
    And – how we know not – all clapped under hatches,
    Where, but even now, with strange and several noises
    Of roaring, shrieking, howling, jingling chains
    And more diversity of sounds, all horrible,
    We were awaked, straightway at liberty;   235
    Where we, in all our trim, freshly beheld
    Our royal, good and gallant ship; our master
    Cap'ring to eye her. On a trice, so please you,
    Even in a dream, were we divided from them,

---

220 *As Pope; . . .* land? / What F   225 SD *Capell; not in* F   226 SD *Capell; not in* F   230 of sleep] F; a-sleep *Pope;* on sleep *Malone*   236 Where] F; When *Dyce*   236 our] F; her *Theobald*

223 three glasses i.e. three hours measured by the hour-glass.

223 gave out split reported wrecked (1.1).

224 tight water-tight.

224 yare prepared, ready (*OED* sv *adj* 1b). *OED* cites this passage under the meaning 'Of a ship: moving lightly and easily . . . easily manageable' (2b), but as they have not set sail this seems wrong.

226 tricksy *OED* cites this under 'playful, sportive, capricious', (sv *adj* 2), but something stronger is perhaps required, suggesting Ariel's resourcefulness.

227 strengthen grow, increase.

232 even now just now, a short while ago. 'Even' should be elided to 'E'en' for the metre.

232 several different, distinct.

233 roaring . . . chains The Boatswain piles up the verbal nouns without connectives (the figure of *asyndeton*) to emphasise the horror of the sound. (One might speculate on why Ariel, or Prospero, should have wakened the lower classes in this way, compared to the heavenly music that rouses the aristocrats.)

236 our trim The garments of the mariners, which, like the ship, are unharmed. 'Trim' is, however, frequently used specifically of a ship – hence Theobald's emendation to 'her trim'.

238 Cap'ring to eye her Dancing for joy as he beheld the ship. 'Caper' could be used generally of dancing, or as a technical term for leaps in a dance.

238 On a trice Immediately, in an instant.

239 in a dream The Boatswain is unspecific about how they were brought, and there is no mention of music leading them as it does virtually all other characters in the play when they are in Prospero's power.

And were brought moping hither.

ARIEL [*To Prospero*]   Was't well done?   240

PROSPERO [*To Ariel*] Bravely, my diligence. Thou shalt be free.

ALONSO This is as strange a maze as e'er men trod,
And there is in this business more than nature
Was ever conduct of. Some oracle
Must rectify our knowledge.

PROSPERO   Sir, my liege,   245
Do not infest your mind with beating on
The strangeness of this business. At picked leisure,
Which shall be shortly single, I'll resolve you,
Which to you shall seem probable, of every
These happened accidents. Till when, be cheerful   250
And think of each thing well. [*To Ariel*] Come hither, spirit,
Set Caliban and his companions free:
Untie the spell.

                                                    [*Exit Ariel*]

[*To Alonso*]   How fares my gracious sir?
There are yet missing of your company
Some few odd lads that you remember not.   255

Enter ARIEL, *driving in* CALIBAN, STEPHANO *and* TRINCULO
in their stolen apparel

---

240 SD *Capell; not in* F   241 SD *Capell; not in* F   246 infest] F; infect *Rowe*   247–8 leisure, . . . shortly single,] F (Which
shall be shortly single*)*; leisure, . . . shortly, single *Rowe*   251 SD *Capell; not in* F   253 SD.1 *Exit Ariel*] *Capell; not in* F
253 SD.2 *To Alonso*] *Oxford*

240 moping 'wandering aimlessly, bewildered'
(*OED* sv *ppl* a).
241 diligence diligent one.
242 maze See 3.3.2 n.
244 conduct conductor, director.
244–5 oracle . . . rectify Because these events
are beyond nature, it will take a supernatural oracle
to correct their understanding.
246 infest trouble, disturb.
246 beating on 'hammering away at', 'insistently
worrying at'.
247 picked leisure at a chosen moment of
leisure.
248 Which . . . single This phrase, enclosed in
parentheses in F, qualifies 'leisure' and means
'which soon will be continuous', but Rowe's emendation of the punctuation, with a comma after

'shortly', so that 'single' means 'individually,
privately', makes for perhaps more straightforward
sense.
248 resolve you explain, make clear to you.
249 Which . . . probable In a way which will
make it seem probable to you.
250 accidents things that have happened (not,
or not primarily, 'chance events').
250 be cheerful Prospero echoes the words he
used earlier to Ferdinand at the end of the masque
(4.1.147).
255 odd (1) extra, unaccounted for (*OED* sv *adj*
9f), (2) strange, eccentric (*OED* sv *adj* 10a, b).
255 SD.2 *in their stolen apparel* This direction,
which may be a scribal elaboration, needs to be
considered in the light of 266–7.

STEPHANO Every man shift for all the rest, and let no man take care
    for himself; for all is but fortune. Coragio, bully-monster, coragio.
TRINCULO If these be true spies which I wear in my head, here's a
    goodly sight.
CALIBAN O Setebos, these be brave spirits indeed!   260
    How fine my master is! I am afraid
    He will chastise me.
SEBASTIAN Ha, ha! What things are these, my lord Antonio?
    Will money buy 'em?
ANTONIO   Very like. One of them
    Is a plain fish, and no doubt marketable.   265
PROSPERO Mark but the badges of these men, my lords,
    Then say if they be true. This misshapen knave,
    His mother was a witch, and one so strong
    That could control the moon, make flows and ebbs,
    And deal in her command, without her power.   270
    These three have robbed me, and this demi-devil –

256–7 *As Pope; Ste. . . . let / No . . . is / But* F   257 bully-monster, coragio] F2 *(coraggio)*; Bully-Monster *Corasio* F
261–2 *As* F; *as one line Steevens*

256–7 These lines are set as approximate verse
in F.
256–7 **Every man . . . himself** Stephano in his
drunkenness reverses the normal phrase which is
'every man shift [provide, manage] for himself'.
257 **Coragio** Courage. The word is also used by
Parolles in *AWW* 2.5.90. The second instance here
is spelt 'corasio' in F, which has been taken to
indicate a drunken slurring on Stephano's part.
257 **bully** 'A term of endearment and familiarity
. . . Often prefixed as a sort of title to the name or
designation of the person addressed' (*OED* sv *n*[1] 1).
258 **If . . . spies** If my eyes are telling me true.
'Spies' literally means 'observers'.
259 **goodly sight** Trinculo echoes Miranda's
observation at 182.
260 **Setebos** Caliban's mother's god (1.2.373).
261 **fine** In his ducal attire.
263 **Ha, ha** Sebastian's laughter is usually
printed to 'complete' Caliban's short line, but since
it does not do so, it is best understood as an extra-
metrical interjection.
264–5 **Will money . . . marketable** Sebastian
and Antonio echo the economic ambitions of
Stephano and Trinculo (2.2.26–8, 63–6) and
reintroduce the perception of Caliban as a fish.
266–7 **Mark . . . true** A nobleman's servants
were identified by wearing the badge of their lord.
Harrison speaks 'of the great trains and troops of
servingmen also, which attend upon the nobility of
England in their several liveries and with differ-

ences of cognizances on their sleeves whereby it is
known to whom they appertain' (p. 231). It is possible that Stephano and Trinculo do indeed have
Alonso's badges on their own costumes, and that
Prospero simply asks if they accurately represent
whose servants they are. But if they are actually
wearing the stolen apparel, then he is pointing out
ironically that they are wearing his livery, not their
'true' one. 'Badge', however, may be used in its
looser sense of any distinguishing emblem or sign,
and Prospero asks whether their dirty external
appearance corresponds truly to their natures (cf.
Mac. 2.3.102: 'badged with blood').
269 **That could** That she could.
269 **control the moon** Power over the moon was
commonly attributed to witches. This is one of the
attributes of Medea in Ovid. It does not figure in
Prospero's earlier speech, where he claims for
himself power over the male sun, leaving the female
moon to Sycorax.
270 **her command** that which she commands
(the tides).
270 **without her power** Two contradictory
senses are possible here, either (1) she could meddle
in some of the areas of the moon's command, but
without her real power or authority; or (2) 'without'
means 'beyond' or 'outside' suggesting that she
'exceeded the moon's power'.
271 **robbed me** i.e. by stealing the clothes which
they now either wear or carry.
271 **demi-devil** As the next line indicates, Pros-

For he's a bastard one – had plotted with them
To take my life. Two of these fellows you
Must know and own; this thing of darkness, I
Acknowledge mine.

CALIBAN   I shall be pinched to death.   275

ALONSO Is not this Stephano, my drunken butler?

SEBASTIAN He is drunk now; where had he wine?

ALONSO And Trinculo is reeling ripe. Where should they
Find this grand liquor that hath gilded 'em?
[*To Trinculo*] How cam'st thou in this pickle?   280

TRINCULO I have been in such a pickle since I saw you last, that I fear
me will never out of my bones. I shall not fear fly-blowing.

SEBASTIAN Why how now, Stephano?

STEPHANO O touch me not! I am not Stephano, but a cramp.

PROSPERO You'd be king o'the isle, sirrah?   285

STEPHANO I should have been a sore one then.

ALONSO [*Gesturing to Caliban*] This is as strange a thing as e'er I
looked on.

PROSPERO He is as disproportioned in his manners

---

277 As Pope; He . . . now / Where . . . wine? F   280 SD *Bevington; not in* F   281–2 *As Pope;* I . . . last, / That . . . bones:
/ I F   287 SD *Malone subst.; not in* F   287 This is as strange a] *Capell;* This is a strange F; 'Tis a strange F3

pero is recalling his account of Caliban's origin at
1.2.320, though the term could be used less specifically as an insult, as it is of Iago in *Oth.* 5.2.301.

274 own acknowledge.

274–5 this . . . mine This line can be interpreted in a variety of ways, from the simplest
acknowledgement by Prospero that just as Stephano
and Trinculo belong to Alonso, so Caliban belongs
to him, to a symbolic acceptance on Prospero's part
of the darkness within himself. (See Introduction,
p. 65.) F's comma after 'darkness', usually omitted
in modern editions, yet usefully suggests a brief
pause before Prospero acknowledges Caliban.

274 thing of darkness This may allude to
Caliban's colour (not elsewhere remarked) as well as
to his diabolic status.

277 where . . . wine where did he get wine from?

278 reeling ripe so drunk that he is staggering.

279 gilded made them flushed, red-faced (*OED*
Gild *v*[1] 6).

280–1 pickle . . . pickle (1) a sorry state, often
specifically a state of intoxication (as in *Eastward
Ho*, 2.1.101, where Golding addresses the spectac-
ularly drunken Quicksilver with 'what a pickle are
you in!' (2) preserving liquid. The first sense is
uppermost in Alonso's mind, but Trinculo puns on
the second.

282 I shall . . . fly-blowing I am so well
preserved that flies will not lay their eggs on me (as
upon a rotting flesh, or a corpse). Trinculo may
refer either to alcohol or to the water of the
stinking pool as his 'preservative'.

285 sirrah A term 'expressing contempt or rep-
rimand' (*OED*). F's question mark has usually been
retained, though an ironic exclamation mark would
also be possible.

286 sore The dominant sense is 'aching' (*OED*
sv *adj*[1] 9a) but playing also on the sense 'sorry, inept'
(*OED* sv *adj*[1] 8).

287 as strange a Though F's reading is not
impossible it is, as Kermode points out, unusually
strained. Capell's emendation makes sense, and
makes the metre of the line more fluent. The
misreading would be an easy one for scribe or
compositor to make.

288–9 as disproportioned . . . shape Prospero
again suggests the commonplace neo-platonic belief
that the outward appearance reflects the inner moral
reality.

288 manners Used with a rather stronger
sense than in Modern English: 'a person's habitual
behaviour or conduct, esp. in reference to its moral
aspect; moral character; morals' (*OED* Manner *n*[1]
4a).

As in his shape. Go, sirrah, to my cell;
Take with you your companions. As you look   290
To have my pardon, trim it handsomely.

CALIBAN   Ay that I will; and I'll be wise hereafter,
And seek for grace. What a thrice-double ass
Was I to take this drunkard for a god
And worship this dull fool!

PROSPERO   Go to, away.   295

ALONSO   Hence, and bestow your luggage where you found it.

SEBASTIAN   Or stole it rather.

                    [*Exeunt Caliban, Stephano and Trinculo*]

PROSPERO   Sir, I invite your highness and your train
To my poor cell, where you shall take your rest
For this one night, which, part of it, I'll waste   300
With such discourse as I not doubt shall make it
Go quick away: the story of my life,
And the particular accidents gone by
Since I came to this isle. And in the morn
I'll bring you to your ship, and so to Naples,   305
Where I have hope to see the nuptial
Of these our dear-belovèd solemnised,
And thence retire me to my Milan, where
Every third thought shall be my grave.

ALONSO   I long

---

297 SD *Exeunt . . . Trinculo*] *Capell; not in* F (*Oxford give Exit Caliban at* 296)   306 nuptial] F; nuptials F2   307 dear-belovèd solemnised] *Pope (*dear-beloved solemniz'd*)*; deere-belou'd, solemnized F; dear-belov'd solemnizèd *Orgel*

289 **Go . . . cell** It is significant that Prospero permits Caliban to return for the first time to the cell from which he had been banished before the opening of the play.

290 **As you look** If (or since) you hope.

291 **trim it handsomely** 'It' refers to the cell, which Caliban must prepare richly (for Prospero's guests).

293 **grace** The word may mean simply 'favour' from Prospero, though its frequent use in theological contexts to describe the free gift of God's grace may strengthen its implication here, as Caliban seeks forgiveness from Prospero, rather than the false 'god', Stephano.

293 **thrice-double** i.e. six-fold.

294 **this drunkard** i.e. Stephano.

295 **this dull fool** i.e. Trinculo.

296 **Hence** Alonso may speak only to his own servants here, especially if Caliban has left immediately after the previous line, as Oxford suggests.

298 **train** retinue.

300 **waste** occupy, pass (*OED* sv *v*¹ 8).

303 **accidents** events, happenings.

306 **nuptial** wedding ceremony.

307 **belovèd solemnised** F's elision of 'belov'd' would require that 'solemnised' be stressed on second and final syllables. Of the four instances in Shakespeare where the word occurs in a line of verse, only one (*LLL* 1.2.42) might require this stress-pattern, the other three (*1H6* 5.3.168, *John* 2.1.539 and *MV* 2.9.6) all unambiguously require the normal modern stress. It would seem likely, then, that the intervention of scribe or compositor was in the wrong word.

309 **third thought . . . grave** To meditate on one's own mortality was a duty enjoined on everyone. Here it perhaps speaks as much of Prospero's abandonment of his aspiration to magic power and recognition of his humanity as it does of any specific sense of his own life coming to an end.

To hear the story of your life; which must   310
Take the ear strangely.
PROSPERO   I'll deliver all,
And promise you calm seas, auspicious gales,
And sail so expeditious that shall catch
Your royal fleet far off. [*To Ariel*] My Ariel, chick,
That is thy charge. Then to the elements   315
Be free, and fare thou well. [*To the others*] Please you draw
   near.

                    Exeunt all [*except Prospero*]

EPILOGUE, *spoken by* PROSPERO

Now my charms are all o'erthrown,
And what strength I have's mine own –
Which is most faint. Now 'tis true

---

314 SD *To Ariel*] Malone *(Aside to Ariel); not in* F   316 SD.1 *To the others*] Langbaum   316 SD.2 *Exeunt . . . Prospero*] Bevington; *Exeunt omnes* F   EPILOGUE 1 Now] F; *Now, now* F3   3 Now] F; *and now* Pope

311 **Take** Affect, captivate.
311 **strangely** wonderfully.
311 **deliver all** give an account of everything.
312 **auspicious** favourable, favouring (*OED* sv
adj 2, citing this passage).
313–14 **so expeditious . . . far off** So swift that
you will be able to catch up with the distant royal
fleet (which, as Ariel said at 1.2.232–5, was bound
'sadly home for Naples' some three hours earlier).
314 **chick** Diminutive of 'chicken', which could
be used in a transferred sense of human offspring
(cf. *Mac.* 4.3.218, where Macduff bewails 'all my
pretty chickens' murdered by Macbeth). Prospero
here, as at 4.1.184, uses a term which suits Ariel's
birdlike qualities, but speaks in a way which
suggests the affection shown to a child.
315 **charge** task, responsibility.
316 **fare thou well** The conventional salutation,
'farewell', is given added force by the personal
pronoun. Especially in recent productions Ariel's
reaction to his freedom has become a focus for
directorial invention. (See Introduction, p. 62.)
   draw near approach (the cell). In some productions Prospero speaks this sentence to the audience,
initiating the Epilogue.
316 SD F simply gives *Exeunt Omnes*, but if
Prospero leaves the stage here then the audience,
thinking the play over, are likely to applaud, thus
rendering Prospero's request for their approval
redundant.

Epilogue
   Few of Shakespeare's plays have epilogues, and
this is the most complex of them, in that the figure
standing before the audience is both the character,
Prospero, and the actor performing the part. There
has been much sentimental reading of this speech
as 'Shakespeare's farewell to the stage', and more
recently it has been adduced as evidence for Shakespeare's Catholicism (David N. Beauregard, 'New
light on Shakespeare's Catholicism: Prospero's
Epilogue in *The Tempest*', *Renascence*, 49 (1997),
159–74). But such readings understate its complexity (see Introduction, pp. 80–1). The Epilogue need
not have been delivered at every performance: the
Epilogue to Jonson's *Bartholomew Fair* was designed only for performance at court, and Tiffany
Stern suggests that, at least after 1611, epilogues
were most often spoken only at the end of first performances (*Rehearsal from Shakespeare to Sheridan*,
2000, pp. 116–19).
   1–3 **Now . . . faint** In the first sentence Prospero
speaks in character.
   3–8 **Now . . . spell** Virtually all editors have
strengthened F's comma after 'Naples' to a full stop,
so that this becomes a statement of fact parallel to
the first sentence. If the comma is retained,
however, 'Now' in this sentence functions not as an
adverb, but as a conjunction, with the meaning
'Now that', and connects Prospero's sense of his
vulnerability with the actor's reliance on the audi-

I must be here confined by you,
Or sent to Naples, let me not,   5
Since I have my dukedom got
And pardoned the deceiver, dwell
In this bare island, by your spell;
But release me from my bands
With the help of your good hands.   10
Gentle breath of yours my sails
Must fill, or else my project fails,
Which was to please. Now I want
Spirits to enforce, art to enchant,
And my ending is despair,   15
Unless I be relieved by prayer
Which pierces so, that it assaults
Mercy itself, and frees all faults.
As you from crimes would pardoned be,
Let your indulgence set me free.   *Exit*   20

---

5 Naples,] F; Naples: F2; Naples. *Rowe*   13 Now] F; For now *Pope*

ence's power to release him. Everything here turns on the actor's delivery of the lines, and either articulation of the relationship of the sequence of statements is possible.

4 here Both the island and the theatre.

7 deceiver impostor, i.e. Antonio.

9 bands bonds, fetters.

10 help . . . hands i.e. by applauding. Noise was thought to break a 'spell'.

11 Gentle breath Either shouts of approval or kind words about the performance.

12 my project The term Prospero used at 5.1.1, but redirected from the aim of the character to the purpose of the actor (or dramatist).

13 want lack (emphatically not 'desire').

14 enforce control.

14 art i.e. magic power (as at 1.2.1), though here also carrying the sense of theatrical art.

15 despair This is a term potentially carrying a theological force. Despair is the ultimate sin against God, denying his power, through grace, to redeem even the worst of sinners. Warburton suggested that 'this alludes to the old stories told of the despair of necromancers in their last moments, and the efficacy of the prayers of their friends for them'. If Shakespeare is gesturing towards the possibility of a Faustus-like despair, however, he is touching it lightly.

17 pierces Compare *An Homily of Common Prayer and Sacraments*: 'the prayer of them that humble themselves shall pierce through the clouds', derived from Ecclesiasticus 35.17.

17–18 assaults Mercy itself Mercy is used as a synecdoche for God, and, as Kermode pointed out, the violence of petitionary prayer is characterised in a similar way in Herbert's poem 'Prayer', which speaks of it as an 'Engine against the Almighty'.

20 indulgence Whilst the word may perfectly well be understood in a general sense as a 'lenient favouring or gentle sufferance' of the actor, it was also a particularly loaded term in the religious disputes of the period, and associated with the Roman Catholic doctrine whereby remission of the penalty for sin in purgatory could be granted by priest or Pope. It is this sense which has been favoured by those who wish to claim Shakespeare as himself a Catholic, but to do so may well be to overload the term in this particular context, which is not about redemption in the next world but release in this. Prospero reminds the audience, echoing the terms of the Lord's Prayer, that it is a duty to pray for others in this world, thereby to declare 'the mutual charity that we bear one towards another' (*Homily of Prayer*).

TEXTUAL ANALYSIS

The editing of any text raises two sets of issues. The first concerns hypotheses about the nature of the printed text and the copy from which it was derived; the second involves a network of assumptions about the nature of the editorial task itself. In both of these areas principles and practices have undergone significant modification over the centuries, and never more so than in recent decades. In the first place, the evolution of the disciplines of bibliography and textual criticism has refined our understanding of the practices of the printers who produced the first published texts, and of the nature of the copy from which they worked. At the same time, however, the old assumption that the primary duty of the modern editor is to recover, as far as might be possible, that original authorial draft, has been questioned. In particular, the evidence of revision in the playhouse – either with or without the co-operation of the author – has led some to argue that the ideal text which one is aiming to recover is that of the first performance, rather than the authorial final draft. As Andrew Gurr puts it in introducing his edition of *Henry V*: 'the target text . . . is what we might loosely call the play-script, the text of the play as it was originally performed'.[1] More extremely, some have argued that all editorial activity is an unjustifiable falsification of the only thing we actually possess – the original printed texts themselves.[2]

It would not be appropriate to conduct a detailed discussion of such theoretical issues here. Current debates, however, in highlighting the fact that editing a text is never a purely objective activity, necessarily lead to a self-consciousness about the underlying assumptions that condition every editorial intervention and, at the same time, direct readers to an awareness of the constructed nature of the texts they read. It is for this reason that this section of the edition – probably that which is least consulted by most readers – is important, and in what follows I have tried to set out as clearly as possible the assumptions that have conditioned my approach to the text, even at the cost of labouring points that might seem obvious to those well versed in textual scholarship, or of simplifying the account of complex and contested matters.

At first sight *The Tempest* is a text which poses few problems. It was first published in the Folio of 1623, and no other complete text survives, either in printed form or in manuscript. Though there are manuscripts which contain songs from the plays, they have no independent authority. The British Library Egerton MS. 2421, for example, transcribes most of the songs, but is almost certainly derivative from F or F2. The play, therefore, presents none of the problems that confront the editor of plays where significantly different printed versions compete for attention and adjudi-

[1] Andrew Gurr, ed., *Henry V*, 1992, p. 56.
[2] For a judicious and dispassionate account of the current state of play in textual criticism see John Jowett, 'After Oxford: recent developments in textual studies', in W. R. Elton and John M. Mucciolo, eds., *The Shakespearean International Yearbook*, 1 (1999), pp. 65–86.

cation. The 'cleanness' of the text has been remarked by all its editors. Nonetheless, the comparatively unproblematic nature of the text of *The Tempest* in the Folio does not, of course, mean that it must therefore be identical to the form in which it left Shakespeare's hand.

Script to print: the copy for the Folio

When an author finished a play, his manuscript in a more or less tidy form (or perhaps in a fair copy by another hand) would be given over to the theatrical company. 'Foul papers' is the conventional term for authorial manuscript, but should not be taken to imply that it must always have been in an untidy or incomplete state. This manuscript, or a transcript of it, would serve as the 'playbook' for performances (this term is to be preferred to 'prompt book', which carries with it implications of theatrical practice from a later age), and from it would be derived the individual parts from which actors learnt their roles.[1] The playbook might be marked up by the book-keeper with early cues for entrances and clarification of exits; with warnings of props that would be needed in the performance and annotation of actors' names. So too, in rehearsal and performance, in the seventeenth century no less than in the contemporary theatre, modifications to the text, including cuts or additions, might be made over a period of time, a process that would be repeated as the play was revived in subsequent years. Some modifications might be required by the Master of the Revels, who licensed the play for performance. Shakespeare himself must have been involved in rewrites and modifications of his text – as he clearly was in the case of *King Lear* and some other plays – but he may well have been content to accept alteration and adaptation that fitted his texts to the company's needs. Since the plays were published after his death, the form in which we now have them could equally reflect changes introduced when he was no longer in any position to control them.

It has at various times been suggested that the text of *The Tempest* is itself a significantly modified 'second thought'. Dover Wilson, among others, contended that the masque in 4.1 was a later addition, supplied when the play was performed at the nuptial celebrations of King James's daughter, Princess Elizabeth, in 1613. On his hypothesis the addition of the masque demanded a recasting of an 'original' play, which would have been much like *The Winter's Tale*, with the material narrated by Prospero in the long second scene originally dramatised in the play's first part. Though Chambers and Kermode effectively demolished Dover Wilson's theories,[2] Irwin T. Smith has resurrected a more limited suggestion of revision for the same occasion, involving only the insertion of the masque of Iris, Ceres and Juno into an originally simpler scene.[3] Smith's case rests on two different kinds of consideration. The first, the suggestion that a masque was added in order to celebrate the royal

---

[1] Tiffany Stern argues for the importance of these actors' parts, suggesting that rehearsals by the whole company together were very few in number, and that revision was likely to derive from these individual parts (*Rehearsal from Shakespeare to Sheridan*, 2000, pp. 46–123).

[2] E. K. Chambers, *Shakespearean Gleanings*, 1944, pp. 76–97; Kermode, pp. xv–xxiv.

[3] Irwin T. Smith, 'Ariel and the masque in *The Tempest*', *SQ*, 21 (1970), 213–22.

THE
TEMPEST.

Actus primus, Scena prima.

A tempestuous noise of Thunder and Lightning heard: Enter a Ship-master, and a Botefwaine.

Master.

Ote-fwaine.

Botef. Heere Master : What cheere ?

Maft. Good : Speake to th'Mariners : fall too't, yarely , or we run our felues a ground, beftirre, beftirre. *Exit.*

Enter Mariners.

Botef. Heigh my hearts, cheerely, cheerely my harts: yare, yare : Take in the toppe-fale : Tend to th'Mafters whiftle : Blow till thou burft thy winde , if roome e-nough.

Enter Alonfo, Sebaftian, Anthonio, Ferdinando, Gonzalo, and others.

Alon. Good Botefwaine haue care : where's the Mafter ? Play the men.

Botef. I pray now keepe below.

Anth. Where is the Mafter, Bofon ?

Botef. Do you not heare him ? you marre our labour, Keepe your Cabines : you do afsift the ftorme.

Gonz. Nay, good be patient.

Botef. When the Sea is : hence, what cares thefe roarers for the name of King ? to Cabine; filence : trouble vs not.

Gou. Good, yet remember whom thou haft aboord.

Botef. None that I more loue then my felfe. You are a Counfellor, if you can command thefe Elements to filence, and worke the peace of the prefent, wee will not hand a rope more, vfe your authoritie : If you cannot, giue thankes you haue liu'd fo long, and make your felfe readie in your Cabine for the mifchance of the houre, if it fo hap. Cheerely good hearts : out of our way I fay. *Exit.*

Gon. I haue great comfort from this fellow : methinks he hath no drowning marke vpon him, his complexion is perfect Gallowes : ftand faft good Fate to his hanging, make the rope of his deftiny our cable, for our owne doth little aduantage : If he be not borne to bee hang'd, our cafe is miferable. *Exit.*

Enter Botefwaine.

Botef. Downe with the top-Maft : yare, lower, lower, bring her to Try with Maine-courfe. A plague——

A cry within. *Enter Sebaftian, Anthonio & Gonzalo.*

vpon this howling : they are lowder then the weather, or our office : yet againe ? What do you heere? Shal we giue ore and drowne, haue you a minde to finke ?

Sebaf. A poxe o' your throat, you bawling, blafphemous incharitable Dog.

Botef. Worke you then.

Anth. Hang cur, hang, you whorefon infolent Noyfemaker, we are leffe afraid to be drownde, then thou art.

Gonz. I'le warrant him for drowning, though the Ship were no ftronger then a Nutt-fhell, and as leaky as an vnftanched wench.

Botef. Lay her a hold, a hold , fet her two courfes off to Sea againe, lay her off.

Enter Mariners wet.

Mari. All loft, to prayers, to prayers, all loft.

Botef. What muft our mouths be cold ?

Gonz. The King, and Prince, at prayers, let's afsift them, for our cafe is as theirs.

Sebaf. I'am out of patience.

An. We are meerly cheated of our liues by drunkards, This wide-chopt-rafcall, would thou mightft lye drowning the wafhing of ten Tides.

Gonz. Hee'l be hang'd yet, Though euery drop of water fweare againft it, And gape at widft to glut him. *A confufed noyfe within.*

Mercy on vs.

We fplit, we fplit , Farewell my wife, and children, Farewell brother : we fplit, we fplit, we fplit,

Anth. Let's all finke with' King

Seb. Let's take leaue of him. *Exit.*

Gonz. Now would I giue a thoufand furlongs of Sea, for an Acre of barren ground : Long heath , Browne firrs , any thing ; the wills aboue be done, but I would faine dye a dry death. *Exit.*

Scena Secunda.

Enter Profpero and Miranda.

Mira. If by your Art (my deereft father) you haue Put the wild waters in this Rore; alay them: The skye it feemes would powre down ftinking pitch, But that the Sea, mounting to th' welkins cheeke, Dafhes the fire out. Oh ! I haue fuffered With thofe that I faw fuffer: A braue veffell

A (Who

marriage, is inherently unlikely, in that *The Tempest* was only one of many plays performed at court in 1613, and there is no evidence whatsoever that it had a special place in the celebrations which would motivate such extensive changes. But Smith also argues from what he perceives as dramatic inconsistencies in the scene as it stands. He notes, for example, that the orders Prospero gives Ariel at the beginning of the scene seem urgent, but are delayed in their execution, and that the masque which is actually performed is not what Prospero seems to demand. He then remarks that Prospero's 'Our revels now are ended' speech at 148 seems remarkably serene for a man in a state of fury. Smith points to real features of the text that might be considered problematic, but they do not seem to me to demand a hypothesis of major revision. The pattern of delay at the beginning of the scene is one which is pervasive in the play; that Prospero does not spell out the nature of the entertainment he proposes makes dramatic sense, and is consistent with the way in which instruction is given to Ariel throughout (even if one does not suppose that Ariel himself is given some agency in arranging the pageant); and though Prospero's speech at the end of the masque challenges an actor to find a coherent emotional path from fury to melancholy meditation, it is a challenge which is surprisingly easy to negotiate on stage. But what is perhaps most revealing in Smith's article is his frequently uttered caveat, 'if the masque is by Shakespeare'. In the end what is most interesting about hypotheses of revision is the insight they give into the assumptions that editors bring to the text. For a long time the court masque was seen as a fundamentally trivial literary genre, and the couplet verse that is employed in the entertainment Prospero provides for Miranda and Ferdinand in Act 4 was regarded as distinctly inferior. The urge to argue for revision, or even for non-Shakespearean authorship of the masque, is but another version of Pope's readiness to banish anything he could not believe his idealised 'Shakespeare' would have written.

Even if one rejects theories of large-scale revision, it is, of course, certain that in many respects the play has been modified during the stages of its transmission from pen to print. We will turn later to the actual printing of the text, but first need to ask what kind of copy it was that the printer had before him. In the case of *The Tempest* there is conclusive evidence that the Folio text derived from a manuscript copy of the play made by Ralph Crane, a professional scrivener. He was an experienced man, over sixty years old when his association with the King's Men began in about 1619 with a transcript of Fletcher and Massinger's *Sir John van Olden Barnavelt*, which may have served as the company's playbook. After 1623 he produced transcripts of plays which were not destined for theatrical use, but served as presentation copies. Different though they are in important respects, these manuscripts, produced before and after the preparation of the copy for the Folio, have enabled scholars to identify characteristics of Crane's scribal habits and establish that he provided the transcripts underlying a number of the Folio's plays.

In an age before consistent spelling and regularised punctuation were considered essential markers of education, every individual had different habits. Trevor Howard-Hill has made exhaustive study of Crane's work, and has identified and tabulated many features of his extant dramatic manuscripts. In the light of his evidence it is generally accepted that Crane worked on *The Tempest*, *The Two Gentlemen of Verona*, *The Merry Wives of Windsor*, *Measure for Measure* and *The Winter's Tale*,[1] and strong arguments have been advanced for his having also provided the copy for *Othello*[2] and *Cymbeline*,[3] and possibly for *2 Henry IV*.[4] It is not necessary to recapitulate Howard-Hill's work in detail, but some of the features that compel recognition of Crane's presence can be summarised. In the first place, Crane punctuated heavily, and in particular he used colons rather than semi-colons, marks of interrogation rather than exclamation marks, had a fondness for hyphens, used parentheses frequently and employed many apostrophes to indicate elisions. All of these features are to be found in *The Tempest*, with a distribution that is comparable to known Crane manuscripts. He had a fondness for particular spellings, and though Howard-Hill found this evidence less decisive for *The Tempest* than some other plays, noting only nine spellings which seem likely to be characteristic of him, Jeanne Roberts added a further pair, including the most significant of them in terms of the text, the spelling 'Princesse' at 1.2.173 which she demonstrates clearly was, for Crane, a spelling for the plural of the male form 'prince'.[5] But perhaps the most striking evidence is that of stage directions. The unusually elaborate directions in this play were at one time taken to be signs of a Shakespeare retired to Stratford providing details for a staging he would not be present to supervise, but this romantic narrative is exploded both by the fact that many of the directions are in fact useless as theatrical directions, and by the consonance between them and Crane's known practices. Other of Crane's scribal habits are of significance for an editor – in particular the lack of clarity in indicating prose and verse, and his readiness to amend the verse where he found it unmetrical, both by elision and by substantive changes to the text. To the editorial consequence of all of these features we will return later. For the moment it is sufficient to accept that the copy the printers received was a manuscript prepared by a scribe who had some experience with theatrical material, but one who was capable also of sophisticating the texts he copied. Howard-Hill concludes that 'his influence was so strong that it obscures evidence of the kind of manuscript which he transcribed'.[6] Nonetheless, it is important to attempt to discern the kind of copy from which Crane was working.

He could have had before him a manuscript in Shakespeare's hand, an earlier scribal transcript of authorial papers, or a copy which had been used as the playbook. It would seem unlikely that the last of these was the case. Though scholars have increasingly questioned the old orthodoxy which claimed that there were clear distinctions to be

[1] See Trevor Howard-Hill, *Ralph Crane and Some Shakespeare First Folio Comedies*, 1972.
[2] See E. A. J. Honigmann, *The Texts of Othello and Shakespearean Revision*, 1996, for the most comprehensive statement of the case.
[3] See Martin Butler, ed., *Cymbeline* (forthcoming) for a summary of the case.
[4] Honigmann supports earlier tentative ascriptions of the copy for the play to Crane (*Texts*, pp. 165–8). He also builds on Howard-Hill's suggestions in 'Shakespeare's earliest editor: Ralph Crane' (*S.Sur.*, 44 (1992), 113–30) that Crane's role in preparation of the copy for the Folio may have extended further, so that he 'must be seen as one of the crucial figures in the preparation of the Folio – and, almost certainly, as part-author of many lines that have passed into literary history as quintessential Shakespeare' (p. 74).
[5] Jeanne Addison Roberts, 'Ralph Crane and the text of *The Tempest*', *S.St.*, 13 (1980), 213–33.
[6] Howard-Hill, *Crane*, p. 138.

made between authorial papers and a theatrical playbook, demonstrating that the company were often content to work with copies that retained much of the indeterminacy once thought to exist only in authorial manuscript, there are nonetheless no obvious signs of a theatrical provenance in the printed text of *The Tempest*.[1] There are no actors' names, for example, or record of props, and the stage directions, apart from their Cranean 'literary' quality, leave a number of loose ends, particularly in the absence of indicated exits, that one might expect would have been tidied up in a text derived from a playbook. Equally, however, there are no unambiguous indications that the copy was an authorial draft including, for example, revisions and second thoughts, interlineations or corrections, or variant speech headings (except, perhaps, in the confused text of 'Come unto these yellow sands'). The absence of such indicators may simply be the product of Crane's thorough tidying up of the text he copied, and John Jowett's suggestion that Crane was transcribing from Shakespeare's 'rough draft' is as plausible as any other.[2] Much of his evidence derives from the analysis of stage directions, making comparison with other late texts believed to have been set from authorial papers which are 'well supplied' with necessary instructions. Perhaps the 'ghost' character of Antonio's son (1.2.437) might be taken as a mark of less than complete revision, as might minor inconsistencies between, for example, Miranda's memory of 'Four or five women' at 1.2.47, and her claim to Ferdinand that she remembers 'no woman's face' except her own (3.1.49–51), but most of the inconsistencies that have been pointed out are visible only to those who require a novelistic consistency in the world beyond and before that of the play itself, matters that simply do not trouble an audience in the theatre. Whilst one might think that the brevity of the play could point to the possibility that the text was still to be fully worked over; whilst one might wish that the feebleness of some of the writing in 2.1 *were* a sign of an early draft; and whilst some of the confusions between prose and verse might further suggest incomplete revision, it does not seem possible to establish with any certainty the nature of the copy Crane transcribed, except to say that it almost certainly had not served as a theatrical playbook and most probably derived from a Shakespearean manuscript.

Printing the Folio

We may now turn to the processes by which Crane's manuscript became the Folio text, and consider the consequences of each stage of that transmigration for the editor. The Folio is made up of quires of three sheets of paper, each folded once, and therefore containing twelve pages. Each quire, then, formed a separate unit in the printing process. The compositors, however, did not begin at the beginning and set the text

---

[1] See, for example, William B. Long, '"Precious few": English manuscript playbooks', in David Scott Kastan, ed., *A Companion to Shakespeare*, 1999, pp. 414–33, Paul Werstine, 'Narratives about printed Shakespeare texts: "foul papers" and "bad" quartos', *SQ*, 41 (1990), 65–86.

[2] John Jowett, 'New created creatures: Ralph Crane and the stage directions in *The Tempest*', *S.Sur.*, 36 (1983), 107–20; p. 119.

sequentially, but set up each of the formes required for the printing of a particular sheet. This means that they would set page one together with page twelve, page two with page eleven and so on. Usually they began with the central sheet of the quire, containing pages six and seven, and worked backwards and forwards from that point. *The Tempest* is an exception to this normal rule, in that pages one and twelve were set first (presumably to allow the first page of the volume to be inspected carefully). The most important consequence of this manner of setting up the type is that the printer had to estimate which parts of the text went where before printing began (a process called 'casting off' the copy), and the compositors then were bound to set exactly and only the portion of text allocated to each particular page, frequently therefore not knowing what came before or after. In practical terms this means that where the casting-off proved not quite accurate then the compositors might be compelled either to compress the material they were given, or to pad it out to ensure it reached the bottom of the page. So, for example, at the bottom of Folio's page 9 (2.2.76) Trinculo's prose speech, 'I should know that voice. It should be –', is set as two 'verse' lines, and the same phenomenon is even more obvious at the bottom of Folio's page 12 (3.2.143–4). It is not surprising that this should occur in prose passages, which are more difficult to estimate exactly than verse, but compositors also on occasion might split verse lines, even omit phrases or whole lines if the page became too crowded, or, conversely, run two lines together to save space – as happened at the bottom of F's page 7, where 2.1.190–1 is printed as a single line.

Printing in this way was necessary for the economical deployment of the time of the compositors who set the text, since it meant that at least two could be employed simultaneously in preparing pages for the press. Charlton Hinman's magisterial work not only established the sequence in which the Folio was put together, but considerably refined the analysis of which compositor set which pages.[1] Using a variety of evidence drawn both from the physical evidence of the type and from analysis of preferred spellings, he concluded that three compositors were engaged on *The Tempest*. His distribution of the text between compositors has been accepted by subsequent scholars, as has his identification of two of them as Compositor B (who set more pages of the Folio than any other workman) and Compositor C. But where he ascribed the third share to compositor A, Trevor Howard-Hill suggested that this was the work of Compositor F, an ascription accepted by Peter Blayney in the second edition of *The Norton Facsimile*. Jeanne Roberts, however, doubted the existence of Compositor F, and the Oxford Shakespeare gives these pages to Compositor D.[2] The matter is not finally settled, but the table lists the Folio pages, their signature, their order of setting and the compositors responsible – leaving open the question of whether D or F was the third. (The latter part of sig. B is occupied by *The Two Gentlemen of Verona*, so the compositors would be setting its first pages in tandem with the last pages of *The Tempest*.)

[1] Charlton Hinman, *The Printing and Proof-Reading of the First Folio of Shakespeare*, 2 vols., 1963.
[2] Roberts, 'Crane', p. 221; Stanley Wells and Gary Taylor, *William Shakespeare: A Textual Companion*, 1987, p. 148.

Folio page	Signature	Order of setting	Compositor
1	A1	1	B
2	A1v	3	D/F
3	A2	11	C
4	A2v	9	C
5	A3	8	B
6	A3v	5	B
7	A4	6	B
8	A4v	7	B
9	A5	10	D/F
10	A5v	12	D/F
11	A6	4	B
12	A6v	2	B
13	B1	23	D/F
14	B1v	21	D/F
15	B2	19	C
16	B2v	17	C
17	B3	15	C
18	B3v	13	D/F
19	B4	14	C

After the compositors set each forme, a single sheet was normally printed and examined for obvious errors. Subsequently, during the printing itself, further pages might be looked at and corrections made. When a volume was bound it therefore could include both corrected and uncorrected sheets. By collation of a large number of surviving copies Hinman was able to show which pages had been corrected during the process of printing, and noted that the first page of *The Tempest* was corrected no less than three times, reflecting 'the special care for appearances thought necessary in the first page of the first play in the volume'.[1] Most of these corrections, however, were of mechanical errors, and almost all the other sheets Hinman noticed as corrected (pages 2, 3, 8 and 17) repair very obvious misspellings – twice of incorrect versions of 'Millaine' – or blemishes of inking. Only two corrections on p. 18 – of 'euens' to 'euents' (5.1.227) and 'Who' to 'Why' (5.1.283) – might suggest a consultation of the original copy, though, as Hinman points out, they are obvious mistakes which do not require reference back to the manuscript. Whereas today an author submits a manuscript to the printers, and then receives a set of proofs which he or she will carefully scan for any departures from the original text (and, no doubt, this is as true of critics who proclaim the 'death of the author' and the 'undecidability of texts' as it is of any other writer) in the seventeenth century such care was by no means routine. Though

---

[1] Hinman, *Printing*, I, 251.

some authors – including Ben Jonson – were beginning to take more scrupulous
responsibility for their texts, such attention was unusual. There is little evidence of
sustained care in the proofreading of the Folio, and virtually none that correction
involved consultation of the original copy from which the text had been set.

The Folio text, then, is the product of successive layers of transcription, in each
of which changes might be introduced, as the compositors set from a scribal manuscript that probably derived from authorial papers. We may now go back through the
layers and attempt to understand the implication of each for the editor.

To begin with the topmost layer: compositors make mistakes, errors which are conventionally categorised as errors of substitution, omission, interpolation and transposition. Scholars have attempted to clarify our understanding of the likelihood of
error, and of the particular tendencies of individual compositors, by examining in
detail the changes that were introduced in Folio copy which they set from extant
quarto texts. John S. O'Connor, for example, has calculated that Compositor C was
not particularly careful, introducing an average of one substantive error in every 21
lines of text he set. He suggests that this should lead editors 'to examine Compositor
C's pages more closely and emend more liberally'.[1] Similarly, though Paul Werstine
has rescued Compositor B's reputation somewhat,[2] Alice Walker's observation that an
editor 'needs always to be on his guard against the readings of Compositor B'[3] remains
wise. In the case of a text like *The Tempest*, however, where there are no quartos to
collate, it has to be recognised and accepted that whilst there is undoubtedly error, it
is not easily identified. A simple example is provided by 4.1.9 where Prospero tells
Ferdinand: 'Do not smile at me, that I boast her of.' The word order is somewhat
unusual, and might suggest that the compositor had transposed an original 'boast of
her'. But 'boast her of' is by no means impossible in Early Modern English. Whether
one emends (as Orgel and Oxford do) or leaves the original to stand is therefore a
matter of editorial judgement of probability. If the page was set by Compositor D
(rather than F), then O'Connor's statistics, showing that transposition was a rare
mistake for him to make, might perhaps incline one to caution – but do not, of course,
rule out the possibility that this is one of his rare errors of this kind. Similar difficulties attend possible errors with final 's'. Compositors certainly did add or omit this
final consonant in contradiction of their copy (Honigmann notes no less than 101 variations of this kind between Q and F *Othello*[4]); furthermore in seventeenth-century
handwriting a final 'es' was sometimes indicated by a single letter form which is easily
confused with a simple 'e' (Crane occasionally used this contraction). Honigmann
further suggests that Shakespeare's own hand was less than clear, especially in the
writing of word endings.[5] Error is therefore probable, and in a case like 3.1.2 no editor
since Rowe has had the slightest hesitation in emending F's 'Delight in them set off'

---

[1] John S. O'Connor, 'A qualitative analysis of Compositors C and D in the Shakespeare First Folio', *SB*,
   30 (1977), 57–74; p. 65.
[2] Paul Werstine, 'Compositor B of the Shakespeare First Folio', *AEB*, 2 (1978), 241–63.
[3] Alice Walker, *Textual Problems of the First Folio*, 1953, p. 93.
[4] Honigmann, *Texts*, pp. 85–6.
[5] Ibid., p. 86.

to 'sets off', nor in accepting F3's correction of 5.1.82 from 'now ly' to 'now lies'. But on several occasions the proper editorial action is less clear, especially where a plural subject has what to modern eyes is a singular verb, as for example at 3.3.2, 'My old bones aches', 4.1.257, 'Lies at my mercy all mine enemies' or 5.1.16 'tears runs'. This construction, though somewhat unusual, was perfectly permissible in Early Modern English, and therefore there can be no compelling reason to change the text, especially since, according to O'Connor, Compositor C (who set all the pages on which these examples occur) was less likely than D to make final 's' errors. In these cases editorial conservatism has no particular consequence for the reading of the text. There are, however, at least two places where a reluctance to make unnecessary emendation involving final 's' is more crucial. At 1.2.7 Miranda appears to note only that there was a singular 'noble creature' on the ship, giving her a developed sense of social hierarchy,[1] but if an error is assumed then the plural 'creatures' (which Theobald first proposed) transforms Miranda's sense of the nobility of the 'fraughting souls' into something rather more inclusive. In the famous crux at 4.1.123–4 (on which more below, pp. 229–30) the fact that Ferdinand uses the verb 'Makes' can be adduced as evidence to support F's reading of the previous line as 'wondered father, and a wise', but it is certainly not impossible that this is a compositorial misreading, rendered more likely precisely if he had misread the manuscript as 'wise', not 'wife'.

These examples indicate that however much one knows about compositorial habits, analysis of them cannot enable emendation in particular cases, even if it offers some guidance on the likelihood of a particular problem being compositorial in origin.[2] Both B and C may have been relatively high-handed with the texts they set, but neither of them was prone to set nonsense; if they transposed or substituted words they generally did so in a way which makes sense, and in the absence of any other text of the play the sense they set must generally be preferred to a hypothetical sense that one might think they had in front of them. This does not, however, mean that all emendation except of the palpably corrupt should be resisted. Four examples are offered here, in each of which there seems to me sufficient reason to justify changing words that deliver a possible meaning as they stand.

work a peace (1.1.19). F's 'work the peace of the present' is comprehensible as it stands (though sufficiently troubling to have provoked emendation by earlier editors), but in searching available databases I have found no use of the phrase anywhere else in the literature of the period, whereas 'work a peace' occurs several times. To substitute the definite article would be an easy error for a compositor to make as he carried the words of the copy in his head, and the emendation provides a reading which is not only simpler, but is in accord with normal idiom of the period.

these words (5.1.156). F's 'Their words' again makes a kind of sense, but seems inappropriate to the drift of Prospero's speech (see Commentary). Capell first suggested

---

[1] Or, as Dover Wilson has it, a fey intuition of the presence of her future husband on board the ship.
[2] The value of compositorial analysis itself has been questioned, notably by D. F. McKenzie, 'Printers of the mind: some notes on bibliographical theories and printing house practices', *SB*, 22 (1969), 1–75, and 'Stretching a point: or, the case of the spaced-out comps', *SB*, 37 (1984), 106–21.

that 'their' was a misreading of the form 'theis' in the copy – a form which Crane used, and which occurs elsewhere in F. Drawn by 'their' as the first word in the line, it would be easy for a compositor to make the substitution, either through misreading the copy or by misremembering it as he set the line. The emendation is plausible in itself, and provides a sense much more coherent in the dramatic situation.

The next two examples both involve the possibility of confusion between the long 's' and the letter 'f', easily mistranscribed either in manuscript or printed copy.

put it to the soil (3.1.47). F's reading 'put it to the foile' has never before been challenged, and it can certainly be made to yield some sense. Editors have generally explicated it as 'overthrew her best virtue' (*OED* Foil *n²* 2), or else as continuing the duelling metaphor which might be implied by 'quarrel', and meaning 'challenged it, as at a fencing match' (Orgel). That editors have not been entirely comfortable with these metaphors, however, is suggested by the invocation in many editions of *OED* Foil *n¹* 6: 'Anything that serves by contrast . . . to adorn another thing or set it off to advantage'. But, as Orgel points out, this is precisely the opposite sense to that required, for the 'defect' does not bestow 'advantage' on virtue, but cancels it out. If, however, one conjectures that the scribe or compositor misread an 's' as an 'f', the resulting 'put it to the soil', with the sense 'moral stain or tarnish', makes appropriate and clear sense – the ladies' best virtues were besmirched by one defect or another. In support of this conjecture one may note not only that *OED* gives this meaning for 'soil' as 'frequent from c.1600–1650', and that Shakespeare uses it in a precisely analogous way in *LLL* 2.1.47–9: 'The only soil of his fair virtue's gloss, / If virtue's gloss will taint with any soil, / Is a sharp wit', but also that the same error is made in Q4 and F of *1H4* 1.2.215 where 'soil' is a misprinting of Qq 1–3, 'foil'. The matter is not, of course, capable of definitive proof, but the gain in clarity and the easy possibility of such error on balance persuades me to adopt this reading.

and a wife (4.1.123). This crux is similar, but much more frequently discussed, and it raises perhaps more significant questions of interpretation. F unambiguously reads 'so rare a wondered father, and a wise'. F2, however, printed 'wife', a reading followed by Rowe, and adopted in most eighteenth-century editions. Though many nineteenth-century editors returned to 'wise', Rowe's reading seemed to be supported by Jeanne Addison Roberts's detection of what appeared to be an 'f' in some copies of the Folio, and her suggestion that the cross-bar of the 'f' was damaged as printing proceeded, until it came to seem like an 's'.[1] But Peter Blayney has argued that the apparent cross-bar is in fact an ink-blot, and so the reading 'wise' is that which the Folio compositors set.[2] It makes sense, and so, it might seem, should be retained. Yet to misread 'wife' as 'wise' would be an easy error by the compositor or by the scribe, and everything turns on editorial judgement of the more persuasive reading in context. My own feeling is that for Ferdinand to add 'and a wise' in praise of Prospero is a redundant amplification, and, crucially, one which contributes nothing to his characterisa-

---

[1] Jeanne Addison Roberts, ' "wife" or "wise" – *The Tempest*, l. 1786', *SB*, 31 (1978), 203–8.
[2] *The Norton Facsimile: The First Folio of Shakespeare*, ed. Charlton Hinman, 1968, 2nd edn with a new Introduction by Peter Blayney, 1996, p. xxxi.

tion of the place as a 'paradise'. By contrast, the 'rich gift' of a wife which Prospero bestows on Ferdinand in this scene can be regarded as the equivalent of God's creation of Eve which, in the period, was seen as 'completing' Adam's paradise in the Book of Genesis.[1] Nonetheless it has to be recognised that the choice of reading here will inevitably owe a good deal to extra-textual assumptions that an editor brings to the task. Stephen Orgel not only adopted the reading 'wife' in his edition, but celebrated it as 'a reading whose time has come'.[2] Jude Kelly, however, in her Leeds 1999 production of the play, instructed Rashan Stone as Ferdinand to adopt the reading 'wise' because she felt that 'and a wife' sounded too much like including Miranda as an afterthought. This is a crux that can never be decided finally one way or the other.[3]

scamels (2.2.149). Whereas the preceding examples are of places where the text as it stands makes sense, this, perhaps the most famous problem in *The Tempest*, since the word is unique to this play, would seem obviously an error, possibly in Crane's manuscript, but more likely introduced in the setting of the printed text. Despite the most energetic efforts of editors over the years no compelling solution has yet been offered. Though it is almost certain that this is one of those 'strange and never heard of words' that Thomas Heywood complained Jaggard's compositors were capable of setting,[4] there is little option but to reproduce F's reading. The scamels cling obstinately to their rock, and Compositor D/F has defeated us all.

One further problem needs to be considered. We know that compositors on occasion omitted words, phrases, even whole lines, in order to deal with technical problems of accommodating the text to the page, or as a consequence of eye-skip or simple incompetence. By their very nature such errors will frequently be undetectable, and even if suspected cannot be repaired. Nonetheless it is possible that problems in one or two places in the text may be the result of such omission. So, for example, editors have wrestled to find a coherent meaning for 2.1.238–9, 'Ambition cannot pierce a wink beyond, / But doubt discovery there' (see Commentary). It is possible that the opacity of meaning derives from error in individual words (though no convincing emendation has been proposed), but it seems to me more likely that a line has been omitted, one which provided an image that paralleled ambition's inability to contemplate any greater possibility than the crown, but led naturally to the second half-line. (One can imagine a line following the formula, 'Nor x do y / But doubt'.) It is possible, also, that the final line of Ferdinand's speech at the beginning of 3.1, another much-disputed passage, is two syllables short because words have dropped out. Obviously an editor cannot remedy such an absence, only note its possibility, even if the addition of 'And are' at the beginning of Ferdinand's line would disambiguate his

---

[1] See Catherine Belsey, *Shakespeare and the Loss of Eden*, 1999, pp. 40–6. Ard3, p. 137, raises as an objection to the reading 'wife' that 'biblical definitions of heaven excluded marriage', but Ferdinand is surely recalling paradise past, not imagining the after-life to come.

[2] Stephen Orgel, 'Prospero's wife', in Margaret W. Ferguson, Maureen Quilligan and Nancy J. Vickers, eds., *Rewriting the Renaissance*, 1986, p. 64.

[3] Richard Proudfoot, however, concludes that the Arden editors were right not to emend the text (*Shakespeare: Text and Canon*, 2001, p. 31).

[4] Quoted from Thomas Heywood, *An Apology for Actors* (1612), by Honigmann, *Texts*, p. 57.

syntax very satisfactorily. The difficulty with hypotheses of omission is that they are untestable. But at the same time they illustrate the way that the proper editorial sequence of first attempting to make sense of the text as it stands, then seeking to repair manifest errors by a process of deduction from the actual words on the page, can never reach to the unpredictable departure from the copy that human scribes and compositors have always been capable of committing.

Verse, prose, elisions and lineation

The Tempest, like most of the plays in F, presents problems of lineation of various kinds. In 1.1., 2.1, 2.2 and 3.2 there is considerable ambivalence over the boundaries between verse and prose; in a number of other places the verse lines as printed are unsatisfactory, with especial difficulties at 1.2.298–305; and there are a number of short lines in the middle of longer speeches, which may or may not signal some corruption in the text. These are problems inherent in the Folio text as it stands, but further difficulty is generated by the normal practice in editions since the late eighteenth century of indicating by 'white space' the links between speeches where a single line is broken into two or more elements. In attempting to come to a principled position from which to approach problems of this kind we need first to be clear about the different possible sources of confusion.

    1. If three pages of *The Booke of Sir Thomas More* are indeed in Shakespeare's hand, then they suggest that the exigencies of space could lead him to run lines together. Beyond this 'evidence', however, there are only inferences that scholars have attempted to draw from printed texts thought to have been set from his papers. Because we know nothing at first hand of his working practices it is impossible to speculate whether the 'near-verse' which characterises some parts of 1.1 and 2.1 in particular is deliberately intended, whether it is a sign of corruption, or whether, indeed, it represents text that Shakespeare himself would have tidied up in a final version. Ben Jonson, after all, claimed that he wrote all his verse first in prose 'for so his master Camden had learned him'.[1] Though Shakespeare's reputation for facility (itself deriving significantly from Jonson) might suggest the contrary, it is not impossible, if the underlying manuscript for *The Tempest* were a 'draft', that some metrical roughness might derive from incompletion. Furthermore, in his later plays Shakespeare wrote with greater metrical flexibility than in his earlier work, employing a much higher percentage of eleven-syllable lines with unstressed endings, and many more short lines at the ends of speeches. He also exhibited a greatly increased fondness for verse in which sense continues over the line break, sometimes producing a quasi-pentameter line which straddles the line-end.[2] This must complicate any notion of 'regularity' in considering the versification of *The Tempest*.

    2. Ralph Crane's manuscript may have contributed to the problem in three different ways. First, he did not continue prose up to the right-hand margin, and conversely,

---

[1] Ian Donaldson, ed., *The Oxford Authors: Ben Jonson*, 1985, p. 603.
[2] See George T. Wright, *Shakespeare's Metrical Art*, 1988.

frequently did not employ upper-case letters to begin a line of verse. Compositors could therefore easily be confused about what was intended as verse or prose. Secondly, as Howard-Hill has demonstrated by analysis of successive transcripts of *The Game at Chess*, Crane was perfectly capable of changing the words themselves in order to achieve what seemed to him a more regular verse line.[1] Thirdly, he frequently indicated with apostrophes elisions that were aimed at generating metrical regularity, even if they did not always achieve it.

3. The compositors, as we have already seen, faced with the technical exigencies of fitting their copy into the space available, might resort to splitting or combining verse lines, and to setting prose as 'verse' or verse as prose to make or to lose space. A single verse line too long to fit the composing stick might be adjusted by the use of variant spellings, abbreviations and elisions, or by turning the final word(s) over to the line above or below. (Generally it seems that whilst compositors might omit or modify words in order to justify prose, they were much less likely to take this drastic step in setting verse.) But, as Paul Werstine has shown, they were also capable of departing from the lineation of their copy for no obvious reason at all.[2]

4. Lines that seem to modern eyes 'unmetrical' may have been much less so to Jacobean ears. Stress-patterns have changed – as is the case with the pronunciation of 'Mìlan', 'ùtensils' or 'exècute' for example. Some words were capable of sustaining different pronunciation – 'devil', for example, could be either one or two syllables, as could 'spirit' (both pronunciations of the latter word seem to be required within a single line at 4.1.120), and many other words, such as 'even', 'heaven' and the like could equally well occur in elided forms as 'ev'n', 'heav'n'. The omission or elision of syllables was recognised as a necessary rhetorical device 'lawfull only to Poets . . . contrary to the true and vsuall wryting or speaking of those wordes, for necessity of number or meeter'.[3] The compositors, like Crane, used elision freely, though their motivation was mostly the purely practical one of fitting a line to the narrow space available.

Faced with such a range of possible sources of confusion, an editor derives some assistance from Werstine's analysis of scribal and compositorial habits, and, on short lines and the lineation of shared lines, from Fredson Bowers's discussion of common practice in the Folio.[4] Where eighteenth-century editors, with their ears finely tuned by the music of the heroic couplet, were perhaps too prone to jump from recognition of rhythmic problems to an assumption that it must indicate corruption in the text, the contrary argument offered by G. B. Harrison and others that Folio lineation preserves Shakespeare's instruction to the actors on how the lines should be delivered

---

[1] Howard-Hill, 'Shakespeare's earliest editor', p. 121.
[2] Paul Werstine, 'Line-division in Shakespeare's dramatic verse: an editorial problem', *AEB*, 8 (1984), 73–125.
[3] Henry Peacham, *The Garden of Eloquence* (1577), sig. EI*. He lists fourteen terms for different kinds of alteration.
[4] Fredson Bowers, 'Establishing Shakespeare's text: notes on short lines and the problem of verse division', *SB*, 33 (1980), 74–130.

derives from ears instructed by modernist free verse, and, as Werstine has shown, is equally unsustainable.[1] In the end, the underlying assumption must be that Shakespeare was likely to write verse that fitted the pentameter model and its normal permissible variants. An editor needs to be aware that the range of those variants increased in his later verse, and must recognise that hypothetical scribal or compositorial omissions and additions are irrecoverable, but it is nonetheless possible to suggest solutions to many of the problems posed in *The Tempest* that have a basis in reason and probability.

VERSE AND PROSE

The scenes involving Stephano, Trinculo and Caliban are printed erratically in F, but in practice pose few serious problems. The general pattern is that Stephano and Trinculo always speak in prose, whilst Caliban, who speaks verse to himself and to Prospero, moves from prose to verse in his conversations with these characters in each scene. In 2.2 his shift to verse as he speaks of the island at line 137 is unambiguous, and seems to suit his fascination with the material world. Things are perhaps less clear in 3.2. After line 46 all his speeches fit comfortably as verse, and are so printed in F. His earlier speeches are less certain. Lines 21–2 are printed as verse, are regular iambics, and could be preserved as such, but since his subsequent speeches cannot be reduced to regularity and must be taken as prose, I have chosen, on the analogy of 2.2 and of 4.1 (where Caliban also begins with prose but swiftly moves to verse), to lineate 21–2 as prose, so that Caliban's move to verse is a decisive one. The other problem here (which belongs with questions of split lines below) is that at 3.2.96 and 107, for example, Stephano seems to be attracted by the music of Caliban's lines to respond with a part-line that completes their rhythm before continuing in clear prose. An actor should certainly be sensitive to the way the relationship of these speeches suggests Stephano's intoxication by Caliban's rhetoric. My choice here to preserve Stephano as a prose-speaker might be to impose an editorial consistency on something more flexible in Shakespeare's practice.

The other scenes embracing both prose and verse involve the lords, and are very much more problematic. There is no simple rule-of-thumb which produces a satisfactory solution, and the specific problems in each scene need separate consideration.

Act 1, Scene 1. The scene begins in prose, spoken both by the Boatswain and the lords, appropriate perhaps to the confusion in social roles that the storm generates.[2] After line 47 the Folio looks like this:

---

[1] G. B. Harrison, 'A note on *Coriolanus*', in James G. McManaway, Giles E. Dawson and Edwin E. Willoughby, eds., *Joseph Quincy Adams Memorial Studies*, 1948, pp. 240–8; Paul Bertram, *White Space in Shakespeare: The Development of the Modern Text*, 1980, are both answered by Werstine, 'Line-division'.

[2] E. K. Chambers, in *Shakespearean Gleanings*, 1944, pp. 81–2, attempted to cast the first part of the scene in approximate verse, but it is not very convincing.

An. We are meerly cheated of our liues by drunkards,
This wide-chopt-rafcall,would thou mightft lye drow-
ning the wafhing of ten Tides.
Gonz. Hee'l be hang'd yet,
Though euery drop of water fweare againft it.
And gape at widft to gluc him. *A confufed noyfe within.*
Mercy on vs.
We fplit,we fplit, Farewell my wife, and children,
Farewell brother : we fplit,we fplit,we fplit.
Anth. Let's all finke with' King
Seb. Let's take leaue of him. *Exit.*
Gonz. Now would I giue a thoufand furlongs of Sea,
for an Acre of barren ground: Long heath, Browne
firrs, any thing; the wills aboue be done, but I would
faine dye a dry death. *Exit.*

There are three distinct questions raised by this passage. In the first place, since Pope the speeches of the lords, until Gonzalo's final speech, have generally been lineated as verse.[1] There are grounds for assuming compositorial error here: this was the first page set, the first encounter of Compositor B with Crane's hand, and some of the uncertainties of capitalisation might be attributed to unfamiliarity with his practice. The apparent prose at 'This wide-chopt . . . drowning' can be explained by a compositorial decision to run on a line which could not be accommodated in the Folio's narrow columns into the next. But the main reason for accepting these lines as verse is, simply, that they work as such.

The second difficulty is posed by the the setting of the lines from the stage direction *a confused noise* to the final 'we split'. Clearly all these words cannot be spoken by Gonzalo, as the Folio implies, and editors have accepted Johnson's conjecture, embodied in Steevens's edition, that all the exclamations, including 'Mercy on us', represent the noises made by the off-stage voices. But this solution is not unproblematic; in particular, it gives Gonzalo no reaction to the noise he hears, and I suggest that Capell was right to assign the first exclamation, which completes a verse line, to Gonzalo. It is best understood as his response to the great shout within, which is then represented in the following two lines. Stage directions in the manuscript copy were set out in the right-hand margin, and might occupy more than one line, leaving their placement up to the compositor. Here he seems to have got it right. We may imagine that the first emanation of 'confused noise' is a shout to which Gonzalo responds with terror, his exclamation 'Mercy on us' accompanied or followed by the differentiated cries which are set out afterwards (there was no clear convention in the period for indicating simultaneous speech). It is curious that the two lines of cries should fit so neatly into blank verse (and some modern editors have chosen to lineate them as prose) – but it is impossible to decide whether this is chance, a witticism on Shakespeare's

[1] Though Ard3 prints them as prose.

part in making confusion conform to metre, or Ralph Crane intervening to regularise the lines.

Thirdly, Gonzalo's final speech reverts to prose, but is, in fact, very close to verse. One could, for example, lineate it like this:

> Now would I give a thousand furlongs of sea
> For an acre of barren ground – long heath,
> Brown furze, anything. The wills above be done,
> But I would fain die a dry death.

It is not impossible that, still unfamiliar with Crane's scribal habits, the compositor misread his copy as prose. But if verse seems appropriate at the end of the scene, the reconstruction offered here is not metrically as secure as the recasting of some of Caliban's apparent prose, and does not justify emendation of the Folio text.

Act 2, Scene 1. Unlike the scenes so far discussed, where the relationship of verse and prose seems purposeful and (virtually) consistent, this scene poses intractable problems. Alonso always speaks in verse, and in the earlier part of the scene the lords for the most part speak in prose when they are engaged in their quibbles and mutual abuse, but sometimes in verse when they address the monarch directly. The latter part of the scene moves decisively into verse. But if this is the general pattern, it is frequently contradicted at the level of detail, and poses significant difficulties for the editor. In many cases these are problems which only become critical because of the editorial practice of indicating shared lines typographically, which will be discussed shortly, but on occasion they generate more complicated difficulties which raise more general questions.

Consider this extract:

> *Alonf.* Prethee peace.
> *Seb.* He receiues comfort like cold porredge.
> *Ant.* The Vifitor will not giue him ore fo.
> *Seb.* Looke, hee's winding vp the watch of his wit,
> By and by it will ftrike.
> *Gon.* Sir.
> *Seb.* One : Tell.
> *Gon.* When euery greefe is entertaind,
> That's offer'd comes to th'entertainer.
> *Seb.* A dollor.
> *Gon.* Dolour comes to him indeed, you haue fpoken
> truer then you purpos'd.
> *Seb.* You haue taken it wifelier then I meant you
> fhould.

The opening of the scene is clearly in verse, and though the first two lines in this passage are rather approximate, Sebastian's second speech appears to be made up of a regular pentameter followed by a short line. Things then become more complicated.

Gonzalo's 'Sir' is presumably a false start, but the first line of his next speech is two syllables short of a regular pentameter, the second is a nine-syllable line. Are they imperfect verse, or mislined prose? Since Sebastian's 'One, tell' is not meant to be heard by Gonzalo, it would possibly be wrong to allow it to complete the line (though there are examples in the play where an unheard speaker still conforms to the metre of other speakers – as, for example, in Prospero's comments on Ferdinand and Miranda in 3.1). Some editors have chosen instead to assume mislineation, and have represented it thus:

> When every grief is entertained that's offered,
> Comes to th'entertainer –

But, as is evident elsewhere, the compositors may have been misled by the copy into setting prose as verse, and the misplaced comma after 'entertained' seems to fit with the habit Werstine notes: 'when compositors divided lines in which there are no pauses they would interpolate punctuation to mark an arbitrary pause'.[1] Something like this may have happened here, and possibly the apparent 'verse' is compositorial, and the lines should be treated as prose. But the problems do not end here. For it would be possible to treat the next four lines as verse, provided one were prepared to accept the addition of significant elisions:

> SEBASTIAN A dollar.
> GONZALO   Dolour comes to him indeed.
>   Y'have spoken truer than you purposèd.
> SEBASTIAN Y'have ta'en it wiselier than I meant you should.

Though this underlines the parallelism of the exchange in a satisfying fashion, and certainly sounds 'right' to my ear, to emend would be to overstep the boundary of acceptable editorial intervention. This passage, then, illustrates the way one decision – to treat Gonzalo's first speech as verse – has potential consequence for the further interventions editors might feel empowered to make.

But, equally, the imposition of an assumption of consistency in the division of verse and prose might lead to a failure to recognise brief moments when Shakespeare's practice tolerates fluid movement between them. So, in a fashion analogous to the pull exerted on Stephano by Caliban's verse, we might see Sebastian's 'Very well' as completing Gonzalo's verse line at 134, and 'Yet he would be king on't' doing the same at 153, though in each case Antonio's subsequent speech is clearly prose. But are editors right to see the responses of Antonio and Sebastian at 138–9 and again at 141 as making up verse lines? Since the first interjections are shared with each other, and not Gonzalo, it seems best to lineate as prose, while the second makes up, as it were, a complete shared line between them, and so is kept as verse. These could well be lineated differently: 'solutions' in this edition, as any other, must be regarded as provisional.

---

[1] Werstine, 'Line-division', p. 81.

There is, however, one place where the Folio's lineation might be crucial in suggesting possible emendation. 75–6 appear in F like this:

> **Seb.** What if he had said Widdower *Æneas* too ?
> **Good Lord, how you take it ?**

The straightforward view might be that Sebastian's speech should be treated as prose, even though the compositor did not justify the text – the first line needs a good deal of crushing to be taken as a pentameter. But the meaning of the speech is not clear. Though only Kermode of more recent editors has noted the difficulty of understanding Sebastian's second sentence, it is a very awkward line, which needs some actorly effort to render plausible. But the fact that there are two separate lines suggests to T. W. Craik the possibility that the scribe or compositor omitted a speech heading from the second, which should be assigned to Antonio. This privately communicated suggestion seems to me to make eminently good sense. Not only does it make for a clearer meaning – Antonio reacts with mock horror to Sebastian's (presumably bawdy) wordplay – it also preserves the dramatic rhythm of this part of the scene in the interchanges between Sebastian and Antonio.

ELISIONS
As has been remarked, both Crane and the compositors had a fondness for elisions. Sometimes these do appear to register an effort to ensure metrical regularity, but often they seem to derive from personal preference or from technical problems of justification. In any event, they are very unlikely in any consistent fashion to reproduce Shakespearean copy. It seems right, then, to remove on occasion an unnecessary elision – as, for example, at 1.2.340, 2.1.273 and 4.1.146. More problematic is whether an editor should attempt to indicate places where additional elision would render a line more smoothly metrical. As is noted above, many words could be taken indifferently as one or two syllables, and Shakespeare must have felt that he could trust his actors to recognise the music of the verse and themselves decide whether 'I have', 'thou hast' and similar locutions should be elided or not. Honigmann sums up the editorial dilemma:

> Even if scribes and compositors introduced some contracted or uncontracted forms that are clearly wrong, there are so many, spread over so many different texts, that we may safely deduce that Shakespeare himself was often responsible. Does that mean that in a modernised text we should break with the QF tradition, lengthening or shortening *I've*, *I have* and the like whenever the metre warrants it? On the assumption that compositors and scribes should be blamed, and also Shakespeare himself, because he didn't care?[1]

He admits that it is a question he ducks. Though feeling that such indications undoubtedly help the modern reader, and are in many respects analogous to the

---

[1] Honigmann, *Texts*, p. 117.

modernisation of spelling or the tidying up of speech headings and stage directions, he concludes that the issue 'will have to be scrutinised by others before we can act upon it. The textual implications are too far-reaching.'[1] Generally in this edition elision of words like 'even' and 'heaven' is not indicated, but I have ventured cautiously to adopt a few contractions into the text where they seem to me unambiguously required, to indicate some others in the notes where the case is less compelling and to place in the collation some few other suggestions made by previous editors. All such interventions are recorded, and though they are inevitably occasional and far from systematic, the intention in raising questions about the realisation of the metre of a line on some few occasions is precisely to alert the reader to the possibility of ambiguity on countless others.

SHORT AND SHARED LINES

The frequency of short lines in Shakespeare's verse increased throughout his career. Most often they occur at the ends of speeches, and on a number of occasions their brevity resonates powerfully – as in Ariel's sombre 'And a clear life ensuing' (3.3.82), or the hauntingly proleptic 'In country footing' (4.1.138) where the short line and missing rhyme seem to predict the vanishing of the masque, and perhaps most strongly of all in Prospero's 'I'll drown my book' (5.1.57). Short lines within a continuing speech are much rarer, though they may be used, as at 1.2.318, to indicate a change of address. Whilst some examples can appear purposeful – notably 'For you are spell-stopped' (5.1.61) – it is difficult to see particular effect in a short line like Ariel's 'Bound sadly home for Naples' (1.2.235). Dover Wilson attempted to use the presence of such short lines as evidence of revision or corruption of the text, but only perhaps at 1.2.253, where 'Of the salt deep' follows a line that the compositor had obvious difficulty in accommodating to the column, might one suspect that something dropped out.

Short lines beginning a speech are much rarer, and there are very few clear examples in *The Tempest* of a short line between two complete pentameters at the beginning of a speech (though, as we shall see, there may be short single-line speeches so encased). The importance of this observation is the guidance that it gives to an editor in deciding how to apportion shared lines. Some might argue that it is an unnecessary, self-inflicted problem, which would disappear if one simply reproduced the Folio's layout, where all speeches are set flush left. But the indication of shared lines, apart from its practical use in facilitating line-counting, assists the reader in perceiving the dramatic effects that can sometimes (even if not always) follow from such linkage. Just as the frequency of short lines increases in Shakespeare's later plays, so does his fondness for shared lines, and throughout most of *The Tempest* there is very little difficulty in deciding the relationship between them.[2]

---

[1] Ibid., p. 124.
[2] Unlike, for example, *Measure for Measure*. (See the Textual Analysis in Brian Gibbons's edition in this series, pp. 205–8.)

The premises upon which this edition operates in less clear cases are as follows:[1]

1. Shared lines will normally exhibit the same degree of metrical regularity as is general in the play as a whole.
2. The general tendency will be for speeches to conclude, rather than begin, with short lines.
3. Where there are short single-line speeches they will be much more likely to attach to a short line at the end of the previous speech than to one which begins the next.
4. Compositors are most likely to introduce their own lineation at the beginning of speeches, and especially in exchanges of short lines.[2]

The operation of these guidelines enables one, for example, to recognise that Sebastian's line at 3.3.13–14, which is set as a single line in F, should be broken, thus completing Antonio's speech, and allowing his response itself to complete a verse line, rather than standing on its own, in contradiction of the second guideline. Folio prints 1.2.192–5 thus:

> On the curld clowds: to thy ſtrong bidding, taſke
> *Ariel*, and all his Qualitie.
>   *Pro.* Haſt thou, Spirit,
> Performd to point, the Tempeſt that I bad thee.
>   *Ar.* To euery Article.

Most editors have attached Prospero's opening half-line to Ariel's concluding short line, following guideline 3. But in doing so they accept Ariel's short-line opening, which goes against guideline 2. Whilst this short line might be defended on the grounds that it is a self-contained observation, the lineation adopted in this edition seems to me much more satisfactory in linking Ariel's reply metrically to Prospero's question, leaving the short line to round out Ariel's first self-congratulatory speech. There are other places where an editorial desire to connect short lines may be over-enthusiastic. Take, for example, 2.1.194–5, where coupling Antonio and Sebastian's remarks generates an improbably licentiate fourteen-syllable line; it is better to accept these as two 'irregular' short lines. Rather similar is the exchange of Ferdinand and Miranda at 3.1.60–1, where to print as two separate observations seems more satisfactory than generating a long and unmetrical single line. There are other places where to entertain the possibility of purposeful short lines suggests a lineation different from the norm. At 3.3.19 Gonzalo's 'Marvellous sweet music' must be taken as a short-line interjection, its brevity appropriately signalling his astonishment. I would argue that a similar possibility should be entertained at 5.1.171. Folio prints this as follows:

---

[1] In these guidelines I am much influenced by Bowers, 'Problems'.
[2] Werstine, 'Line-division', p. 79.

As much, as me my Dukedome.
Here Profpero difcouers Ferdinand and Miranda, play-
ing at Cheffei
Mir. Sweet Lord, you play me falfe.
Fer. No my deareft loue,
I would not for the world. (wrangle,
Mir. Yes, for a fcore of Kingdomes, you fhould
And I would call it faire play.

Generally editors have attached Ferdinand's first half-line to Miranda's accusation, and left the second as an uncompleted short line (again, in line with guideline 3). If, however, we take Miranda's outburst as a single short line it is then followed by two regular pentameters and a short line completed in the normal way by the opening of the next speech. This seems to me both metrically and dramatically much more persuasive – and it perhaps has a basis in the practicalities of printing, since one could argue that the compositor, aware of two long lines coming up, chose to break the first and turn up the second.[1] The same logic might assist in a more complicated passage at 2.1.128–32. Folio prints it thus:

Mo widdowes in them of this bufineffe making,
Then we bring men to comfort them:

(This is at the foot of a column, and continues:)

The faults your owne.
Alon. So is the deer'ft oth'loffe.
Gon. My Lord *Sebaftian,*
The truth you fpeake doth lacke fome gentleneffe,

This is a passage unambiguously in verse, but we are faced with an eight-syllable line followed by three short lines before regularity is restored. Editors have generally accepted F's lineation, representing Alonso's speech as completing Sebastian's verse line, with the cluster of contractions preserving the rhythm. Ard3, however, links it to Gonzalo's short opening line. This seems to me mistaken, first because Alonso's pained rejoinder clearly belongs with Sebastian's rebuke, secondly because Gonzalo's

---

[1] There is a question here to which, as far as I am aware, bibliographers have not provided an answer. To turn a line up at its end would seem a much more difficult operation than to turn it down, requiring the compositor either to anticipate difficulties or else to reset an already completed line. Yet of the twelve turned-over lines in *The Tempest* eight are turned up, five of them in places where to turn down would have been perfectly possible. It does not seem, on the limited evidence of this play, to be a matter of compositorial preference. It may be that elsewhere in F, as I believe is the case here, the decision to turn a line up or down may have knock-on effects on the immediately contingent lines.

short line does follow Bowers's claim that such lines almost always have a 'structural or rhetorical purpose' and 'contain a distinct break after them' (easily imagined as Gonzalo reacts with shock to Sebastian's indecorous rebuke). Both solutions, however, leave Sebastian's octosyllabic line untouched. My suggestion is that mislineation shifted 'The fault's' to the next line, after which Crane, or possibly the compositor, clustered elisions in order to make the line conform. If this be allowed as a possible hypothesis, then repairing the short line and removing the elision generates a very effective emphasis on the words 'Your own', and, to my ears at least, a very much to be preferred fluency in the delivery of Alonso's line.

But metrically the most problematic passage in the whole play is 1.2.298–305.

> Thou haſt howl'd away twelue winters.
>   *Ar.* Pardon, Maſter,
> I will be correſpondent to command
> And doe my ſpryting, gently.
>   *Pro.* Doe ſo : and after two daies
> I will diſcharge thee.
>   *Ar.* That s my noble Maſter :
> What ſhall I doe? ſay what? what ſhall I doe?
>   *Pro.* Goe make thy ſelfe like a Nymph o'th' Sea,
> Be ſubieƈt to no ſight but thine,and mine : inuiſible
> To euery eye-ball elſe : goe take this ſhape
> And hither come in't : goe : hence
> With diligence.   *Exit.*

This cluster of irregularity has led some to speculate that the passage is corrupt, and most modern editors, with varying degrees of desperation, to attempt relineation. This seems a case where no rigorous application of rules can generate a satisfactory answer. Though it is possible to construct a narrative whereby confusion in Shakespeare's manuscript led first the scribe and then the compositors on their own initiative to attempt solutions which themselves compounded the problem, this would inevitably be a back-formation fabricated to endorse an answer arrived at on the basic ground that if regularity is possible, then it is likely to have been present in Shakespeare's mind and ear. The lineation offered in this edition has the merit of being metrically reasonably satisfactory and dramatically appropriate in the rhythm of its exchanges without requiring substantive emendation of the text. (Line 298 would be 'regular' if 'spriting' were expanded to 'spiriting', and though in 302 I have adopted F2's plausible correction 'Like to', the line could also be made regular by expansion of the elision 'o'th'Sea'.)

Decisions such as these must, in the end, be a matter of editorial judgement, and therefore open to question and alternative realisation. In the Commentary I have tried always to indicate where significant decisions have been taken so that readers can make up their own minds. But I do not believe that a modernised edition should duck the need for decisions that the conventional demand for clear indication of lineation generates. It is important to be able to hear, for example, the way in which emphatic single-syllable interjections gain their power by their completion of an iambic pentameter. (See, for example, the Commentary at 5.1.129, and consider Prospero's enigmatic 'Well' at 4.1.56, or Antonio's emphatic 'O' at 2.1.219.) It makes a difference, however small, whether one takes Miranda's 'Alas, now pray you' at 3.1.16 as completing, unmetrically, Ferdinand's short line, or as a short-line interjection made more powerful by its brevity. Examples could be multiplied indefinitely – but the basic point remains that in the increasingly subtle music of his later verse Shakespeare tests his listeners' ears in a variety of ways, and a modernised edition should endeavour to assist readers to hear that music.

Spelling and punctuation

This edition follows the conventions of the series in the modernisation of spelling. Generally there are no problems, though perhaps the modernisation of 'Millaine' to 'Milan' and 'Argier' to 'Algiers' has some unfortunate effect in rendering the stress-patterns anticipated by the verse more elusive, since they both need to be stressed on the first syllable. On one or two occasions there is a choice of possible modernisations – 'human/humane' at 1.2.347 'lose/loose' at 2.1.120, 'travel/travaile'at 3.3.15 for example. In each case modern spelling imposes a choice, where the original leaves both senses in play, and these are indicated in the Commentary. Only in two instances have the normal series rules been set aside. First, in the spelling of 'wrack' and its derived forms I have chosen to keep the Folio's universal spelling (much the commoner in the period) since, as *OED* makes clear, it is not simply a spelling variant of 'wreck', but a word etymologically distinct. Secondly, though 'mushrumps', 'vild' and other spelling variants which earlier editors found hard to discard have not been retained, I have chosen to keep 'debosh'd' at 3.2.24 for the reasons explained in the Commentary.

Modernising punctuation poses rather different, and more serious, problems and cannot be considered merely as adaptation of indifferent 'accidentals'. The little that can be inferred of Shakespeare's own habits suggests that he punctuated lightly. The intervention of Crane – who punctuated heavily – and of the compositors means that nothing in the Folio text can be safely taken to represent an original authorial intention. Nonetheless, Michael J. Warren (amongst others) has argued that 'intelligent respect must be paid to the punctuation of original texts since nothing else has comparable authority'.[1] At one level this proposition is a sensible one, for we might assume that Crane and the compositors punctuated in ways which seemed to them appropriate, and that their contemporary reading of Shakespeare's manuscript ought to command at least some of our attention. But Honigmann argues fiercely against this

[1] Michael J. Warren, 'Repunctuation as interpretation in editions of Shakespeare', *ELR*, 7 (1977), 155–69, p. 157.

view, claiming that Folio punctuation, no less than modern, 'misrepresents the fluid-ity of Shakespeare's dramatic dialogue', and 'inspires no confidence whatsoever'.[1] Vio-lently opposed though they are, however, both Warren and Honigmann are appealing to notions of 'authority', whether located in the physical object which is the Folio or in the sadly irrecoverable Shakespearean manuscript. Both would probably assent to Greg's observation, cited by Warren, that 'the flow of [Shakespeare's] thought is often more easily indicated by the loosely rhetorical punctuation of his own day than by our more logical system'.[2] Both would argue that modern punctuation is 'directive'. But I do not believe that even Shakespeare's original punctuation, were it to be recov-erable, would be a guide to his 'thought' rather than to his culturally conditioned prac-tice, nor do I accept that the punctuation of Crane and the compositors is essentially 'rhetorical'. It is frequently arbitrary, or at least if it has 'rules' they are not consis-tently derived from attention to possible oral delivery of the lines.[3] Moreover, the absence, quite as much as the presence, of punctuation is 'directive'. If Shakespeare indeed punctuated very lightly then it might, positively, leave syntactical relationships 'fluid' as Honigmann suggests, but it might equally leave them confused, and a modern (if not a seventeenth-century) actor or reader struggling to find a route through a sentence. Whilst some might think it better to leave readers to sort out the problems themselves rather than for an editor to 'impose' a solution, it seems to me wrong to assume that all the ambiguities left by a refusal to take editorial decision are therefore part of a Shakespearean 'intention' which modernisers betray. At a practi-cal level, to strip out what might be assumed to be scribal or compositorial 'additions' to the Shakespearean original is as arbitrarily a consequence of individual editorial reading as to add new punctuation. In this edition, then, I have tried to treat the punc-tuation as it exists in the Folio neither as unauthorised addition (as Honigmann would see it) nor as 'infinitely superior in authority' (as Warren would have it), but simply as a possible guide to reading that needs to be considered carefully and weighed on its merits. The collation and Commentary, therefore, point more often than is some-times the practice to cases where punctuation has an important effect upon under-standing. To collate all of the many hundreds of variations from the Folio is unnecessary and impractical (and to do so on a historical basis would be a recipe for madness[4]); my aim is only to alert readers from time to time to the ways in which punctuation controls our sense of the words, and therefore to the need for them to consider all punctuation as provisional.

---

[1] Honigmann, *Text*, pp. 134, 127.
[2] Quoted from W. W. Greg, *The Editorial Problem in Shakespeare*, 1954, by Warren, 'Repunctuation', p. 155.
[3] Bruce R. Smith, in the most thoughtful recent consideration of these problems, argues that the punctu-ation of the period was poised between two systems, the older founded on the performative breath, the newer on syntactic principles. '"Prickly characters"' in David Bergeron, ed., *Reading and Writing in Shakespeare*, 1996, pp. 25–44.
[4] Though Peter Holland makes interesting observations on the variations in Rowe's practice in 'Modern-izing Shakespeare: Nicholas Rowe and *The Tempest*', *SQ*, 51 (2000), 24–32.

Stage directions

If punctuation may be at one level considered as a guide to performative reading, the same is much more obviously the case with stage directions. Whilst it would seem that Shakespeare in his last plays tended to provide more elaborate directions than had been his earlier practice, it is generally acknowledged that Ralph Crane intervened significantly in their formulation, as John Jowett has most fully demonstrated.[1] His evidence derives from a number of different sources. First, from the evidence of Crane's later dramatic transcripts which indicate that he was capable of varying, adding to and deleting directions present in his copy; secondly, from the fact that a number of directions in *The Tempest* use vocabulary that is not found elsewhere in Shakespeare, but can be paralleled in Crane manuscripts; thirdly, from a recognition that some of the directions give information that might be of use to a reader in imagining the scene, but are of no practical use in the theatre (3.3.52 SD, *with a quaint device the banquet vanishes*, is but the most obvious such case). *The Tempest* does not, however, include the 'massed' stage directions listing all those who were to appear in a scene at its opening which are characteristic of Crane's later transcripts, and this may indicate that the transcript for this play was prepared earlier than those for *The Winter's Tale*, *The Merry Wives of Windsor* and *The Two Gentlemen of Verona*. There are, however, some directions which it might be argued are placed a line or two early – something that seems to have been his occasional habit.

There can be no secure means of disentangling what might be Crane's variations of the stage directions in his copy from their original. There are, however, occasions when Crane seems to have run stage directions together – as at 3.3.17 and 19 and 4.1.138 and 142, for example – and it seems best to separate them out clearly. Even here, however, it may be that editors have on occasion been too ready to assume Crane's intervening hand. At 1.1.31 the Folio stage direction is printed like this:

> *Botef.*Downe with the top-Maſt : yare, lower, lower,
> bring her to Try with Maine-courſe. A plague————
> *A cry within.*   *Enter Sebaſtian, Anthonio & Gonzalo.*

Editors have generally separated the two elements of this direction, and placed the entry of the lords after the word 'office' at line 33. At the same time the long dash after the word 'plague' was suggested by Kermode as a possible indication that oaths that would justify Sebastian's abuse of the Boatswain had been omitted. Though it is possible that Crane, who appears to have had a personal distaste for oaths of all kinds,[2] might have deleted words he thought objectionable, it is much more likely that the arrangement here is a product of compositorial difficulty in fitting copy to the page (see illustration 24). The long line which contains the stage direction is the only example of such an interruption of a prose speech at the bottom of a column any-

---

[1] Jowett, 'Directions', though he recognises that it remains 'an unproved hypothesis' (p. 120).
[2] Howard-Hill, 'Shakespeare's earliest editor', pp. 123–4.

where in the Folio. The long dash is used generally to indicate interrupted speech and here it must represent a compositor's best effort to accommodate marginal stage directions (which in this case no doubt stretched over more than two lines in the manuscript) in a place where the justification of the prose speech allowed little room for manoeuvre. But the joining of the two elements of the stage direction in a single line may represent rather more than compositorial convenience, or Crane's habits. Clearly the direction *A cry within* is needed before the Boatswain responds with 'A plague upon this howling.' But it makes dramatic sense also that the entrance of the lords should begin before the Boatswain's complaint about his passengers, in order to motivate Sebastian's vitriolic response to him.[1] Crane may not, then, have been running directions together, but representing intelligently what lay in his copy.

The same is true of the pattern whereby *others* are indicated as attendants for Alonso in 1.1, 2.1 and 3.3, but not in 5.1. Orgel assumes that these were 'erroneously included in Crane's text', but as Appendix 3 makes clear, they provide a perfectly rational pattern for the casting of the play. Usually such 'permissive' directions are taken to indicate that an authorial manuscript, rather than a theatrical playbook, was being transcribed, and though recent studies have shown that such directions were tolerated in manuscripts used in the theatre, the balance of probability here is that they do indicate a Shakespearean original.

In exploring the nature of Crane's contribution Jowett echoes others in suggesting that 'it is almost certainly necessary to postulate that he was familiar with the play on the stage'.[2] But it seems to me that his observation that 'Crane must have given some thought to his additions, and was probably in the habit of looking forward through his copy in search of apposite words' is in fact perfectly sufficient to explain the adjectives and phrases that we might conjecture the scribe added to his copy. Nonetheless the hypothesis that the stage directions in some way record memories of an actual theatrical performance powerfully conditions editorial response to the most controversial of them – the direction *Juno descends*, which, in the Folio, is set beside lines 4.1.72–3, though neither Iris nor Ceres show any awareness of Juno's presence until line 101, when Iris declares: 'Great Juno comes.' There are a number of possible explanations:

1. The stage direction is misplaced in F. This was the assumption of most editors until relatively recently. The problem is in providing any hypothesis which would explain how such misplacement might have come about. Since there is no other evidence of theatrical provenance for the text of the play, it is most unlikely that this is a book-keeper's direction placed early as a warning. One is forced, then, to try to construct a narrative of misreading or of erroneous guesswork on the part of the scribe or the compositors, or to posit a Shakespearean error in the underlying manuscript. Since normal scribal practice was to insert stage directions after completing the copying of the text of a page, some kind of error is always possible, though a scenario

---

[1] It is probably true that, especially in the large open space of the Globe, actors often entered before the point indicated in the text. See Andrew Gurr and Mariko Ichikawa, *Staging in Shakespeare's Theatres*, 2000, ch. 4, 'The ins and outs of stage movement'.
[2] Jowett, 'Directions', p. 114.

is difficult to imagine in which a stage direction was misplaced by what must have been virtually a whole page. It is possible that setting the direction here represents a Shakespearean first thought, not fully worked out, and in effect discarded as Juno enters at 101, or a direction inserted originally with thought of production at the Globe or Blackfriars, a staging which then had to be reimagined in the light of court performance, where descents would have been much more difficult to arrange. In short, if a direction existed in the copy at 101 but was misplaced by thirty lines, then one has to fall back on the possibility of a scribal or compositorial mistake that simply cannot be deduced from the physical evidence. A more likely hypothesis might be that there was no direction at all for Juno's entry in the authorial manuscript, and that Crane, who was certainly capable of inventing new stage directions, lit upon the line 'Here peacocks fly amain' (as it reads in F) to suggest a stage direction.

2. If, however, the stage direction is correctly placed and accurately describes a possible performance, then Juno begins her descent (presumably in a carriage) at line 71, and hovers above Iris and Ceres until finally lowered to stage level at or about 101. This is Jowett's solution (anticipated in general terms by Barton) and rests on evidence that such 'floating deities' were possible on the Renaissance stage. But in both *Women Beware Women*, 5.1, and Chapman's *The Widow's Tears*, 3.2, which might be suggested as parallels, the descending deity is acknowledged by those on stage, and soon speaks to them. In *Cymbeline*, 5.5, Jupiter speaks as he descends, is accompanied by thunder and lightning and hurls a thunderbolt, all of which no doubt assisted in covering the noise which the machinery for descents was likely to generate.[1] The further extension of Jowett's hypothesis, enthusiastically adopted by Oxford and Orgel, suggesting that Juno does not disembark from her carriage but summons Ceres to her, and that both are raised above the level of the stage to sing their song of blessing, runs flat in the face of the text, however ingeniously explained.[2] But the central problem with this hypothesis remains that it is hard to imagine that Iris and Ceres unconcernedly speak to one another without registering the fact of Juno's descent.[3]

3. James Knowles has suggested an alternative explanation in which Juno first appears 'above' in the gallery at line 72, but 'descends', as masquers most frequently did in the earlier Jacobean masques, by simply walking down the steps at the back of the stage, to emerge from the stage doors, on foot, at 101.[4] This proposal has the merit of reconciling the early direction for Juno's appearance above with Iris's apparently belated 'Great Juno comes, I know her by her gait', which clearly implies an entrance at stage level. It also suits with court practice at the date of the known performances

---

[1] See, for example, the unfavourable comments of the Agent of Savoy on the screeching 'like a portcullis' which accompanied the descent of the masquers in Campion's *Somerset Masque* (1613), and complaint that no music was provided to cover the noise. (John Orrell, 'The Agent of Savoy at the *Somerset Masque*', *Review of English Studies*, 28 (1977), 301–4.)

[2] Though it has been adopted in some performances.

[3] As Irwin T. Smith argues, in *Shakespeare's Blackfriars Playhouse: Its History and Its Design*, 1964, p. 416. Pauline Kiernan, however, thinks the absurdity is intentional, satirising the performance (*Shakespeare's Theory of Drama*, 1996, pp. 87–9).

[4] 'Insubstantial pageants: *The Tempest* and masquing culture', in Jennifer Richards and James Knowles, eds., *Shakespeare's Late Plays: New Readings*, 1999, pp. 108–25.

of *The Tempest* there, but still leaves unexplained the specificity of the stage direction *descends*, since one might have expected *Juno enters above*.

Though I am drawn to the last of these explanations, none of them is entirely convincing. It seems therefore wrong to supply additional editorial directions in the text which privilege one of them over the others. Since the only unequivocal certainty is that Juno must appear at 101, and that a stage direction is unambiguously required there, I have chosen to move *Juno descends* to that point, though preserving the original formulation precisely to signal that there is a problem.

In the course of this edition a number of additional stage directions have been supplied, sometimes to provide for places where there are obvious gaps in the Folio directions, but mainly to indicate who is speaking to whom. These are, inevitably, 'directive', and it is important that their provisionality is recognised. As is the practice in the New Cambridge Shakespeare all additional directions are enclosed within square brackets.

Songs: 'Come unto these yellow sands', 'Full fathom five'

The first of these songs (1.2.375–86) is printed thus in the Folio:

> *Enter Ferdinand & Ariel, inuisible playing & singing.*
> *Ariel* Song. *Come vnto thefe yellow fands,*
>   *and then take hands :*
>   *Curtfied when you haue, and kift*
>   *the wilde waues whift :*
> *Foote it featly heere, and there, and fweete Sprights beare*
>   *the burthen.* Burthen difperfedly.
> *Harke, harke, bowgh wawgh : the watch-Dogges barke,*
>   *bowgh-wawgh.*
> Ar. *Hark, hark, I heare, the ftraine of ftrutting Chanticlere*
>   *cry cockadidle-dowe.*

As it stands this lyric is chaos. The lineation, especially of the fifth line, ignores the shape of the verse and it is not clear which words belong to the 'burthen', nor where it begins and ends. It is not obvious, furthermore, what the function is of the additional speech heading for Ariel at the ninth printed line, and the problem of interpretation is compounded by the various possible meanings of 'burthen' as either a continuous undersong, or as a refrain (see Commentary). It seems clear that there were difficulties here for Crane in making sense of his copy, and likely that the problems were further compounded by the compositors. In attempting a solution the central hypothesis must be that Shakespeare wrote a shapely lyric, and one which he anticipated could be accommodated to the prevailing musical styles with which he was familiar. (In the last song of the play, 'Where the bee sucks', for example, the structure, with its movement to a triple-time conclusion, is well prepared for a conventional musical pattern.)

In this last respect the fact that a setting survives for 'Full fathom five' which is certainly close to the date of the play's performance and may well have figured in its first staging is helpful. It is not, of course, conclusive evidence, since composers were and are perfectly capable of taking liberties with the texts they set. But F's text for this second song also places the instruction for its 'Burthen: ding dong' in the margin, and sets it before the final line of the lyric.

Sea-Nimphs hourly ring his knell.
Burthen: ding dong.
Harke now I heare them, ding-dong bell.

It is possible that Shakespeare may have imagined 'ding dong' as a kind of drone or repeated bass line running under and beyond Ariel's final sung line, 'Hark, now I hear them, ding dong bell', but in Johnson's setting the only possible realisation of the early scores (consisting of a solo vocal line and bass part only) which would answer to the play's implied request for the burden to continue as Ferdinand speaks is that which is revealed in the later three-part version printed in Wilson's *Chearfull Aires* (1660), and reprinted in Appendix 1, p. 252. The canonic imitation in three parts of the phrase 'ding dong bell' initiated by Ariel fulfils the theatrical requirements admirably. It is possible, then, that the Folio simply prints the instruction for the burden one line too early. Given that it was probably an instruction written in the right-hand margin of the manuscript, and, perhaps, given a rather literal-minded scribe or compositor who assumed that there had to be an audible 'ding dong' before Ariel's injunction to 'Hark' to it, the misplacement, if that indeed is what it is, is understandable.

Unfortunately no setting of 'Come unto these yellow sands' survives, but nonetheless the possibility that the burden was intended to function in this song in a fashion analogous to 'Full fathom five' might usefully be entertained. This would suggest that Ariel, as the Folio implies, restarts his singing after the burden of dogs; it also suggests that the off-stage spirits imitate both dogs and cock in sequence. As in 'Full fathom five' it is possible that the marginal instruction for the burden is inserted early, one or two lines before it is required. By analogy with the second song, too, we might assume that 'Hark, hark' is sung by Ariel, rather than being part of the refrain; it is an imperative verb concluding a sequence of imperatives. This then suggests that the first 'Bow wow' is not necessarily sung by him, but by the off-stage spirits. Many modern editors have come thus far, and have separated out the 'Bow wow' as an interjection in Ariel's line, printing it as follows:

> Hark, hark!
>   [*Burden dispersedly*] Bow wow
> The watch-dogs bark.
>   [*Burden dispersedly*] Bow wow.[1]

---

[1] Ard3 takes a different course by giving all of the two lines 'Hark . . . bow wow' to 'Spirits'.

This is a possible solution, but the more radical alternative I propose is that the compositors misplaced the instruction for the 'dispersed' refrain, and that either they or the scribe then misplaced the first 'Bow wow'. (If, for example, the instruction '*Burthen dispersedly* Bow wow, bow wow' were all placed in the margin in the original manuscript, running down three lines, such misplacement would be easy to make.) Additionally it seems to me likely that the parallel injunction to 'hark' to the cry of the cock should similarly be answered off stage. If editors have generally felt that some clarification of the Folio is necessary here, few recently have followed the emendation of the fifth line to 'the burden bear' first introduced in Shadwell's 1674 make-over of Dryden and Davenant's *The Enchanted Island*, and later resurrected by Capell. But taken as it stands, editors have struggled to find a satisfactory metrical form for this part of the lyric. One popular answer, adopted by both Kermode and Orgel, is to relineate as:

> Foot it featly here and there
> And sweet sprites bear
> The burden. Hark, hark
> The watchdogs bark

This generates, in effect, a second four-line grouping which appears to repeat the rhyme-scheme of the first four lines. But though the first two lines here might be read as continuing the alternation of trochaic and iambic rhythm of the opening four lines, the parallel collapses in the next two lines, the first of which is an irregular five syllables. Furthermore the enjambement uneasily yokes 'the burden' to 'Hark, hark', where a musical break and fresh start seem to be required.[1]

To assume transposition in 'bear the burden', and to emend and relineate accordingly, allows the first part of the lyric to fall into an entirely satisfactory and conventional six-line stanza, and permits a natural break where it seems musically to be required. The pattern of alternation which then follows between Ariel and the echoing spirits is one which is consonant with that of the following song. This 'solution' makes no claim to be final, but it seems to me to represent something much more likely than existing versions – though, of course, it remains entirely possible for composers to realise the song as they will. (It would be possible, for example, for the first 'burden' to be followed by a recapitulation of some or all of the opening six lines, continued into the second refrain.)

At the beginning of the Textual Analysis I remarked on the double set of issues raised by any edition. The network of assumptions about the editorial task that underlie this edition are, in the end, as in almost all editions, mixed, since one is both attempting to represent the text as accurately as possible, and yet at the same time to re-present it for a modern reader. At the level of individual words, in the absence of any indication that the copy for *The Tempest* had theatrical provenance, the aim is to recover as best one can the authorial manuscript from which Crane transcribed. In

---

[1] Even less satisfactory is the solution which rhymes 'there' and 'bear' but leaves 'burthen' perched in its own unrhymed, unmetrical space (e.g. Ard3).

taking decisions about lineation the motive is only partly to reconstruct that copy in line with assumptions about authorial intent, for in significant respects the practice of a modern edition introduces questions and problems of which the original authorial and scribal manuscripts took no cognisance. In repunctuating, and in supplying supplementary stage directions, there is no question of appeal to some idealised original. These interventions are guided only by the desire to represent the text in a fashion that makes it accessible to the modern reader, while respecting the cues and clues provided by the original printed text. In an age when the Folio text is more readily available in facsimile than ever before, it seems to me that there is no need to apologise for such editorial intervention; its provisionality must be recognised, but it is not therefore disqualified. Editions, like stagings, are performative.

APPENDIX 1. THE SONGS

Settings of two of *The Tempest*'s songs survive in versions by Robert Johnson (c. 1582–1633). He was one of King James's lutenists, and also served as a musician to Prince Henry and to Prince Charles. He contributed settings to a number of Jacobean court masques, performed in some of them, and was also associated as a songwriter with the King's Men. Settings survive for plays from *The Tempest* to Beaumont and Fletcher's *The Lovers' Progress* (1623), including a particularly dramatic setting of 'Oh, let us howl' for Webster's *The Duchess of Malfi*. Since he published no book of songs it is extremely likely that many of his songs do not survive. It is impossible to assert with absolute confidence that his *Tempest* settings were used in the first, or early, performances of the play, but there is nothing in them that suggests that they could not have been so employed.

Both songs were first printed in John Wilson's *Cheerful Ayres* (1660) though they also survive in a number of earlier manuscript copies. Wilson's publication offered the songs in two forms. As was customary in the period the solo song version is supplemented by additional vocal parts, created to satisfy the market for domestic ensemble singing. (Campion, in his address 'To the Reader' which prefaces his *Two Books of Ayres* (c. 1613), observed that though the songs were written for one voice, 'they have since beene filled with more parts, which who so please may use, who like not may leave. Yet do we daily observe, that when any shall sing a Treble to an Instrument, the standers by will be offring at an inward part out of their owne nature; and, true or false, out it must, though to the perverting of the whole harmonie'.[1]) The songs have been edited by Ian Spink[2] in the form of solo songs, with bass and editorial continuo part. Here 'Where the bee sucks' is given simply as tune and bass, but for 'Full fathom five' I have chosen to offer a speculative reconstruction in which the first part of the song is represented as solo and bass line, but the arrangement of the 'burden', or refrain, derives from Wilson's three-part arrangement. The point here is not to insist that this is how the song was first heard, but only to demonstrate that Johnson's setting *could* readily be realised in a form which fits the requirements of the dramatic situation, where the spirits dispersedly echo the refrain 'ding dong bell'. (See the Textual Analysis, p. 248, for further discussion).[3] The verbal underlay is editorial, since it is vaguely marked in the original.

[1] Walter R. Davis, *The Works of Thomas Campion*, 1969, p. 55.
[2] *The English Lute-Songs* (Second Series), 17 1961, revised edn 1974, pp. 24–7.
[3] Peter Holman arrives, independently, at a similar realisation in the performance, with the Parley of Instruments, on the CD *Hark! hark! the lark* (*Hyperion* 66836, recorded 1997).

Full fathom five

Full fa-thom five thy fa - ther lies, Of his bones are cor - al made; Those are

pearls that were his eyes; No-thing of him that doth fade, But doth suf-fer a

sea - change In-to some-thing rich and strange. Sea-nymphs hour-ly ring his knell.

Hark, now I hear them, Hark, now I hear them, ding dong bell.

Ariel /1st Spirit

Ding dong ding dong bell; ding dong ding dong

2nd Spirit

Ding dong ding dong bell; ding dong ding dong

3rd Spirit

Ding dong ding dong bell; ding dong bell;

bell; ding dong ding dong bell.

bell; ding dong ding dong ding dong bell.

ding dong ding dong bell; dong bell.

Where the bee sucks

Where the bee sucks, there suck I; In a cow-slip's bell I lie;

There I couch when owls do cry; On the bat's back I do fly Af-ter sum-mer mer-ri-ly.

Mer-ri-ly, mer-ri-ly, shall I live now, Un-der the blos-som that hangs on the bough.

Mer-ri-ly, mer-ri-ly, shall I live now, Un-der the blos-som that hangs on the bough.

APPENDIX 2. PARALLEL PASSAGES FROM VIRGIL AND OVID

Virgil

THE DESCRIPTION OF SWIMMING SERPENTS

ecce autem gemini a Tenedo tranquilla per alta
(horresco referens) immensis orbibus angues
incumbunt pelago pariterque ad litora tendunt:
pectora quorum inter fluctus arrecta iubaeque
sanguineae superant undas; pars cetera pontum
pone legit sinuatque immensa volumine terga.

and lo! from Tenedos, over the peaceful depths – I shudder as I tell the tale – a pair of serpents with endless coils are breasting the sea and side by side making for the shore. Their bosoms rise amid the surge, and their crests, blood-red, overtop the waves; the rest of them skim the main behind and their huge backs curve in many a fold.

(*Aeneid*, 2.203–8. Loeb translation by Frank Justus Miller)

THE HARPIES

tristius haud illis monstrum, nec saevior ulla
pestis et ira deum Stygiis sese extulit undis.
virginei volucrum voltus, foedissima ventris
proluvies, uncaeque manus, et pallida semper ora fame.

. . .

          tum litore curvo
exstruimusque toros dapibusque epulamur opimis.
at subitae horrifico lapsu de montibus adsunt
Harpyiae et magnis quatiunt clangoribus alas,
diripiuntque dapes contactuque omnia foedant
immundo; tum vox taetrum dira inter odorem.

. . .

          invadunt socii et nova proelia temptant,
obscenas pelagi ferro foedare volucris.
sed neque vim plumis ullam nec volnera tergo
accipiunt, celerique fuga sub sidera lapsae
semesam praedam et vestigia foeda relinquunt.
una in praecelsa consedit rupe Celaeno,
infelix vates, rumptique hanc pectore vocem:
'bellum etiam pro caede boum stratisque iuveneis,
Laomedontiadae, bellumne inferre paratis
et patrio Harpyias insontis peller regno?
accipite ergo animis atque haec mea figite dicta.
quae Phoebo pater omnipotens, mihi Phoebus Apollo
praedixit, vobis Furiarum ego maxima pando.

Italiam cursu petitis, ventisque vocatis
ibitis Italiam portusque intrare licebit;
sed non ante datam cingetis moenibus urbem,
quam vos dira fames nostraeque iniuria caedis
ambesas subigat malis absumere mensas'.

No monster more baneful than these, no fiercer plague or wrath of the gods ever rose from the Stygian waves. Maiden faces have these birds, foulest filth they drop, clawed hands are theirs, and faces ever gaunt with hunger . . . then on the winding shore we build couches and banquet on the rich dainties. But suddenly, with fearful swoop from the mountains the Harpies are upon us, and with loud clanging shake their wings, plunder the feast, and with unclean touch mire every dish; then amid the foul stench comes a hideous scream. . . . My comrades charge, and essay a strange combat, to despoil with the sword those filthy birds of ocean. Yet they feel no blows on their feathers, nor wounds on their backs, but, soaring skyward with rapid flight, leave the half-eaten prey and their foul traces. One only, Celaeno, ill-boding seer, alights on a lofty rock, and breaks forth with this cry: 'Is it even war, in return for slaughtered kine and slain bullocks, is it war ye are ready to bring upon us, ye sons of Laomedon, and would ye drive the guiltless Harpies from their father's realm? Take then to heart and fix there these words of mine. What the Father omnipotent foretold to Phoebus and Phoebus Apollo to me, I, eldest of the Furies, reveal to you. Italy is the goal ye seek; wooing the winds, ye shall go to Italy and freely enter her harbours; but ye shall not gird with walls your promised city until dread hunger and the wrong of violence towards us force you to gnaw with your teeth and devour your very tables!'   (*Aeneid*, 3.214–17, 223–8, 240–57.)

Ovid

MEDEA'S INCANTATION

'Nox' ait 'arcanis fidissima, quaeque diurnis
aurea cum luna succeditis ignibus astra,
tuque, triceps Hecate, quae coeptis conscia nostris
adiutrixque venis cantusque artisque magorum,
quaeque magos, Tellus, pollentibus instruis herbis,
auraeque et venti montesque amnesque lacusque,
dique omnes nemorum, dique omnes noctis adeste,
quorum ope, cum volui, ripis mirantibus amnes
in fontes rediere suos, concussaque sisto,
stantia concutio cantu freta, nubila pello
nubilaque induco, ventos abigoque vocoque,
vipereas rumpo verbis et carmine fauces,
vivaque saxa sua convulsaque robora terra
et silvas moveo iubeoque tremescere montis
et mugire solum manesque exire sepulcris!
te quoque, Luna, traho, quamvis Temesaea labores
aera tuos minuant; currus quoque carmine nostro
pallet avi . . .'

Metamorphoses, 7.192–209 (Loeb)

O trustie time of night
Most faithfull vnto privities, O golden starres whose light
Doth jointly with the Moone succeede the beames that blaze by day

And thou three headed Hecate who knowest best the way
To compasse this our great attempt and art our chiefest stay:
Ye Charmes and Witchcrafts, and thou Earth which both with herbe and weed
Of mightie working furnishest the Wizardes at their neede:
Ye Ayres and windes: ye Elves of Hilles, of Brookes, of Woods alone,
Of standing Lakes, and of the Night approche ye everychone.
Through helpe of whom (the crooked bankes much wondring at the thing)
I have compelled streames to run cleane backward to their spring.
By charmes I make the calme Seas rough, and make the rough Seas plaine,
And cover all the Skie with Cloudes and chase them thence againe.
By charmes I rayse and lay the windes, and burst the Vipers jaw.
And from the bowels of the Earth both stones and trees doe draw.
Whole woods and Forestes I remove: I make the Mountaines shake,
And even the Earth it selfe to grone and fearfully to quake.
I call up dead men from their graves: and thee O lightsome Moone
I darken oft, though beaten brasse abate thy perill soone.
Our Sorcerie dimmes the Morning faire, and darkes the Sun at Noone.

> Translation from Arthur Golding, *Ovid's Metamorphosis*, 1567, 7.263–77

APPENDIX 3. 'AND OTHERS': CASTING THE PLAY

The Tempest's stage directions, though heavily mediated through the improving hand of Ralph Crane (see Textual Analysis), retain at least one feature which can be taken to indicate the presence of an authorial manuscript: the frequent vagueness concerning the number of supernumerary characters in many scenes. We have 'Mariners' in 1.1, the court party accompanied by unspecified *others* in 1.1, 2.1 and 3.3, *several strange shapes* who bring in the banquet in 3.3, and *certain* nymphs and reapers in 4.1. These 'permissive' directions may suggest an author leaving to his company the detailed task of finding what bodies they could to fill in the blanks. Stephen Orgel goes further in suggesting that the specifications for *others* in the earlier entrances of the court party, but absent from their entrance in 5.1, are a Cranean addition, and he removes, as do the editors of the Oxford edition, all mention of these extras from 2.1 and 3.3 (though leaving 1.1 untouched). It is frustrating to the imagination of the reader that there should be this imprecision in the designation of the numbers of attendants, shapes, spirits and the like. For to know the number of Mariners in the opening scene might have some effect on our visualisation of the chaos of the storm, and to have some sense of the number of participants in the masque's dance could affect one's sense of the relationship between the 'vanity' of Prospero's art, and the court masque proper which it recalls and plays against.

It might seem that the double disqualification of the stage directions as evidence for the original staging – that they may well have been significantly modified by the scribe, and that, anyway, they are only an authorial first thought, to be clarified in the practice of the playhouse – invalidates any attempt to pursue the matter further. But the inevitable focus in textual criticism on stage directions primarily as signs of the nature of the copy available to the printer has tended to inhibit what might otherwise seem to be a key test of their reliability: whether or not they give instruction for a viable casting and performing of the text as we now have it. When *The Tempest*'s directions are considered in the light of recent work on the company and casting of the plays, they actually provide a remarkably satisfactory guide to the likely casting of the play as a whole, and therefore enable us to speculate with a degree of conviction about the stage picture in these scenes. Underlying this case is a belief that even if the text as we have it derives from authorial papers, it is inherently unlikely that Shakespeare, intimately connected throughout his professional life with the practicalities of the stage, would not have had some sense of the possibilities of casting in mind as he drafted his play, and would have calculated fairly precisely on what was possible and achievable given the number of actors available in the company.

David Bradley suggests that there are five basic propositions that should guide any attempt to reconstruct the casting of a play from the text:

1. That plural calls for attendants may be satisfied by the appearance of two actors, unless the text clearly indicates otherwise.
2. That an actor who leaves the stage last in one scene will not normally re-enter at the beginning of the next.
3. That boys will not normally double with men. To which we may add that men will not normally play female roles.
4. That if, in a single scene, the demands made on the cast suddenly swell out of proportion to those made by the next largest limiting scene, and beyond the evidence of cast size in any crucial scenes there may be, we may suspect the presence of gatherers or stand-ins.
5. That speaking actors were not normally cast for two *alternating* roles in the same play.[1]

With these principles as a guide it is possible to reconstruct a minimum casting for *The Tempest* which is consistent with what is known about the size of the company at the time of its composition.

It is necessary to begin with those scenes which call for the maximum number of actors on stage at once – what Bradley calls 'limiting' scenes. In this play there are two such scenes, which each set different limits for the supernumerary figures. 5.1 requires the maximum number of speaking parts, whilst 4.1 requires, in the performers of the masque and the spirits who chase out Caliban and his co-conspirators, the maximum number of 'extras'. In 5.1 the plot requires that all the major characters be called successively to attend the comic resolution. The arrival of the court party is described in these terms:

Here enters ARIEL *before; then* ALONSO *with a frantic gesture, attended by* GONZALO; SEBASTIAN *and* ANTONIO *in like manner attended by* ADRIAN *and* FRANCISCO. *They all enter the circle which Prospero had made, and there stand charmed; which Prospero observing, speaks*:

The precision of the allocation of attendants – Gonzalo to Alonso, Adrian and Francisco to Sebastian and Antonio – might suggest that Ralph Crane had engaged in a characteristic amplification and 'tidying up' of the direction he found in his copy. Nonetheless, it is the absence of any mention of *others* as attendants in this direction which persuades some recent editors to remove them from the earlier entrances of the same court party. Yet, if the requirement for *others* is tracked through the play, then a simpler, practical reason might account for their absence here – that there were simply no *others* available to swell Alonso's train.

In 1.1 the court party is defined as '*ALONSO, SEBASTIAN, ANTONIO, FERDINAND, GONZALO and others*'. In 2.1 appear '*ALONSO, SEBASTIAN, ANTONIO, GONZALO, ADRIAN, FRANCISCO and others*', and this direction is repeated in 3.3 with *others* represented as *etc.* The appearance of the two additional names, Adrian and Francisco, is simply explained. Two hitherto silent attendants burst into speech for

[1] David Bradley, *From Text to Performance in the Elizabethan Theatre: Preparing the Play for the Stage*, 1992, pp. 41–2.

the first time, and so require naming. Though only Adrian is actually addressed by name by another character, and it has proved an easy matter over the years to reassign Francisco's two speeches to Adrian or Gonzalo, nonetheless, as Kermode points out in his note to 2.1.109, 'lords appear in couples'. We may assume that in the dramatist's mind those simply described as *others* in the opening scene acquire names as they are needed, and, once named, do not revert again in Act 5 (where they say nothing) to anonymity. But it still leaves open the question of whether the intervening plenitude of Alonso's retinue is merely authorial or scribal indifference. Since, however, these *others* disappear in the scene when the Master and Boatswain, having been apparently absent from the stage for the whole of the rest of the play, reappear, one possible answer is simply that these actors doubled as supernumeraries, until the point where they were once again required to appear in their original shape.

If this hypothesis holds, then it perhaps also suggests why in Act 5 the Mariners of the first scene are not brought back on stage. If, for the moment, at least, one assumes that these Mariners were played by men, rather than boys, then a neatly reciprocal answer suggests itself – if the *others* disappear from the final act because the actors are no longer available, then perhaps the absent Mariners are a sign that those who performed their parts are now required in speaking parts – namely in the persons of Stephano and Trinculo.

Mention of the boy actors leads to the second major question posed by the casting of the play – how many spirits form Ariel's 'quality'? Act 4 sets the problem clearly. If, as is probable, Ariel's statement that he 'presented Ceres' indicates that he actually doubled in the part, then the masque proper requires two boys as Iris and Juno, and then needs at least two each of the nymphs and reapers who perform the dance at its end. Then, shortly afterwards, a number of dogs are required to chase out Caliban, Stephano and Trinculo, and, if Prospero and Ariel's naming of Mountain, Silver, Fury and Tyrant is to be taken as indicating the actual number of performers, then a minimum of four actors would be required. The total of up to eight 'extras' required in this scene raises the most acute practical problems in envisaging an economical casting for the play. Bradley suggests that up to six boys might form the normal complement of the company, of whom two are clearly demanded for the parts of Ariel and Miranda. It would be possible for four remaining boys to perform the other two named parts in the masque, and the roles of the female nymphs in the dance. We are left, then, with the reapers to find; and again, the Master and Boatswain would be available to double as the male reapers in the dance. The dogs might simply have been performed by four boys – but if Iris and Juno were at all elaborately costumed, as in the court masque itself, then a quick change might have been difficult to achieve (though Ariel as Ceres is required to make an equally swift transformation). It might be possible that the adult actors again doubled as two of the dogs.

But in any case, we must assume that these same four supernumerary boys played the *shapes* of 3.3. Whether or not the boys also doubled as Mariners in the opening scene is an open question. Bradley's intuitive feeling that boys did not double in 'adult' roles is not necessarily an absolute rule. Apart from the fact that the oldest of the 'boys' could well have been approaching adult status, even a demand for verisimilitude might permit there to be younger Mariners on board. All of this can be summed up in the following chart:

	1.1	1.2	2.1	2.2	3.1	3.2	3.3	4.1	5.1
ADULTS									
1 Master	*		'others'				'others'	reaper/dog	*
2 Boatswain	*		'others'				'others'	reaper/dog	*
3 Alonso	*		*				*		*
4 Sebastian	*		*				*		*
5 Antonio	*		*				*		*
6 Ferdinand	*	*			*			*	*
7 Gonzalo	*		*				*		*
8 Adrian	['others']		*				*		*
9 Francisco	['others']		*				*		*
10 Prospero		*			*		*	*	*
11 Caliban		*		*		*		*	*
12 Trinculo	[Mariner]			*		*		*	*
13 Stephano	[Mariner]			*		*		*	*
BOYS									
1 Miranda		*			*			*	*
2 Ariel	*	*				*	*	*+Ceres	*
3 Spirit		?Mariner					'shape'	Iris	
4 Spirit		?Mariner					'shape'	Juno	
5 Spirit		?Mariner					'shape'	nymph/dog	
6 Spirit		?Mariner					'shape'	nymph/dog	

T. J. King offers a rather different pattern of doubling, which generates a less economical requirement for 15 adult actors, and eight boys.[1] In particular he leaves the Boatswain with nothing to do between the first and last acts, gives a similarly scanty role to the boy playing Iris, and assumes a further actor for the part of Ceres. He does, however, manage to find a further nymph and reaper. Keith Sturgess, feeling that a still larger number of dancers would be required, argued that 'especially in the masque scene the normal company would be overstretched' and claimed that 'the King's Men could draw on a number of trained extras to fill the ranks', suggesting that the Chapel Royal might have supplied these choreographed extras.[2] It is certainly possible that extras could have been drafted in, but the point of this chart is not to insist that this is how the play *must* have been staged, only to indicate that it *could* be mounted by a cast of normal size, and that the stage directions as they stand are consistent and 'playable'.

In whatever ways Ralph Crane may have sophisticated the stage directions of his copy, then, the designation of *others* in 1.1, 2.1 and 3.3 and their absence from 5.1 is entirely consistent with theatrical necessity. Making such an assumption clarifies two specific further issues. It makes it more probable that Ariel's statement that he 'pre-

---

[1] T. J. King, *Casting Shakespeare's Plays*, 1992, pp. 23–4.
[2] Keith Sturgess, *Jacobean Private Theatre*, 1987, pp. 77–8. He parallels this with the requirements of the pastoral scene in *The Winter's Tale*.

sented Ceres' does indeed mean that he took the part. There is no obvious thematic reason why he should do so, but a clear practical imperative that required the principal singer in the play to take one of the singing parts in the masque. More contentiously it might be argued that the ghostly presence of Antonio's 'brave son', alluded to by Ferdinand at 1.2.437, but never appearing thereafter, represents a first thought that was cancelled, at least in part, as a consequence of the problem that finding a further boy actor to fill the part, especially in 3.3, would have posed.

READING LIST

This list is not a comprehensive index of books cited in the Introduction and Commentary, but a selection of some of the critical works which might be most useful to students in developing their approach to the play. Anthologies of criticism which might be especially convenient starting-points are those of Vaughan, and White.

Barker, Francis, and Peter Hulme. 'Nymphs and reapers heavily vanish: the discursive con-texts of *The Tempest*', in John Drakakis, ed., *Alternative Shakespeares*, 1985, pp. 191–205

Bate, Jonathan. *Shakespeare and Ovid*, 1993

Berger, Jr, Harry. 'Miraculous harp: a reading of Shakespeare's *Tempest*', *S.St.*, 5 (1969), 253–83

Berger, Karol. 'Prospero's Art', *S.St.*, 10 (1977), 211–39

Breight, Curt. '"Treason doth never prosper": *The Tempest* and the discourse of treason', *SQ*, 41 (1990), 1–28

Brower, Reuben A. *Fields of Light*, 1951

Brown, Paul. '"This thing of darkness I acknowledge mine": *The Tempest* and the discourse of colonialism', in Jonathan Dollimore and Alan Sinfield, eds., *Political Shakespeare: Essays in Cultural Materialism*, 2nd edn 1994, pp. 48–71

Callaghan, Dympna. *Shakespeare Without Women*, 2000, ch. 4

Frey, Charles. '*The Tempest* and the New World', *SQ*, 30 (1979), 29–41

Frye, Northrop. *A Natural Perspective*, 1965

Fuchs, Barbara. 'Conquering islands: contextualizing *The Tempest*', *SQ*, 48 (1997), 45–62

Gibbons, Brian. '*The Tempest* and interruptions', *Cahiers Elisabéthains*, 45 (1994), 47–58

Gillies, John. 'Shakespeare's Virginian masque', *ELH*, 53 (1986), 673–707

Graff, Gerald and James Phelan, eds. '*The Tempest*': *A Case Study in Critical Controversy*, 2000

Greenblatt, Stephen. *Learning to Curse*, 1990, pp. 16–39

Griffiths, Trevor R. '"This island's mine": Caliban and colonialism', *The Yearbook of English Studies*, 13 (1983), 159–80

Gurr, Andrew. '*The Tempest*'s tempest at Blackfriars', *S.Sur.*, 41 (1989), 91–102

Hamilton, Donna B. *Virgil and 'The Tempest': The Politics of Imitation*, 1990

Hirst, David L. *The Tempest: Text and Performance*, 1984, pp. 41–68

Hulme, Peter, and William H. Sherman, eds. '*The Tempest*' *and its Travels*, 2000

Hulme, Peter. *Colonial Encounters*, 1986

James, Heather. *Shakespeare's Troy: Drama, Politics and the Translation of Empire*, 1997

Kahn, Coppélia. 'The providential *Tempest* and the Shakespearean family', in Murray M. Schwartz and Coppélia Kahn, eds., *Representing Shakespeare: New Psychoanalytic Essays*, 1980, pp. 217–43

Kastan, David Scott. *Shakespeare After Theory*, 2000, ch. 10

Knapp, Jeffrey. *An Empire Nowhere*, 1992

Leininger, Lorie Jerrell. 'The Miranda trap: sexim and racism in Shakespeare's *Tempest*', in Carolyn Lenz *et al.*, eds., *The Woman's Part*, 1980, pp. 285–94

Lindley, David. 'Music, masque and meaning in *The Tempest*', in Lindley (ed.) *The Court Masque*, 1984, pp. 47–59

'Tempestuous transformations', in Shirley Chew and Alistair Stead, eds., *Translating Life: Studies in Transpositional Aesthetics*, 1999, pp. 99–121

Linton, Joan Pong. *The Romance of the New World*, 1998

Loomba, Ania. *Gender, Race, Renaissance Drama*, 1992

Miola, Robert S. *Shakespeare and Classical Comedy: The Influence of Plautus and Terence*, 1994

Mowat, Barbara. *The Dramaturgy of Shakespeare's Romances*, 1976

'Prospero, Agrippa, and hocus pocus', *ELR*, 11 (1981), 281–303

'Prospero's book', *SQ*, 52 (2001), 1–33

Neill, Michael. 'Remembrance and revenge: *Hamlet*, *Macbeth* and *The Tempest*', in Ian Donaldson, ed., *Jonson and Shakespeare*, 1983

Nevo, Ruth. *Shakespeare's Other Language*, 1987

Nixon, Rob. 'Caribbean and African appropriations of *The Tempest*', *Critical Inquiry*, 13 (1987), 557–78

Norbrook, David. ' "What cares these roarers for the name of King?": language and Utopia in *The Tempest*', in Gordon McMullan and Jonathan Hope, eds., *The Politics of Tragicomedy*, 1992, pp. 21–54

Nuttall, A. D. *Two Concepts of Allegory*, 1967

Orgel, Stephen. 'Prospero's wife', in Margaret W. Ferguson, Maureen Quilligan and Nancy J. Vickers, eds., *Rewriting the Renaissance: The Discourses of Sexual Difference in Early Modern Europe*, 1986

Palfrey, Simon. *Late Shakespeare: A New World of Words*, 1997

Schmidgall, Gary. *Shakespeare and the Courtly Aesthetic*, 1981

Singh, Jyotsna G. 'Caliban versus Miranda: race and gender conflicts in postcolonial rewritings of *The Tempest*', in Valerie Traub *et al.*, eds., *Feminist Readings of Early Modern Culture*, 1996, pp. 191–209

Skura, Meredith Anne. 'Discourse and the individual: the case of colonialism in *The Tempest*', *SQ*, 40 (1989), 42–69

Strier, Richard. ' "I am power": normal and magical politics in *The Tempest*', in Derek Hirst and Richard Strier, eds., *Writing and Political Engagement in Seventeenth-Century England*, 1999

Sundelson, David. ' "So rare a wonder'd father": Prospero's *Tempest*', in Murray M. Schwartz and Coppélia Kahn, eds., *Representing Shakespeare: New Psychoanalytic Essays*, 1980, pp. 33–53

Tudeau-Clayton, Margaret. *Jonson, Shakespeare and Early Modern Virgil*, 1998

Vaughan, Alden T., and Virginia Mason Vaughan. *Shakespeare's Caliban: A Cultural History*, 1991
Vaughan, Alden T., and Virginia Mason Vaughan, eds. *Critical Essays on Shakespeare's 'The Tempest'* 1998
Warren, Roger. *Staging Shakespeare's Late Plays*, 1990
White, R. S. *Let Wonder Seem Familiar: Endings in Shakespeare's Romance Vision*, 1985
White, R. S. ed. *The Tempest: William Shakespeare* (New Casebooks), 1999
Wood, Nigel, ed. *Theory in Practice: The Tempest*, 1995